Employee Relations in an Organisational Context

Kathy Daniels teaches at Aston Business School and is a tutor for ICS Ltd in employment law and related topics. She is also a tutor on the Advanced Certificate in Employment for the Chartered Institute of Personnel and Development. She is a lay member of employment tribunals, sitting in Birmingham. Prior to these appointments she was a senior personnel manager in the manufacturing sector.

The CIPD would like to thank the following members of the CIPD Publishing Editorial Board for their help and advice:

- Pauline Dibben, Sheffield University

- Edwina Hollings, Staffordshire University Business School

- Caroline Hook, Huddersfield University Business School

- Vincenza Priola, Keele University

- John Sinclair, Napier University Business School

Employee Relations in an Organisational Context

Kathy Daniels

Chartered Institute of Personnel and Development

Published by the Chartered Institute of Personnel and Development
151 The Broadway, London, SW19 1JQ

This edition published 2006

Typeset by Curran Publishing Services, Norwich, Norfolk
Printed in Great Britain by Cromwell Press, Trowbridge, Wiltshire

British Library Cataloguing in Publication Data
A catalogue of this publication is available from the British Library

ISBN 1-84398-138-6
ISBN–13 978-1-84398-138-1

The views expressed in this book are the author's own and may not necessarily reflect those of the CIPD.

The CIPD has made every effort to trace and acknowledge copyright holders. If any source has been overlooked, CIPD Enterprises would be pleased to redress this for future editions.

Chartered Institute of Personnel and Development
151 The Broadway, London, SW19 1JQ
Tel: 020 8612 6200
Email: cipd@cipd.co.uk   Website: www.cipd.co.uk
Incorporated by Royal Charter.   Registered Charity No. 1079797

Contents

Contents

List of figures

List of tables

Guided Tour

Objectives of the chapter outline the key learning outcomes of the chapter. This feature is designed to help students focus their learning and evaluate their progress.

Tables and figures are used to illustrate key concepts in a detailed and illustrative way to serve as memorable learning aids.

Activities encourage students to reflect on the concepts being addressed or require students to find out how specific issues are addressed in their own organisation.

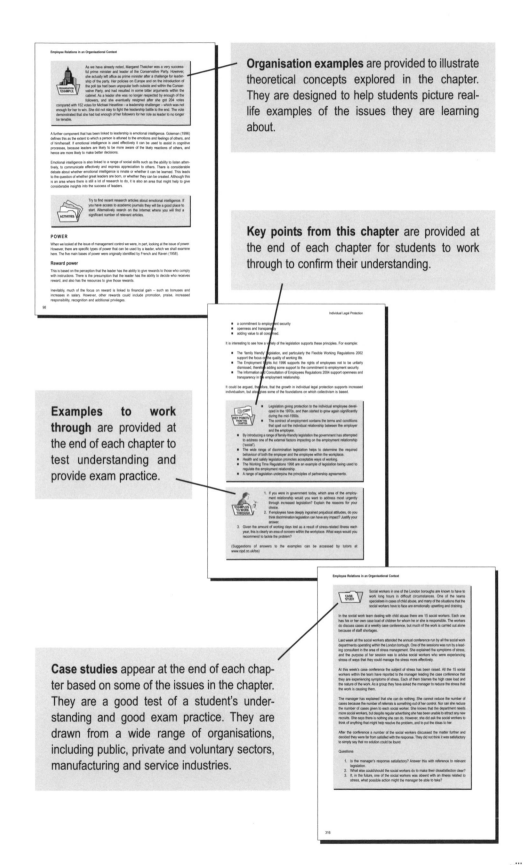

Organisation examples are provided to illustrate theoretical concepts explored in the chapter. They are designed to help students picture real-life examples of the issues they are learning about.

Key points from this chapter are provided at the end of each chapter for students to work through to confirm their understanding.

Examples to work through are provided at the end of each chapter to test understanding and provide exam practice.

Case studies appear at the end of each chapter based on some of the issues in the chapter. They are a good test of a student's understanding and good exam practice. They are drawn from a wide range of organisations, including public, private and voluntary sectors, manufacturing and service industries.

Introduction

This book has been written for students studying employee relations as part of an undergraduate or postgraduate course, or as a CIPD specialist elective. A key emphasis of this book is looking at the subject of employee relations in the context of the organisation. An organisation consists of a group of employees, and the success of the organisation is directly related to the success of that group of employees. One of the key factors in determining the success of those employees is the relationship that they have with the employer. If that relationship is poor and employees are demotivated and dissatisfied, the organisation is likely to be less successful. It is essential, therefore, to place the subject of employee relations in context, which is what this book sets out to do.

CIPD STANDARDS

This book covers all of the CIPD standards for the Employee Relations specialist elective. For teaching purposes, the mapping of the chapters against the standards is as follows:

1. Employee relations management in context (addressed in Chapters 1, 2 and 3).
2. The parties in employee relations (addressed in Chapters 4, 5 and 6).
3. Employee relations processes (addressed in Chapters 7, 8, 9, 12 and 13).
4. Outcomes (addressed in Chapters 1, 2 and 8).
5. Employee relations skills (addressed in Chapters 8, 10 and 11).

GUIDE TO THE CONTENT

The content of the book is structured as follows.

Chapter 1

In the first chapter we start by looking at the history of employee relations, and consider the move from 'industrial' relations to 'employee' relations. We then consider different theoretical approaches to the topic, and the way that these help us to understand the changes that have occurred.

It is important to understand that employee relations operate differently in different organisations, and we examine this by looking at the impact of different organisation structures, organisational features, culture, values, the identification of decision-makers and also how employee relations operates within a system.

In this chapter we also take the first look at the important concept of the psychological contract.

Chapter 2

In this chapter we move on to look at the external factors that can impact on the employment relationship. We do this by looking at key issues under each of the headings from the PESTLE framework for analysis: political, economic, social, technological, legal and ethical/environmental.

We also consider how organisations react to the impact of external factors, and the different strategies that they can put in place to address such factors.

Chapter 3

In this chapter we continue to look at external factors, and focus specifically on the impact of the government, the European Union and globalisation. In doing this we look at the role of the government as an employer, and how this has changed and adapted over recent years.

We also look at some key external bodies that can be influential in issues relating to employee relations.

Chapter 4

Having identified the internal and external factors that impact on the employment relationship, we now focus on the parties within that relationship. We start by looking at the specific factors affecting management. To do this we explore the definition and roles of management and of leadership. In doing this we look at concepts of power, control and obedience as well as empowerment and leading employees through a period of change.

In this chapter we also look at different styles of management specifically in the context of employee relations.

Chapter 5

We now move on to look at the role of employees in the employment relationship. We do this by looking at the employee as an individual, and at theories of motivation that might help to explain some differences between employees. In looking at this we also consider the important issue of work–life balance.

We then move on to look at employees within a group, and how groups develop. In considering the impact of groups we examine the issues of conformity, prejudice and group diversity.

Chapter 6

In this chapter we look at the role of the trade unions. We define trade unions, and examine the structure and operation of them. In doing this we also look at the role of the TUC and the ETUC. We also look at key statistics giving us an insight into the membership of trade unions. Having looked at those statistics we consider the reasons for the overall decline in trade union membership over recent decades.

In looking at the future for trade unions we consider the impact of European Works Councils, recent legislation on information and consultation and the move towards partnership agreements.

Chapter 7

This chapter introduces us to different processes that are used in employee relations, and focuses on the specific issues of employee involvement and participation. We start by looking at the history of these processes and their relevance today. We then look at specific examples of employee involvement and participation, and examine their advantages and disadvantages.

In looking at the issue of employee participation we further explore the issue of European Works

Councils as well as other initiatives. We end by considering the factors that determine whether employee involvement and participation is a success.

Chapter 8

In this chapter we move on to the process of collective bargaining and negotiation. We start by defining collective bargaining and examining the way that the process works, how it is structured and the extent of its use. We then move on to look at the process of negotiation and the skills required to negotiate successfully.

We end this chapter by considering why conflict can occur within these processes, drawing on the understanding we gained in Chapters 4 and 5 of the role of management and employees.

Chapter 9

We now move on to look at the process for dealing with grievances. We start by understanding what a grievance is, the most common types of grievance and how they develop. In doing this we look at issues associated with the development of attitudes and behaviours. In looking at the management of grievances we examine the Statutory Grievance Procedures, and the skills required to manage grievances effectively. We also look specifically at the issues of harassment and bullying.

We end this chapter by a look at the role of the employment tribunal in addressing grievances that are not resolved within the organisation.

Chapter 10

In this chapter we examine the process of managing reward and the impacts that this has on the employment relationship. We start by understanding the range of impacts and revisit the issues of motivation and the psychological contract. We then look at the different ways that reward can be structured, and the impact that the different structures can have on the employment relationship.

We also look at inequalities in pay, how they develop, and the law that exists to try to remove unfair inequalities.

Chapter 11

We now move on to look at the law and its impact on employee relations, and we begin by looking at the law relating to a key process, that of discipline and dismissals. We examine the use of discipline and the procedures required to use it fairly. We then move on to look at dismissals, examining potentially fair reasons for dismissal, constructive dismissal, automatically unfair reasons for dismissal and wrongful dismissal.

We end the chapter by examining the process of redundancy, considering both the legal requirements and the way to manage such a process with the minimum damage to the employment relationship.

Chapter 12

In this chapter we look at the law specifically relating to employee relations. Hence, we return to the issue of trade unions and consider the law relating to trade union recognition, collective bargaining and protection for the trade union member. We also look at the law relating to other trade union duties.

We then move on to look at the law governing industrial action and associated issues.

Chapter 13

We end the book by looking at the development of employment law, and how this development has affected employee relations. In doing this we look at how the law can be used to promote individuality, address external factors in the employment relationship, determine acceptable behaviour, promote ways of working and underpin the move to partnership deals.

FEATURES OF THE BOOK

This book has a number of features that are designed to make the learning experience more interesting and more enjoyable. The features are as follows.

Activities

The activities are designed to encourage you to participate in active learning, alongside reading the textbook. There are a range of different activities, including suggestions of further reading, encouragement to reflect on the concepts being addressed or requiring you to find out how specific issues are approached within your organisation, or an organisation with which you are familiar. Although it might not be possible to complete all the activities it is strongly recommended that you try a significant number.

Examples to work through

At the end of each chapter there are three examples to work through. It is recommended that you think about these examples, because they will help to test your understanding of the material that you have read. The examples could also be useful practice before an examination.

Case studies

At the end of each chapter there is a case study based on some of the issues covered within the chapter. Again, these are a useful test of your understanding as well as good practice for examinations. (Tutors should note that guidance on the answers for these three features is available at www.cipd.co.uk/tss.)

Key points from this chapter

At the end of each chapter the key points covered in the chapter are listed. It is advised that you work through these points and confirm to yourself that you have understood each of the points that are listed.

Organisation examples

Throughout each chapter there are a number of organisation examples that have been provided to illustrate the theoretical concepts that are being explored. A useful learning activity is to think of further examples that you would give to illustrate the issue.

Tables and figures

Throughout the book there are a number of tables and figures presenting such information as statistical data or research findings. These illustrate key concepts and give further detailed information. (See pages ix and xi for a full list.)

Objectives of the chapter

At the start of each chapter the objectives are set out. This will help you to understand the material that is to be covered in the chapter. At the end of each chapter it is useful to return to those objectives to check that you are confident you have met them all.

FURTHER DEVELOPMENTS IN EMPLOYEE RELATIONS

Finally, it is important to emphasise that employee relations is an ever-evolving and fast-moving topic. It is important, therefore, that you read a good HR journal or magazine (such as *People Management*) alongside this textbook. It is also recommended that you regularly read a good quality newspaper to keep abreast of issues that occur in organisations that affect employee relationships, and to see the theory you will learn through reading this book being applied. Throughout the book a number of relevant websites are cited. It is strongly recommended that you take time to look through these websites to understand concepts and issues in more detail.

What is the Employment Relationship?

CHAPTER 1

The objectives of this chapter are to:

- explain the employment relationship
- give an overview of the history of employee relations
- explore the different approaches to defining the employee relations
- outline how employee relations impacts on the strategic outlook of the organisation
- consider the impact of different organisational structures on employee relations
- explore the role of employee relations within a system
- provide an overview of corporate culture and how this impacts on employee relations.

The purpose of this chapter is to introduce the topic of employee relations. We start by looking at the history of employee relations. Although many might argue that the present is more important, it is very useful to see how the past has shaped the present. We shall do this through examining different approaches that have been taken to employee relations, and understanding what insight they give us into how employee relationships operate.

However, it is not possible to apply a particular theory of employee relations to an organisation or to a situation without understanding the context in which the relationships are operating. In the next chapter we shall focus primarily on the external factors that impact on the employee relationship, and in this chapter we will look at the internal factors. We do this by looking at the features of organisations, such as their structure, size, sector, culture and values. We shall also note that just looking at the structure of the organisation is a somewhat limited approach, because it does not necessarily explain who is the decision-maker in the organisation.

THE HISTORY OF EMPLOYEE RELATIONS

If this textbook had been written 20 years ago it is almost certain that the title would have included the term 'industrial relations' rather than 'employee relations'. Although this change in title might be little more than a change in fashions within human resources, there is also an important point to be made.

As noted by Lewis *et al* (2003), the term 'industrial relations' suggests declining industries and blue-collar workers, with the emphasis being on collective bargaining between trade unions and employers. However, the term 'employee relations' suggests that a wider range of employment is encompassed, with equal importance being placed on white-collar workers and non-union employment issues.

If one looks back at the development of employment over recent years there is plenty of evidence to suggest that the term 'employee relations' is more relevant to today's organisations:

- The manufacturing sector, the employer of many blue-collar workers, has declined significantly and is no longer the largest employment sector in the UK (as it was in the 1960s–70s). In winter 2003 14 per cent of the workforce was employed in manufacturing, compared with 28 per cent in the public sector and 20 per cent in hotels and restaurants (source: www.statistics.gov.uk). This suggests that the key industry supporting the term 'industrial relations' is no longer as relevant to today's world of employment.
- There has been a significant decline in trade union membership. In 2004 the rate of trade union membership amongst all workers was 26.0 per cent. This was a fall of 0.6 per cent compared with 2003 (source: www.statistics.gov.uk). Union membership reached its peak in 1979 when 57 per cent of those in employment were trade union members. This decline suggests that trade union membership is less important to employees today, and hence a fundamental part of the definition of 'industrial relations' is declining.

Apart from these two main attacks on the concept of 'industrial relations' there are also many reasons that the term 'employee relations' has become more relevant:

- There is an increase in white-collar workers – as shown by the statistics quoted above.
- More people are going to university, and hence are looking to work in typical white-collar professions.
- The increase in legislation offering individual protection to employees has meant that employees are less likely to see the need for collective bargaining.
- The recent trends in reward are very focused on paying for individual contribution, be it performance, competencies or skills. Again, this leads employees to seeing less need for collective bargaining.

ACTIVITIES

Understanding the history of employee relations is a useful starting point for understanding some of the issues that are of particular importance to employees today. Talk to someone you know who was in employment 20–30 years ago, and try to gain an understanding of the differences in the workplace between then and now.

DIFFERENT APPROACHES TO EMPLOYEE RELATIONS

Now we have seen that employment has developed and changed, it is important that we understand the concept of employee relations today. Before we consider the various theoretical approaches to gaining this understanding it is interesting to consider the nature of relationships.

We all have a variety of relationships, with friends, partners and colleagues. Although these relationships vary in a number of ways, there are some features that are likely to be common. However, the differences in the relationships will be caused by both internal and external factors:

- Different influences will alter our relationships. External factors such as redundancy, marriage and bereavement all have an impact on our existing relationships.
- Relationships mature. The initial excitement of a new partnership can mature into a stable relationship.
- People change. As we age our priorities change, and we change as a result of major impacts on our lives, for example becoming a parent.

- Expectations change. We might start a relationship with great demands on the other person, but these might decrease as time passes.
- Difficult times occur. All relationships have periods when there is conflict.
- Different types of relationships suit different people. We have all looked at other people and wondered how they tolerate a specific type of relationship.

In the same way that our personal relationships change and develop, so do employment relationships. It is very important that we realise that employment relationships are dynamic and not static:

- **Different influences.** In Chapter 2 we look at the range of external factors and how they impact on the employment relationship. A good example is the economy. In a time of a growing economy employees can demand more of an employer, because if the employee is not satisfied it is relatively easy to get a job elsewhere. In a time of declining economy the employer can make more demands, because employees do not have the same ability to seek work elsewhere if they are not satisfied with what they are being offered.
- **Relationships mature.** As employer and employee continue to work together they gain an understanding of the needs of each other, and they learn to work together. This takes time, and is part of the maturing of a relationship.
- **People change.** In an employment relationship this might quite literally mean change. Employees do leave organisations and new employees arrive, and each time the employer has to build a new relationship. In addition people's values, beliefs and demands can change over time.
- **Expectations change.** As we shall see later in this chapter, the psychological contract comprises the unwritten expectations of the employer and the employee. This psychological contract changes and develops.
- **Difficult times.** When all is going well in an organisation both employer and employee are more likely to be relaxed and ready to 'give and take' within the relationship. However, difficult times – particularly difficult trading situations – will change this. If the employer has to decide whether employee can retain their job, the whole dynamic of the relationship will change.
- **Different types of relationships.** As we shall see in Chapter 4, employees have different styles, as do managements. Some employees will want to work closely with the employer, and be consulted about decisions. Other employees will want to do as they are told, and not be involved in planning and decision-making.

We see, therefore, that in defining 'employee relations' there can be no one definition that works for every relationship. We also see that a definition that fits a relationship at one time might cease to fit as time passes. It is important that we remember this as we look at the various theoretical approaches that have been developed. It is also important that we identify the different internal and external factors that impact on the employment relationship. In this chapter we are focusing on internal factors; we look at external factors in Chapter 2.

We shall start our exploration of the employment relationship by looking at two theoretical approaches. The two approaches to employee relations that are most often cited are unitarism and pluralism, first defined by Fox in 1966.

Unitarism

The key theme of unitarism is harmony between employer and employee – having a common purpose or goal to work towards.

- The concept has teamwork as an essential component.
- There is a single source of authority – that is, management.
- Harmony is expected and conflict does not occur, because everyone is working towards the same goals.
- If conflict does occur it must be the result of poor communication or a troublemaker deliberately stirring up problems.
- There is no need for a trade union representative, because there is harmony, and there are no conflicts to resolve.

The primary weakness of this theory is that it does not see that employees and employers will inevitably have different objectives, even if the overall company mission and direction is agreed between them. The employer is driven by achieving the company targets, be they profits or levels of service. The employee has a mix of objectives, likely to include personal gain (salary and benefits), career development (the job might just be a stepping stone to the next career goal) and achieving a balance between work and outside interests.

It is easy to see how conflict can occur when these different objectives exist. If the employer is driven by getting the work done, however long it takes to achieve that, and the employee wants to achieve a better work–life balance, then it is likely that there will be conflict between them.

If there is conflict of this nature the unitary approach would suggest that it needs to be removed as quickly as possible. Palmer (1983) refers to this as the need to remove deviancy – probably by removing the employee involved.

Another weakness of this theory is that it presumes that the employer will be making the right decisions. If the employer makes a wrong decision then it is possible that conflict will arise because employees will not respect that decision.

Pluralism

Pluralism grew as an explanation for employee relations that addressed some of the weaknesses of unitarism. As Halsey (1995) notes, society in prosperous post-war Britain had changed, and pluralism tried to address these changes.

Fox (1966) saw pluralism as the organisation having several sectional groups with different interests. A central body tries to ensure that all these groups work together to achieve a common goal.

This theory is largely seen as more relevant to the workplace today, in comparison with unitarism. It recognises that employees and the employer do have different interests. Indeed there is also a range of interests amongst employees. As we shall see later in this chapter when we look at different organisation structures, organisations themselves often have a range of different and diverse functions.

It should be noted, however, that there is still a very important and central role for management to play. It is management that is the central body trying to ensure a common goal for the various parties, and it is also management that has the responsibility for managing any conflict that occurs.

In recognising that there are different groups and interests within the organisation the pluralist approach also recognises that there is a real possibility that conflict will occur. Organisations then develop their own processes for dealing with this.

As well as these two approaches it is also worth considering the Marxist approach. Although this might not be a 'traditional' ER approach, it still offers an interesting insight into the relationships of people at work.

Marxism

The theory of Karl Marx, who lived in the 1800s, is often seen as irrelevant today. The principles of the theory are focused largely on the conflict between different classes within society.

McLellan (1999) summarises the key points of Marxism as:

- Class conflict is the result of an uneven distribution of wealth and economic power within society.
- Other conflict, such as social and economic conflict, is the inevitable result of this uneven distribution of wealth.
- The conflict affects a wide range of factors, including an uneven access to such things as education and healthcare.

ORGANISATION EXAMPLE

The miners' strike of 1983–84 is often quoted as an example of a group of employees trying to apply Marxist principles to a work situation. The strike took place at a particularly prosperous time for much of the UK. A large number of employees, particularly within sectors such as finance, were experiencing considerable growth in income, and a new sense of financial security. The strike also took place when a growing number of people owned their own homes for the first time.

Against this growing prosperity whole communities were facing redundancies, with little prospect of re-employment in other industries. Not only were they facing the reality of poverty, they already came from communities where the newfound prosperity of the middle classes was not being experienced. There was a clear divide between the 'haves' and the 'have nots'.

In many of his speeches during the miners' strike the NUM (National Union of Mineworkers) leader, Arthur Scargill, spoke openly of his desire for the strike to result in a redistribution of wealth within the country. He openly admitted that part of the goal of the strike was to bring down the government of the time (Conservatives, led by Margaret Thatcher) and to see real changes in society.

In the end the resolve and the planning of the government meant that the miners did not win the battle. (The government had seen that there was an economic need to close many pits, and had realised that there would be an inevitable battle to achieve this. One part of their planning had been to stockpile two years' worth of coal to be used during the dispute. Hence, the strike never resulted in a dangerous shortage of coal.)

An alternative way to viewing what happened in this strike is to leave aside the Marxism and see it as a real battle for job security. Indeed, with the benefit of knowing what went on to happen, we can see that the concerns of Arthur Scargill for the jobs of his members were very relevant, and that what he feared went on to be realised. Maybe the conflict

> could have been avoided by both parties seeing the inevitability of the decline of the mining industry in the UK and working together to find solutions for those affected.

An interesting comparison is with the demise of the MG Rover Group in the UK in 2005. Although the trade unions did work hard to try to protect the jobs of their members there was no industrial action. Rather, the management, external agencies and the trade unions realised the inevitability of the situation and are now working together to try to find solutions for the difficulties faced by former MG Rover workers.

Although there might be a general acceptance amongst most commentators that Marxism is no longer a relevant model of employee relations for the twenty-first century it would be a mistake to presume that some of the ideals of Marxism are no longer supported. In an article in the *Daily Mail* (Friday 19 July 2002) it was highlighted that a number of trade union leaders are currently members of the Socialist Party, which adopts many Marxist ideals. It was suggested that the battles fought and lost by the miners are still the subject of battles being fought in other industries today.

Collectivism and individualism

At the start of this section we examined the difference between industrial relations and employee relations. In explaining the relevance of the term 'employee relations' we noted that there were a number of reasons that collective bargaining has become a less significant part of the relationships between employees and the employer. This is a reflection of the move away from collectivism towards individualism.

As Kelly (1998) explains, collectivism involves workers mobilising their interests through collective action. This relates very well to the traditional view of the trade unions – groups of employees gathering together to add weight to their arguments.

Clearly, for collectivism to be relevant the group of workers need to have common interests that they want addressed. A well-used example of this is the annual pay negotiation, when all employees have a common interest in getting a significant increment on their current pay.

However, as already noted, the increased focus on individual reward has lessened the relevance of collective bargaining. As noted by Armstrong (2002), the success of collective bargaining largely depends on the amount of pressure that the trade union or other representative body can bring on the employer. However, if the number of employees represented by that body is small, the amount of pressure will be reduced accordingly.

It should also be noted that the increase in employment legislation has meant that employees have less need for collectivism, because the law offers increased individual protection. We look at the range of legislation in later chapters, but it is sufficient to note at this point that there is considerable breadth to the legislation and it is an ever-growing area of protection.

There is also an increased availability of information for employees, which lessens the need for collectivism. In past years an important role of bodies such as the trade unions has been informing employees of their rights. With the growth of the Internet, and readily available information, employees have more ability to represent their own interests.

Collectivism is not an irrelevant concept, however. There are occasions where the very nature of the event will result in employees having common needs and experiences, which will lead to an element of collectivism.

ORGANISATION EXAMPLE

In 2005 the demise of the MG Rover Group was announced, with 5,000 workers being given notices of redundancy. Although there seemed to be nothing left to fight for (there was no point trying to oppose the decision, because there seemed to be no options left) there was a clear sense of collectivism appearing.

This is because the 5,000 workers all faced very similar problems. Although they might have had differing financial situations, and have had differing skills, they were all facing a very uncertain future. Hence, they were largely being treated as a group, and there was a definite reporting of 'collective experience'.

The growth of individualism is also symptomatic of the society that was described in the case study on the miners' strike. In the 1980s a 'have it all' message was portrayed to society, and this was very much focused on personal wealth and prosperity. In addition, the higher levels of education that many employees now experience gives employees greater confidence to deal with their own issues.

Individualism can be seen as attractive to employers, because a major difficulty of collectivism is the potential strength that a group has compared with an individual. However, there are initiatives that seem to promote collectivism.

In April 2005 the Information and Consultation Directive 2002 became part of UK legislation. This directive requires employers with more than 150 employees to put in place a framework for communicating and consulting with employees. (Businesses with 100 or more employees will need to comply by March 2007 and businesses with 50 or more employees must comply by March 2008.)

There are clearly many positive aspects to this – communicating with employees has been shown to improve employee relations (see Chapter 7) and consulting with employees has the purpose of reducing or avoiding conflict. However, by taking this approach of consultation the directive encourages a more collective approach.

In addition, a common theme of successful organisations is the effective use of teamwork. A look at the *Sunday Times* survey of 100 best companies to work for 2005 illustrates this again and again:

- *Asda*: 'Three quarters of staff say their immediate colleagues go out of their way to help them, making it clear that teamwork is high on the Asda agenda.'
- *WS Atkins*: 'Team spirit is good: 78 per cent say they laugh a lot together.'
- *WL Gore and Associates*: 'You've got to be a team player at Gore. Your team ranks your contribution on a scale of one to six, and that's one of the things your salary is based on.'

However, teamwork is bringing employees together as a collective group, rather than encouraging them to operate as individuals.

ACTIVITIES

Reflect on the importance of teamwork within your organisation, or an organisation with which you are familiar. How important is teamwork to that organisation? Do you think that the organisation is an example of an individual or collective approach? Does this fit with the emphasis on teamwork?

EMPLOYEE RELATIONS WITHIN THE ORGANISATION STRUCTURE

A key internal factor that impacts on the employment relationship is the organisation structure within which the relationship is operating. Employment relationships happen within the context of the organisation. The organisation is a group of people who are working together towards a common goal. The achievement of that goal determines the success of the organisation. If employees and the employer are not working effectively together, it is more likely that the organisation will fail.

It is important, therefore, that we understand the different formats that organisations can take, and how they impact on employee relations.

The actual structure of the organisation can influence the success of the activity that takes place to transform the inputs into outputs. There is no one best way to structure an organisation. However, we will take a look at the structures that underpin the structure most commonly used in organisations, and consider the impact that they can have on employee relations.

Functional structure

One of the most commonly used structures is the functional structure. Employees are grouped according to the type of work that they do. A typical structure for an engineering company is shown in Figure 1.1.

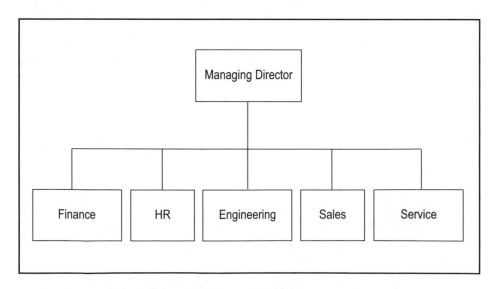

Figure 1.1 Typical structure for an engineering company

This structure results in the needs for the following relationships:

- relationships within the function
- relationships between functions
- relationships between the function and the managing director.

The success of the relationship can be affected by:

- The perceived importance of the function. If sales think that engineering is the only function that is ever listened to, they could feel that they are a less important function.
- The understanding of different functions. There could be the view that finance is only for specialists, and hence the function becomes somewhat isolated from the rest of the organisation.
- Having a common goal. If the different functions have goals that do not all point towards the same organisational goal, there is likely to be some conflict between the different functions.

As stated by Duncan (1979), clear weaknesses of this type of structure are that employees are likely to have a partial view of the organisational goals, they are less likely to be innovative, and there is the potential for poor horizontal co-ordination (ie between functions). However, the structure does allow individuals to develop in-depth knowledge and skills, and is probably the best way for functional goals to be achieved.

Divisional structure

One way to address the rather blinkered mentality that can occur with a functional structure is to develop a divisional structure. In this type of structure the employees are grouped according to such things as products or market sectors. This is particularly effective when there are significant differences between the different sectors. For example, the Virgin Group has a number of different product lines including an airline, a mobile phone company and financial products. There is definite logic in grouping employees according to the division within which they work.

Alternatively, the divisions could be based on the country in which the employee works. Coca-Cola, for example, is present in over 200 countries. Although the logo and the product are universally used, there are differences in the ways that the product is marketed in different countries. Sales and marketing, therefore, could be best structured on a divisional basis according to country.

A divisional structure, therefore, might look something like the structure in Figure 1.2.

This structure results in relationships needed between each division and the managing director, and within divisions. There is the need for some interaction between divisions, but they could have individual goals, albeit directed towards the same overall goal for the organisation.

It is possible that this structure is more efficient for effective employee relations, because employees are working within a division where the goals can be clearly seen, and innovation can be encouraged. However, as Duncan (1979) points out, there is the possibility that it will result in poor co-ordination across product lines.

One way to address this lack of co-ordination can be to encourage mobility between the different

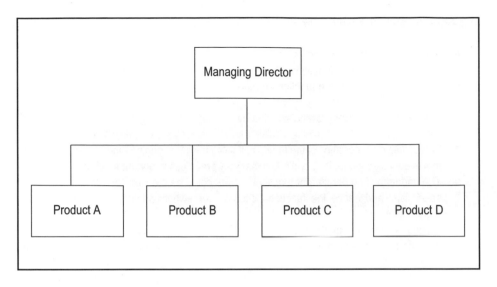

Figure 1.2 A divisional structure

divisions. If employees build up strong relationships within the division, then they will have a point of contact when they move to another division.

It cannot be assumed that all divisions within the organisation are equally attractive to employees, and this can cause conflict in the relationships between employees as well as in the relationship between the employer and the employee. This is demonstrated by looking at a portfolio management system that is used by some employers to identify which areas of the organisation to develop and grow, and which to close.

The Boston Consulting Group Matrix is such a tool. This tool places organisations into one of four boxes, as shown in Figure 1.3.

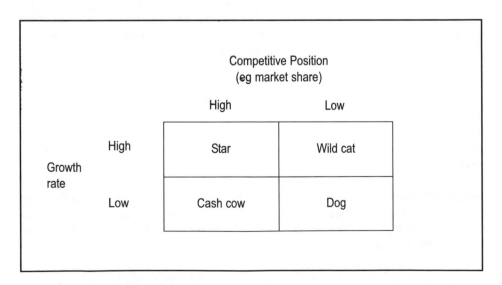

Figure 1.3 The Boston matrix

The Boston Consulting Group define the groups as follows:

- **Stars:** Businesses that are profitable and have a dominant market position. Working within these businesses brings good prospects of promotion and competitive salaries
- **Cash cows:** These are companies that are mature and have a large market share, but are growing slowly. They are secure but not particularly challenging for employees. Promotion is typically only available when people leave, but salaries are comfortable. There is always the possibility that these businesses will start to decline steadily eventually.
- **Wild cats:** These are risky businesses. The market share is still low, but there is a high growth rate. The work can be innovative and exciting and there are likely to be considerable opportunities for career progression and promotion.
- **Dogs:** These businesses are failures. There is a low market share and low rate of growth, and no potential for this situation to change.

Clearly, no employee will want to work in a division that is seen to be a 'dog', and there are likely to be a lot of employees wanting to work for the 'star' division(s). If an employee is denied an opportunity to join a star this will have a negative impact on the employment relationship.

Matrix structure

The matrix structure attempts to address weaknesses of both the divisional and functional models. In this structure employees are based in a functional group that reflects their area of expertise, and are then allocated to work in a particular division. Figure 1.4 explains this structure.

In this structure the relationships are constantly changing. For example, an employee from the finance function might be assigned to Product A for three months, and then to Product D for six months before moving on to Product C. The relationships become fragmented and never fully develop.

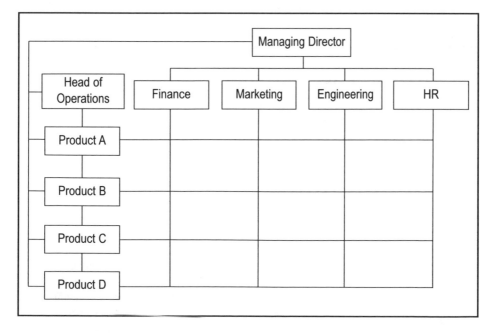

Figure 1.4 Matrix structure

However, there is a clear focus on the goal of each division. It is also a very economic way to deploy staff, because people are sent to the division where they are needed, rather than being under-occupied in one division while another division is struggling to meet deadlines. Another difficulty with this structure is that employees end up having two managers. They are responsible both to the manager in charge of the division, and to their functional division. This can lead to split loyalties, and can also be confusing if instructions from the two managers differ.

What we see from looking at these three examples of organisation structures is that the term 'employee relations' is somewhat confusing. It is typically used to suggest a relationship between an employee and the employer. However, from looking at these structures we have been able to identify two key points:

1. Within the organisation there are ranges of relationships, all of which must be operating effectively if the organisation is to work successfully. It could be concluded, therefore, that concentrating our examination of employee relations solely on the relationship between employee and employer is a limited approach.
2. If we do conclude that the focus is solely on the relationship between the employer and the employee, then we have to acknowledge that it is not always easy to identify who the 'employer' is. In the structures we have looked at, is it the managing director who is the 'employer' – or is that role too remote from the daily operations of the employee? If the role is too remote, then is the key relationship the one between the employee and the head of the function/division? If this is the case, then what is the key relationship in the matrix structure?

Try to find out the organisation structure used by the following organisations: McDonald's, Barclays Bank, Honda, Asda. Explain why these structures might have been chosen. Do you think they are the most effective approaches for efficient employee relations?

EMPLOYEE RELATIONS WITHIN A SYSTEM

Having identified the organisation structure, we also have to understand how the organisation operates. This process of operation is another key internal factor in the employment relationship.

According to Daft (1998), it is important to view the organisation as a system. The system is a number of interacting elements. Inputs come from the environment, the organisation transforms those inputs, then outputs are discharged to the external environment. This model of a system presumes that people and departments must work effectively together. If one part of that system breaks down then the organisation will be unable to function.

A good example of how a system can break down was demonstrated by the industrial action that was taken in the Royal Mail in October/November 2003. Initially there was a series of unofficial strike action within London and the surrounding areas relating to a variety of issues, from a dead rat that was found in a toilet to the suspension of a trade union representative. However, around

> one-fifth of all post handled by the Royal Mail passes through London, and gradually the impact of the industrial action spread across the country.
>
> The system of delivering the mail broke down, and gradually post office workers in other areas of the country stopped working.

It is important that the employer understands the nature of the system in this situation. If the employer does not resolve a problem that erupts at one stage of the system, the whole system can quickly decay. Hence, there is a need to address problems efficiently and effectively as they arise. It is also interesting to note that the employees are aware of how the system operates. They are aware that industrial action in just one part of the system can quickly broaden its impact, because of the nature of the system. Hence, they can bring most of the system (in the example, the postal network) to a standstill just by taking action in one part of the country.

In viewing the organisation as a system Thompson (1967) suggested that there are two types of system, closed and open. A closed system is independent of the external environment. The external environment is stable and unchanging, and hence all management attention is given to the internal systems. In reality this type of organisation does not exist. As we shall see in Chapter 2, there are wide ranges of external factors that can potentially impact on an organisation, and this lack of stability cannot be ignored.

However, the concept of the closed system is the basis on which much of the work of F. W. Taylor (1856–1915) was based. Taylor developed a scientific approach to management. His view was that organisations were machines, and the people who worked within them were the source of variation within an organisation, and were largely unreliable. Hence, he identified the need to focus on reducing the unreliability and variability of employees, presuming that if this was addressed, the organisation as a whole would be more productive.

Although we have not the space here to look at all of Taylor's work in depth, it is interesting to see some of the measures he put in place to manage employees. His approach was to scientifically analyse the work that was to be done, and to break it down into small component parts of the overall job. Then he recruited workers who were best suited to the job, and trained them in the small tasks that he had identified. Managers were then required to plan the work and give precise instructions to employees each day. Employees were required to follow those instructions precisely, and if they achieved their work within the specified time limits they were given an increase on their ordinary wages.

This scientific approach resulted in a significant level of hostility from employees. The jobs were broken down to such a level that they were mundane and monotonous. Employees were typically seated so that they could not communicate easily with each other, because that would distract them from the achievement of the tight time targets. This led to employees feeling isolated and humiliated.

Although it is not necessary to employ such rigid methods as those developed by Taylor, working within a closed system can stifle the creativity of employees. This is because the challenges provided by the external environment are being ignored, and the emphasis is on refining internal processes.

In such an environment the employee relationships are likely to be very focused on the manager telling and the employee doing. This is because the manager needs to retain control over the internal processes.

ORGANISATION
EXAMPLE

Henry Ford used the basis of Taylor's work on scientific management when planning his car plants. He identified the time needed to carry out each small component of the assembly of a car, and identified ways in which that time could be reduced by more efficient organisation of the assembly process.

While he accepted that many of the jobs were monotonous, he concluded that no harm would come to any of his employees if they did monotonous work, and they always had the option of leaving if they did not like it.

One could argue that the car plants worked effectively because of this very rigid style of management. Alternatively, one could argue that allowing employees to add in their own creativity and improvements would have produced better work more effectively in the longer term.

From this philosophy, much of the assembly line approach that has been so common in manufacturing was developed. However, the system did not allow for any variation in the system – and this is almost inevitable. For example, if there is a variation in the temperature or humidity some processes will operate differently. This adds weight to the suggestion that, in reality, a closed system does not operate within an organisation. A more modern approach focuses on the innovation and creativity that employees do possess, and a consideration of how this can be captured to improve the internal processes, and to help address issues resulting from external factors. Hence, more modern approaches acknowledge the existence of an open system and try to use the positive aspects of this type of system for the benefit of the organisation.

An open system needs to interact with the external environment. If it is to survive it must adapt and change in accordance with the demands of the external environment. The great majority of organisations are open systems. They need to be constantly aware of the changes in demands from customers, the activities of competitors, and so on, and they need to adapt accordingly. If they do not adapt then they are likely to fail.

Working within an open system can be a very exciting experience for employees. However, it is also an experience that can lead to difficult relationships as changes have to be introduced which employees are not happy with, or which affect the security of the employees' jobs.

ORGANISATION
EXAMPLE

The Royal Mail faces a difficult time with its monopoly on mail delivery due to be removed in 2006. Already facing significant losses, and the changing habits of customers (using e-mail and texting instead of writing letters), the employer has to take action if it is to survive. This has led to a number of disputes with employees, particularly over changing working practices.

In this situation, the system has got to change to address the new working conditions. The Royal Mail is a good example of the system being forced to change by external factors (such as the removal of the monopoly).

Source: www.bbc.co.uk/news.

Chaos theory

Although there are significant differences in the definitions of open and closed systems, in both concepts there is the assumption that the changes that occur in either the external or the internal environment are somewhat manageable. However, as Daft (1998) states, the world is complex and full of randomness and uncertainty, and the organisation needs to operate within the chaos that this creates.

It is important that organisations are able to respond to the unpredictable, and in doing this they need to be prepared to change the ways that they do things. Chaos theory suggests that the role of the manager is to ensure that all employees clearly understand the mission and values of the organisation. The employees are then empowered to act within those mission and values, requiring them to take on additional responsibility for decision-making that would previously have been shouldered by management.

This chaos demonstrates the fragility of the employment relationship. If it is accepted that organisations do have to operate in some degree of chaos, it must also be accepted that there is no longer such a thing as a 'job for life', and that employees need to be prepared to learn new skills in order to remain employable. This results in both employers and employees having expectations and needs that might be unspoken, but have a significant impact on the employment relationship.

Psychological contract

One way that these unspoken demands have been explained is through the concept of the psychological contract.

The psychological contract was first described by Schein (1988), who suggested that it contains three kinds of individual expectations:

1. The need to be treated fairly. Employees want to see that they are treated equally to others, and also want information about any changes that might take place.
2. Employees want some level of security and certainty in return for giving loyalty to the employer.
3. Employees have a need for fulfilment, satisfaction and progression. Employees want to know that organisations place a value on their current contributions, prior successes and on their relationships.

Heriot (1995) showed how the different expectations of the employee and the employer within the employment relationship have changed over time. His conclusions have been summarised in Table 1.1. In the 1970s many employees worked for one employer throughout their working career, and in return for this experienced a level of security and care that satisfied their needs.

Table 1.1 How the different expectations of the employee and employer have changed over time

The individual offers:	The organisation offers:
1970s	
loyalty	security
compliance	promotion
good citizenship	care
1980s	
accountability	a job
flexibility	higher salary
long hours	
2010s	
learning	employability
learning to learn	flexible contract
clear added value	individualised rewards

In the 1980s there was a significant recession and the expectations of the employment relationship changed. The concept of jobs for life started to disappear, and the concept of loyalty to one employer was also eroded. This led to the 1990s when the primary requirement from the employee was for a job and, as the recession ended, for a high personal salary. However, the employee started to realise that more was expected by the employer than loyalty. Hence, the emphasis moved to be on accountability, flexibility and working long hours.

When Heriot devised this table 10 years ago he predicted that, by 2010, the emphasis would be primarily on learning, flexibility and the individual. He is largely correct.

Organisations today operate in a very fast-moving and competitive environment. There is also a move towards a knowledge economy, where ideas and creativity are important. Hence, employees need to keep learning – so that they are constantly able to bring new and up-to-date ideas to the organisation to help it retain its competitiveness. This concept of lifelong learning is definitely part of the expectations of the employer and the employee.

In return the employee is demanding increased flexibility – and an improved work–life balance. We will explore both of these concepts later in the book. There is also, as we have already noted, an increased move towards individualism away from collectivism.

THE IMPACT OF ORGANISATIONAL FEATURES ON THE EMPLOYMENT RELATIONSHIP

In looking at the organisation structure, and the organisation as a system, we have been looking at internal factors at a macro level. However, it is also important to see how individual features of an organisation can impact on the employment relationship. Although a number of organisations might operate with the same approach, individual organisations will have specific features that impact on the way that they conduct their relationships with employees. These include the following.

Size

If the employee is working in an organisation of just 10 people the relationships are likely to be much closer and much more intense than in an organisation of 100,000 people. In a small organisation it is much easier to identify the employer and the employee, and it is much easier to determine who is in charge. As already noted, in a larger organisation there are likely to be a number of people who hold positions of responsibility, and hence it is more difficult to precisely define the employer/employee relationship. It is obviously easier to communicate effectively in a small organisation.

Locations

If the employee is working at the same location as all other employees, and at the same location as the manager, then the employment relationship will typically develop more quickly and more effectively. If the employee has very little contact with the employer then it becomes more difficult to build up a rapport and understanding.

Shift patterns/flexible working

It is possible for the employer and the employee to work at the same location, but not see each other because they are not there at the same time. This is partly due to the increased demands from customers, particularly of the service sector, for availability to products and services around the clock, and it is also due to the increased availability of flexible working.

Sector

Different sectors result in different goals for employees, and this can have an impact on the nature of the employment relationship – because it impacts on the priorities placed on the employee by the employer. In the private sector it is very likely the goal is increased sales and profits. However, in the voluntary sector the goals will be much more focused on meeting a particular need of a group, which can lead to a much more collaborative approach between employer and employee.

Strategy

Throughout this chapter we have made reference to the organisation aiming to achieve some form of goal. The strategy is the process by which this goal will be achieved. Key parts of the strategy are often determined by the competition.

Porter (1990) defines three different competitive strategies, all of which have implications for the way that employees behave within the organisation.

1. A low-cost leadership strategy is characterised by a strong central authority, close supervision and limited employee empowerment. The relationship here is one of 'tell and do'. Employees are not encouraged to be creative and innovative. For some employees this is a comfortable way of working, but for others it is frustrating. The different reactions of employees to the way of working can lead to intragroup conflict – with some of the group wanting things to change, and others resisting that change. There can also be conflict with the leadership – with employees feeling undervalued and under-utilised.

2. A differentiation strategy is when organisations attempt to show how their products or services are different from the competitor, setting themselves apart as unique in some way. The unique factor could relate to such things as price, features of the product or the actual product/service itself. This results in an employment relationship that is categorised by wanting greater creativity from employees. This will lead to increased employee involvement (see Chapter 7), which often leads to increased motivation and commitment. However, some employees will flourish in this environment while others will struggle to be creative, or might not feel able to contribute. This can also lead to intragroup conflict and conflict with management.

3. A focus strategy is when the organisation makes the decision to concentrate on a specific market or buyer group. Within this narrowly defined market the organisation will attempt to obtain an advantage, either through price or through differentiation of the product/service. This encourages employees to develop customer loyalty, and requires them to focus clearly on specific areas of activity. The development of such a strategy clearly has an impact for employees who previously worked on peripheral markets, and some employees can find the narrower approach dull and uninspiring.

Flexibility

In looking at the psychological contract we acknowledged that the concept of flexibility is a key topic for the twenty-first century. However, the concept of flexibility can also impact on the security of employment that employees enjoy.

Atkinson (1984) developed the flexible firm model. In this model an organisation employs a number of core workers who are employed on standard contracts. In addition to this core a number of peripheral workers are employed through a variety of means (temporary contracts, fixed term contracts, sub-contractors, and so on). To retain efficiency the employer can alter the number of peripheral workers in accordance with the demands on the organisation.

This approach has weaknesses for both the employer and the employee. The employee never gains any security, and hence any relationship that is built up with the employer rarely has any depth of loyalty within it. In return the employer has little ability to retain the peripheral workforce, because no security is being offered. Hence, the employer might invest time and money in training workers only to find that they leave as soon as they find more secure employment.

In addition, the model presumes that there is a pool of peripheral workers available to the employer. Whilst this might be true of areas of high unemployment, this is not necessarily true at other times. The model also presumes that the skills required by the employer are available within the pool that exists.

Think of an organisation with which you are familiar. Describe the organisation in relation to the features that have been listed in this section. How do you think those features impact on the relationships between the employer and the employee within that organisation?

THE DECISION-MAKER AND THE EMPLOYMENT RELATIONSHIP

When we looked at the variety of structures that an organisation might use, we noted that it is not always clear who the employment relationship is between. This can become increasingly difficult when it is not clear who is actually making the decisions that affect the employment relationship

In the winter of 2002/03 the FBU (Fire Brigade Union) took industrial action. This was as a result of their request for a 40 per cent pay increase being refused by the management.

The FBU was negotiating the deal with the Local Government Association. However, at the same time the government, and particularly the deputy prime minister (John Prescott) were seen to be influencing the ability of the Local Government Association to reach an agreement. This was demonstrated when, in the early hours in November 2002, the FBU and the Local Government Association reached an agreement that both parties were willing to accept and which, therefore, would have resulted in no strike action being taken. However, when John Prescott was informed of the detail of the agreement he is reported as refusing to allow it to go ahead. At this point talks collapsed and the FBU did go on to take strike action.

This is an unusual example, but it still demonstrates how it was not clear who the two sides to the employment relationship were. Clearly, the FBU was representing the employees, but it was not clear who they really needed to reach an agreement with.

In this case, the focus needed to be on the relationship between the employee and the paymaster, rather than the relationship between the employee and the person who, on a daily basis, was seen to be the employer. As we note in Chapter 3, the role of the government as an employer does add some complexities into the employment relationship.

Source: www.bbc.co.uk/news.

To a lesser extent this can be the case in many organisations. If the managing director is the 100 per cent owner of the organisation it can be presumed that s/he has full control over the decision making process. However, in most organisations that is not the case, and it is possible that the most senior employee does not have full decision-making powers. It could be argued that this is the case for all public limited companies (plcs), because the companies are owned by the share-holders and hence they have the final say over key business decisions through their ability to vote on propositions at the AGM.

It is also very possible that the most senior person in Organisation B is reporting to a senior person in Organisation A, which actually owns Organisation B. This is increasingly true given the mergers and acquisitions that take place. Although the most senior person in the organisation is likely to have a large discretionary power to make decisions, there could be agreements reached with employees that are overruled at a later stage.

This does cause a difficulty for employees, and particularly for those negotiating on the behalf of a group of employees. Clearly, the whole process is seen as a waste of time and effort if those involved in the relationship do not have the power to reach an agreement.

THE IMPACT OF CULTURE AND VALUES ON THE EMPLOYMENT RELATIONSHIP

The last internal factors that we look at in this chapter are the culture and values within the organisation. In the Sunday Times survey of 100 best companies to work for 2003 many of the descriptions referred to the culture of the organisations. Two examples of this are:

- *Richer Sounds*: 'You only have to step into Richer Sounds' head office in southeast London to realise that making work fun is a concept that Britain's largest hi-fi retailer takes very seriously indeed. Among the desks and computers and hard-working employees you can find a whole army of wacky artworks, including a life-size Elvis and Fido.'
- *Timpson*: 'The company believes in praising 10 times more than criticising, and area managers issue so many prizes that many carry a permanent stock in the boot of their cars.'

The culture of the organisation is a mix of the beliefs, values, mission, approaches to thinking and understandings. It is often communicated to employees, and to the wider world, in the format of a mission statement. It is a description of how the organisation should operate, and the reasons why specific issues are of importance to the organisation.

The culture of the organisation helps employees to know how they should behave within the organisation. It also informs customers of the values that are most important, and can be used as a competitive edge.

ORGANISATION EXAMPLE

The Body Shop has the following five clear values:

- We consider testing products or ingredients on animals to be morally and scientifically indefensible.
- We support small producer communities around the world who supply us with accessories and natural ingredients.
- We know that you're unique, and we'll always treat you like an individual. We like you just the way you are.

- We believe that it is the responsibility of every individual to actively support those who have human rights denied to them.
- We believe that a business has the responsibility to protect the environment in which it operates, locally and globally.

Source: www.thebodyshop.com.

If an employee is thinking of applying to the Body Shop and shares these values, he or she is likely to find it easier to fit into the organisation and make effective relationships – because s/he will be making relationships with like-minded people. If an person has dramatically opposed values to the Body Shop, he or she is unlikely to enjoy working there, or to make effective relationships (and it is unlikely that the Body Shop would make an offer of employment).

However, not all organisations have values that are as emphatically expressed as The Body Shop. Daft (1998) suggests that there are four different models of corporate culture that organisations fit into:

1. **Adaptability/entrepreneurial culture.** This type of culture is focused on the need for flexibility and change in order to meet customer needs. As well as adapting to the changes required as a result of pressures from the external environment, there is also the encouragement to be innovative and create change.

   Employees who enjoy risk-taking, creativity and innovation will thrive in this type of organisation. Relationships are likely to be ever-changing, as job roles and people within those roles change.

   Examples of this type of culture are found in fast-moving and developing industries, such as mobile phone companies. The functionality and pricing structures of mobile phones are constantly developing. A mobile phone company that does not innovate will die, and a mobile phone company that follows and does not innovate will lose market share as it will always be a follower.

2. **Mission culture.** This type of organisation does not have the same need for rapid change. There is a greater focus on achieving specific goals (eg profits, sales). The organisation is relatively stable and hence there are likely to be clear rewards for employees who perform in accordance with the organisational goals.

   This type of organisation will suit the employee who does not like to take risks, but prefers to have some stability at work. The relationships are likely to be steady and there is likely to be less change of personnel within the organisation. There are likely to be clear reporting structures with individuals having clear roles.

   Examples of this type of culture are the high street banks. Although they have changed greatly over recent years there is a certain stability about their purpose and their products/services.

3. **Clan culture.** The key feature of the clan culture is the involvement and participation of employees. The culture focuses on the needs of employees, and sees that commitment to employees will lead to a greater commitment to the organisation. The external environment is likely to place ever-changing demands on the organisation.

   This will suit an employee who is uncomfortable with the level of risk taking in the adaptability/entrepreneurial culture, but wants something a little more change-oriented than the mission culture. There are likely to be close bonds drawn up between employees, and between employer and employees, through the process of involvement.

Examples of this type of organisation are often found in those involved in creativity – such as the fashion industry. The product (clothes or accessories), is constant but the need to innovate is high.

4. **Bureaucratic culture.** In this culture there is a strong focus on internal systems and there is likely to be a stable environment. There is a methodical approach to doing the job, and a high level of consistency and conformity. The organisation is typically efficient, and relationships and status are clearly defined.

   Although many employees might see this to be a stifling culture, other employees enjoy the structure and the security that it brings. There is a clear understanding of the expectations, and employees learn how to interact with each other. An example of this is the Civil Service, which is very structured and where relationships and status within the service is clearly defined.

SO WHAT IS EMPLOYEE RELATIONS?

We started this chapter with the task of understanding employee relations. We have shown by looking at the various impacts on the employment relationship that it is very difficult to define. It is difficult to define because it is affected by the features of the organisation that an employee works in, the structure of the organisation, the culture and values of the organisation, and by who is making the decisions within the organisation.

Although we might therefore reach the unsatisfactory conclusion that it is not possible to give a clear definition of the employment relationship, what we have seen is that the relationship is complex and dynamic.

We have also seen the importance of the employment relationship to the success of the organisation. If the relationship fails then the organisation cannot achieve its goals, and ultimately might also fail.

KEY POINTS FROM THIS CHAPTER

- Employee relations is more relevant to today's organisations than industrial relations.
- The key theme of unitarism is harmony between the employer and employee.
- Pluralism is seeing the organisation as having several sectional groups with differing interests.
- Marxism is largely focused on the conflict between different classes within society.
- Collectivism is mobilising the interest of a group through collective pressure, whereas individualism is promoting one's own individual interests.
- The structure of the organisation determines the primary relationships within that organisation.
- The matrix structure attempts to address the weaknesses of the functional and divisional structures, but can leave the employee with conflicting relationships.
- Organisations are a type of system, and a system can be described as open or closed.
- Chaos theory suggests that we work in a world full of randomness and uncertainty.
- The psychological contract contains the unwritten expectations of employer and employee.

- Size, location, working patterns, sector, strategy and flexibility are features of an organisation that can all impact on employment relationships.
- It is important to define who is the decision-maker within the employment relationship.
- The type of culture within the organisation will impact on the types of relationships that develop.

EXAMPLES TO WORK THROUGH

1. You work in an organisation that operates according to a functional structure. There have been a number of incidences when projects have not been completed on time, and this is thought to be a result of the lack of communication and co-operation between different functions. You have been asked to advise how the organisation could be adapted to stop these sorts of incidences occurring. Advise the organisation.

2. Identify organisations that are examples of each of the four types of culture as defined by Daft. Justify the examples that you have given.

3. Write out the psychological contract that is likely to have been experienced by the employer and the employee in the following situations:
   - members of the FBU and employers during the fire strike of 2002/03
   - an individual employee of Rover Group on being made redundant following the collapse of the organisation.

(Suggested answers for example questions can be accessed by tutors at www.cipd.co.uk/tss).

CASE STUDY

Banking is a sector that has experienced significant change over recent years. The major changes have included:

- a number of building societies changing to become banks
- a number of supermarkets creating banks.
- a number of online banks setting up (such as 'Egg') which only deal with customers online, and do not have any branch networks
- some significant mergers between the big-name banks, such as NatWest and the Royal Bank of Scotland and the formation of Lloyds TSB.

Another major change has come from the introduction of new technology. Before the age of computers a lot of staff resource was employed simply to process all the paperwork and to handle the large amounts of cash. Now, computers have replaced many of the 'backroom jobs', and customers use less cash, relying more on the use of credit cards for transactions.

In addressing the many challenges that these changes have brought about, one of the key concerns for the sector has been customer service. Customers have more choice then ever before about where to bank, and hence providing excellent levels of service has become mandatory, rather than optional.

Premium Bank has become increasingly concerned about this issue of customer service, following a steady increase of complaints. Most of the complaints are not about major errors, rather they are complaints about the manner in which problems have been dealt with. Premium Bank has commissioned some research and the results have now been presented to them.

The consultants have concluded that there is a direct link between the levels of customer service and the relationship between Premium Bank and its employees. They have investigated this further, and found that employees who were reported to give poorest levels of customer service where also the employees who felt dissatisfied with work at Premium Bank. It was also interesting to note that these groups of employees had received less communication from the bank than other groups, and also had less interaction with other departments within the bank. The results were summarised well by the comment one employee wrote on her questionnaire:

> No, I don't really care about customer service. But then, why should I? I come to work, do my job and go home again. No one from head office ever tells us anything, and I do not feel of any value to the bank. If they valued me then I would value their customers.

The consultants have suggested that part of the problem could be the organisational structure that the bank operates. It is a functional structure. There are the following main functions:

- Branch network
- HR
- Accounts
- Marketing
- Sales

Each of these functions has a senior director who reports directly to the chief executive. All senior staff are based at the headquarters of the bank, which is in Swindon.

Another suggestion that has been made is that the problem lies with the ways that the employees operate:

Customer service is primarily dealt with within the branch network. Each branch has a manager, and the number of staff within the branch depends on its size and the area of the country that it is covering. The smallest branch has five staff, and the largest has 48. The branch staff all have clearly defined roles, and have little interaction with any other Premium Bank employees outside the branch. They all have individual targets to reach, which are based on sales of products. They have very little discretion in the types of products that they are allowed to sell. This is partly due to regulation with the financial services industry, and partly due to the product focus determined by the bank.

Over 60 per cent of the staff do not work regular full-time hours. Many staff work part-time hours, with a variety of shifts that are agreed individually with the branch manager.

Premium Bank is determined to improve its levels of customer service, but it has been persuaded by the consultants that it has employed that the solution is not just a matter of exhorting the employees to do better. The bank has been persuaded that it needs to review the way that it operates, and to address the low levels of motivation and satisfaction. The bank believes that if it achieves this, customer service will automatically improve.

The difficulty is the bank does not know what to do. Hence, it has asked the consultants to come back and make suggestions about what it could do to address those problems. You are the lead consultant.

Answer the following questions that have been posed by the bank:

1. Would it help to address the problems if we changed our organisation structure? If so, what structure would be best to change to, and why? If you think we should keep our current structure, how can we improve it to help address the problems we are experiencing?
2. Do you think that we need to change the way that our employees work? If so, what changes do you think would have the biggest positive impact on the relationship between the employer and the employee, and also within groups of employees?

External Factors and their Impact on the Employment Relationship

CHAPTER 2

> The objectives of this chapter are to:
>
> - explore how the external environment impacts on employment relations
> - outline the political impacts than can affect employee relations
> - outline the economic impacts that can affect employee relations
> - outline the social impacts that can affect employee relations
> - outline the technological impacts that can affect employee relations
> - outline the legal impacts that can affect employee relations
> - outline the ethical/environmental impacts that can affect employee relations.

In the last chapter we looked primarily at the internal factors that can impact on the employment relationship. In this chapter we move our focus to look at the external factors.

An effective way that many students are taught to examine the external environment is to carry out a PESTLE analysis – looking at the political, economic, social, technological, legal and ethical/environmental factors that have an impact. In this chapter we follow this outline.

As well as the issues that we look at in this chapter there are some specific external factors such as the impact of the government, the European Union and globalisation. These areas are given a more detailed examination in Chapter 3.

THE EXTERNAL ENVIRONMENT

In Chapter 1 we looked at a number of factors that can impact on the employment relationship. However, it would be wrong to assume that all an organisation has to consider is what is happening within it. Indeed, we acknowledged this when we considered the difference between open and closed systems. An organisation does not operate in isolation from the events of the outside world.

This is well illustrated by the impact of the tragic events of 11 September 2001, involving the hijacking of a number of aeroplanes and the ultimate destruction of the twin towers of the World Trade Center. Prior to this date airline companies would have had strategies and plans in place. Then, as a result of those events all the planning and strategies had to be changed – and in place came a struggle for survival, which some airlines did not achieve.

Another example is the foot and mouth crisis of 2001. However well planned and run organisations within the farming industry were, all of a sudden external events happened which had a catastrophic impact on many farms.

It is very easy to be simplistic in thinking about the impacts of such events and presume it is just about job loss. It is true that many of those affected by the two events lost jobs, but there are also other lasting effects. Wheatley (2003) reports that leadership styles within organisations affected by 9/11 have changed to become more controlling and commanding. She equates this to the perception that organisations believe that more control is needed at time of risk.

As well as acknowledging that external events can impact on the organisation, we also have to acknowledge that the events can happen at different levels within the external environment. Salamon (2000) identifies these different levels as being within the industry (for example, the decline of the manufacturing industry), nationally and internationally. It might seem appropriate to split the international impact in two – the impact of the European Union within which the UK needs to operate, as a member, and the wider international scene.

The degree of influence from external factors will vary from organisation to organisation. This degree of influence will depend upon a number of dimensions (Daft 1998) which we now examine.

Stability

The stability of the organisation depends on the extent to which the external environment is ever-changing. For some industries the demands do change constantly. For example the telecommunications industry has seen great change over recent years. We have moved from relying on land-line phones, to relying on mobile phones, to developing videophones. The demands of customers and the product developments result in a lack of stability for organisations.

Complexity

Complexity refers to the number of external factors that are impacting on the environment. For example, a hospital has become an increasingly complex environment. External factors include the government setting targets and introducing a range of changes, customers (ie the patients), the range of medical staff and the need to recruit accordingly, and the increased complexity of many medical procedures resulting in the need for new equipment and processes. However, a small corner shop that has passed down from generation to generation and is probably only impacted on by customers (many long-standing and loyal) and a few suppliers is not a complex organisation (although it might be struggling to survive in an ever-competitive market place).

Dispersed

An organisation that has many subunits that are dispersed either nationally or internationally will have a greater range of external factors imposing on it compared with an organisation that is based on location only. Take an organisation such as McDonald's, which operates in 119 countries. In each country there are different laws and regulations that have an impact on McDonald's. Compare this with a restaurant that has just one outlet in one place in the UK – clearly a much smaller range of impacts are evident.

ACTIVITIES

Consider each of the following organisations, and determine the extent that it is affected by the external environment in relation to complexity, stability and dispersion: Marks & Spencer; the university or college in which you are studying; the police force; Lastminute.com; and Oxfam. On the basis of your analysis, which organisation do you think has the greatest number of external impacts?

THE IMPACT OF THE EXTERNAL ENVIRONMENT ON EMPLOYEE RELATIONS

Now we have seen that different types of organisations experience different ranges of impacts from the external environment, our next consideration is what impact this has on employee relations.

Thompson (1967) reports that the traditional approach to coping with a range of uncertainty in the environment was to create buffer departments. These departments deal with the uncertainty, leaving the core of the organisation to get on with making the product or providing the service. However, this protection of the core of the organisation from external impacts such as the customer and the supplier can lead to a less responsive organisation. It also takes away some of the responsibility from employees for innovating and understanding what the customer wants. This can lead to a monotonous job for the employees in the core, and also the feeling of a lack of trust from those in the buffer departments (and a lack of trust from management in considering that buffer departments are required). If we think back to the psychological contract we considered in Chapter 1, we could presume that employees might offer increased loyalty in response to increased trust. Many organisations have now removed any buffers, and trust employees to be more exposed to customers and employees.

ORGANISATION EXAMPLE

W L Gore and Associates (manufacturers of Gore-tex, a breathable, water-resistant fabric) is singled out in the *Sunday Times* survey of 100 best companies to work for 2005 for its approach to innovation. Within the organisation there are no directors, managers or operatives – everyone is an 'associate' and is accountable to each other. Team members even influence each other's pay. As a result of this approach the survey found that nine out of every ten employees think their manager trusts their judgement.

This structuring of the organisation has clearly removed all buffer departments, and has made all employees accountable. Although it is maybe an extreme example of an approach that can be taken, it is the organisation that was found to be 'number one' in the survey.

It is interesting to consider whether this approach would work for all organisations. Without the rules and structures that we more commonly associate with organisation structures, would some organisations decay into chaos?

Another approach that can be taken to dealing with an organisation that has many external impacts is to create specialists within that organisation. Lorsch (1970) refers to this as differentiation. This links back with the functional approach to organisation structures that we saw in Chapter 1. This does allow experts to be created and developed within an organisation, but it also gives employees a narrow experience within the organisation. It can also lead to poor relationships between functions, because employees within each function do not understand or appreciate the work of other functions.

Daft (1998) identifies the importance of boundary-spanning roles. He identifies boundary spanning as the process of gaining information about the external environment and bringing this information into the organisation, and also promoting the organisation favourably in the

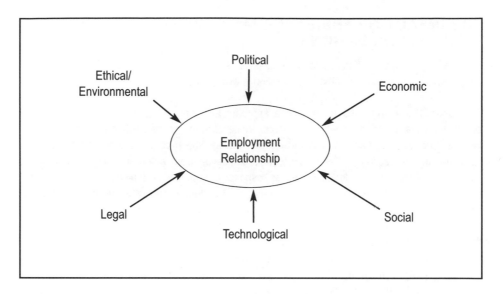

Figure 2.1 External factors impacting on the employment relationship

external environment. Schwab *et al* (1985) suggest that the greater the complexity of the organisation, the more important the role of boundary spanning.

It is possible to see how this process of boundary spanning could help some of the isolation experienced by those working within the kind of functional structure that is needed to grow experts in a complex environment. If the information that is gathered from the external environment is clearly and widely communicated there is likely to be a more cohesive organisation, and a greater understanding of the purpose of the different roles within that organisation. As a result of this some of the negative impacts caused on the employment relationships could be eliminated.

Now we have seen that the external environment can impact on the way that organisations structure, and hence on the experiences of individuals within those organisations, we look at external impacts in more detail.

THE IMPACTS OF POLITICAL FACTORS ON EMPLOYEE RELATIONS

The government impacts on employee relations through developing legislation relating to employment, through policies affecting economics and social factors (as we shall see as we progress through this chapter) and through the management of the public sector. We examine the role of the government as an employer in Chapter 3, but it is important to note here that the government is a huge employer in the UK, with one in five of all people working in the public sector (Philpott 2005b).

In recent history one of the biggest changes brought on employment through politics was the election of a Conservative government in 1979. Prior to this there had been a significant unsettled period in employee relations, culminating in the 'Winter of Discontent' in 1978/79 when a number of major trade unions went on strike. This prolonged period of industrial action is largely seen as the event that brought down the Labour government of that time.

The Conservative government focused on promoting individualism and private enterprise. Home ownership, for example, grew to new and unprecedented levels during this period of government. The Conservative government also focused on reducing the perceived imbalance of power between employers and employees, by introducing legislation that made it more difficult for employees to take industrial action. We will examine the detail of this legislation in more detail in Chapter 12, but the introduction of it was definitely significant in reducing the impact of unrest that had been apparent.

The Conservative government distanced itself somewhat from the European Union, and refused to sign the Social Chapter of the Maastricht Treaty 1992. This Treaty set out a number of basic rights relating to employment, living and working conditions, social security, training and social cohesion. Although the UK already met many of these standards there were implications of signing the chapter, such as the requirement to introduce a national minimum wage.

In 1997 the period of Conservative government came to an end and Labour returned to government. It was largely expected that the Labour government would reduce some of the stringent requirements on employees in relation to taking industrial action. Traditionally, the Labour government had been supported by trade unions and hence it was expected to take actions to redress the balance of power in favour of the employee.

However, the Labour government promoted itself as 'New Labour' and the old-style attitudes of the Labour Party were not as apparent. It did introduce the Employment Relations Act 1999, which made some adjustments to the legislation introduced by the Conservative Party, but this was largely seen as 'tinkering round the edges' rather than making fundamental changes.

A part of the Labour Party manifesto had been to sign the Social Chapter, and the government did this soon after being elected. As already referenced, this resulted in a number of changes in employment legislation, including the introduction of the national minimum wage in 1998.

ORGANISATION EXAMPLE

When the national minimum wage was introduced in 1998 there was much concern that organisations would be forced to cut jobs to cope with the resultant increase in wage costs. Generally speaking, that has not occurred. However, there is a range of organisations, most notably the Trade Union Congress (TUC), that do not believe that the minimum wage is high enough for employees to achieve an acceptable standard of living.

In April 2005 the mayor of London was convinced by these arguments and declared that, with immediate effect, there would be a living wage level of £6.70 for all those employed by the Metropolitan Police Authority, the London Development Agency and Transport for London. It will also apply to companies that carry out contract work for the Greater London Authority

Source: www.tuc.org.uk.

In the run-up to the 2005 General Election each of the political parties published its manifesto. It is interesting to see if the different policies of the three main parties have significantly different impacts on employment issues.

Although the parts of the manifestos relating to employment were all wide-ranging and rather complex, it is probably most interesting to focus on just three areas: diversity, productivity and skills.

Diversity

All of the three main political parties clearly stated that they wanted to fight discrimination (but as most potential areas of discrimination are unlawful according to existing legislation these were not particularly notable statements!). However, the differences came in their approach to the management of immigration. We look at this issue in more detail later in this chapter. However, it is interesting to note that all parties saw it as an issue that needed to be addressed – the Labour Party through a points system, the Conservative Party through a quota system and the Liberal Democrats through matching an agreed number of work permits to different categories of skills.

The Labour Party placed considerable emphasis on the need for immigrants to fill skills shortages. (Indeed, without employees from overseas it is difficult to see how the UK would be able to recruit sufficient people to jobs such as nursing and teaching.) However, the Conservative Party argued that the focus should be on retraining those who were unable to find work, rather than relying on the migrant community to fill skills shortages. Clearly these issues have a direct impact on unemployment levels within the UK.

Productivity

All parties saw productivity as an issue, with the Labour Party stating that UK prosperity was likely to depend on the capacity to translate scientific research into innovative products and better services. The Labour Party identified five key drivers: improving competition, promoting enterprise, supporting science and innovation, raising skills levels and encouraging investment. The Conservative Party focused on the need to ensure that profits were not unreasonably taxed and that there was the right level of skills and management. The Liberal Democrat Party focus was on the need to open up trading opportunities and to reduce regulatory burdens.

Skills

This is another area that all parties saw as important. The Labour Party referred to the New Deal and the fact that more than 1 million people had got work through this programme (more details about the New Deal are available at www.newdeal.gov.uk). It also proposed giving every adult the entitlement to gain a level 2 qualification (equivalent to GCSE standard) by 2006/07. It promised that where employers were prepared to offer low-skilled employees paid time to train, the costs would be fully subsidised. The Conservative Party stated that the future was a knowledge economy, but not necessarily an all-graduate economy. It emphasised that there was a need for people to do jobs with lower levels of skills. It proposed a flexible model for people to develop further skills while still working. The Liberal Democrat Party proposed to scrap university tuition fees. It stated that there was a need to ensure vocational training and business needs were aligned without eroding first-class academic research, talent for innovation or freedom of choice. (Source of detailed analysis: Philpott (2005a).)

Although there was little detail about how any of the proposals might be achieved, it is clear how the political approaches could impact on employers and employees. For example, if the government makes training free and more attractive to employees, they will be encouraged to take part in that training. In addition, if employers are given incentives to ensure that employees participate in training, there is likely to be more enthusiasm to make it happen.

Try to identify how the organisation you work for, or an organisation with which you are familiar, has been affected by specific political policies. How significant do you think any impact has been?

THE IMPACT OF ECONOMIC FACTORS ON EMPLOYEE RELATIONS

Economic growth results in the creation of employment. However, economic growth also depends on the human capital within the economy. Price (2004) defines this human capital as the investment in the skills of the labour force, including education and vocational training to develop specific skills. Hence, to grow a more successful economy there has to be a link to investment in employees. This is particularly true when there is a reliance on a knowledge economy, rather than an economy dominated by employees performing manual tasks.

The obvious way that the economic climate affects employee relations is in the number of jobs available and the level of pay and benefits that employers are able to provide to their employees. However, it is a very narrow approach to just view the impact of economics in this way.

A government will always have policies with regard to:

- employment
- inflation
- taxation and spending (fiscal policies)
- interest and exchange rates (monetary policies).

Different governments will have different priorities, but broadly they will all be trying to achieve:

- price stability
- full employment
- economic growth
- a balance of payments surplus.

However, the approach that different governments take to achieve these aims does vary. As we have already noted, the government is the largest employer in the UK and hence one way to keep control on the economy is through the careful management of public sector pay increases. Private sector pay increases are affected by what happens in the public sector – if high pay increases are offered in the public sector there is often an increase in demands from the private sector.

In 2002/03 there was an ongoing dispute between the Fire Brigade Union (FBU) and the government (represented by the Local Government Association) over pay. The initial pay claim from the FBU was for a 40 per cent increase. The union claimed that the job of fire fighter had been undervalued over many years, and was seeking to address this issue.

Clearly, any group of workers claiming a 40 per cent increase is unlikely to succeed easily, especially at a time of relatively low inflation. However, a particular issue that the government had to consider was the knock-on effect of agreeing to any such increase. It would have been very likely that other groups within the public sector would have expected the differential between their pay and that of the fire fighters to be maintained, resulting in additional large pay claims from other groups. In addition, if the fire fighters had been successful (they were not), it is very likely that groups of employees within the private sector would have expected comparable increases to maintain pay differentials. So, in considering the pay claim, the government could not just think about the individual situation but also had to consider the wider ramifications of any agreements it came to.

From the 1940s through to the early 1990s one way that successive governments attempted to manage income levels was through a variety of different incomes policies. These policies restricted pay increases to reduce pressure on costs and prices, particularly during periods of high inflation. Blyton and Turnbull (2004) refer to income policies as the most expedient solution to the economic ills that faced the UK during the post-war period.

However, incomes policies do bring with them increased frustrations in the employment relationship, and often led to trade unions being marginalised because the policies left them with little opportunity to negotiate pay on behalf of their members.

The last wages council was abolished in 1993. Today the only 'income policy' is the national minimum wage – although many would not view it in that way.

In addition to the direct management of the cost and increase of wages, the approach that governments take to the management of the economy has an impact on employment. Here we shall examine fiscal and monetary policies:

Fiscal policies

In 1970 there were 600,000 unemployed people in the UK. Compared with the high rates of unemployment that were reached in the 1990s this figure seems low, but at the time it was the highest figure for two decades and hence was a cause of great concern. To try to resolve this situation the government of the time (Conservative, led by Edward Heath) altered its fiscal policy.

Fiscal policy is the policy taken on tax and spending, and in this case the decision was taken to cut taxes. The result of this was that all taxpayers had more disposable income, because they were paying less in tax. This meant that they were likely to spend more, and by spending more they increased the demand for products and services, which meant that the suppliers of these products and services needed to employ more people to meet the demand. That reduced the level of unemployment.

Another approach that could have been taken would have been to increase spending (another aspect of fiscal policy). By increasing spending on public services such as education and health the government could create new jobs (for example, for teachers or nurses). If the government creates more jobs, clearly that will have a positive effect on employment levels.

Alternatively, a government might increase social benefits, giving more spending money to people receiving benefits. As with reducing taxes, people with more money buy more products, services and so on, and hence more jobs are created to meet this demand.

These two examples are very simplistic, as they do not take into account any other variables that could affect the level of unemployment. However, they do illustrate the use of fiscal policies.

Monetary policies

Monetarism was a feature of the economic policy of the Conservative government of 1979–97. The strategy used by this government used financial rather than fiscal tools to manage the economy.

The government recognised that excessive demand for goods and services led to price inflation, which reduced competitiveness and resulted in the failure of businesses and increased unemployment. Monetarists believe that in order to reduce these risks demand can be effectively managed by financial instruments – primarily interest rates and the supply of money in the economy – rather than fiscal ones (tax and spending). An increase in interest rates reduces consumer spending and investment by companies, slowing the general level of economic activity and therefore reducing any upward pressure on prices. Conversely, a reduction in interest rates stimulates economic activity and can prevent recession.

The Conservative government also believed that economic stability and prosperity would be maximised by focusing on the productive capacity of the economy. Therefore, a key government strategy must be to increase the supply of goods and services to the market. According to Gennard and Judge (2005), the government of 1979–97 tried to achieve this by:

- creating an environment conducive to private enterprise
- creating incentives for individuals to work
- creating incentives for firms to invest, produce goods and services, and employ workers
- liberalising product markets
- privatising publicly owned enterprises
- reducing taxation
- deregulating labour markets.

So, from this overview of the economic factors we can see that the range of issues that can impact on employers and employees is far greater than job availability and levels of pay and benefits.

The impacts for the employer include:

- Costs of providing products and services – which has an impact on the competitiveness of the employer, which then has an impact on the ability to employ and pay employees.
- Wage costs.
- The availability of workers in the market place.
- The cost of materials and the cost of borrowing. Interest rates have a direct impact on this, which can have a serious effect on the profitability of the company. Again, this affects the ability to employ and pay employees.

The impacts for employees include:

- The availability of jobs – as unemployment rises then employees have less choice about the type of job they take, and less power to bargain over terms and conditions of employment.

As we saw in Chapter 1, this has a direct impact on the psychological contract between the employer and the employee.

■ Wage rates.
■ The amount the employee has to spend on goods and services – this impacts on the standard of living the employee enjoys. If the employee perceives that the standard of living has fallen there is going to be more pressure on the employer to pay more to bring that standard back to where it was once perceived to be.
■ The cost of borrowing (personal loans and mortgages) – this also impacts on the perceived standard of living. It also impacts on the importance of job security. If the cost of borrowing is high it is likely that employees will be more fearful of being unemployed because of the inability to meet the higher levels of repayment. Again, this affects the expectations of employees, and hence has an impact on the psychological contract.
■ The amount of tax the employee pays – which also impacts on the standard of living.

In this past section we have referred to the psychological contract on a number of occasions. Write down the expectations on both sides of the contract (employer and employee) during times when:

■ unemployment is high
■ unemployment is low
■ the cost of borrowing is high.

THE IMPACT OF SOCIAL FACTORS ON EMPLOYEE RELATIONS

In looking at the impact of economic factors we have highlighted one of the key social factors that impacts on employee relations, unemployment.

Unemployment

Inevitably, unemployment levels tend to follow economic trends. Hence, high periods of unemployment were seen in the recession years of 1985–86. In recent times unemployment has been more stable, at around 5 per cent. Caution has to be exercised in interpreting this statistic. If unemployment is 5 per cent it is incorrect to make the conclusion that employment levels are 95 per cent. In fact, employment levels are running relatively stable at around 75 per cent (source: CIPD 2005a).

That leaves 20 per cent of people of working age who are not working, and who are not registered as unemployed. These people will include those who:

■ are studying full-time
■ are not looking for work for personal reasons (for example, women who have decided to stay at home full-time for childcare reasons)
■ are claiming incapacity benefit (that is, are registered as suffering from long-term sickness)
■ have taken early retirement.

The 5 per cent unemployed figure refers to those who are actively seeking work. Alongside the unemployment figures, jobs opportunities have been growing (185,000 in the service sector and

41,000 in construction offsetting the 124,000 job losses in manufacturing and 2,000 job losses in other production industries in the year to September 2004). In the CIPD Survey (2005a) 55 per cent of employers reported were anticipating recruitment difficulties, 66 per cent because of the lack of specialist skills and 54 per cent because of a lack of relevant experience. More than two in five employers reported receiving no applicants for vacancies that they had advertised.

As well as reflecting the economic climate the unemployment levels also reflect the type of work available, and the fit between the skills held by the unemployed and the jobs that are available. An area that has been of particular concern to the current Labour government has been the number of young people who are unemployed. Hence it introduced the New Deal programme.

The New Deal programme is a key element of the government's strategy for getting people off benefits and into work. Although the programme is mandatory for young jobseekers aged 18 to 24 and for those aged 25 and over who are claiming Jobseeker's Allowance, it is also available to people of all ages who are long-term unemployed. The idea behind the scheme is to make the unemployed more employable by providing them with new skills

The New Deal works through giving the unemployed an opportunity to do some work while still receiving benefits, which could lead to a permanent job – or will at least result in the person having new skills to market. There are four New Deal options.

1. A job with an employer– under which employers receive £60 per week for up to six months towards employment costs.
2. Work with a voluntary sector organisation – providing work with training in the voluntary sector for up to six months.
3. Work with the environment task force – offering up to six months work on tasks designed to improve the environment.
4. Full-time education or training – aimed primarily at young people without NVQ/SVQ level 2 or equivalent. This option may last up to one year, to enable completion of the chosen course

(source: www.newdeal.gov.uk).

This New Deal programme is part of the process of ensuring that the UK meets with 'Pillar one' of the 1999 European Union employment guidelines (www.europa.eu.int). These guidelines were drawn up with the aim of the European Union becoming the 'most competitive and dynamic knowledge-based economy in the world, capable of sustainable economic growth, with more and better jobs and greater social cohesion' (Bolkestein 2000).

Pillar one is 'employability', and puts particular emphasis on ensuring that young people especially have the skills necessary to find jobs in today's working environment, although all the long-term unemployed are included.

Immigration and emigration

As we have already noted when considering political issues, the topics of immigration and emigration were important topics in the 2005 general election campaign. Although immigration was the main area of concern that was expressed, it is also important to consider the impact of emigration.

In 1993, 266,000 people left the UK to live elsewhere. This compares with 359,000 people who left in 2002. During the decade to 2002, 2.8 million people left the UK to live elsewhere. Of the people who left in 2002, 125,000 went to other EU countries. Around half of those leaving the country were aged between 25 and 44 years. Males made up about 55 per cent of those leaving the country (source: www.statistics.gov.uk).

The reasons that people leave the country vary. The groups that give greatest concern are those with valuable skills who are leaving to seek employment opportunities in other countries. For example, there have been a significant number of academics leaving the UK to pursue research opportunities that are better funded in countries such as the United States.

You may recall that the manifesto of the Conservative Party for the 2005 General Election, which we looked at earlier in this chapter, referred to the UK as a 'knowledge economy'. This refers to an economy where there is more importance placed on the knowledge of workers, rather than on the manual work that they do. The more complex the knowledge, (eg leading-edge research) the higher the value that is placed on it. Hence, if leading academics leave the UK to pursue research elsewhere there is a potential impact on the competitiveness of the UK knowledge economy, because some of the knowledge is being removed from the UK and taken elsewhere.

This is a constant difficulty for organisations, because much of the 'knowledge' that is being referred to is that which is in employee's heads. Although information can be recorded, the way that it is interpreted and used often relies on the particular skills of the individual. Hence, if a key knowledge worker leaves an organisation a significant percentage of the knowledge that was being used by the worker goes too.

Of course, not all emigration relates to employment opportunities. There are also those who decide that they would prefer to live in sunnier climates – indeed, there are areas of countries such as the south of Spain that have a high concentration of British expatriates.

Understanding immigration figures is not easy, because there are so many different figures quoted. In addition, it seems that no one is certain of the number of illegal immigrants that are in the UK at any one time. However, according to the Office of National Statistics (www.statistics.gov.uk) the number of applications for British citizenship in 2003 rose by 21 per cent on the previous year, to 139,315. The number of people actually granted British citizenship in 2003 rose by 3 per cent on the previous year to 124,315. Of those that were granted citizenship 44 per cent were granted citizenship on the basis of residency, 30 per cent were granted citizenship because of marriage to a British citizen and nearly 24 per cent were children (minors).

The main countries of origin of those granted citizenship were Pakistan, India and Somalia. People of Asian origin accounted for 40 per cent of those granted citizenship, whereas people from Africa accounted for 32 per cent.

A specific issue relating to immigration is asylum seekers. Asylum seekers come into the country without the legal papers that are required in order for them to stay. Typically they request asylum at the immigration control at an airport or port. They then have to make a formal application for asylum which is considered by the government. Their application is based on the declaration that it is unsafe for them to return to their home country – for some reason their lives are at risk.

According to the Office of National Statistics, in the third quarter of 2004 (July to September) there were 8,605 applications for asylum. This was 9 per cent higher than the previous quarter, but 29 per cent lower than the same quarter in 2003. The top five nationalities requesting asylum in this

Table 2.1 Response to requests for asylum, 2002 and 2003

	2002 (%)	2003 (%)
Asylum granted	10	6
Exceptional leave to remain allowed/ discretionary leave	24	6
Humanitarian protection given	n/a*	5
Refused	66	83

* Humanitarian protection and discretionary leave replaced the one category of exceptional leave to remain from 1 April 2003.

quarter were Iranian, Chinese, Somali, Zimbabwean and Iraqi. In total 49,405 applications for asylum were received in 2003, compared with 84,130 in 2002.

The response to the requests for asylum over 2002 and 2003 is shown in Table 2.1.

There are a number of complex issues to be considered here. There is the accusation that a number of asylum seekers specifically target the UK because it is seen as relatively easy to gain entry, and there is immediate access to the benefits system. Clearly, the more people accessing the benefit system has an impact on government spending, which can result in the wider impacts that were studied in the last section.

However, it is a mistake to view all immigration as a problem. This has been shown historically. In the 1950s and 1960s there were severe labour shortages in the UK, and there was active recruiting of people overseas. Indeed, London Transport had recruiting offices in the West Indies, and the Department of Health had recruitment campaigns for doctors and nurses overseas.

In the twenty-first century there is still a need to attract specific skills to the UK, to fill skill gaps that are not currently being met from within the population. Examples of professions that need to seek overseas for skills include nursing and teaching. However, there is also the need to increase training in such skills within the UK. Various schemes have been put in place to attract people to the professions, but with relatively low unemployment there are not large numbers of people wanting to undergo the training.

ORGANISATION EXAMPLE

According to a report made to the Royal College of Nursing conference in April 2005 around 50,000 nurses left the profession in 2004, with 20,000 joining having completed their training, and a further 12,000 nurses coming to the profession from overseas.

The report went on to say that 45 per cent of the nursing intake into the NHS over the past four years has come from nurses trained overseas.

The reasons that were reported for nurses leaving the profession include dissatisfaction with pensions and pay, inflexible working practices and fear of violence. This is in addition to those who leave the profession through retirement or for reasons relating to childcare responsibilities (source: www.rcn.org.uk).

Just looking at the figures here shows that, if there were not nurses coming into the profession from overseas, it would be impossible to replace the vacancies created by those leaving the profession. However, there is the need to consider the issue from a short-term and a long-term perspective. Recruiting from overseas might be promoted as a short-term measure, but are enough nurses being trained to address the long-term issue? Is it more realistic to presume that the need to recruit from overseas is also the long-term solution, and if so, is there the need to improve the system of that recruitment?

ACTIVITIES

Identify a profession other than nursing that relies significantly on overseas workers. Why do you think there is a particular issue that results in the need for recruitment overseas? What solution would you offer to the problems that this profession faces?

Family issues

The third social issue that we shall look at is the issue of the changing family structure in the UK. With the increasing rates of divorce there are increasing numbers of one-parent families, resulting in more women needing to work for financial reasons. In addition, there are more women opting to establish themselves in careers before starting families.

The suggestion would be, therefore, that the statistics relating to men and women in employment are relatively similar. However, that is not the case. First, there is a significant difference in the employment rates of men and women. In 2003, according to the Office for National Statistics, 69 per cent of women of working age were in employment, compared with 79 per cent of men. In addition, there is significant difference between the numbers involved in part-time work (see Table 2.2).

Table 2.2 Percentage of all those working part-time in each age range

Age (years)	Female	Male
16-24	45	29
25-34	33	4
35-44	47	3
45-54	42	4
55-64	56	13
65+	89	69

Table 2.3 Percentage of men and women in selected occupations, 2003

	Female	Male
Taxi cab drivers	8	92
Security guards	12	88
Software professionals	14	86
ICT managers	16	84
Police officers, up to sergeant	22	78
Marketing and sales managers	25	75
IT operations technicians	32	68
Medical practitioners	39	61
Solicitors, lawyers, judges and coroners	42	58
Shelf fillers	48	52
Chefs and cooks	49	51
Secondary school teachers	55	45
Sales assistants	73	27
Waiters and waitresses	73	27
Cleaners and domestics	79	21
Retail cashiers	82	18
General office assistants and clerks	83	17
Primary and nursery school teachers	86	14
Care assistants and home carers	88	12
Hairdressers and barbers	89	11
Nurses	89	11
Receptionists	96	4

Source: Labour Force Survey 2003.

An obvious explanation for this difference is the fact that many women balance work with child-care and other caring responsibilities. It is maybe more interesting, therefore, to look at the gender differences within certain occupations (see Table 2.3).

Here we see evidence that there are still jobs that are dominated by men, and others that are dominated by women. Daniels and MacDonald (2005) suggest the reasons for this might be:

- **Stereotyped jobs.** There is still the idea that some jobs are 'more suitable' for one particular gender. These stereotypes affect young people as they make their career choices.
- **Parents.** The career of their parents is a significant influence when young people make career choices, primarily because it is the career they know best. It is also more likely that they will be able to gain some work experience in a field where a parent works, and it is possible that a parent might be able to help a child gain access to his/her career. This results in gender stereotyping being reinforced through the generations.
- **Flexibility.** There are some jobs where it is simply easier to have flexible work. Women are more likely to want flexible working, and hence they are more likely to be attracted to these jobs.

British Airways v *Starmer (2005)*

An example of the difficulty of flexibility in certain careers is illustrated by the case of the British Airways pilot, Jessica Starmer. After having her first child Starmer asked British Airways if she could work 50 per cent part-time, so that she could balance childcare responsibilities and work. British Airways refused her request on the grounds of safety.

They said that there was a requirement (actually introduced after Starmer made her request) that all pilots should have flown for at least 2,000 hours before they were allowed to fly part-time. This equated to around three years of full-time flying. BA stated that this was essential to ensure that pilots had the depth of experience necessary and to ensure that safety standards were met.

Starmer brought her case before the Employment Tribunal under the Flexible Working Regulations 2002 and the Sex Discrimination Act 1975 (we will look at both pieces of legislation in more detail in Chapter 10). They reached their judgement in April 2005, finding Starmer was the victim of unfair indirect sex discrimination. At the time of writing British Airways has stated that it intends to appeal against the judgement.

- **Aptitude.** There is debate about whether different genders have different aptitudes, which affect their career choices.
- **Discrimination.** Although discrimination on the grounds of gender is unlawful (Sex Discrimination Act 1975), it still happens. There are instances of women being refused entry to a career based on the discrimination of recruiters.

It would be wrong to assume that issues relating to childcare only affect women. The Employment Act 2002 introduced increased rights for fathers through the introduction of paternity leave, and there are proposals to allow a mother and father to 'swap' a portion of maternity leave. These provisions are explored in more detail in Chapter 10.

Think about the career you have chosen to follow. Why have you chosen that career? If you had the opportunity to start again would you still choose the same career? Why/why not?

THE IMPACT OF TECHNOLOGICAL FACTORS ON EMPLOYEE RELATIONS

Technology is an ever-growing area, but it is important to remember that one of the most significant step changes in this area was the introduction of personal computers. It is very easy to be dismissive about the impact of this area of technology on employees, because it seems that we have had personal computers around for so long. However, as quoted by Lewis *et al* (2003) the first personal computers only became available in the mid-1970s.

Those who started work in the early 1970s (before the introduction of personal computers) are today in their 50s, and very likely to still be part of the working population. Although many people of this age have become very familiar with the use of computers, others have found it difficult to adapt. We can see, therefore, that although there is a significant proportion of the working population who have started work since the introduction of personal computers, it would be wrong to assume that the entire workforce is familiar and comfortable with the use of personal computers.

Again, we can see how this can impact on the psychological contract. If the employer expects flexibility to use new technology, and the employee feels unable or is unwilling to undergo the required learning, there becomes an imbalance between the expectations of the employer and the employee, which can cause conflict within the employment relationship.

Moving on from the introduction of personal computers, technology now allows employees to work remotely from the workplace through the use of technology such as mobile phones and laptop computers. According to a CIPD survey on flexible working (2005b), 55 per cent of organisations surveyed had employees working from home on a regular basis, with 27 per cent engaged in mobile working. This is largely possible because of the use of technology.

There are advantages and disadvantages to this approach to work. Advantages include the ability to fit work around other responsibilities, such as childcare – and the considerable time saved in not commuting to work. However, according to the CIPD survey quoted above, 54 per cent of managers reported difficulties managing flexible working. It can be more difficult to manage employees if there is not face-to-face contact, and there has to be a certain level of trust that work is actually happening.

It is interesting to return again to the psychological contract. The assumption of the successful working of the psychological contract is that the employer and the employee become aware of the expectations of each other. One could argue that, with reduced contact between the employer and the employee, there is less ability to become familiar with those expectations and hence there can be a lack of understanding of the expectations of each other.

ORGANISATION
EXAMPLE

A controversial use of technology can be found in call centres. Here, sophisticated use of technology allows the management to monitor the number of calls answered by each operator, the number of calls waiting to be answered and the overall productivity of each team. A research report commissioned by the Health and Safety Executive (2003) found that the risk of mental health problems is higher for call handlers than for benchmark groups of employees in other occupations. It also found that not all call centres were equally affected, and those worst affected included those who had their performance monitored either constantly or rarely. The report recommends that employees are given more opportunity to manage their own work demands.

These are interesting findings, particularly the conclusion that monitoring performance rarely had negative impacts on the employees, as well as monitoring constantly. The over-all conclusion seems to be that, when the technology is available to monitor performance it should be used carefully, giving consideration to the potential impacts on the employees involved. However, how can monitoring be carried out 'carefully'?

A further effect of increased technology that has had negative impacts for some employ-ees is the ability to work from any area of the world. Clearly there are huge benefits to be able to e-mail colleagues in other countries, particularly those in other time zones. However, this has resulted in a number of jobs being moved to other countries where labour is cheaper than in the UK.

Again, this has had a significant impact on call centres. Many large companies in the UK (including Tesco, Abbey National, Prudential and Aviva (formerly Norwich Union)) have moved part or all of their call centre operations to India.

The change in communication methods has also impacted on the way that people work. Maybe the most influential of all these methods is the use of e-mail. E-mail has become a very quick and cost-effective way of communicating with people. However, it is also a way to avoid difficult conversations, indeed there have been reports of employees being dismissed through an e-mail message.

A survey conducted by the British Computer Society (2003) found that managers spent an aver-age of 1.7 hours each day reading and writing e-mails. Managers reported that they received an average of 52 e-mails each day, with 7 per cent reporting that they received more than 100. Of the e-mails received 35 per cent were read for information only, 25 per cent were immediately deleted, and 30 per cent were classified as essential.

The excessive amount of time that many managers are spending concentrating on e-mails results in less time being available to build up relationships with employees. There is also the temptation to conduct employee relationships electronically, which clearly reduces the ability to interact personally.

An organisation that has been hit particularly hard by the increased use of e-mail and sending texts is the Royal Mail. It is quite easy to understand why. Think about how many letters you have sent recently, and then think about how many e-mails and text messages you have sent. It is very likely that you have sent many more e-mails and texts than letters. It is also likely to be true that not all the e-mails and texts would have resulted in letters – some would never have been sent, and some information would have been communicated over the telephone. However, it is not difficult to see the potential impact on the Royal Mail. In addition, the loss of the monopoly on mail delivery will further impact on the volume of business for the Royal Mail.

A look around the Royal Mail website (www.royalmail.com) shows the range of products it now offers, partly reflecting a need to diversify in order to survive. In addition, there have been organisation changes, such as the move to just one delivery a day. All of these changes are partly the result of changes in technology.

ACTIVITIES

How has technology affected your job? Identify a variety of impacts. Then think about the impact that this technology has had on your employment relationships. Try to identify both positive and negative impacts.

THE IMPACT OF LEGAL FACTORS ON EMPLOYEE RELATIONS

We look at the legal context in which employment operates in detail in the last three chapters of this book. However, it is a significant external factor that impinges on organisations, and hence we take a brief look here at the evolution of employment legislation, and the type of changes that have taken place.

If we go back just over 30 years there was very little legal protection for employees. The first significant change to this was the introduction of legislation relating to unfair dismissal in 1971. This was followed by the introduction of the Health and Safety at Work Act in 1974. The first piece of discrimination legislation was the Sex Discrimination Act 1975, which was followed by the Race Relations Act 1976.

The full range of employment legislation that is now on the statute book is immense. However, what is particularly interesting is the growth over the past 10 years. One area of particular growth has been in the area of discrimination, including legislation to make discrimination unlawful on the grounds of:

- disability (Disability Discrimination Act 1995)
- transsexuality (Sex Discrimination (Gender Reassignment) Regulations 1999)
- sexual orientation (Employment Equality (Sexual Orientation) Regulations 2003)
- religion or belief (Employment Equality (Religion and Belief) Regulations 2003).

There has also been a significant range of legislation introduced to support parents at work, including:

- the right to request flexible working (Flexible Working (Eligibility, Complaints and Remedies) Regulations 2001)
- improved maternity leave provisions (Employment Act 2002)
- the introduction of adoption leave (Employment Act 2002)
- the introduction of paternity leave (Employment Act 2002)

- the allowance of unpaid leave to deal with issues relating to childcare (Maternity and Parental Leave regulations 1999).

Health and safety legislation has also grown, with detailed provisions included in the following:

- Workplace (Health, Safety and Welfare) Regulations 1992
- Personal Protective Equipment at Work Regulations 1992
- Health and Safety (Display Screen Equipment) Regulations 1992
- Manual Handling Operations Regulations 1998
- Provision and Use of Work Equipment Regulations 1998
- Management of Health and Safety at Work Regulations 1998
- Working Time Regulations 1998.

This is by no means an exhaustive list of all employment legislation that has been introduced in the past 30 years, but hopefully it illustrates the considerable growth that there has been in legislation.

The legislation serves to protect employees, and there are employers who would complain that it is restrictive and results in their being constrained unnecessarily. In understanding this debate it is useful to reconsider the section we studied on political factors. Here we saw that, when the Conservative government was elected in 1979, there was a perception that the balance of power in the employment relationship was tilted too far in favour of the employee. Hence, legislation was introduced to realign that balance. The question then becomes whether the range of legislation that has now been introduced has actually altered the balance of power again – back in favour of the employee.

Interestingly, if the argument that the balance of power is tilted towards the employee is accepted we can see that there is a distinct difference from the situation of the 1970s. In the 1970s the big issue was collective power – that employees were using the existing legislation (or lack of legislation) in their favour to take collective action against employers. If the balance is now tilted towards the employee it is much more focused on individual protection. If you look back at the list of legislation at the start of this section, all of it relates to the rights of the individual.

THE IMPACT OF ETHICAL/ENVIRONMENTAL FACTORS ON EMPLOYEE RELATIONS

An area of growing concern to many employees and employers is corporate social responsibility (CSR). CSR is defined by the European Commission (2001) as 'a concept whereby companies decide voluntarily to contribute to a better society and a cleaner environment'. The concept of CSR goes beyond compliance with the minimum legal standards, and considers broader obligations to employees, the wider community and shareholders.

As we will see in Chapter 6, the impact of globalisation on organisations has increased interest in how organisations should behave, and increased concerns about health and environmental issues.

An interesting example of the impact of globalisation is the movement of labour between countries. As we have already noted, the UK has a significant shortage of recruits into nursing, and therefore relies on a certain percentage of nurses coming from overseas. However, is this a socially responsible approach if it leaves developing or underdeveloped countries short of nurses because they have come to work in the UK?

In addition, much interest has been placed on organisations moving operations overseas, such as call centres, which we looked at earlier in this section. There is pressure on organisations to pay such workers fairly, even though accepted pay rates are lower than in the UK.

According to the CIPD paper on CSR (2003), issues such as these affect decisions that customers and suppliers make about who they want to do business with. Hence, CSR becomes relevant in terms of positioning in the market place, protecting an organisation's reputation and building credibility with customers and employees.

In addition to this 'voluntary' adherence to high ethical standards, there are also legal require-ments placed on employers. This is particularly relevant with relation to the environment, with increased legislation and taxation on practices that negatively affect the environment.

ACTIVITIES

Find out if the organisation you work for, or an organisation with which you are familiar, has a corporate social responsibility policy. If it has, ask for a copy so that you can understand the priorities your organisation has set. If it has not, try to find out if corporate social responsibility has been considered, and how important it is to the organisation.

KEY POINTS FROM THIS CHAPTER

- All organisations are affected by the external environment.
- The extent of the effect of external factors will depend on the stability, complexity and dispersion of the organisation.
- Some organisations introduce buffer departments to absorb the impact of the external factors.
- The policies of different political parties can alter the external environment in which organisations operate.
- All governments have policies on employment, inflation, taxation and spending, interest and exchange rates – and the way that they manage these can impact on the organisation.
- Significant social factors impacting on the organisation are unemployment, immigration and emigration and family issues.
- Technology can enhance the working experience, but can also introduce negative impacts.
- Employment legislation has grown considerably over the past 30 years, and some would argue has resulted in the balance of power being in the employees' favour.
- Corporate social responsibility is an area of growing concern for organisations.

EXAMPLES TO WORK THROUGH

1. Your managing director has asked for you to give advice on the employment issues to be considered when relocating the call centre within your organisation overseas. Explain the issues that you would highlight in your response.
2. Carry out a PESTLE (political, economic, social, technological, legal and environmental/ethical) analysis of the main issues

that are currently impacting on your organisation. Link each factor to the impact that it has on the employment relationship.

3. Look at the structure of your organisation and try to determine how this structure helps to deal effectively with the external factors that impact on it. Is there a way that the structure could be improved to enable external factors to be dealt with more effectively?

(Suggestions of answers to the examples can be accessed by tutors at www.cipd.co.uk/tss.)

In this chapter we had a brief look at the problems that resulted in industrial action from the Fire Brigade Union (FBU) in 2002–03. Although the industrial action is often referred to as being an issue over pay, it was about more than that. It was also about the modernisation of the fire service, and differences of opinion about what this should involve.

When the dispute was finally settled a pay offer of 16 per cent, payable over three years, was accepted. However, payment of each stage of the increase was dependent on certain modernisation targets having been agreed. Many of the fire fighters were reported to be unhappy about the conclusion to the dispute, believing that their leadership had accepted a deal that fell short of what they had been fighting for. Indeed, in May 2005 the members of the FBU ousted Andy Gilchrist (who had been the leader during the dispute) in favour of Matt Wrack, who had argued against accepting the deal that ended the industrial action.

Here we are going to look at a number of external factors that impacted on the industrial action at the time. Once you have read through the list of external factors, and added any more of your own, you will be required to consider the impact of these factors on employee relations. If you want to gain a greater understanding of the events surrounding the dispute before completing the case study, a useful source of information is www.bbc.co.uk/news, search on 'fire strike'.

To analyse the external factors we shall use a PESTLE approach:

Political

- The Labour government was torn between working with the trade unions (a more traditional role of the Labour party) and being tough.
- After the tragedies of 9/11 fire fighters were well respected by the public.
- At the time it was expected that a war with Iraq would develop, and hence the army was needed for that purpose and did not need to be distracted by covering for the fire fighters.
- The industrial action happened at a time of heightened security in the country, when emergency services are crucial.

Economic

- The cost of the requested increase (40 per cent) would have been huge.

- If the 40 per cent increase had been agreed then other public services would probably have sought similar sized increases.
- If the fire fighters had received an increase taking their annual earnings to around £30,000 per annum there would have been pressure from people in a variety of professions for increases in pay as they compared their earnings to the £30,000 mark.
- The industrial action did result in some events being cancelled and some high-rise buildings not being used, due to security risks. There was a cost associated with that.

Social

- The reaction of the public was important – firstly one of support, but this diminished as time passed.
- A number of fire fighters had second jobs, and the proposed reforms would have made it difficult to continue with these.
- Fire fighters generally work a certain amount of unsocial hours, and expect to be compensated for this.
- Society has a very high expectation of service after having dialled 999.

Technological

- The introduction of new fire engines had made the fighting of fires more effective, but had also increased the skill levels required.
- There was a request for fire fighters to train to use equipment such as defibrillators and other paramedic equipment – adding to the skills required to do the job.
- Technology had improved the communications available on the red fire engines (not available on the 'green goddesses' used by the Army during the dispute).

Legislation

- The fire fighters had to abide by employment legislation determining how a strike should be called.
- There were threats from the government to pass legislation that would have made it illegal for fire fighters to take industrial action.

Ethical/environmental

- Lives were at risk when fire fighters went on strike.

Questions

1. Which of these factors do you think would have been most influential in prolonging the industrial action?
2. When the industrial action was over many of the above factors were still relevant. Which do you think would have had the most negative impact on ongoing employee relations?
3. How would you address the factors that you have identified in response to the last question?

The National and Global Context

CHAPTER 3

The objectives of this chapter are to:

- explore the role of the government as an employer
- examine the impact of the European Union on employee relations
- consider the role of key external bodies in employee relations
- look at the impact of globalisation on employee relations
- consider the specific issues affecting multinational organisations.

In Chapter 2 we looked at the external factors impacting on an organisation, broadly following the PESTLE framework. Adding these together with the internal factors identified in Chapter 1 we have started to get a much clearer understanding of the nature of the employment relationship and the complexity within it.

In this chapter we look in more detail at some specific external factors. These include the government, the European Union and globalisation. Although these factors fit well within the framework of the last chapter, they are areas of significance that need additional thought.

When we reach the end of this chapter we shall have finished looking at the internal and external factors that impact on the nature of the employment relationship and we shall move on to look at the parties within that relationship.

THE GOVERNMENT AS AN EMPLOYER

In Chapter 2 we noted how political factors could impact on the employment relationship. We also noted that the government is a significant employer in the UK. In this section we look in more detail at the role of the government as an employer, and the impact that this has on employee relations within the public sector, and more widely on the private sector.

It is useful to start by reflecting on the range of jobs that are included within the public sector. Broadly speaking, they can be divided into four main categories:

The Civil Service

This section is primarily concerned with the administration of central government, and hence the majority of employees are based in London. However, because of the costs of living and working in London there are an increasing number of sections moving outside of London, and there are a number of key roles in other major cities in the UK.

Traditionally, the key feature of employee relations in this part of the public sector has been based on loyalty and responsibility to the state, because of working in jobs that are involved in developing policies of the state. However, as we will see later in this section, that loyalty can no longer be taken for granted by the government.

Local authority workers

Typical jobs in this category included those involved in education, social services and refuse collection. Traditionally, the terms and conditions of employment of these groups have been negotiated and agreed centrally, although there has been a gradual move towards decentralisation since the 1980s.

As a result of privatisation some of the jobs in local authorities have been put out to tender, and hence the employees involved have moved away from the public sector and into private sector employment.

State agencies

The main groups of employees within this category are in the police services, the fire services and the National Health Service (NHS). As we saw in Chapter 2 when we looked at issues surrounding the dispute involving the fire services, the government appoints bodies to deal with employee relations (in the case of the fire services, the Local Government Employers Association). However, it still retains much influence.

Although much of the management of terms and conditions of employment has traditionally been carried out centrally, there is a move towards decentralisation, particularly through the creation of individual NHS trusts within the NHS.

Nationalised industries

During the period of Conservative government from 1979–97, 21 national industries were privatised. This has resulted in very few nationalised industries remaining, the Royal Mail being one that does remain. The major privatisations are listed in Table 3.1.

Now we have seen the structure and the breadth of the public sector, we consider the role of the government as employer.

Table 3.1 Major privatisations 1979–97

1984	British Telecom
1987	British Airways
1988	British Steel
1989	Regional water authorities
1990	Area electricity boards and National Grid Company
1991	National Power and Powergen
1994	British Coal
1995	British Rail
1996	British Energy

The role of the government as employer

At the time of the Conservatives being elected in 1979 the perception of the government being a stable employer, which people wanted to work for, was starting to erode. Among the positive perceptions were job security and benefits that were often better than the private sector. These included a pension, enhanced sick pay and annual increments to an individual's salary. However, among the negative perceptions was the growing belief that employees in the private sector were being paid more, and that comparable jobs in the public sector were being undervalued.

As we have already noted, part of the culmination of this growing unrest was the 'Winter of Discontent' in 1978/79. The key feature that is typically reported of this time is the amount of industrial action that took place – including essential services such as refuse collection and workers within hospitals. However, maybe more importantly for the Labour government of the time, there was a growing perception that the government was unable to manage the economy effectively, because it had lost control of the ability to manage the public sector pay bill. It is largely thought that this perception was a key part of the Labour government's downfall in the 1979 elections (Rowthorn 1986).

Prior to defeat in 1979 the Labour government established a Standing Commission on Pay Comparability. The purpose of this standing commission was to investigate the pay differences between public and private sector workers, and to advise on awards that should be made to address any differences that had arisen. However, the Labour government was defeated at the election, and never saw any benefit from the investigations.

As we noted in Chapter 2, a key part of the manifesto promises of the Conservative government that was elected in 1979 was the rebalancing of the power between employees and employers. The government did let the standing commission complete its investigations, and did implement the recommended pay alterations for nurses, teachers and manual workers in the NHS and local authorities. However, it did not support the ongoing work of the commission, and it was abolished in 1991.

The Conservative government introduced an approach that was based much more on individualism, rather than collectivism. However, there is evidence that the acceptance of individualism was tainted with growing class inequality. Edwards (1998) argues that the real change was that people no longer saw any purpose in mass protest, rather than mass protest no longer being wanted by most people.

ORGANISATION EXAMPLE

Maybe the best remembered example of conflict from the time of the Conservative government of 1979–97 was the miners' strike of 1984–85. The strike was the result of an announcement by the government that it intended to allow 20 uneconomic pits to close, with the proposed loss of 20,000 jobs. The result was a lengthy and bitter strike, which ended when miners started to return to work.

The financial struggle that many miners' families endured during the strike was a dramatic contrast to the increasing wealth and affluence that many people were enjoying in London and the south-east. This increase in personal prosperity is an outward sign of increased personal opportunities – a result of individualism. However, the miners were very reliant on collectivism – all miners working together towards the same aim, and sharing the same struggles.

One of the reasons that the miners' strike was not successful was that most pit workers in the Nottingham mines continued to work. This defiance of the strike broke the ties of collectivism and weakened the overall strike. It also resulted in violent scenes on picket lines, as striking miners tried to stop working miners going in to work.

However, this was a dispute that the government was ready for, and had planned for. Margaret Thatcher (the prime minister at the time) had arranged for two years' supply of coal to be stockpiled in the months leading up to the strike – and hence the country never ran out of coal. The government had also identified supplies of coal from overseas that could be purchased if required. The government simply held its ground and waited for the miners to give in – which is exactly what happened eventually.

ACTIVITIES

The miners' strike is one of the most extreme examples of industrial conflict in recent history. It is a fascinating story, and many accounts of the conflict have been written. Search on the Internet for 'Miners strike 1984–85' and read some of the many references you will find. Do you think that such a bitter and prolonged dispute could happen today? Why/why not?

Despite the doubts that individualism was truly occurring in the 1979–97 period, there were definite moves to encourage and facilitate individual wealth and creativity. Two ways that specifically encouraged this were housing and privatisation of nationalised industries.

The Housing Act 1985 allowed people who had previously been living in local authority housing to buy the property through specifically created 'right to buy' legislation. During this period more people than ever became homeowners – with the later rises in house prices leading to increased personal wealth.

The privatisation of national industries encouraged individuals to buy shares, many for the first time. There were large advertising campaigns supporting the selling of industries such as British Telecom, and many people made large amounts of money quickly, by buying shares and selling them as the share price quickly rose. As well as increasing personal wealth, the privatisation of national industries meant that large numbers of public sector employees were moved into the private sector. As Farnham (2000) notes, this meant that there were fewer employees to demand higher wage settlements from the government, and any claims for increases to terms and conditions of employment had to be driven by the financial success of the organisation. Hence, the wage determination of significant numbers of employees was taken out of the political equation.

In taking these actions, and in moving towards a more individualistic society, the Conservative government dramatically altered the psychological contract between employers and employees. Prior to this time the psychological contract had been very much based on group expectations, rather than individual expectations, which had put a lot of pressure on employees to agree to the expectations. However, with the more individualistic approach the psychological contract became more personal between the employer and the employee, resulting in much more individual expectations. Hence, employees had to take individual responsibility for meeting the expectations of their employer (for example, hard work, loyalty) and only in achieving this could they realise their own expectations (for example, job security and higher pay).

In 1997 the Labour Party was elected to government. It inherited a trade union movement that had been weakened, by legislation and by losing key battles (such as the miners' strike) and an economy that was gaining stability after a significant period of recession in the 1980s.

The Labour Party carefully positioned itself as being different from the traditional Labour Party, which had largely been seen as the political arm of the trade union movement. 'New Labour' as it called itself needed to appeal to a wider range of people than just traditional trade union members. New Labour also saw the benefit of the focus on individuality, and among its manifesto promises were the increases of individual rights, such as the introduction of a national minimum wage.

Tony Blair, the prime minister, summarised his approach in a document entitled *The third way* (1998), which outlined four key values:

- *equal worth*: a commitment to ensuring equality between all individuals
- *opportunity for all*: ensuring all had opportunities regardless of their backgrounds
- *responsibility*: the encouragement of people to take personal responsibility
- *community*: emphasising the importance of groups to support individuals in meaningful relationships.

The emphasis here is very much on the equality of opportunity for all. Hence, policies such as the New Deal (explained in Chapter 2) are important to the Labour government because they give a second chance to people who have not found equality of opportunity on leaving school.

The 'third way' was also the basis for the employment policies of the Labour Party when it came into government in 1997. As Farnham (2000) notes, the fundamentals of the British economy at this time remained weak. There was the perception of low pay, low skills and low-quality jobs. These fundamental problems were the basis of the employment policy, which included:

- higher skills and standards being achieved in schools and colleges
- partnership with business to raise investment in infrastructure, science and research in order to help small firms to grow
- minimum standards of fair treatment – which included the national minimum wage
- a welfare-to-work programme to get the long term unemployed back to work (which included cutting social security costs).

One way that the Labour government tried to address the raising of standards was by the setting of targets for public sector employees. This had long been the practice in many private sector organisations, and an attempt was made to import this approach into the public sector. There are significant difficulties with this approach. Private sector organisations usually have one main goal – to make a profit. However, the public sector cannot make a profit – it is focused on providing a service.

The actual setting of standards had been in place for some time. In 1982 the then Conservative government had introduced the Financial Management Initiative, which monitored the progress and efficiency of all departments. In 1991 there was the Citizens Charter requiring parts of central government to publish data about their efficiency. However, a key part of the focus of the target setting of the Labour government was league tables. Different schools, or different hospitals, or different police forces, for example, score points according to different achievements (eg performance of children on examinations, number of fatalities following operations, number of crimes solved) and are ranked accordingly.

The main criticism of such league tables is that the performance is not put into context. For example, a school that manages to achieve high examination results when drawing children from wealthy and affluent homes arguably has less of a challenge than a school drawing children from one of the poorest and most deprived areas of the country.

In addition, the introduction of league tables can direct performance towards achievement of specific standards, rather than seeing the overall picture. For example, a hospital might score better on the league tables if it carries out many low-risk operations. That might discourage it from taking on more difficult, high-risk patients – resulting in a lack of care for such patients, and the lack of development of higher levels of skill needed for such operations.

Again, it is interesting to look at the psychological contract of employees working to targets in the public sector. For example, take the surgeon who is giving a target of no more than 0.5 per cent fatalities amongst all operations undertaken – this is the expectation of the employer. However, if the surgeon is tackling difficult operations with a lower rate of survival, that expectation will not be met. This can result in an uncomfortable lack of balance within the contract, which can be very distressing for the individual concerned.

However, the setting of individual targets is important to increase skills and performance – a key part of the basis for the Labour Party's employment policy in 1997. The difficulty occurs when the performance against those targets is also linked to the pay of the individual, especially if the perception of that individual is that he/she has no control over the targets. We examine this in more detail when we look at the role of reward in the employment relationship in Chapter 9.

ORGANISATION EXAMPLE

On 21 July 2003 the Public Administration Committee completed a report into the setting of public sector targets. For schools, it suggested that the government concentrate on having a smaller number of national aims, with individual benchmarks being set by schools. Its findings suggested that head teachers were more focused on achieving targets, than on ensuring that an all-round education was provided. The report suggested that the targets were the basis for a blame culture developing, with allegations of cheating being commonplace, and distortions of facts occurring in the pursuit of a better place in the league tables.

However, the Department of Education commented that there would not be a return to a time when no targets were in place. It insisted that it is important that there is a framework in place to assess the progress of children, and to ensure that the drive to improve standards remains.

This leaves us with the question of whether targets are useful or not. The impact of the targets on the employees who are working to try to achieve them also needs to be considered.

Identify the advantages and disadvantages of targets in the public sector. Now reflect on the list that you have written, and think what recommendations you would make regarding the future of such targets. What would you do differently, if anything?

Private finance initiative (PFI)

The private finance initiative (PFI) is an approach that was introduced by the Conservative government of 1979–97 and has been developed by the Labour government. PFI is means of funding major capital investments without using public money. Consortia are put together, typically involving major construction organisations, and they fund the building and management of major projects – for example, a new school or a new hospital. The building is then leased back to the public sector, typically over a period of 30 years.

This approach draws the public and private sectors together, a move that is seen as increasingly important by the Labour government. Another example of bringing the two sectors closer together is seen in the use of business process outsourcing, with the largest provider of such services in the UK being Capita (www.capita.co.uk). Such providers will run such systems as the administration processes for organisations, freeing them to manage the main activities of the organisation.

Job security

Another important change in the employment relationship between the government and the public sector employee has been the issue of job security. In his 2005 budget speech the chancellor of the Exchequer (Gordon Brown) announced that 104,000 jobs in the public sector were to go. In addition, a number of jobs would move out of London and the South East to other areas of the country. He also announced that 35 government agencies would be merged into just nine, in a bid to cut costs.

The programme of job cuts will take place over a period of time, but it will include compulsory redundancies – something that was once unheard of in the public sector. This led to strike action being taken on Friday 5 November 2004.

On Friday 5 November 2004 the Public and Commercial Services union (PCS) organised a day of industrial action over the proposed job cuts in the public sector. The action resulted in museums being closed, job centres being disrupted and driving tests being cancelled. The main argument of the employees was that a lot of work had been put in place to improve public services, and the reduction of so many jobs would actually reduce standards.

However, the chancellor of the Exchequer remained adamant that the wage bill of the public sector is too high. He insisted that more money was needed to invest in education, health, transport and the fight against crime – and that the money saved by the cutting of the jobs would result in more nurses, teachers, doctors and police being trained and employed.

In reality the public sector workforce has grown by around 100,000 since the start of 2004 (Philpott 2005), and the growth is expected to continue for at least the next two years. The Gershon Review of 2004 recommended that £22 billion of efficiency savings needed to be paid in the public sector, but the savings generally represent not a cut in public spending but a reallocation of spending within the current budget. The argument then is whether the jobs being created are 'front-line' or further administrative and management support. Philpott suggests that around 25 per cent of the net rise in public sector employment is accounted for by front-line professionals, with a similar number being accounted for by managers and administrators. The remaining 50 per cent are classed as 'intermediate staff' such as teaching assistants and care support workers.

Another area where there has been a threat to the government as a 'model' employer relates to the provision of pensions.

In 2004 the government announced proposals to raise the pensionable age of public sector workers from 60 to 65 years, and to base the pension on average earnings during employment within the public sector, rather than on final salary as it currently is calculated. The government said that this approach was fairer for the lower-paid employees, and not a cost-saving measure.

However, the proposals sparked a strong reaction and the PCS joined with the Amicus, UNISON and TGWU trade unions to plan a day of strike action on 23 March 2005 in protest at the proposals. As this date was in the run-up to the general election the proposed strike action was very politically sensitive. Eventually, the strike never happened because the deputy prime minister agreed not to implement the changes (which had been planned for 1 April 2005) and to further review the situation.

Now we have seen that job security and pensions are under threat, it is of concern that there is significant unrest amongst certain groups of public sector employees regarding their levels of pay.

In April 2004, 90,000 workers at the Department of Work and Pensions (DWP) took industrial action over their level of pay. Although there was not agreement between the government and the PCS trade union, the PCS claimed that the overall value of the pay award that had been offered was less than inflation.

The PCS claimed that one in four civil service workers earned less than £13,750 while 41 per cent earned less than £15,700. The starting salary in the DWP is £10,300.

The actual figures (Philpott 2005) show that at the start of 2003 average public sector earnings were rising at an annual rate of 5.1 per cent compared with 3.7 per cent in the private sector (excluding bonuses). By the start of 2004 growth had slowed in both sectors, but was still ahead in the public sector (4.2 per cent compared with 3.5 per cent). Philpott reports that private sector workers on average earn £27.60 more per week than public sector workers. However, the distribution of pay within the private sector is much wider – and when the median is compared, public sector workers achieve £12 per week more than private sector workers. It is only in the top 25 per cent of the earnings distribution that private sector workers clearly earn more than the public sector.

We see, therefore, that there is considerable unrest among public sector employees at this current time. The role of the government as an employer that provides secure employment, good pay and benefits and a secure pension has all but disappeared. Although many would argue that this has simply brought the public sector more into line with the private sector, others would argue that the problems with the introduction of such things as targets and league tables have shown that the public and private sectors cannot be brought into line with each other.

THE IMPACT OF THE EUROPEAN UNION ON EMPLOYEE RELATIONS

The UK joined the European Community (EC) in 1973. At that time the EC consisted of Germany, Italy, France, Belgium, the Netherlands and Luxemburg. Ireland and Denmark joined at the same time as the UK, and they were followed by Greece in 1981 and Spain and Portugal in 1986. Further expansion has resulted in there now being 25 member states.

The EC became the European Union in 1993 as a result of the Maastricht Treaty, which widened the remit of the group. The principal aims of the EU are to:

- promote a harmonious and balanced development of economic activities
- respect the environment
- promote high levels of employment and social protection
- raise the standard of living and quality of life
- promote economic and social cohesion and solidarity among member states
(source: www.europa.eu.int).

As already noted, the Labour government signed the Social Charter on coming into power in 1997. This followed a refusal to sign it by the previous Conservative government. The Social Charter is a declaration that the member state will adhere to a basic level of rights as spelled out in the 1957 Social Chapter. These basic rights include a right to a basic wage; the rights to join or not join a trade union; the right to strike and the right to be consulted by employers. The Social Chapter is important, because it is the basis for many of the directives that have been introduced by the European Union.

For the Social Charter to be adopted there needed to be unanimous acceptance by the member states of the EU. With the UK refusing to sign (it was the only member state that did refuse) the Social Charter had no legal status, and was no more than a statement of intent of the member states. In 1991 the member states apart from the UK decided to reach their own agreement, which was known as the Social Protocol Agreement on the Social Agreement. This was attached to the Treaty of Maastricht 1992.

When the Labour government did sign the Social Charter it resulted in a range of legislation being introduced into the UK. This included the National Minimum Wage Act 1998 and the Working Time Regulations 1998. Both these pieces of legislation are examples of the basic levels of rights that were spelt out in the 1957 Social Chapter.

European law is given precedence over UK national law. Therefore, if there is any dispute between UK national law and European law the European law will always be enforced. If there is doubt over the interpretation of the law then the matter is referred to the European Court of Justice (see below).

There are four main sources of European law:

- The primary sources of all European law are *treaties*. A treaty is a framework within which a member state can implement legislation. The first treaty was the Treaty of Rome (1957) that created the European Economic Community (as it was then named). Subsequent treaties include the Maastricht Treaty (1992) and the Treaty of Amsterdam (1997).
- The European Commission creates *regulations*, which automatically become part of the national laws of member states. There might be the requirement for the member state to pass legislation to incorporate them. Examples of regulations are the Working Time Regulations 1998 and the Part-time Workers (Prevention of Less Favourable Treatment) Regulations 2000.
- Whereas a regulation automatically becomes part of national law, a *directive* lays down objectives that the member state is directed to implement. The member state achieves this by making the directive part of national law. Each member state decides exactly how it will achieve this. There is usually a time period given in which to carry out this implementation, and there have been occasions where an extension to this time period has been negotiated. If the member state does not implement the directive in the given time period it can be forced to pay damages to any individual who has suffered loss as a result of the non-implementation. Examples of directives are the Working Time Directive 1993 (which went on to become the Working Time Regulations in 1998) and the Information and Consultation Directive 2002 (which went on to become the Information and Consultation Regulations in 2004).
- *Decisions* relate to specific member states, individuals or organisations. They are binding.

There are five key institutions within the European Union:

1. *European Commission (www.europa.en.int/com)* The European Commission is the executive body of the EU and proposes measures and ensures that they are implemented in accordance with the agreements that are reached. The Treaty of Nice 2003 capped the size of the European Commission at 27.
2. *European Parliament (www.euorparl.org.uk)* The European Parliament has a considerably less influential role than the UK Parliament has in the UK. The European Parliament has the right to be consulted over any proposals but, unlike the UK Parliament, cannot introduce any proposals. Its purpose is to act as the main consultation body for the EU. Each member state elects Members of the European Parliament (MEPs), who hold their post for five years. The number of MEPs from each member state depends on the size of that state.
3. *Council of the European Union (www.coe.int)* The Council of the European Union has one representative from each member state. It is the decision-making body of the EU, and primarily adopts the proposals from the Commission for inclusion by the member states.
4. *European Court of Justice (www.curia.eu.int)* As already noted, the European Court of

Justice (ECJ) has an important role in defining and interpreting EC law. The final court of appeal in a member state (in the UK this is the House of Lords) can refer a case to the ECJ for an interpretation of a specific aspect of European law. The ECJ makes the ruling and then returns it to the courts in the member state for that ruling to be acted upon. The ECJ is the final level of appeal in any dispute.

The ECJ carries out a number of additional functions including:

- Hearing challenges that the member state has failed to fulfil some aspect of a treaty. An individual or a group of individuals can bring these challenges.
- Hearing complaints regarding the way in which European law has been interpreted and applied.

5. *European Court of Human Rights* (www.echr.coe.int) The European Court of Human Rights (ECHR) is the court that hears any claims that an individual, or groups of individuals has suffered a violation of the European Convention on Human Rights 1950. In the UK, much of this convention has been incorporated into the Human Rights Act 1998. The rulings of the ECHR are then managed in much the same way as rulings from the ECJ, with any legislation of a member state that is found to be incompatible with European Law being referred back to the government of the member state for amendments to be made to national legislation.

The Treaty of Maastricht 1997 allowed EU representative bodies to have a role in the EU legislative process. There are three main bodies, which are known as the 'social partners':

1. *European Trade Union Confederation (ETUC) (www.etuc.org)* The ETUC represents the interests of trade union members at European level. The national trade union confederations of each member state are affiliated to the ETUC as full members. In addition the ETUC comprises 11 European sectoral trade unions known as European Industry Federations. These federations represent individual trade unions from particular sectors and are recognised as the sectoral employees' social partners.
2. *The Union of Industrial and Employers' Confederations of Europe (UNICE) (www.unice.org)* This is the main voice of employers within the EU and comprises 35 members and four observers from throughout Europe. Its aim is to promote policies and legislation that supports employers throughout Europe.
3. *The European Centre of Enterprises with Public Participation and of Enterprises of General Economic Interest (CEEP) (www.ceep.org)* CEEP represents the interests of employers within the public sector throughout Europe.

Clearly, there is a detailed structure within the EU, but the question remains whether the EU really has any impact on employee relations in the UK.

The answer must surely be 'yes'. First, there is the area of employment legislation. As we have already noted, legislation relating to the national minimum wage and working time comes as a result of membership of the EU. As we shall see in the last three chapters of this book, there are many other areas of legislation that have been influenced by the EU.

Being a member of the EU also means that a resident in one of the member states can seek work in any other member state. This has opened up more employment opportunities for individuals, and has also resulted in organisations moving into other European countries. This brings specific challenges to the employment relationship, including managing a disparate work force and overcoming language barriers.

Membership of the EU has also meant that employees are required to consult and communicate with their employees in a formal way. We will look at these requirements in Chapter 5.

 Membership of the EU definitely has an impact on employee relations in the UK. To gain more understanding of the range of areas touched on by this membership look on the websites of the various bodies within the UK (all addresses have been given above). Try to understand the breadth of activities and involvement that occur.

ACTIVITIES

THE ROLE OF EXTERNAL BODIES IN EMPLOYEE RELATIONS

Although the main focus of the employment relationship is on the two parties of the employer and the employee, there are times that an external body can offer valuable help. In this section we look at the role of such bodies.

Acas (Advisory, Conciliation and Arbitration Service) www.acas.org.uk

Acas was established in 1974. It is a service that is funded by the government, but is independent of any government control. It is run by a council of 12 members who represent business, trade unions and the independent sector. The 800 employees of Acas work from 11 regional offices and a head office in London.

The traditional view of Acas is of an organisation that enters into disputes between the employer and the employee when they have reached a deadlock, and tries to help the two parties reach a solution. However, in its 2003/04 annual report Acas reported on the changing focus that it is developing.

The focus of Acas is now on working together with those involved in the employment relationship to bring about effective workplaces. The focus has moved from being reactive, to being proactive in developing healthy employment relationships. Acas describes the key features of this vision of effective workplaces as having:

- ambitions, goals and plans that employees understand and are familiar with
- managers who listen and value the input of employees
- employees who are confident to give their views
- everyone treated equally with differences being valued
- encouragement of innovation and initiative
- acknowledgement that employees have commitments outside of work and an attempt to help employees balance work and their other commitments
- a fair and consistent reward system
- a healthy and safe place of work
- as much employment security as possible
- a culture where employees are encouraged to learn new skills to use in their current job, or alternative employment
- a good working relationship between management and employee representatives
- fair procedures for dealing with disciplinary issues, grievances and disputes.

To help support the achievement of this vision Acas has divided its work into four sections: information, advice, training and working with organisations.

A key part of the work of Acas remains advising people about employment related matters. Anyone, employer or employee can phone Acas for advice, and there is no charge for the advice. In 2003–04, 796,649 calls were received and answered. Of those making the calls 55 per cent were employees, 36 per cent were employers and 9 per cent were people representing someone else.

This statistic links back to the increased individualism that we see in the employment relationship. A level of 55 per cent of calls coming from employees suggests that employees are aware that there is a source of advice that they can seek on an individual basis.

The top three topics that were discussed in the calls for advice were discipline (19 per cent), contracts of employment (18 per cent) and lay-offs, short-time working, redundancy and transfers of employment (17 per cent).

Acas also plays an important role in trying to resolve individual conflicts that occur between the employer and the employee. When an employee puts in a claim to an employment tribunal, Acas has a statutory duty to contact both parties (employer and employee) and try to reach a conciliated settlement. In 2003/04 Acas dealt with 102,559 such applications to the employment tribunal, with only 24 per cent of cases going on to a tribunal hearing. In the Acas annual report the organisation comments that the problem in most cases was a breakdown in communication between the two parties.

Acas plays an important role in such situations in identifying where the breakdown in communication has occurred, and in helping each party to clarify any misunderstandings. This can then result in some form of conciliation being reached.

In addition to these primary roles, Acas was involved in 69 trade dispute arbitrations and helping with 1,245 collective conciliations (source of data: www.acas.org.co.uk).

CAC (Central Arbitration Committee) www.cac.gov.uk

The CAC is an independent body with statutory powers, whose specific role is to determine the outcome of applications relating to the statutory recognition or derecognition of trade unions for collective bargaining purposes. We look in detail at this issue in Chapter 11. Although this is the primary purpose of the CAC, it is also responsible for determining the outcome of disputes between employers and employees over the disclosure of information for collective bargaining purposes, and in dealing with complaints relating to the establishment of works councils in the UK.

The committee consists of a chairperson, 11 deputy chairpersons, 21 members representing workers and 23 members representing employers. The secretary of state for trade and industry appoints the committee after consulting with Acas. The composition of the committee is designed so that opinions and experiences of both sides of the employment relationship are considered in decision-making.

According to the 2003/04 annual report CAC received 107 applications relating to trade union recognition, and 6 relating to disclosure of information during the 2003/04 period.

The remaining three bodies that we shall look at all relate to the issues of discrimination. Although we examine their roles separately here, it is important to read on to the end of the section, where we shall see that the bodies are to be brought together in 2007 as one body.

EOC (Equal Opportunities Commission) www.eoc.org.uk

The EOC is an independent statutory body, funded by grant-in-aid. It is independent from the government, although it is responsible to the equality minister.

The EOC was set up as a result of the Sex Discrimination Act (1975) to work towards the elimination of discrimination on the grounds of sex or marriage and:

- to promote equality of opportunity for women and men
- to keep under review the Sex Discrimination Act (1975) and the Equal Pay Act (1970)
- to provide legal advice and assistance to individuals who have been discriminated against.

To achieve its aims the EOC:

- provides up-to-date advice on rights relating to equality to both employers and employees
- runs high-profile campaigns and lobbies decision-makers at every level
- carries out relevant research and publishes the results
- represents employees at landmark legal cases under the Sex Discrimination Act (1975) and the Equal Pay Act (1970).

CRE (Commission for Racial Equality) www.cre.gov.uk

The Commission for Racial Equality is a publicly funded, non-governmental body set up under the Race Relations Act (1976) to tackle racial discrimination and promote racial equality.

It works in both the public and private sectors to encourage fair treatment and to promote equal opportunities for everyone, regardless of their race, colour, nationality, or national or ethnic origin. It:

- provides information and advice to people who think they have suffered racial discrimination or harassment
- works with public bodies, businesses, and organisations from all sectors to promote policies and practices that will help to ensure equal treatment for all
- runs campaigns to raise awareness of race issues, and encourage organisations and individuals to play their part in creating a just society
- makes sure that all new laws take full account of the Race Relations Act and the protection it gives against discrimination.

DRC (Disability Rights Commission) www.drc-gb.org

The Disability Rights Commission (DRC) is an independent body, established by Act of Parliament to eliminate discrimination against disabled people and promote equality of opportunity. The DRC:

- provides an advice and information service for disabled people, employers and service providers
- supports disabled people in securing their rights under the Disability Discrimination Act (DDA)
- supports legal cases to set new precedents and test the limits of the law through representing and/or advising applicants
- campaigns to strengthen the law so that it works better and protects more disabled people

- organises campaigns – such as the Educating for Equality campaign – to change policy, practice and awareness so that disabled people get a fairer deal
- puts on events and conferences to raise public awareness of disability issues
- produces publications about rights for disabled people and good practice for employers and service providers
- publishes policy statements and research on issues that affect disabled people.

In January 2003 the government introduced the Equality Bill. Part of that bill proposed that the work of the Equal Opportunities Commission, the Commission for Racial Equality and the Disability Rights Commission be brought together as a single body to be known as the Commission for Equality and Human Rights (CEHR). As well as the areas of discrimination covered by these existing three bodies the CEHR will also have responsibility for ensuring equality in the areas of age, religion and belief and sexual orientation. It will be established in October 2007, but will not take over the work of the CRE until April 2009.

The purpose of the new body is to promote equality and human rights through the giving of advice, undertaking research and through publishing Codes of Practice. According to the Department of Trade and Industry, the vision for the core purpose of the CEHR is to:

- build and nurture respect for equality, diversity and human rights
- work towards compliance with equality and human rights legislation
- promote good relations between communities.
(source: www.dti.gov.uk).

Inevitably there is some concern that the forming of one body will dilute some of the emphasis that is given to individual areas of discrimination by the current organisations. However, there is also the argument that a larger body will have more influence over decision-making.

ACTIVITIES

In the time building up to October 2007 when the CEHR is established there are very likely to be reports on it in the business and personnel press. Follow the reports, trying to understand the reasons for its establishment, and some of the concerns related to it.

GLOBALISATION AND THE IMPACT ON EMPLOYEE RELATIONS

Globalisation is the opening up of an organisation to operate on an international basis. Although globalisation has been a trend for many years (according to Lewis *et al* (2003), Ford have been making cars outside the United States since the 1920s) the growth in electronic communication, and developments in transport have made it easier for organisations to operate on an international basis.

Perhaps due to the importance of technology in facilitating globalisation, the multinationals that have expanded most spectacularly are in industries employing advanced technology. However, although multinational enterprises have an advantage in the advanced technology sector, they are not restricted to it, as they have also made inroads into areas like food products, motor vehicles and cosmetics – for example, firms like Coca-Cola, General Motors and Unilever.

According to the United Nations Conference Report 1997 over 80 per cent of world trade comes from multinational corporations, with the top 200 multinational corporations controlling approximately one third of global production. The report goes on to highlight some of the growing difficulties of globalisation:

- Overall the world economy is growing too slowly to generate sufficient employment with adequate pay, and hence to alleviate poverty.
- Gaps between developed and developing countries are slowly widening.
- The rich have gained everywhere, especially in terms of the distribution of income.
- Increased job and income insecurity is spreading. Shedding labour and wage repression has become common in all areas of the world.
- The growing wage gap between skilled and unskilled labour is becoming a global problem.

From this we can see that, although globalisation might bring job security and increased opportunities to those employed within an organization, worldwide it can exacerbate differences that already exist in the fortunes of developed and developing countries.

Multinational organizations have also been accused of taking advantage of the differences between their home country and the country in which they are operating (known as the host country), to the disadvantage of the employee. This can be done through pursuing policies in the host country that are not to the best advantage of those working in that country – for example, paying very poor wages because there is no legislation in the host country to prevent that from happening. Some organizations have also been accused of registering offices overseas to avoid conforming to legislation in their home country.

However, given the size of many multinationals, host countries can be reluctant to protest against any practices that are not seen to be fair because of the fear that any investment by such multinationals might be withdrawn, taking with it the associated job opportunities. Blyton and Turnbull (2004) cite the competition between multinationals as being translated into an 'international race to the bottom' in respect of wages and the terms and conditions of employment of workers.

The recognition of the problems that multinationals can cause led, in 1976, to the Organisation for Economic Co-operation and Development (OECD) formulating guidelines that were designed to control the situation. These guidelines included the following.

- tougher 'anti-bribery' provisions (a number of multinationals were involved in 'bribery allegations' and 'scandals' earlier in 1976)
- rules stipulating the extent to which governments can demand multinationals to disclose information pertaining to their business
- taxation agreements designed to make it more difficult to control 'transfer pricing'.

As we saw in Chapter 2, another aspect of globalisation that has been of particular note recently is the moving of parts of an organization to an area of the world where the labour is cheaper. As we saw, this has been evident in the moving of call centres to countries such as India.

Perlmutter (1999) identified forces that support global harmonization, and those that oppose it. These are summarised by Naylor (2004) in his book *Management*:

Forces that support global harmonisation:

- political systems that can work alongside each other, and are willing to co-operate
- an open world economy with a reduction of trade barriers
- increased awareness of different cultures and consumer tastes and an increased sharing of ideas
- developments in communications – both in transport and in electronic communication
- common concerns of the consequences of operating, such as environmental concerns.

Forces that oppose global harmonization:

- uneven distribution of natural resources and differing/shifting climates
- contrasting stages of economic development, and contrasts between rich and poor within nations
- differing levels of education, and the outflow of well-educated people from poorer countries
- conflicting cultures and differing values
- differences in language, and increasing divergence within languages.

Given the various difficulties associated with globalisation, one could question why it is a process that is growing. One of the key reasons for this is organizational survival.

- Relying on the home market only can be restrictive. If a significant number of competitors operate in the same market this could damage the long-term survival of the organization. By operating in just one market the organisation also restricts itself to being influenced by the state of the national economy, and could suffer accordingly. For example, if one economy is in recession this will affect the organisation. However, the impact can be lessened if it is also operating in a stable economy.
- If an organisation does not look to overseas opportunities it could be restricting the opportunity to grow.
- In some situations global expansion will occur because trade restrictions are lifted. Organisations might feel the need to take advantage of this, because if they do not competitors will.
- There might be decreased costs from operating in other countries, as illustrated already with the example of organisations moving their call centres overseas.

ACTIVITIES

Think about the organisation you work in, or an organisation with which you are familiar. Is it a national organisation or a multinational? Are there any plans to move into more markets, or to retreat from any markets? How do you think that the decisions on multi-national expansion have impacted on employee relations?

ORGANISATION EXAMPLE

The reaction of the government to globalisation can seem to be rather mixed, and this can be demonstrated by looking at the car industry. Foreign investment can be actively welcomed, as it was when Nissan (in Sunderland) and Toyota (in Derby) decided to build new factories in the UK. However, not long after this the government watched Jaguar being sold to Ford and MG Rover being sold to BMW, both of which are foreign companies.

> In this example we see two different issues being addressed. The move of Nissan to Sunderland was specifically encouraged because of the demise of the shipbuilding industry in that area, and the associated unemployment.
>
> However, the foreign investment in struggling UK companies was welcomed to help keep jobs in the UK. In the case of MG Rover the foreign investors, BMW, were not able to change its fortunes and eventually sold it to a UK consortium (Phoenix). Even under this ownership it continued to lose money, and the eventual result was the collapse of the MG Rover Group with the initial loss of 4,000 jobs.

The question that is of specific interest to us here is what impact globalisation has on employee relations. Some of the key impacts are:

- *Greater potential for career development.* In some organisations employees can become very demotivated and dissatisfied because the career opportunities are limited. In a multinational organisation there are potentially a broader range of development opportunities.
- *Greater job security.* This can be an advantage, because a large organisation has more ability to absorb the need for job loss through natural turnover. However, the very process of globalisation can result in job loss if, for example, an organisation decides to relocate to another country.
- *Cost of labour.* Another impact on job security is the cost of labour. If employees work in a country where labour costs are high they are more likely to face job insecurity.
- *Language barriers.* The ability to progress in an organisation can be limited due to language ability amongst employees. Both employees and employers need to be willing to address these issues.
- *Remote management.* It is possible that a manager in one country reports to a manager in another country. This is likely to be very true for the most senior managers in countries where the head office is not located, reporting into the head office wherever that might be. It can also be true for functional reporting – for example, the most senior finance manager in one country might report into the general manager in that country, as well as to a senior finance manager in the head office. It can be more difficult to build relationships when there is a physical remoteness between the two parties to the relationship.

The globalisation of the organisation can lead to an additional aspect to the psychological contract. This is particularly true in the case of remote management when it is much more difficult to identify and understand the expectations of each side of the contract. In addition, there can be a sense of increased helplessness on the side of both the employer and the employee as the more complex demands of globalisation lead to both parties feeling a lack of control of the expectations.

GLOBAL ORGANISATION STRUCTURES TO SUPPORT EMPLOYEE RELATIONS

Global organisations typically grow from a domestic organisation. For example, McDonald's started from one restaurant in Illinois, USA and now has restaurants in over 100 countries worldwide. Daft (1998) summaries the four stages that organisations go through as they become fully global. They are:

- *Domestic*: The market for goods or services is primarily in the home country. There may be some exports, and if there are, this takes place through a home-based export department.
- *International:* The company starts to take exports seriously and has specialists to deal with sales and service in different countries. The export department is replaced by an international division.
- *Multinational*: At this stage the organisation has marketing and production facilities in different countries, and more than one-third of sales occur outside the home country.
- *Global*: The company consists of a number of subsidiaries, and the company is the driver, rather than the country in which the company originated.

Although the growth of an organisation from domestic to global might seem to be heavily based on the growth of products and services, it is totally dependent on the people within the organisation. To ensure successful expansion, the employees must work together effectively and be supportive of the global goal. To ensure this happens successfully, attention needs to be given to:

- *The organisation structure*. In a domestic organisation, a functional structure works well, because employees have specific jobs to do within a relatively simple market place. However, when the organisation grows to become international the structure is likely to change to a divisional structure – with employees needing to focus their efforts on the demands of different markets. This is particularly true when there are different regulations that need to be adapted to in different countries.

    As the organisation becomes global it is likely that the structure will move to a matrix structure, with each country having its own support functions (eg finance, marketing, HR) which need to operate in accordance with the demands of the specific country and report to the local manager. However, there is also the need for the organisation to have some overall control of such operations, and hence there is likely to be a dual reporting role to a head office function.

    The creation of the most suitable structure within the organisation is very important for employees, as it defines the key working relationships. However, any change in the structure needs to be carefully managed so that the perceived status of different employees is either maintained or, if it has to be altered, is carefully explained. Employees who perceive that they have been demoted will be less committed and motivated to the goals of the organisation.
- *Appropriate skills*. A common mistake that is made when an organisation is expanding is to presume that employees who have been successfully working in a domestic organisation have the skills to work in a global organisation. Organisations need to ensure that they provide the relevant training opportunities, but will also need to recruit some expertise from outside of the organisation. This can damage employee relationships if the perception is that employees who have worked loyally within the organisation are undervalued.
- *Common goals*. An organisation that is successful has all parts of that organisation working towards the same goal. In a divisional structure, particularly one that has goals set for each division (or country in the case of a global organisation), managers must learn to cooperate as well as to compete (Harrigan 1987). This adds another dimension to the employment relationship for some employees – relationships between divisions/countries, as well as up to the line manager and over to the functional specialist in the head office.

Figure 3.1 summarises the range of relationships that an employee can need to manage.

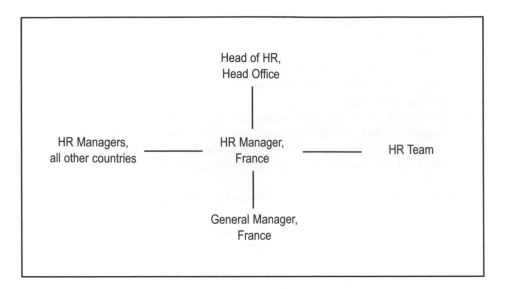

Figure 3.1 Example based on the relationships being managed by an HR manager of a French subsidiary of a global organisation

A survey by Hall (2005) looked at the specific difficulties faced by the conflicting relationships that exist in a global organisation. The survey involved 2,400 people working in multinationals across 17 countries. As a result of the survey Hall suggested that there is a need to think in terms of three distinct groups of employees, each of which have different needs.

The 'global group' are a small group of senior people who focus on global activities. Hall suggests that one way to keep their focus on global activities is to recruit people in proportion to the business of the organisation. So if 10 per cent of the business is in Spain, 10 per cent of the managers should be Spanish. However, to ensure that there is a true global perspective it is important to move managers around to work in different countries, otherwise they will never really develop a global perspective.

The second group is 'locally loyal'. Hall suggests that even in the most global organisations, at least 80 per cent of employees will have jobs that are rooted in local activities. He suggests that they should be encouraged to have pride in the international aspect of the organisation, but should focus on finding local solutions to local problems – why make their relationships more complex than they need to be?

The third group is the 'matrixed middle'. This is the group of people with complex relationships interfacing between the local and the global. As shown in Figure 3.1, they have multiple reporting lines as well as needing to develop and maintain a variety of working relationships. Difficulties that can occur are too many meetings (reporting progress to too many people), too much communication (again a facet of over-reporting) and too much teamwork, rather than empowering individuals to do the job. It is important to develop effective ways of working for this group, rather than to try to impose local or global methods which do not fit the complexity.

The primary message that comes across about managing employees in a global organisation is that there are complexities to the relationships. However, not all employees need to have complex relationships – and for those that do there need to be put in place processes that allow them to manage the complexities, which might need to be unique to their situation.

KEY POINTS FROM THIS CHAPTER

- The government is the major employer in the UK.
- Traditionally the government has been seen as a model employer, a view that is now challenged.
- During the period of 1979–97 the Conservative Party emphasised individualism.
- From 1997 to the present the Labour Party has focused its employment policies on the basis of equal opportunity for all.
- A key part of the process for managing public sector workers has been the use of target setting.
- The role of the government as a model employer is specifically being challenged in terms of job security, pensions and levels of pay.
- The UK signed the Social Charter in 1997.
- European law takes precedence over UK law.
- Acas's focus has become much more proactive, based on working together with organisations.
- It is proposed that the Commission for Equality and Human Rights will replace the Commission for Racial Equality, the Equal Opportunities Commission and the Disability Rights Commission.
- Globalisation is the opening up of an organisation to operate in international markets.
- Globalisation can be necessary for an organisation to survive.
- When globalisation occurs, structures need to change to reflect the changing relationships.
- Within a global organisation it is suggested that there are three groups of employees – the global group, locally loyal and matrixed middle.

EXAMPLES TO WORK THROUGH

1. You have listened to an argument between two friends about the use of target setting in the NHS. One has argued very strongly that target setting is not an appropriate way of managing the NHS, whereas the other has argued that there must be some form of accountability. You can see sense in both arguments. What other approaches might there be that could be used to manage employees in the NHS?
2. Your managing director makes the rather sweeping comment that the European Union has no real effect on employees within the UK. Do you agree with her? Why/why not?
3. Referring back to the survey by Hall (2005), think about some of the difficulties faced by the group termed the 'matrixed middle'. What processes could be put in place to help sustain and improve employee relationships amongst this group?

(Suggestions of answers to the examples can be accessed by tutors at www.cipd.co.uk/tss).

One of the largest groups of employees in the public sector are those employed by the National Health Service. Although, obviously, the NHS employs a large number of medical professionals there are actually a huge range of jobs covering all sorts of occupations.

As part of an ongoing attempt to improve terms and conditions of employment within the NHS, the 'Agenda for Change' has been introduced. This is seen as the most radical change to the NHS pay system since the NHS was formed in 1948. The Agenda for Change applies to over one million employees within the NHS, with the exception of doctors, dentists and the most senior managers.

As part of the Agenda for Change, a job evaluation scheme has been developed specifically for the NHS. The main focus is that employees will be paid on the basis of the jobs that they are doing, and for the skills and knowledge that they bring to these jobs. The new pay system aims to ensure fair pay and gives employees a clearer system by which they can understand career progression opportunities.

The job evaluation scheme includes a knowledge and skills framework that is linked to annual development reviews and personal development plans. This approach replaces the old system, where employees could progress by taking on new responsibilities. The idea is that employees are rewarded for the skills and knowledge that they have, and that this will allow jobs to be designed around patient and staff needs. Overall it is expected that this will improve productivity and employee satisfaction with their jobs. The new system also introduces standard arrangements for hours of work, annual leave and overtime.

Although one of the main focuses is on fairer pay, the new system also provides more flexibility for employers. They will be able to:

- design jobs around the needs of patients, rather than around grading definitions
- define the core skills and knowledge that employees are required to develop in each job
- pay extra if they face recruitment or retention difficulties.

According to the NHS the benefits of the new scheme are:

- It is a system that is fair and transparent.
- There is recognition and reward for the skills and competencies that staff acquire throughout their careers.
- There will be greater employer flexibility.
- Team working will be supported more effectively through harmonised conditions.
- There will be the flexibility to pay a premium when there are recruitment or retention difficulties.
- This should be an easier system to administer.
- The system should improve recruitment and retention of staff, and help to make the NHS a model employer.

(source: www.nhsemployers.org).

Questions

a) Do you think that the Agenda for Change is indicative of the approach that the current Labour government has taken to being an employer? Why/why not?
b) How do you think that the Agenda for Change will contribute to improved employee relations? Justify your suggestions.
c) If you had been part of the team developing the Agenda for Change, what other proposals would you have made? Explain the reasons behind these proposals.

The Role of Management in Employee Relations

CHAPTER 4

> The objectives of this chapter are to:
>
> - explore the function of management
> - examine the different management styles in employee relations
> - examine the impact of different approaches to management
> - explore the difference between management and leadership
> - consider how power can be used and abused in the employment relationship
> - examine the process of managing change.

In the first three chapters of this book we have been focusing on the internal and external factors that impact on the employment relationship. In the next three we shall be looking in more detail at the parties within the employment relationship and the issues that impact on them.

Chapters 4 and 5 look at the role of management, and Chapter 6 looks at the role of employees. As the two main parties in the employment relationship it is inevitable that the issues that concern one of these parties will also be of interest to the other party. Hence, the chapters should be read with this overlap in mind.

We shall start this examination by looking in this chapter at the role of management. It is important to understand the different management styles within employee relations, and we shall start at this point. However, to understand the employment relationship we have to look more broadly than this and consider different approaches to management, the role of leadership and how such things as power are used and abused. We will, therefore, open up the debate about the role of management to cover these areas.

THE FUNCTION OF MANAGEMENT

In Chapters 1, 2 and 3 of this book our focus has been very much on the organisation. In this chapter we narrow our focus and concentrate on the role of management in the employment relationship.

The role of management, and the relationship between employees and their managers, can have a significant impact on the job satisfaction expressed by the employee. In turn, this has a significant impact on whether the employee is likely to stay with the organisation. Hutchinson and Purcell (2003) found that the behaviour of front-line management has a direct impact on the commitment, motivation and satisfaction reported by employees. They state that a poor relationship with a line manager can often be a key reason that employees leave an organisation, but this is not always demonstrated in data collected in exit interviews, because the interviews are often conducted by the line managers.

Although there is a wide range of potential reasons for relationships between an employee and the manager breaking down, a common reason relates to the very purpose of having a manager.

This is the issue of control. Managers are typically responsible for ensuring targets are met, standards are reached and that there is order and stability. However, many individuals dislike the idea of being told what to do, and hence the approach that the manager takes to being in control can be the factor that determines whether the manager/employee relationship breaks down.

Huczynski and Buchanan (1991) suggest that control starts at the organisational level with three different connotations:

1. *Economically necessary*. If control does not exist then resources will be wasted and money can be spent unnecessarily. Hence, control is a means of ensuring efficiency and the most effective use of resources.
2. *Psychologically necessary*. Control can be used to produce predictability, which can lead to psychological well being. Lack of control can lead to uncertainty, ambiguity and disorder.
3. *Political process*. The use of control is a means of perpetuating inequalities in power and in other resources within the organisation. Within the political process there are certain powerful individuals and groups who dominate others.

As is shown with these definitions, some level of control is necessary within an organisation. The suggestion is that, without control, some level of chaos will develop.

Think of different managers that you have worked for. How did they take control? Do you think that their approach to control enhanced their role as manager or did it made them unpopular with employees?

There are several examples of managers who have taken a very strong approach to being in control, but maybe one of the most commonly cited examples is Margaret Thatcher, who was the leader of the Conservative Party from 1975–90.

She was nicknamed the 'Iron Lady' by a Soviet newspaper in relation to her tough stance on the cold war, but this nickname was extended to reflect her tough stance on most issues that she faced. As we have already noted, she is particularly renowned for her tough stance against trade unions, and specifically the National Union of Mineworkers.

She was in control. Prior to her election as prime minister there had been significant discontent (leading to the Winter of Discontent), and she addressed the issues very clearly and by ensuring efficient use of the resources that were available. She was very clear about her aims, and even if people disagreed with her they clearly knew what she aimed to achieve.

In addition, she was clearly a powerful individual. Today her period as prime minister is often referred to as the 'Thatcher government' – rather than the Conservative government. It was clearly her time, and she was clearly in control.

Taking control as a manager spans a range of different aspects, and Hellriegel and Slocum (1978) suggest that there are six management control strategies that are commonly adopted.

Organisation structure

As we saw in Chapter 1, there are a number of different organisation structures that can be adopted. However, what is common to them all is that they define relationships. As we saw, they can define a relationship between a manager and a subordinate – and they can also define a relationship between two different teams. However, what is common to all traditional organisation structures is that status can be determined by studying them.

One way that managers can exercise control is by relying on the status that is prescribed by the structure of the organisation. Hence, if I have a higher status than you, you must do as I say.

Some organisations have recognised this as a negative impact on employee relationships, and have moved to a teamwork structure where status is not as easily defined. However, even within such a teamwork structure there is still likely to be a team leader – even if this is not emphasised.

Despite the potential conflicts, having a clear understanding of status can give security to the employment relationship. If an employee feels insecure in his/her own judgement or abilities, then knowing that there is someone more senior who will take overall responsibility for the outcomes of any decisions is reassuring. There are also some situations where having clear levels of status is essential for safety.

ORGANISATION
EXAMPLE

In the armed forces there is clear level of rank, with respect shown for all superiors. Although some might find this a rather dated way of behaving, it is important to remember why the armed forces exist.

If the armed forces go into battle, it is essential that all those within the armed forces obey orders quickly and efficiently. Lives could be lost if time was spent with subordinates questioning the orders that have been given.

Recruitment and training

Managers are typically responsible for choosing who to recruit to work in their department, and for deciding who should receive what type of training. As Price (2004) states, employees who are wrongly placed into jobs are often unhappy, bored and anxious about being unable to do the job well. By recruiting the wrong people, therefore, managers can create an employment relationship that is characterised by dissatisfaction.

There is also the danger that managers will perpetuate what they see as the best way to approach tasks, and will not recruit new ideas and innovation into the department. This can be by recruiting people who have similar characteristics to the manager, or who have some other striking characteristics that are appreciated by the manager. This is known as the 'halo effect', a term first used in 1920 by the psychologist Edward Thorndike.

Rewards and punishments

The psychologist B F Skinner (1938) worked with rats and pigeons, manipulating their behaviour through a series of rewards and punishments. He concluded that rewards tend to increase the frequency of desired behaviours, whereas punishments suppress or decrease the frequency of undesired behaviour.

The use of rewards and punishments can be a key way for managers to reinforce the behaviours that they want. For example, bonuses can be paid in return for achieving particular targets, or praise can be given for the display of desirable behaviours (we will look at the issue of reward in more detail in Chapter 9). Punishment can take the form of disciplinary warnings, non-payment of bonuses and negative criticism of performance.

If the manager has the ability to determine rewards and punishments then there is inequity in the employment relationship. If the employee perceives that the manager is not fair in determining the rewards or punishments, there is likely to be conflict within the employment relationship.

ORGANISATION
EXAMPLE

The result of inappropriate use of punishment is illustrated in the case of *Stanley Cole (Wainfleet) Ltd* v *Sheridan* (2003). Sheridan had been an employee for more than five years, and had no record of disciplinary action. She had a heated discussion with a colleague which upset her, and she then left the office for one and a half hours (which included her half-hour lunch break). She returned, and her line manager suggested that she go home because she was clearly still upset. She then went absent on the grounds of ill health. Disciplinary action was taken against her for leaving the office without permission, and she was issued with a final written warning (the last stage of the disciplinary procedure before dismissal). Her appeal against the decision was rejected. She resigned and claimed constructive dismissal. (If the employer's conduct is such that it breaches the contract of employment, and that breach goes to the very root of the contract the employee can terminate the contract of employment and claim constructive dismissal.)

The employment tribunal found that the severe penalty of a final written warning for a first (and relatively minor) offence amounted to a breach of the contract of employment because it breached the implied term of trust and confidence or/and the implied term that the disciplinary procedure would be used fairly. Her claim for constructive dismissal was upheld.

We see, therefore, that in this case the use of inappropriate punishment caused irretrievable breakdown of the employment relationship.

Policies and rules

Employees are required to abide by company rules, because they typically become incorporated into the contract of employment. Managers can use rules and policies to define the types of behaviours and attitudes that they want to see in the organisation.

Most rules are accepted by employees. However, if a rule is introduced that an employee finds it difficult to abide by (such as the introduction of a no smoking rule, which can be hard for smokers to abide by), then conflict can result in the employment relationship.

The level of conflict will depend on the willingness of management to help employees address any difficulties they might have in abiding by the rules.

Budgets

Part of the budgeting process is to set targets – seen as a key management function. However, if employees do not believe that the targets are reasonable then tension can be created. An approach to target and objective setting that is commonly used is to ensure that they are 'SMART':

Specific

Measurable

Achievable

Realistic

Timebound

However, using this acronym does not ensure targets that are acceptable to all, because the assessment of such things as achievable and realistic is largely subjective.

ORGANISATION EXAMPLE

One of the ways that management often decide to cut costs is through the loss of jobs. However, this can lead to conflict if employees do not believe that the targets set for the remaining staff are achievable.

This was part of the reason for industrial action that was taken by employees of the BBC in May 2005. BBC management had announced that there was to be the loss of 3,780 jobs – a 15 per cent cut across most departments. Employees took industrial action because compulsory redundancies had not been ruled out and because they did not believe that meaningful consultation had taken place. They did not believe that it was possible to achieve the proposed workload (ie the targets) with such a severe reduction in staffing.

Source: www.bbc.co.uk/news, 22 May 2005.

Machinery

Machinery can be used by management to replace jobs, but it can also be used to gather information about employee performance. We have already noted how this can take place in a call centre, with information being gathered about employee performance in answering and dealing with calls.

ORGANISATION EXAMPLE

In October 2003 allegations were made that employees of the directory enquiries service 118118 (known as 'The Number') were cutting callers off before they had fully answered their queries in a bid to earn extra bonuses by reducing the average length of call. The call centre equipment recorded the performance of each member of staff. After an investigation Oftel, the telecommunications regulatory body, was satisfied that The Number had taken action swiftly, including the dismissal of staff at the centre of the allegations.

Source: www.bbc.co.uk/news, 2 October 2003.

From looking at the six different control strategies we see that there are a number of different ways that managers can take control. All of these can cause conflict within the employment relationship if it is abused in any way.

ACTIVITIES

Think about at least two managers that you have worked for. Work through the six control strategies that we have explored in this section. Can you think of any examples of how the managers have exercised control using any of these strategies?

OBEDIENCE

One reason that managers are able to take control is that some subordinates will obey them simply because of their status. This is demonstrated to a frightening level in a classic psychological study by Milgram (1963).

Milgram's interest in obedience stemmed from the need for some explanation after millions of people were slaughtered in concentration camps by the Nazis during the Second World War. He wanted to understand why Nazis working in the concentration camps obeyed instructions to act in such an abhorrent way.

His experiment was to make a 'shock generator'. The generator had a number of switches with labels from 'slight shock' to 'danger: severe shock'. The switches also had a voltage marked against them, moving in 15-volt steps from 15 to 450 volts.

The experiment involved a 'victim' (known as the learner) being given a series of word pairs that he was required to memorise. The participants in the experiment were told that the 'victim' was a fellow participant and that the experiment was looking at the role that punishment plays in learning. They were told that they would randomly be assigned to the role of teacher or learner by taking a slip of paper with one of the roles written on it. (In fact they were always assigned the role of teacher, and the victim was always assigned the role of learner.) The victim was actually working in collaboration with Milgram.

The learner was strapped into a chair and the experimenter explained to the learner and the teacher that the shocks can be extremely painful, but they will cause no permanent tissue damage (!). The participant was then given a shock of 45 volts to enhance the authenticity of the experiment.

The teacher read out a word from one of the pairs and gave the learner a choice of four possible answers (ie four possible pairs to that word). The learner showed his response by pressing one of four switches that lit a light on top of the shock generator. If the learner gave the correct answer the teacher moved on to the next word on the list. If the answer was incorrect the teacher gave the correct answer and told the learner the amount of punishment he was going to receive (ie the number of volts' shock he was going to be given). Each time an incorrect answer was given, the teacher was required to increase the level of shock that was given.

As required by the experiment, the learner gave a number of wrong answers and hence received a series of electric shocks. Each time the teacher increased the level of shock s/he could hear the learner protest and complain about his discomfort. Of course, in reality there were no shocks and the cries the teacher heard were actually a tape recording.

Forty participants took part in this experiment, with three having 'full-blown uncontrollable seizures' as a result of taking on the role of teacher. One of these three had such a violent seizure that the experiment was halted. All of the 40 students obeyed up to the administering of 300 volts (the 20th switch).

Milgram was amazed by the level of obedience displayed in this task (which would be seen as highly unethical today). He suggested a number of potential reasons for it, but primarily he suggested that if people are given a task to do by someone who is in authority, and the task seems to be legitimate, then people tend to continue and complete that task.

Although electric shocks are unlikely to be administered in the workplace, this study does raise some interesting points about the relationship between a subordinate and a person who is seen to be in charge. If employees accept the authority of the manager, they might go on to obey all instructions without question.

ACTIVITIES

Can you think of a time that you have obeyed an instruction from a manager although you were not happy that it was the right thing to do? Alternatively, can you think of a time that you have refused to do what a manager told you because you did not think it was the right thing to do? What was the ongoing result of your actions?

Another factor that can impact on the obedience of the employees is the perceived success of the manager.

ORGANISATION EXAMPLE

Andy Gilchrist was the leader of the Fire Brigade Union (FBU) during the industrial action of 2002–03. However, there were a significant number of members who were not happy with the deal that he negotiated over pay, terms and conditions of employment, and modernisation of the fire service.

In the union leadership elections of 2005 Andy Gilchrist was ousted from his position as FBU leader, and replaced by Matt Wrack, who had opposed the strike settlement. Wrack was elected by 12,833 votes compared with 7,259 votes for Gilchrist.

Although there is potentially a range of reasons for the election of a new leader, one real possibility could be that Gilchrist had lost the respect of his followers because of the deal he had brokered. Once respect has been lost, the followers are less likely to be loyal to the leader.

Source: www.bbc.co.uk/news, 6 May 2005.

This issue of respect is also shown in the following example.

ORGANISATION
EXAMPLE

British Leyland was a motor manufacturer that was frequently hit by industrial action in the 1970s. The leader of the trade unions at that time was Derek Robinson (known as 'Red Robbo' because of his extreme left-wing political views).

In 1977 Michael Edwardes was appointed as the new managing director following a £2.4 billion loan to the organisation. He was ordered to turn the ailing business into a profitable business at any cost. His approach to doing this led to many conflicts with the trade unions.

In November 1979 Robinson was dismissed for distributing Communist leaflets on the shop floor. This resulted in hundreds of workers laying siege to the main factory site in Longbridge, and production line staff walking out. At one stage one-third of the workforce were on strike. Despite Robinson insisting that this was a fight he intended to win, workers returned a week later, and in February 1980 Edwardes decided not to reinstate Robinson.

Robinson held a mass meeting in Cofton Park, near the Longbridge site, a few days later. He attempted to 'rally the troops' but was humiliated by his speech being met with derision, and he was pelted with rotten fruit. He had gone from being a highly influential leader to one who was jeered by his ex-colleagues. He had lost the respect of his colleagues, and hence he was no longer an influential leader.

Source: *Birmingham Post*, 9 April 2005.

In looking at the Milgram experiments it is important not to end with the view that management is a negative concept that is characterised by abuse of power. Indeed, effective management can lead to the effective management of situations to reduce conflict, and can result in a positive approach to dealing with disciplinary and grievance situations. Through clear and effective management there is the possibility of a strong and positive working relationship being created.

Indeed, many would point to the UK armed forces (already cited as an example in this chapter) as a very positive example of effective working relationships that result in very positive results. This is definitely an example of strong management, and there are many highly motivated and committed people serving in the armed forces.

STYLES OF MANAGEMENT IN EMPLOYEE RELATIONS

So far, in this chapter, our exploration of approaches to management has been somewhat general. In this section we focus specifically on styles of management in managing employee relations.

Purcell and Sisson (1983) identified five different styles of managing employment relationships, and we shall now examine these.

Traditionalists

This style of management is where employees are treated most poorly, and where there is likely to be most control from management. Employees are likely to be treated as a piece of equipment – something to get the most out of, without any consideration of the welfare of the employees. There is likely to be a drive towards keeping costs low, so employees will be paid as little as possible, and there are unlikely to be any additional rewards such as bonuses, or any benefits associated with the employment.

Because of the strong nature of the control, there is likely to be little employee involvement. Employees are not expected to suggest any ideas, they are just required to do the job. Because trade unions fight for the improved welfare of their members, traditionalist managers are unlikely to welcome trade union recognition.

ORGANISATION EXAMPLE

It is difficult to give a specific example of this type of management, as no employers would want to agree that this description fits the way they treat their staff. However, it would be very wrong to reach the conclusion that such a style of management is not used in the UK.

This is highlighted by a campaign run by the mayor of London and the Trades Union Congress, which resulted in the Mayor of London declaring in April 2005 that there would be a living wage level of £6.70 an hour in London with immediate effect. Research by the mayor's living wage unit had found that one in five London workers received less that the proposed living wage. One in seven of all workers were living on less than £5.80 an hour. The level of the living wage was set following research that had been commissioned from Queen Mary College, London to find out the level of income that was needed for a family of two parents (one working full time and one working part time) with two children to live above the poverty line without claiming any state benefits.

In its report on the London living wage the TUC website specifically relates the issue of low wages to privatisation, outsourcing of local services and insecure employment in sectors such as hotels, restaurants and tourism. Although it is certainly true that sectors such as hotels and restaurants are often associated with the traditionalist style of management, we must be careful not to put a label on all organisations within these sectors.

Source: *People Management*, 21 April 2005.

Given the rather gloomy picture that is painted of this style of management, it is interesting to consider why employees would want to work in such organisations. The simple answer is probably that they do not want to work in such organisations, but they are unable to find work anywhere else. A lot of part-time employment is concentrated in these types of organisation, and if an employee can only work part-time he or she might not be able to find many employment opportunities elsewhere. In addition, a lot of migrant workers fill jobs in such organisations, and they might be less aware of their rights than UK workers.

Sophisticated paternalists

This is a management style that links with the unitarist approach to employee relations, and hence does not recognise trade unions. Employees are treated generously, and management does not see that there is any need for trade unions to be involved. There are typically well-developed HR policies such as training and career progression, and employee involvement is encouraged.

This management style is characterised by the manager and employees working together towards a common goal, and achieving this without the help of any outside parties.

Although there might be an emphasis on not recognising trade unions, if sufficient employees want a trade union to be recognised they can trigger a recognition process (see Chapter 11). However, sophisticated paternalists would not expect this to happen.

ORGANISATION EXAMPLE

Marks & Spencer does not recognise a trade union, and sees no need to do so. The founders of Marks & Spencer believed that building good relationships with employees, suppliers and the wider community was the key to success, and Marks & Spencer still has that ethos as central to the organisation.

Marks & Spencer was one of the first UK organisations to set up a European works council (see Chapter 7) and states that it uses this and business involvement groups to communicate and consult with employees locally, regionally and nationally. They also have regular business updates and team briefings.

Although Marks & Spencer's financial performance has been poor in recent years, it is still seen as a good employer to work for, largely because of the way that it treats employees.

Sophisticated moderns (constitutionalists)

This is the management style of organisations that do recognise trade unions, but do so reluctantly. It is a common style of organisations within the manufacturing and engineering sector – and part of the reluctance could be linked to an increased likelihood of industrial conflict in these sectors. This leads to a link to the pluralist approach to employee relations.

There are likely to be well-used consultation processes that have led to formal and detailed agreements between management and employees. Bargaining is taken seriously, with the results including clear winners and losers. The management style is linked to the pluralist approach to employee relations.

Although the recognition of trade unions is not welcomed, there is an acceptance that it is inevitable, and hence there is unlikely to be any attempt to challenge the recognition in any way. Indeed, the legal ability to challenge the trade union recognition would rely on a low interest amongst the workforce, which is unlikely to occur (see Chapter 11). Hence, most managers will accept the inevitable and will work with the trade unions in an attempt to benefit from their presence.

It is interesting to note that no major manufacturing or engineering organisations are listed in the *Sunday Times* survey of the 100 best companies to work for 2005.

ORGANISATION EXAMPLE

Although the MG Rover Group collapsed in April 2005 it was a good example of this style of management. Around 90 per cent of the workforce were members of recognised trade unions. For a number of years the management and trade unions had been working together in an attempt at meeting the needs of both the management and the employees.

In 1992 a 'New Deal' agreement was negotiated that took away unnecessary status differences and revised formal communication channels. An MG Rover Group Joint Negotiating Committee was put in place, which consisted of a management team of relevant business managers, employment relations directors, senior line managers and 35 senior trade union representatives from all sites. The approach was seen as a real attempt of a highly unionised organisation tackling issues such as competition and productivity with the full co-operation of the unions. Unfortunately the company did not meet with success.

Source: www.dti.gov.uk.

Sophisticated moderns (consultors)

This management style is related to organisations where trade unions are willingly recognised. There is a welcome to the trade unions to join in with the management of the employment relationship. Rather than seeing bargaining as 'someone wins and someone loses', it is seen as a way of solving problems together. HR policies are developed to encourage employee commitment.

The standard of support given to employees is very similar to that related to the sophisticated paternalists, but the key difference is that the consultors recognise trade unions. Consultors want to work together with trade unions, hence they are likely to provide information to the trade unions to help them with their work, whereas constitutionalists who do not really want trade unions present are likely to be more sparing with any information that they give.

Blyton and Turnbull (2004) suggest that this style of management is typical of many of the Japanese industries that have built sites within the UK. Initially there was some suspicion about the role of trade unions, and a reluctance to recognise them. However, most Japanese industries in the UK have moved on to work effectively with trade unions, with single union deals ensuring greater clarity of the route for communication, and an emphasis on employee involvement and single status agreements.

ORGANISATION EXAMPLE

Following on from the reference to Japanese industries, a good example of the consultor style of management is Nissan. Nissan first started production in UK in Sunderland in 1984. It agreed a single union deal and has proceeded to work with trade unions in a range of ways.

> An example of working with the trade unions was when a 35-hour working week was introduced. Rather than just reducing the 39-hour week to 35 hours, the trade unions agreed to a deal whereby employees take an extra two week's holiday each year, at a time that suits the organisation.
>
> Source: www.bbc.co.uk/news, 24 September 2004.

Standard moderns

This style of management relates to organisations that recognise trade unions, but with a rather ambivalent attitude – they do not really have any strong opinion about whether they exist or not. They tend not to have very formalised ways of dealing with employee relations, but just address issues as and when they occur.

Organisations that tend to have this style have often grown rather erratically through acquisitions and mergers, and hence might not have a very clearly defined profile. When organisations merge and acquire other organisations, there are inevitably different styles of management and approaches to a range of issues. If this happens on a number of occasions, a potential result can be a lack of a clearly defined organisation.

Many of the large conglomerates could fit this definition, although not all display the lack of formal approaches to employee relations. However, it is interesting to look at some of the conglomerates and see the variations of organisations within them, and consider how difficult it must be to get a uniform approach to the management of employee relations.

For example, GKN has six primary divisions (Driveline, Powder Metallurgy, AutoComponents, OffHighway, Emitec and GKN Aerospace). Not only does it have a range of activities, there are 39,000 employees working in 30 different countries. It is probably inevitable that an organisation this broad will not have formalised approaches to employee relations.

Look back at the five styles of management of employee relations that we have just explored. Try to think of at least two more examples of organisations to illustrate each of the styles of management.

Table 4.1 provides a broad summary of the differences between the styles we have examined.

This summary, albeit brief, does highlight some of the difficulties of the classifications. For example, within the category of 'non-union' there is only the model of organisations with generous treatment of employees and well-developed policies. There is no model for an organisation that is

Table 4.1 Differences between the different styles of management

	Unions	Treatment of employees	Approach
Traditionalists	Anti	Poor	No policies for ER
Sophisticated paternalists	Non-union	Generous	Well- developed policies
Constitutionalists	Recognise reluctantly	Formal	Formal policies
Consultors	Willingly recognise	Good	Clear ER policies
Standard moderns	Recognise	Good	React to ER issues, rather than plan

'non-union' and treats employees poorly. Lewis *et al* (2003) suggest that the majority of organisations that fall into this unrecognised category are small and medium-sized firms. They quote research by McLoughlin and Gourlay (1994) suggesting that there is no predominant style for this group of organisations.

Interestingly, McLoughlin and Gourlay (1994) found that there was little support for the model of sophisticated paternalism. They found that the primary determinant of management style was the skills of employees, particularly when there were scarce skills.

One of the main weaknesses of the model developed by Purcell and Sisson (1983) is the broad categorisation. If we think back to the internal and external factors that we have examined in Chapters 1, 2 and 3, we have seen a wide range of factors that impact on the employment relationship. It is perhaps inevitable, therefore, that one model with five categories cannot hope to capture the complexities of the employment relationship.

Alternatively, one can take the view that the five categories identified by Purcell and Sisson are looking at a spectrum of examples within each category, and should not be interpreted so rigidly. Hence, the category of 'anti-union' as applied to traditionalists should be interpreted as expressing a range of attitudes to trade unions rather than that such a negative view that is implied.

ORGANISATIONS REPRESENTING MANAGERS

Most people are familiar with the role of trade unions in representing employees. However it is important to note that there are also organisations representing the interests of employers. The most well known of these is the Confederation of British Industry (CBI). It represents employers in both the public and private sectors, employing a total of around 10 million employees.

The CBI's mission is to help create and sustain the conditions in which businesses in the UK can compete and prosper for the benefit of employers and employees. The CBI does this through working with the UK government, international legislators and policy-makers to help influence issues that affect the effective competition of UK businesses. The CBI has offices around the UK, in Brussels and in Washington, DC.

ACTIVITIES

The CBI is often quoted on the news. Listen out for any references to it. Also, gain a greater understanding of the range of activities the CBI is involved in by browsing through its website – www.cbi.org.uk.

As well as the CBI there are specific bodies that represent different sectors of management. One of the largest of these is the British Retail Consortium (www.brc.org.uk), which represents the whole of the retail sector, from small independent stores to the large multiples.

The purpose of all the employers' organisations is to represent the interests of the employers. This might be in giving opinions on policy-setting (such as the level at which the minimum wage is set) or on the introduction of new legislation (such as the impact of flexible working on employers). Unlike the trade unions, the influence is exerted through lobbying and involvement, without the potential use of industrial action if the outcome is not as desired.

LEADERSHIP

ACTIVITIES

Before we start to explore the issue of leadership it is useful to think of some great leaders that you admire. List at least five. Then write down why you think these people are/were great leaders. What attributes do/did they have that make/made them special?

In this chapter so far we have been focusing on the role of managers. However, many commentators today would suggest that successful organisations need leaders, not managers. This does give rise to some difficulty, because there is significant overlap in the two definitions, however there are some significant differences also, which we shall attempt to understand.

Brodbeck *et al* (2000) define leadership as:

> having and being seen to have the ability to influence, motivate and enable others to contribute toward the effectiveness and success of a working group or an organisation.

From this definition we see that there is emphasis on influencing, motivating and enabling rather than on telling and instructing. Although a leader is still responsible for the outcomes, the leader achieves this by working alongside people rather than by going ahead and determining the direction, as a manager would do. This difference between the manager and leader is further emphasised by looking at the different functions related to the two roles.

According to Huczynski and Buchanan (1991), the primary functions of the manager are to:

- establish overall purpose and policy
- forecast and plan for the future
- allocate duties and responsibilities and generally organise work
- give orders and instructions
- take control, checking that performance is according to plan
- co-ordinate the work of others.

In contrast, they define the primary functions of the leader as including:

- *enabling* people and groups to achieve their objectives
- setting and *communicating* objectives
- *monitoring* performance and giving feedback
- establishing basic *values*
- clarifying and *solving* problems for others
- organising resources
- administering rewards and punishments
- providing information, advice and expertise
- providing social and emotional *support*
- making decisions on behalf of others
- *representing* the group to others
- *arbitrator* in disputes
- *father figure*
- *scapegoat.*

In listing these definitions I have italicised the key words that separate out a leader from a manager. Although the leader is still required to take responsibility for ensuring that work is done and standards are met, there is much more emphasis on supporting and enabling the workforce in their achievement of this, rather than in telling the workforce what to do.

We see, therefore, that a key difference is in the exercise of control that we examined at the start of this chapter. Although the leader still has ultimate responsibility for the group of people or the area of work, this is not achieved through taking control – but in supporting the workforce to achieve their best.

An inevitable question, therefore, is whether managers can be leaders. One approach to answering this question is to look at features of great leaders, and see if they describe a special kind of person, or simply list processes that managers are engaged in as part of their regular duties. The approach that has attempted to do this is known as trait theory, first developed by Stogdill (1948).

Trait theory attempts to identify the personality traits that are associated with a successful leader. Stogdill's studies placed emphasis on above-average intelligence, dependability, activity, social participation and socio-economic status. However, a key weakness of trait theory is it presumes that there is one style of leadership that will be successful in all situations. There is also a weakness with many of the studies in that they primarily look at people who are leaders, and hence it is not clear whether the traits have been developed because of the leadership role, or whether the traits were present prior to the leadership role.

It is important to consider the impact of different styles of leadership in employee relations. For example, consider again the success of the trade union leader at Rover, Derek Robinson. Although he was ultimately humiliated by his own trade union members, he led them strongly for many years. However, his style of 'rallying the troops' and taking a very adversarial stance worked in manufacturing. It might have been very unsuccessful had he been trying to lead a trade union in a different sector. The same could be said of Arthur Scargill, the leader of the National Union of Mineworkers during the bitter strike of 1984/85. Would his style of leadership have been successful in all sectors? It is unlikely.

It is also an error to presume that 'leadership' is a term that covers just one style. Within the rather vague term of leadership a number of different styles have been identified. Lewin *et al* (1939) and Lippitt and White (1959) carried out research into three different styles of leadership:

- *Democratic leadership*: This style of leadership involves discussing and deciding approaches to be taken to issues facing the group. It involves allowing everyone a say, and going along with the majority view.
- *Laissez-faire leadership*: A laissez-faire leader plays a passive role and allows the group complete freedom to make their own decisions. Indeed, it could be argued that no real leadership takes place.
- *Authoritarian leadership*: The authoritarian leader takes charge. He/she makes decisions for the group and he/she decides the direction that the group is going to take.

Although these styles of leadership are very different, we can see how they would be suitable in different situations. For example, if a leader was leading a team of experts in a particular field it would be inappropriate to take an authoritarian style of leadership – and it would also have the potential for stifling some of the creativity that the group could produce. However, a leader of the army in a war needs to have an authoritarian style. This does not mean that some of the key char-acteristics of a leader (motivating, inspiring, enabling and influencing) cannot be present – it simply means that the leader is making decisions and taking charge.

Wilson (2004) refers to this as situational leadership. Effective leadership depends on the ability of the leader to accurately understand the specific situation and to act appropriately given that situation. This would suggest that a leader might use more than one style of leadership, maybe taking an authoritarian style in some situations but a more democratic style in other situations.

Brodbeck *et al* (2000) report on the leadership and behaviour attributes that have been identified as effective in 22 European countries through the GLOBE programme (Global Leadership and Organisational Behaviour Effectiveness). They report that the leadership style that can really transform organisations is the charismatic/transformational style.

This style was first identified by Burns (1978) and was developed further by Bass (1985). The transformational leader alters the goals of those being led, introducing new goals that are of a higher and more challenging level. These goals are clearly related to the overall success of the organisation and the people working within it. The transformational leader clearly communicates a vision to the followers, resulting in a set of aspirations that are shared by all, and that guide the activities of all the followers. The transformational leader has the key characteristics of inspiring, stimulating individuals intellectually, and having charisma to communicate the vision.

If you look back at the leaders that you identified in the activity at the start of this section, it is very likely that you have identified transformational leaders. This is because this style of charisma and inspiration is the style that we most commonly associate with successful leadership. Brodbeck *et al* comment that the reason that this style of leadership works is because it is closest to the perception of 'ideal' leadership than other styles. Research has shown that the better the match between the perception that an individual has of what leadership is and the actual style of the leader, the more likely the individual is to let the leader exert influence over him/her.

In ensuring that the relationship between the employee and the leader is effective, this evidence from Brodbeck *et al* is very important. If the employee does not perceive that the leader has the appropriate style to lead successfully, the employee is less likely to let that leader have influence. By taking a stance of some level of non-co-operation with the leader, the employee makes it much more difficult for the leader to be successful. We can see, therefore, that the ultimate success of the leader is partly determined by the attitude of the followers towards that leader.

Of course, there are also times when a leader needs to be appointed who will make unpopular decisions, because the organisation needs radical change. An example of this relates back to British Leyland in 1977, when the government appointed Michael Edwardes as chairman. Although his leadership style involved introducing a new vision and making significant changes, those he was attempting to lead were involved in considerable conflict with him. However, the reasoning was that if he did not take these difficult decisions, the organisation would fail.

Although there are different styles of leadership, Yukl (2001) suggests there are a number of attributes that help to predict leadership effectiveness. These are:

- *High energy level and stress tolerance.* Leaders have to be prepared to work long hours and work at a fast pace. They also have to be prepared to work under a high level of stress, primarily because of the responsibility that they have to take for decision-making.
- *Self-confidence.* If leaders do not have self-confidence they are less likely to make decisions and are less likely to be able to influence others. Leaders without self-confidence are also less likely to attempt difficult tasks and set challenging objectives.
- *Internal locus of control.* Those with a strong internal locus of control believe that events are the result of their own actions, rather than chance. Therefore, they are more likely to take responsibility for their own actions as they believe that they can control the results of doing so.
- *Emotional stability and maturity.* Those who are emotionally mature have a more accurate understanding of their own strengths and weaknesses and have more self-control.
- *Personal integrity.* Leaders need to have respect. If followers find that they have been dishonest or that they do not keep promises, they will lose that respect and hence will become less effective leaders.
- *Power motivation.* Those who want to influence people and want to have some power are more likely to seek positions of leadership. If people are shy of having power they are unlikely to want to be leaders, and might be ineffective if they are appointed to such a role.
- *Achievement orientation.* Successful leaders want to excel, they want to achieve success and they are motivated by seeking that achievement.
- *Low need for affiliation.* Leaders typically do not need to be liked and accepted by others. They are unwilling to let relationships interfere with the need to get the job done and to be successful.

It is interesting to note that most of these attributes are very centred on the individual leader, and not on the overall success of the organisation. Leadership is often a rather remote and lonely role. However, if followers are not satisfied with a leader they can be rather brutal, as we saw in the example of Derek Robinson.

As we have already noted, Margaret Thatcher was a very success-ful prime minister and leader of the Conservative Party. However, she actually left office as prime minister after a challenge for leader-ship of the party. Her policies on Europe and on the introduction of the poll tax had been unpopular both outside and within the Conser-vative Party, and had resulted in some bitter arguments within the cabinet. As a leader she was no longer respected by enough of the followers, and she eventually resigned after she got 204 votes compared with 152 votes for Michael Heseltine – a leadership challenger – which was not enough for her to win. She did not stay to fight the leadership battle to the end. The vote demonstrated that she had lost enough of her followers for her role as leader to no longer be tenable.

A further component that has been linked to leadership is emotional intelligence. Goleman (1996) defines this as the extent to which a person is attuned to the emotions and feelings of others, and of him/herself. If emotional intelligence is used effectively it can be used to assist in cognitive processes, because leaders are likely to be more aware of the likely reactions of others, and hence are more likely to make better decisions.

Emotional intelligence is also linked to a range of social skills such as the ability to listen atten-tively, to communicate effectively and express appreciation to others. There is considerable debate about whether emotional intelligence is innate or whether it can be learned. This leads to the question of whether great leaders are born, or whether they can be created. Although this is an area where there is still a lot of research to do, it is also an area that might help to give considerable insights into the success of leaders.

Try to find recent research articles about emotional intelligence. If you have access to academic journals they will be a good place to start. Alternatively search on the Internet where you will find a significant number of relevant articles.

POWER

When we looked at the issue of management control we were, in part, looking at the issue of power. However, there are specific types of power that can be used by a leader, which we shall examine here. The five main bases of power were originally identified by French and Raven (1958).

Reward power

This is based on the perception that the leader has the ability to give rewards to those who comply with instructions. There is the presumption that the leader has the ability to decide who receives reward, and also has the resources to give those rewards.

Inevitably, much of the focus on reward is linked to financial gain – such as bonuses and increases in salary. However, other rewards could include promotion, praise, increased responsibility, recognition and additional privileges.

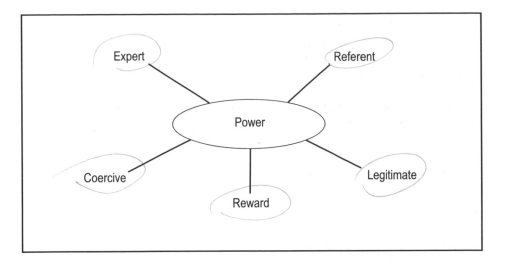

Figure 4.1 Five bases of power

If the employees perceive that the leader has no control over rewards, this form of power will not be effective. Additionally, if the leader is offering rewards that the employee does not desire, this type of power will not be effective. For this type of power to be effective the rewards must be ethical, desirable and they must be understood. If employees are rewarded and do not understand why, there will be no power exercised by the leader in giving the reward.

Reward power is particularly evident at the time of a pay review, when leaders are determining increases and bonuses.

Legitimate power

This type of power is based on authority and hierarchy. The employees perceive that the leader has the right to influence them because of the position that the leader has in the organisation. Legitimate power is also known as position power, because it depends on the position within the organisation structure and not on any personal relationship between the leader and the employee.

This type of power can become ineffective if employees do not respect the hierarchy within the organisation – possibly because a leader has been promoted to a role that the employees do not understand, or the employees do not believe that the leader should have received that promotion.

Legitimate power is particularly evident in organisations such as the police or the armed forces, where respect for hierarchy is fundamental to the smooth running of the organisation.

Expert power

A leader who has expert power is perceived by employees as having some special knowledge or expertise in a particular area that is superior to the knowledge of the employees. The work of the expert must be credible, and there must be clear evidence of the superiority of the leader for this type of power to be effective.

This type of power is particularly evident in high-technology industries where people can have very specialist and detailed knowledge about a particular area. Expert power is often very narrow in focus.

Referent power 參照权

This type of power is based on identification with the leader. The leader can influence the employees because s/he is seen to be particularly attractive, or has personal characteristics that are specifically liked, or a reputation as being a particularly good leader. It is based largely on charisma.

It is possible that the leader that has referent power is not able to give rewards, and might not be an expert. However the employees like the leader and hence are prepared to follow and respect the leader.

If you look back at the leaders you identified in an earlier activity, it is likely that a number of them are well liked – because these are the leaders that often stick in our memory.

Coercive power 强制权

This type of power is based on fear. It is based on the perception that the leader can punish those who do not obey, or can bring about undesirable outcomes of not complying. This could include withholding pay rises and promotions, giving undesirable tasks or responsibilities, withholding support or using formal reprimands through the disciplinary process.

Although coercive power can be effective in controlling the behaviour of employees, it will lead to a considerable amount of dissatisfaction and demotivation. If an organisation's employee retention rate suddenly changes it is possible that this type of power is being used.

MANAGING CHANGE

One of the tasks that leaders are often required to do is to manage change. This might be to turn around a business that is failing, or it might be to introduce new technology. In looking at the different approaches to leadership we have seen how change could be managed effectively.

First, it is important to consider why change might be necessary. Reasons could include:

- *Because a business is failing.* For example, there is a need for Marks & Spencer to change its image because of falling profits. In May 2005 it announced it was to change the green colour used in stores to red, black and white as part of an image change.
- *Because of external factors.* For example, many airline companies had to make significant numbers of employees redundant after the tragic events of 9/11 and the resulting reluctance of people to travel.
- *Because of the introduction of new technology.* For example, a typical car assembly plant uses several hundred robots to build and paint vehicles, replacing many jobs that used to be done by hand.
- *Because of costs.* For example, a number of organisations have moved call centres to countries where labour costs are lower than in the UK.

Once it has been identified that change is needed, it is necessary to determine the approach that should be taken. A number of models have been developed that try to identify different approaches. One of the most commonly used models was created by Lewin (1951). Lewin suggested that there are three basic mechanisms involved in managing change:

- *Unfreezing*: This involves creating a certain level of dissatisfaction with the current situation, hence creating a situation in which change will be more acceptable.

- *Changing*: This involves creating the change and putting in place the resources so that the change can be successful.
- *Freezing*: This is the process of imbedding the changes into the organisation.

Whatever change model is used, it is important not to underestimate the role of the leader. It is the leader who is ultimately responsible for ensuring that the change happens and is successful. Hence, success of the change process can be ensured:

1. *By having the right type of leader for the situation*. It is important to choose a leader who fits with the type of organisation. This might be in terms of leadership style (authoritarian, laissez-faire or democratic), but it could also be in terms of expert knowledge that the leader has.
2. *By having a transformational leadership style*. Although different styles might fit different organisations in terms of being authoritarian, laissez-faire or democratic, research has shown that leaders with a transformational leadership style are better at inspiring people and creating a vision. Arguably that is a key aspect of managing change, and hence it could be argued that the leader who is most likely to successfully achieve change will have a transformational leadership style.
3. *By the effective use of power*. It is important that power is not abused in the change process, because many employees will be very unsettled during a period of change. To try to achieve this through using fear, or through inappropriate use of reward, could result in change being achieved, but in an unsatisfactory way.
4. *Through effective communication*. We shall look at the issue of communication in more detail in Chapter 7, but we have already noted its importance in understanding the strength of the transformational leadership style. If the employees do not understand the vision they are likely to be less co-operative in working towards its achievement.

It is also important to understand why change programmes can fail. Reasons for this can include:

- no clear vision, or a vision that is poorly communicated
- fear of employees, particularly if the change is linked to any job loss
- the failure of previous change programmes, bringing a lack of belief that this change will be successful
- a leader who is not respected
- a misunderstanding of what is required
- a lack of preparation and planning, which leads employees confused about what they should be doing.

Sir John Stevens was the Police Commissioner for the London Metropolitan Police (the Met) from 2000–05. He was largely credited with turning round the fortunes of the Met after it was named as 'institutionally racist' following the Stephen Lawrence enquiry.

He was asked about his style of leadership that resulted in the required change being achieved, in an article for *People Management* in 2005. He defined leadership as:

> Good leaders are people who can see things with vision and who have integrity. I have worked for some of the biggest bullies ever. Yet I've also worked for people who you would give your right arm for.

Stevens used his strong leadership style to help change the attitudes of staff, primarily focusing on allowing them to feel pride in their jobs. He also communicated clearly with all the staff, using a consistent message and outlining his vision for the Met. Under his leadership the Met made £310 million of efficiency savings, grew from 25,000 to 30,000 officers, and sickness absence fell from 13 days per person to seven days.

THE IMPORTANCE OF THE LEADER

Throughout this chapter we have considered different aspects of leadership and management. However, the consistent message throughout has been about the importance of the leader. If a leader is not effective within the organisation, then that organisation is likely to be less successful. In the next chapter we look at the other side of the employment relationship – the employees.

KEY POINTS FROM THIS CHAPTER

- The primary role of the manager is to take control.
- Obedience to a manager can be related to the perception of the status of that manager.
- A manager or leader needs to be respected by the subordinates.
- There are five styles of management in employee relations – traditionalists, sophisticated paternalists, constitutionalists, consultors and standard moderns.
- Leadership and management have both similarities and differences.
- Trait theory is an attempt to identify the personality characteristics of successful leaders.
- A transformational leadership style is most often associated with creating change within an organisation.
- Emotional intelligence has been linked to successful leadership.
- There are five types of power used in leadership – reward, legitimate, expert, referent and coercive.
- Managing change requires an effective leader and a clearly planned approach.

EXAMPLES TO WORK THROUGH

1 You have been asked to give a presentation on the topic 'Anyone can be a manager, but not everyone can be a leader'. Write an outline for this presentation.

2 You work as the HR manager in a manufacturing organisation. The manufacturing director of the organisation is largely disliked by the employees, and commands little respect. Following a recent quality audit, concerns have been expressed about the quality of production, and the levels of productivity. The managing director wants to keep

the manufacturing director because of his knowledge of the processes, but is aware that something needs to be done. What would you advise?

3   After the collapse of the miners' strike of 1984/85, Arthur Scargill remained leader of the National Union of Mineworkers until his retirement several years later. Why do you think that a leader who was associated with failure of the strike was able to retain respect?

(Suggestions of answers to the examples can be accessed by tutors at www.cipd.co.uk/tss).

CASE STUDY

Stephens Steel Company is a manufacturing company based in the Black Country, an area within the West Midlands. It is one of three organisations owned by the Stephens family within the area.

Stephens Steel makes a range of products from steel, ranging from quite small fixings to large frameworks for machinery. Stephens Steel employs around 500 people. The majority of the employees are directly involved in the manufacturing process. Male employees make up 98 per cent of the workforce. The remainder of the employees work in support functions (such as administration and accounts), 80 per cent of these employees are female.

Stephens Steel is a traditional manufacturing company. There is clear demarcation of jobs – the employees come to work and do a very clearly defined series of operations. They will not do anything that is not in their job description, and are very rarely asked to do anything outside their job description. The employees work individually: there is no team-work. Most of the operators are long-serving, with the longest service currently being 48 years, and the shortest being 9 years.

The management structure is also traditional, with a hierarchy of different levels of super-vision. At the top of the hierarchy is a manufacturing director. He reports to the general manager of all the Stephens organisations, who is based at a different site. Hence, it is the manufacturing director who really runs the Stephens Steel on a daily basis. Reporting to the manufacturing director are two production managers. Reporting to them are three senior foremen. There are then six more foremen who oversee the daily operations.

Stephens Steel has not been performing well over recent years. This is partly seen to be caused by a drop in demand for traditional steel products. Raw material prices have also risen, meaning that the prices that Stephens Steel have been forced to charge for their products has become uncompetitive.

The general manager is determined not to see the Stephens empire collapse, and he appointed an HR manager six months ago to try to address some of the people issues. His view is that the employees are not motivated and determined to succeed, and he wants this to be addressed. He also wants to introduce new working practices into the factory, but so far has been met with blatant refusal from the employees.

The HR manager has spent the last month working at Stephens Steel and has reported that, in his opinion, most of the problem lies with the manufacturing director. At a meeting with the general manager this morning, the HR manager gave a very candid description of the style of the manufacturing director, with a number of specific examples. The key issues that have been reported include:

- The manufacturing director only ever seems to communicate by shouting.
- In the month that the HR manager has been there he has seen the manufacturing director tell at least 18 people that they 'were sacked'. All of them just carried on working, and ignored him!
- Each time someone was told they 'were sacked' it was for some minor transgression and was shouted out in front of all the other employees.
- The manufacturing director held a morning meeting each day with all his managers and supervisors. Each day he humiliated them in front of each other by listing their personal faults.
- The manufacturing director routinely called 'important meetings' at 5 pm (the day's work finished at 4 pm) for the managers, and on three occasions kept them waiting for an hour – before telling them that the meeting was cancelled.
- No one told the manufacturing director if something went wrong. The HR manager estimates that the production managers spent about 75 per cent of their time working out how to hide facts from the manufacturing director.

However, the manufacturing director is very highly skilled in steel manufacture – and is recognised as being extremely knowledgeable. The general manager does not want him to leave, but the HR manager is adamant that, in the current climate, there is no possibility of motivating the employees to work better, or gaining their co-operation in changing working practices.

The HR manager has suggested that either the style of the manufacturing director must change, or the manufacturing director must go. However, the HR manager is concerned that it would take a lot of time for the employees to trust that the manufacturing director's style really had changed (if he agreed to try to change it), and he is concerned that this is time that the organisation does not have.

The general manager now needs to decide what to do:

1 Explain the management style of the manufacturing director, in light of the knowledge that you have gained from this chapter.
2 Do you think the HR manager is right? Do you think that significant change is impossible with the current style of the manufacturing director? Why/why not? If the manufacturing director did change, do you think that wider change could then be introduced? Why/why not?
3 Do you think it is possible for the manufacturing director to change his style of management? Justify your answer.

The Role of Employees in Employment Relations

CHAPTER 5

The objectives of this chapter are to:

- explain the role of the employee in the employment relationship, both as an individual and as part of a group
- evaluate the impact of the different personalities of employees
- explore the different factors that impact on the motivation of employees
- explore the impact of the search for a work–life balance
- explain how groups develop
- consider why employees conform within a group
- outline how prejudice develops.

Having looked at the role of management in the employment relationship in Chapter 4, we shall now focus on the other party in the relationship – the employee. The employee interacts within the relationship in two different ways, as an individual and as part of a group. We start by looking at the employee as an individual, and then look at the employee as part of a group.

As an individual an employee has to develop his/her own relationship with management, and this will be partly influenced by such issues as personality and motivation. When the employee becomes part of the group, motivation and even personality attributes might become less important, and the overall group cohesiveness might become more important.

EMPLOYEES AS INDIVIDUALS

It is very difficult to make any generalised statements about how employees behave within the employment relationship. This is because employees have different reasons for being at work, have different motivators to perform and have different personalities.

Some significant work in explaining the differences in personalities amongst employees has been carried out by Belbin (1996). Belbin identified five different styles of subordinate:

Receptive subordinate

The receptive subordinate adheres to instructions and deadlines. This individual likes to work with clear directions from above. This type of personality is often related to the shop floor in a manufacturing environment where, traditionally, employees are given clear instructions of what to do and there is little opportunity to add in any variation or personal interpretation of the instructions.

Self-reliant subordinate

The self-reliant subordinate prefers to work without any constraints. These individuals have their own ideas and enjoy the opportunity to develop them with minimal intervention. This type of personality is often linked to creative work, such as designing new products or work in marketing and architecture. The employee is employed to bring new ideas and to develop them.

Collaborative subordinate

The collaborative subordinate also has many ideas to contribute, but prefers to discuss them with others and to be part of a team in developing the ideas. The employee enjoys trying new approaches, rather than staying with conventional methods. This type of employee will happily work in a creative environment, but rather than working where ideas are developed individually, prefers to work where ideas are developed as part of a team.

Informative subordinate

The informative subordinate likes to be involved in decision-making, but will accept the final decisions even if they are contrary to personally held views. Again, this is likely to relate to an employee working within a team – and is unlikely to be a subordinate that is taking any leadership role within that team.

Reciprocating subordinate

The reciprocating subordinate is not afraid to speak up and is undeterred by status. In many ways this employee is the opposite of the receptive subordinate, because the employee does not like direction and is more likely to be managed through persuasion. The employee might be very stubborn, but is focused on completing the task.

Eysenck and Wilson (1975) also looked at the differences in personalities, and suggested that there are two major dimensions of personality: the extroversion–introversion dimension (known as the E dimension) and the neuroticism–stability dimension (known as the N dimension).

Eysenck and Wilson defined the extroverts as being tough-minded individuals who need varied and strong external stimulation. They suggested that there are seven personality traits that describe this personality type, and they are:

- expressiveness
- impulsiveness
- risk-taking
- sociability
- practicality
- irresponsibility
- activity.

They defined introverts as tender-minded people who do not need the constant and intense external stimulus, and who are likely to experience strong emotions. The seven personality traits that Eysenck and Wilson linked with this personality type are:

- carefulness
- responsibility
- control
- reflectiveness
- unsociability

- inhibition
- inactivity.

On the N dimension Eysenck and Wilson described neurotics as having a low opinion of themselves and tending to be pessimistic, depressed and disappointed with life. The seven personality traits that they linked with this personality type are:

- low self-esteem
- anxiety
- guilt
- obsessiveness
- hypochondria
- unhappiness
- lack of autonomy.

They defined stable individuals as being self-confident, optimistic, easy-going and realistic. They are positive about the future and the past. The seven personality traits that they linked with this personality type are:

- self-esteem
- calm
- guilt freedom
- casualness
- sense of health
- happiness
- autonomy.

In reality very few people fall neatly into any of the categories proposed by Eysenck and Wilson, but their research is interesting to us because we see how greatly the employees in any organisation can differ. In defining their two dimensions (E and N) they have suggested 28 different factors of personality, the combinations of these in any one person can demonstrate to us the great number of differences that can exist between people.

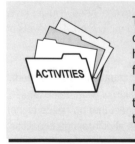

ACTIVITIES

The subject of personality is one that has occupied many psychologists over the years – and we have only scratched the surface here. If it is an area that interests you, a vast range of sources for further study are listed at hhtp://pmc.psych.nwu.edu. Even if you do not want to read any of the research papers it is a useful website to look at, as it gives a clear explanation of the various approaches to the study of personality.

The impact on the employment relationship of the research by both Belbin and Eysenck and Wilson is that the manager or leader needs to try to understand the personality of the employee in order to develop a relationship that results in getting the very best from the employee. Some organisations do this through the use of personality assessments, partly to understand employees and their development needs, but also to develop teams of people who (theoretically) will work effectively together.

Leary-Joyce (2004) reports that, in her research of companies listed in the *Sunday Times* survey of 100 best companies to work for, every manager or leader that she spoke to emphasised the significance of getting to know their people. She quotes the example of a leader at Honda who starts each Monday morning by walking slowly through the office, chatting as he goes. He does this to gain an understanding of what his employees do outside work, and also to build up a relationship with them.

EMPLOYEES AND MOTIVATION

The implication of understanding that all people are different is that the manager has to have an individual relationship with each employee. Later in this chapter we look at employees operating within a group. However it is still important that the manager has an individual relationship with each group member.

This links back to the concept of the psychological contract. This is a personal contract between the employee and the manager – and is very closely linked to the type of person that the employee is and the needs that he/she has. In describing how the psychological contract develops, Heriot (1995) suggests that the first stage is an exchange of information. He suggests that each party needs to understand what the other party wants and can offer. If the manager does not know the employee well, the suggestion is that the psychological contract cannot be formed successfully.

As well as understanding the personality of the employee, for a psychological contract to be successfully formed the manager must understand what motivates the employee. There have been various attempts to explain motivation, and here we look at some of the most commonly quoted theories:

Maslow's hierarchy of needs model

Maslow (1954) suggested that individuals have a hierarchy of needs. He suggested that each level of need has to be satisfied before individuals move on to the next level of need. If lower level needs remain unfulfilled, then the higher levels cannot form the basis of motivation. The levels of needs that he identified are shown in Figure 5.1.

There are a number of difficulties in applying Maslow's work to the work situation. First, the model refers to a number of factors that are likely to be affected by events outside of work. For example, if the employee is experiencing a relationship break-up this would suggest that no needs higher than safety could be addressed. Also, as we have seen from a brief look at different personalities, employees place different values on different things. So, for example, an extrovert might place a lot of emphasis on social needs, which would not necessarily be emphasised by an introvert. Another key difficulty is that some rewards at work satisfy a range of different needs. For example, an increase in pay could affect esteem as well as physiological needs.

Herzberg's two-factor model

Herzberg's theory (1957) is based on the theory that there are two distinct groups of factors, one that gives rise to job satisfaction and the other that gives rise to job dissatisfaction.

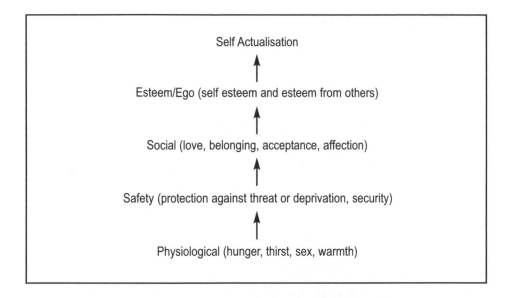

Self Actualisation

Esteem/Ego (self esteem and esteem from others)

Social (love, belonging, acceptance, affection)

Safety (protection against threat or deprivation, security)

Physiological (hunger, thirst, sex, warmth)

Figure 5.1 Maslow's hierarchy of needs

The first set of factors is known as the hygiene factors. They have the potential to dissatisfy if they are not met, but once they are met they become reasonably irrelevant to motivation, because increasing them further will not increase motivation. They are things such as supervision, working conditions, status, security, and relationship with peers. The other set of factors are known as satisfiers or motivators. They are things that are intrinsic to the job such as achievement, the work itself, and responsibility and growth. As they increase, so will motivation.

Although there has been criticism of this theory, primarily because of the rather limited research (it was based on research conducted solely with engineers and scientists), it offers a useful insight into how motivation is affected by a variety of different factors. It also offers an interesting link back to the personality theories. For example, responsibility is important to the self-reliant subordinate, but is not particularly important to the informative subordinate. Therefore, increasing responsibility for the self-reliant subordinate might increase his/her motivation, but might actually demotivate the informative subordinate.

Adam's equity theory

Adams (1965) suggested that people would be better motivated if they perceive that they are being treated equitably (fairly), and they will be demotivated if they perceive that they are being treated inequitably. This perception of fairness is gained by making comparisons between the treatment that the individual sees that s/he is receiving, and the treatment given to comparable groups. It is important to emphasise that it is based on comparisons. It is not presuming that everyone should be treated equally, because there might be good reasons why, for example, one person is paid more than another. However, motivation decreases if the perception is that people are not being treated fairly.

This theory adds an extra dimension to the need for a manager to develop an individual relationship with the employee. There also needs to be some element of horizontal integration with the way that the manager is treating other employees, so that the perception of fairness is maintained.

Vroom's expectancy theory

Vroom (1964) suggested that motivation is a function of two factors, valency and expectancy. Valency is the desirability that an individual places on achieving a particular outcome. The more desirable an individual perceives the outcome to be; the more motivated he or she will be on achieving it. Expectancy is the belief that the outcome will actually happen. Hence, if employees believe they will receive a desired promotion if they work hard and achieve particular targets, they are likely to be more motivated than if they do not believe a desired promotion will take place.

The desirability is the factor that is most likely to be affected by the personality of different employees. For example, if the self-reliant employee believes that s/he will be given more freedom to act upon successful completion of a particular task, there is going to be greater motivation to achieve successful completion. However, if the employee has an informative style and perceives that the result of successful completion will be additional responsibility, there is likely to be less motivation to succeed, because the outcome is less desirable.

Latham and Locke's goal theory

Latham and Locke (1979) suggested that motivation and performance are directly linked to the goals that have been set. Motivation increases when specific goals are set, when they are difficult but accepted, and when there is feedback on performance. They suggest that participation is important in the goal-setting. However, this might not fit with the receptive subordinate style employee, who prefers to be told what to do, although it would fit well with the collaborative subordinate style.

They also suggest that there must be difficult goals, and achieving them should be helped by guidance and advice. This would fit with the receptive subordinate style employee, but not with the self-reliant subordinate style, who is unlikely to want the guidance and advice.

They also suggest that feedback is essential, particularly because this can aid employees in achieving even higher goals in the future.

 Think through these different theories of motivation and try to find examples when you have seen them used in an organisation (intentionally or unintentionally). Which theory do you think is closest to explaining what really motivates employees in organisations today?

These different theories of motivation suggest that there are a variety of factors that might result in the motivation of employees. Understanding how to motivate different employees is part of the process of developing the individual employment relationship.

 In reading the *Sunday Times* survey of 100 best companies to work for, it is interesting to see the variety of unusual benefits offered by organisations – presumably as motivators. Examples include:

- *The Carphone Warehouse*: Holds a ball once a year with free drinks, food, accommodation and travel for all employees.

> - *WS Atkins*: Arranges snowy adventures (tobogganing and discounted ski trips to Switzerland) as well as regular theatre trips and matches involving two football teams based at the headquarters.
> - *Severn Trent Water*: Staff enjoy alternative therapies such as Hopi ear candles and reflexology.

If organisations are able to offer a range of different motivators, it is possible that all employees will find something that fits with their needs, and hence motivates them. Alternatively, it could be that employees seek employment in an organisation that fits with their personalities, and hence is more likely to provide motivators that meet their needs.

WORK–LIFE BALANCE

Work–life balance has become a very topical issue in recent years. As well as being of key importance to organisations, it is also an issue that is indicative of the individual nature of the employment relationship. This is because the view that employees take of their work–life balance is very personal to them. The view will be partly determined by the importance of leisure activities, family caring responsibilities and the attitude to work. The view will also vary at different stages of the employee's career and life.

The Employers and Work–Life Balance Group suggests that one of the primary reasons that work–life balance is, and will remain, an issue is that the structure of the labour market in the UK has changed dramatically over the last few years and will continue to change. The evidence for this is that:

- We remain in full- or part-time education until we are older, while more of us are opting to retire at an earlier age.
- The largest growth in labour market participation between 1990 and 2000 occurred among mothers with young children.
- It is projected that 66 per cent of the increase in the UK population between 2000 and 2025 will be attributable to immigration.
- Generation Y (those born after 1978) has entered the workforce: these young workers look at an organisation's track record on corporate social responsibility and are not afraid to negotiate flexible working terms.

The types of work we do and the nature of work itself have also changed dramatically over the past 20 years:

- Jobs in the service sector have risen by 36 per cent while manufacturing jobs have fallen by 39 per cent.
- The intensity of work has increased: average working hours are shorter but work is carried out faster. Intensification affects all countries in the EU, all industry sectors and all occupational categories.
- Changes in technology (IT and telephony) give employers more flexibility in terms of the way they ask people to work.

(www.employersforworklifebalance.org.uk).

Find out how the organisation you work for, or another organisation that you are familiar with, has adapted or introduced new initiatives to address the changing needs of work–life balance. Do they think that the initiatives have been successful? What evidence do they have of the successes?

A lot of research and commentary on work–life balance has focused on the need to balance caring responsibilities (usually relating to childcare) and work. However, this view is limited, and presumes that it is only parents (and primarily mothers) who are concerned about their work–life balance. A broader definition of work–life balance is given by Bratton and Gold (2003), where they describe it as the need to 'balance work and leisure/family activities'. The leisure activities might include such things as the desire to travel, the desire to be involved in community activities and the need to care for older relatives (an issue that is increasing in relevance as people live longer).

A fuller definition is given by Clutterbuck (2003) as:

- being aware of different demands on time and energy
- having the ability to make choices in the allocation of time and energy
- knowing what values to apply to choices
- making choices.

We see here the emphasis on choice. We live in a society where increasingly services are available 24 hours a day, seven days a week. In order to provide those services there need to be employees working 24 hours a day, seven days a week – and it is this demand on employees that many are finding difficult to absorb.

Platt (1997) suggested that a happy medium needs to be found between the demands of work and home. He suggested that there literally needs to be a 'balance' between work and life. The balance needs to reflect the different aspects of work and life, such as:

Work	Life
Deadlines	Hobbies
Travel	Childcare
Responsibilities to others	Time for the family
Meeting customer expectations	Care for older relatives
Competition with others	Travel
Promotion	Community involvement
Desire for increased reward	Holidays

The government has identified the need to address this issue, and has primarily done this through legislation. As we shall examine in some detail in Chapter 12, the government introduced the Employment Relations Act 1999 which gave employees with children born on or after 15 December 1999 the right to unpaid parental leave, and then introduced the Flexible Working (Procedural Requirements) Regulations 2002 which gave parents with a child aged under six years (under 18 years if the child is disabled) the right to request flexible working.

Table 5.1 The most common forms of flexible working offered by organisations

Work pattern	Male	Female	Total
Part-time	38	71	53
Variable hours (coming in/leaving late/early)	49	52	51
Job sharing	23	34	28
Working from home	21	20	20
Term-time only working	14	26	19
Annualised hours	17	18	18
Nine-day fortnight	10	10	10
Other	2	5	3
None	26	12	19

Indeed, the way that most employers have attempted to address the issue of creating an acceptable work–life balance for employees is to increase the flexibility in the design of the working day. There are a wide range of different working patterns that have been designed to fit individual needs. The CIPD survey *Flexible working and paternity leave* (2004) looked at the most common forms of flexible working offered by organisations. Table 5.1 lists the most popular forms.

Flexible working is increasingly difficult to define, as organisations have had to move away from traditional nine to five working patterns in order to cope with customer demand for 24-hour, seven days a week access to services. However, flexible working is typically defined as a pattern of working in an organisation that is different from the normal working patterns in that organisation.

If we return to the legislation that introduced the right to request flexible working if the necessary requirements are met, it is important to note that the flexibility that employees can request does not just relate to hours of work. The flexibility also relates to time of work (for example, the time of day that an employee completes his/her allotted hours) and also the place of work (which could also be linked to a request to work from home if this is appropriate).

However, flexible working is not the only way in which organisations can help employees to achieve their desired work–life balance. The CIPD (2004) fact sheet on work–life balance suggests that other approaches the organisation can take include:

- career breaks for carers
- sabbaticals
- study leave
- secondments.

Extra support can also be offered through:

- employee assistance programmes
- financial services (eg subsidised insurance or loans)
- loans/allowances to help pay for childcare
- workplace facilities such as crèches or medical centres.

ORGANISATION EXAMPLE

Marks & Spencer is an organisation that has developed a wide-ranging strategy in addressing work–life balance issues. It has a range of different initiatives available for different categories of employees:

- *For all employees*: Flexible working patterns, career leave (employees who have up to two years' continuous service may be entitled to up to nine months' leave), domestic emergency leave (paid or unpaid, depending on the circumstances) and access to a welfare helpline.
- *For parents*: Enhanced maternity, adoption and paternity leave, support during IVF treatment, support during fostering, extended parental leave, time off to take a child to school on their first day, and after five years service parents can take up to a five-year child break.
- *For carers*: Dependency leave (unpaid or paid) and dependency break (for employees with two years' or more continuous service)
- *For people who help in the community*: Support for magistrate duties, support for other public duties and a break in service for potential political candidates.

The main business benefits that Marks & Spencer report from taking such initiatives are in increased productivity, and a greater recruitment pool.

Source: www.employersforworklifebalance.org.uk.

Despite organisations increasingly offering additional flexibility at work, not all employees will take up the opportunities. Kodz *et al* (2002) conducted research into organisations that had promoted work–life balance initiatives, and still found that the take-up rate of the initiatives was relatively low. The main concern they found was the perceived impact on career prospects. Employees were concerned that taking up work–life balance initiatives would be interpreted as a lack of commitment to the organisation, and hence would have a negative impact on their chance of promotion.

There was also the concern that taking up work–life balance initiatives would result in a negative reaction from other employees. A CIPD survey (2003) found that 47 per cent of employers are concerned that staff without children resent their colleagues benefiting from rights relating to flexible working.

The difficulties that are being experienced here relate back to the individual nature of employees. When we considered the relevance of the equity theory of motivation we noted that it is important for the manager to consider the horizontal integration of the relationship with one employee, compared with others – is the manager treating all employees fairly?

Here we see another impact of the perception of fairness. If employees consider that they are having to work extra hard, or to cover duties that are not typically theirs, because of the flexibility that has been offered to other employees, there is likely to be the perception of unfairness. Hence, in considering ways to assist employees with their work–life balance there needs to be consideration of both the vertical impact (the impact on the organisation) and the horizontal impact (the impact on other employees).

The benefits of work–life balance have been recorded in a number of surveys. The Employers for Work Life Balance (EfWLB) association lists the benefits as including:

- increased productivity
- improved recruitment and retention
- lower rates of absenteeism
- reduced overheads
- an improved customer experience
- a more motivated, satisfied and equitable workforce
  (source: www.employersforworklifebalance.org.uk).

A report by the DTI (2004a) surveyed 50 companies of all sizes and sectors that had introduced flexible working. They reported that they had seen improvements in customer service and performance, reduced staff stress and absenteeism. A further report from the DTI (2004b) found that flexible working will motivate staff, save on recruitment costs, reduce staff turnover, reduce absenteeism, attract and retain a talented workforce, and improve customer service.

Work–life balance is certainly an issue that will continue to be topical, as organisations try to compete for the best employees, and employees are increasingly attracted to the organisations that meet their needs most effectively. However, it would be wrong to assume that simply offering increased work–life balance initiatives will address the issues, because the needs of employees are so clearly individual.

ACTIVITIES

Go to the website for Employers for Work–Life Balance (www. employersforworklifebalance). Browse through the variety of material that is available about work–life balance.

EMPLOYEES WITHIN GROUPS

As we noted at the start of this chapter, employees exist within an organisation both as individuals and as part of groups. We now move our focus to look at the employee as part of a group.

The need for managers and leaders to develop relationships with employees as groups is important. Although we have already noted that the focus of employee relations has changed somewhat from a collective to an individual approach, employees do still operate in groups within the workplace. Indeed, the use of teamworking has grown considerably in organisations over recent years. Although employees might address conflict within the employment relationship on an increasingly individual basis, they are still likely to work within clearly defined groups.

Just as different individuals have different needs and expectations, so do different groups of employees. Indeed, the challenge in developing a relationship with a group is particularly challenging for the manager because groups go through a series of changes as they develop. Part of this change will be the group settling down and becoming effective, but there will also be the change that results from members leaving a group and others joining it.

Tuckman and Jensen (1977) suggested that all groups go through five stages in their development, outlined in Figure 5.2.

Forming

This is when the team are getting to know each other and developing an identity. Team members are finding out about each other and establishing ground rules. It is at this stage that different members will be finding out who has a similar background to them, and groups within the team will also be established. Here is where intergroups can be formed that might affect the overall performance of the team.

Storming

This is the stage at which conflict occurs in the group. People are making individual goals and objectives clear, and there can be conflict as a result. This could also be the time at which conflict occurs between different intergroups, and the successful resolution of these conflicts is key to the ongoing success of the team.

Norming

The team now work out ways to work together, and agreed expectations are sorted out. It is possible for some teams to never reach this stage because they never resolve the conflicts.

Performing

This is also a stage that some teams might never reach (although they might successfully reach the norming stage). This stage is when the team start to get on with the job. However, if

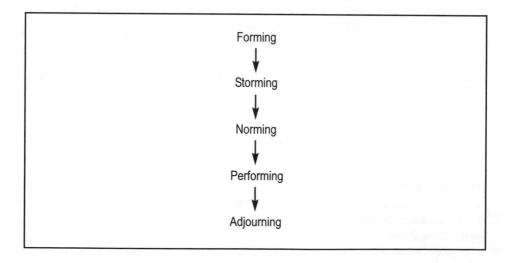

Figure 5.2 The five stages of the development of groups

the team are still stuck in conflict and have not worked out a way to work together, they will never perform successfully.

Adjourning

This is when the team disband, typically because the task they were set has been completed.

As we have just noted, some teams will never perform successfully. Within the employment relationship a key role of the manager is facilitating the successful performance of the team.

ORGANISATION EXAMPLE

In January 2005 a breakaway group of members of the trade union Aslef (Associated Society of Locomotion Engineers and Firemen) formed a new trade union, the Associated Train Crew Union (ASTC). ASTC was formed by a group of train drivers after a number of concerns and conflicts in Aslef.

Aslef national organiser Andy Reed dismissed the new union with the comment:

> Over the past 12 months we have had problems with a handful of members who refuse to accept democratic decisions and trade union principles. Rather than reconsider their attitudes, they have set off on the hopeless task of taking over our union's membership.
>
> (*People Management*, 27 January 2005)

It is largely seen that the potential success of the new trade union will be whether the employers agree to recognise it, and hence consult and negotiate with it (see Chapter 11). However, as this is an example of the breakdown of a group, only the members of the group could really say whether it ever got to the 'performing' stage, or whether it has been stuck at the stage of storming or norming for some time.

Just as we noted that individuals have different personalities, different team members are likely to adopt different roles within a team. Part of the role of the manager is to ensure that the team has a variety of different roles within it, hence making it more likely to succeed.

Belbin (1981) defines team roles as 'a tendency to behave, contribute and interrelate with others in a particular way'. He identified a number of different team roles:

- *Plant*: This role contributes creative and imaginative ideas, and is likely to solve difficult problems. However, the person does not always communicate effectively.
- *Co-ordinator*: This is the chairperson. The person is mature and confident and is able to clarify goals, promote decision-making and delegate effectively. However, the person can be seen to be manipulative and to offload work s/he does not want to do.
- *Monitor/evaluator*: This person is strategic and discerning and looks carefully at all options. The person is good at making accurate judgements, but might lack drive and the ability to inspire others.
- *Implementer*: This person is disciplined, reliable and efficient. Ideas are turned into practical actions, although s/he might be somewhat inflexible in responding to new ideas.
- *Completer/finisher*: This person is very detail-conscious, painstaking and conscientious.

The person will ensure that the work is delivered on time, but is inclined to worry and is reluctant to delegate.

- *Resource investigator:* This person is extrovert, enthusiastic and communicative. The person is likely to have a lot of contacts that he or she uses effectively, but can be over-optimistic.
- *Shaper:* This person is challenging and dynamic and thrives on pressure. The person has the drive and courage to overcome obstacles, although there is a tendency to offend others.
- *Teamworker:* This person is co-operative, perceptive and diplomatic. The person listens, builds and tries to avert problems, but can be indecisive in difficult situations.
- *Specialist:* This person is single-minded and self-starting. The person has knowledge and skills that are generally in short supply, and are important to the team. However, the breadth of contribution is rather limited and the person tends to dwell on details and technicalities.

Just as we noted when looking at different subordinate styles, people tend to have an element of more than one team style in the way that they operate. However, it is important that a variety of team roles are represented within a team. If nobody, for example, is a completer/finisher, a lot of good work can take place – but it might never get completed!

Think about groups that you have been part of. Can you identify that the stages described by Tuckman and Jensen have been passed through? Think of the different styles identified by Belbin. Can you identify particular group members who represented those styles?

ACTIVITIES

CONFORMITY

One of the interesting phenomena of a group is the way that people adapt and change their views in order to become part of that group. This process of conforming was the subject of two classic psychological studies.

Asch (1955) carried out research using a group of students who were told they were taking part in a 'psychological experiment in visual judgement'. They were told they would be required to compare the length of lines that would be shown to them.

All the students were shown two white cards. On one was a vertical dark line – the standard that was to be judged. On the other card there were three vertical lines of various lengths. One of the lines on the second card was the same length as the single line on the first card; the other two were significantly different lengths. The students were asked to choose which of the three lines was the same length as the single line – and to call their judgement out loud.

Although the students were led to believe that all the group participants were students carrying out the same task, there was actually only one participant in the experiment in each group. The rest were fellow experimenters. On selected trials these experimenters gave incorrect answers.

On the occasions that the fellow experimenters gave an incorrect answer, around 75 per cent of the 123 students went along with the majority at least once. Under the pressure of the group, the students accepted the judgement of the majority on 37 per cent of the trials. There were significant individual differences. Some students never agreed with the majority, while others agreed with the majority most of the time.

After the interview the students were interviewed. Some said that they had total confidence in their own judgement, which is why they never agreed with the majority. Others believed the majority was correct but continued to disagree because they felt the pressure to report what they saw. Those that yielded to the group pressure felt they were deficient in some way and just went along with the rest of the group.

This is a fascinating study because it shows how people feel discomfort when they disagree with a group, and experience a pressure to conform to the majority view. This might be relevant when employees are involved in potential industrial action. Although they might not agree with the proposed action, and might even have voted against it in a ballot, it takes a lot of courage to stand apart from the rest of the group and act differently.

The impact on individuals of going against the group majority was bitterly demonstrated during the 1984–85 miners' strike. Nottinghamshire miners did not join the strike, and their leader Neil Greatrex suffered a number of threats against himself and his family. The divisions caused by this industrial action split whole communities, particularly in areas where the strike action was initially 100 per cent, and then miners started to return to work. Young children were seen on picket lines being taught to shout 'scab' at those returning to work. Even today, 20 years later, there are still family members who will not speak to each other as a result of individuals going against the majority and working before the strike had ended.

ORGANISATION EXAMPLE

Another classic psychological study demonstrated how individuals conform to roles that they expect particular team members to play. Zimbardo (in Haney *et al* 1973) placed an advertisement in a newspaper asking for male volunteers to take part in a psychological study of prison life. From the 75 respondents they selected 24 participants through a series of interviews and psychological tests.

Zimbardo *et al* made a simulated prison at Stanford University. The participants were randomly assigned to be guards or prisoners. They were paid a small daily amount for participating and were guaranteed basic living needs. However, they were told that they could not be guaranteed any privacy.

The guards were told that their task was to maintain a 'reasonable degree of order' in the prison. They were not allowed to use physical aggression. The prisoners were kept in the prison for 24 hours a day. The guards worked in teams of three on eight-hour shifts. They were allowed to go home after their shifts.

Both the guards and the prisoners were given uniforms that reflected their different status. The local police station assisted in the study by unexpectedly arresting the subjects. They were charged with burglary or armed robbery, advised of their rights, handcuffed, searched and taken to the police station. At the station they were fingerprinted and locked in a police cell. They were then driven to the mock prison whilst blindfolded. Here they were stripped, deloused, stood alone and naked in the prison yard and then given their uniform, allocated to a cell and told to remain silent.

The prison warden read them rules, which they had to memorise, and then gave them a prison number which was used instead of their name for the remainder of the experiment. They were allowed three meals a day, three supervised toilet visits, two hours for reading and writing, two visit times a week, exercise periods and film rights. They were also required to carry out some work and line up for counting at the start of each new shift of guards.

The participants all began to adopt their new roles. The prisoners showed that they believed they really were prisoners. Five had to be released early due to extreme emotional reactions. As the experiment progressed the guards became increasingly aggressive. The prisoners started to refer to themselves and each other by their numbers. The simulation became so real that the decision was taken to end the experiment early – after six days instead of 14.

In this experiment we see how people conform to the roles that they are given. Although the nature of this experiment was somewhat extreme, we can see how employees within a work situation might conform to a role. Hence, if the manager tells them to get on with their work and not ask questions, over a period of time the employees might adopt this submissive role and put aside any creativity that they could have brought to the role.

Another way in which employees are seem to conform was explained by Janis (1982) using the term 'groupthink'. Groupthink is when group members are influenced by the desire for cohesiveness and by a dynamic leader. The group ignore the external realities and impacts of the decisions that they make, because they are driven by a desire to achieve consensus at any cost. This situation often occurs where there is some sort of external threat, and the stress that results from this results in group members striving to reach agreement and not considering all the options carefully. Inevitably flawed decisions often result.

Janis noted five characteristics of groupthink:

1. The members of the group felt they were invulnerable, that they were beyond critics.
2. The group believed that what they were doing was right.
3. Any information that was contrary to the decision of the group was discredited.
4. There was a strong pressure on all group members to conform.
5. There was a negative stereotype attached to any individuals or groups who opposed the group.

ORGANISATION EXAMPLE

In his research Janis gave a number of examples of situations where he believed that groupthink had occurred. These included the Bay of Pigs invasions of Cuba (which was when President Kennedy supported a misguided invasion of Cuba by Cuban exiles), the Watergate scandal (when President Nixon helped cover up a robbery of the Democratic Party headquarters) and NASA's decision to launch the *Challenger* space shuttle despite engineers' warnings that there were dangers related to the cold weather. In each case the group had made flawed decisions, but all the group members had been convinced that what they were doing was right.

PREJUDICE

One of the dangers of group conformity is that the group members adopt flawed attitudes and behaviours. An example of how this occurs is the development of prejudice within groups.

In understanding why prejudice occurs it is useful to start by thinking about how people react within different social or work groups. Research by Sherif (1956) has shown that we quickly develop a great loyalty to a group that we belong to, and in doing so develop a negative attitude towards other groups. Sherif worked with boys aged 11 and 12 years old in a summer camp setting. The boys were unknown to each other at the start of the camp. After a few days they divided the boys into two groups, and observed that the groups quickly developed their own identities, with special jargon and secrets, leaders emerging and all members being forced to pull their weight. Sherif then introduced conflict between the two groups in a series of games. The boys refused contact with the other group and gave negative ratings to boys in the other group. Sherif had shown that simply by separating people into two groups and introducing some conflict, hostilities could be produced. In the next stage he introduced tasks that required the two groups to work together, and he found that the boys did work together and formed new friendships with those in the opposing group. He had shown that the hostility that had been created could be made to disappear just as easily.

Further research by Tajfel (1970) has shown that merely being categorised as a group member can produce a negative attitude towards other groups. Tajfel worked with 64 boys aged 14 and 15, who all knew each other well before the experiment. In the first experiment the boys were told that the experiment was about visual estimation. They were shown a series of pictures with a number of dots, and asked to estimate how many dots appeared. The boys were then divided into two groups. They were told that one group comprised the 'over-estimators' and the other the 'under-estimators', whereas the allocation to groups was actually completely random. They were then asked to give rewards of small amounts of money – to any boys. Tajfel found that a significant majority of boys elected to give more money to boys in their own group, rather than to boys in the other group. Tajfel concluded that it was actually very easy to provoke negative attitudes towards other groups.

This has an interesting impact on our understanding of why prejudice occurs. If we belong to a group (such as those who are male, or white) then we develop a sense of loyalty and pride in that group. In doing so we can develop a negative attitude towards other groups (such as the female or non-white), and that negative attitude can lead to prejudices. Once those prejudices have developed they become deeply held attitudes and can be difficult to change.

Prejudice also occurs because groups have a lack of understanding about each other. This is probably particularly evident in tensions between different racial groups. Here there are often outward signs of differences (eg dress, diet, language, religion), and a lack of understanding of the reasons behind these differences can lead to misconceptions developing about the other group. Hence, education about different groups is an important part of the fight against prejudice.

Another important factor in the development of prejudice is the amount of contact that people have with the 'out' group. Research by Van Dick et al (2004) showed that the negative attitudes towards other groups significantly decreased if those with the negative attitudes had opportunities to have acquaintances and make friends with those in the 'out' group. This is an important factor, because if people discover for themselves that negative views are wrong, this is much more powerful than simply being told that they hold wrong views and beliefs about others.

In putting groups together, therefore, there is the temptation to group people together who have similar attitudes, as this is likely to result in there being little, if any, prejudice between group members and in there being more agreement within a group.

What are your prejudices? How have they developed? Has the influence of a group been part of the formation of your prejudices?

ACTIVITIES

One way that prejudice has been demonstrated within groups has been through the development of institutional racism.

ORGANISATION
EXAMPLE

The phrase 'institutional racism' became widely publicised as a result of an investigation into the handling by the Metropolitan Police (the Met) into the murder of Stephen Lawrence. The MacPherson Report (1999), set up to investigate this incident concluded that there was evidence that the Met was institutionally racist. The report defined this as:

The collective failure of an organisation to provide an appropriate and professional service to people because of their colour, culture, or ethnic origin. It can be seen or detected in processes, attitudes and behaviour which amount to discrimination through unwitting prejudice, ignorance, thoughtlessness and racist stereotyping which disadvantage minority ethnic people.

The definition suggests that specific prejudice relating to racism had become part of the culture of the organisation. It is not suggesting that there was necessarily any deliberate racism, rather that the practices and attitudes towards racism were disadvantaging people, probably without anyone being truly aware of these disadvantages.

In the MacPherson Report 70 recommendations were made for changes to the Met in order to combat institutional racism. Some of the recommendations that are of more general interest are:

- to recruit a workforce that reflects the cultural and ethnic mix of the area in which the organisation operates
- to monitor statistics relating to equal opportunities in order to identify any examples of unintentional discrimination
- training for employees in the understanding of discriminatory practices and how to prevent them occurring
- making the use of language that is specifically offensive to a minority group a disciplinary offence.

These are all recommendations to try to educate and train people so that prejudice within the group is reduced.

When trying to prevent anything from occurring it is useful to consider why the problem occurs in the first place – it is often more effective to address the causes rather than just try to change the outward manifestations. So, why does institutional racism occur? To answer this, one approach might be to consider how attitudes develop (Michener *et al* 2004).

Instrumental conditioning would suggest that the negative attitude is learned because of a negative experience with a particular group, or as a result of information about that group that has been supplied by other people. This attitude is reinforced by praise or reward from the group, when an individual expresses attitudes or displays behaviours that fit with the negative attitude. It is this second approach that is of particular interest here. Applying it to the police force, if a new police officer joins the force and hears a regular message that a particular ethnic minority is a problem, that officer will eventually learn this attitude. If he/she is praised or rewarded by colleagues when he/she expresses this attitude, the learning will be reinforced. If this attitude is widely held throughout the force, through instrumental conditioning it will become an attitude held by the whole police force – and now we have institutional racism.

Classical conditioning would suggest that there is some form of stimulus and response. So, if the new police officer learns that the rest of the force react in a certain way to an ethnic minority group, the officer will learn that response to the group. As the stimulus and response are linked more regularly, the learning will become stronger.

The other approach to the development of attitudes is observational conditioning. If a new officer sees people of certain ethnic group being treated in a particular way, or being spoken of in a certain way, that officer will learn that this is the way this group behaves towards the ethnic group. The new officer then learns the behaviours and attitudes of the existing group, hence reinforcing institutional racism.

From this analysis we can see that the way to address the prejudice that has resulted in institutional racism is to challenge the attitudes and behaviours that are being learned by new entrants to the police force. If officers learn a different way of thinking about and interacting with ethnic minority groups, this institutional racism will not be passed from officer to officer.

It should be noted that, since the MacPherson Report, the Met has made huge efforts to address the problems that were raised. The Met has developed a diversity strategy, with the main intentions being defined as to:

- ensure that victims and their families have a clear understanding and certainty regarding the standards of service they will receive
- build fair practice and no prejudice into the force through training, management and measurement
- increase the number of officers from ethnic minorities through new approaches to retention and recruitment
- increase the transparency of what happens in the force by the greater involvement of lay people
- make it very clear to all employees of the Met that there is no room for racism in the organisation, and to actively target and address any examples of poor performance or bad behaviour.

DIVERSITY WITHIN GROUPS

Diversity within a group has both negative and positive effects. Research by Watson *et al* (1993) has shown that increased diversity leads to increased creativity and improved decision-making. Research by Tsui *et al* (1992) has shown that there is reduced interpersonal liking, psychological commitment and intergroup communication as a result of diversity. Further research has shown that diversity can have a negative effect on group cohesion (Smith *et al* (1994) and increased group conflict (Jehn 1995). The research has shown that these negative impacts of diversity decrease as time passes.

Research by Riketta and Van Dick (2005) has shown that people tend to have a stronger attachment to their workgroup than to the overall organisation. This research emphasises the importance of teamwork, and the effective development of teams. A further study by Richter *et al* (2004) found that the more individuals identified with their organisation, the less conflict their group developed with another group that they worked most closely with.

However, we have already noted that diversity can lead to reduced group cohesion and greater levels of conflict within the group. We have to question, therefore, whether the reliance on teamworking actually has a positive impact on diversity.

In the previous section we briefly touched on research by Sherif and Tajfel into social identity and social categorisation. We shall return to this research to try to understand what might happen within a team.

Sherif and Tajfel both suggested that people quickly become loyal to the group of which they are part – and see that group as superior to any other groups. This would suggest that if people are placed in a work team they will usually develop loyalty to that work team, and see it as superior to other groups. As stated by Van Dick (2004), the more individuals identify with a group, the more their attitudes and behaviours will be governed by the group membership.

However, that conclusion ignores the loyalty that the team members might have to other groups to which they belong. For example, if the team is composed of men and women, the men in the team already belong to a 'gender group' and might have the attitude that their gender group – men – is better than the other gender group – women. Hence, there is potential for a split within the team between men and women. This could lead to a reduced cohesion in the overall team. The same explanation can be given to explain subgroups that can be formed within a team relating to racial groups, disability and other less obvious issues such as status within the organisation.

West (2002) suggests that one of the results of this split within the team is that individuals do not have the psychological safety that is needed in order to contribute creative ideas without the fear of ridicule. (That is, a member of another subgroup might deride a contribution.) This would suggest that there is a negative correlation between diversity in teams and team innovation.

However, another theory is that diverse teams actually perform better than non-diverse teams because they have a greater range of knowledge and cognitive skills to draw on. Polzer *et al* (2002) found that diverse teams have a greater variety of information, perspectives, knowledge, abilities and skills to draw on, and hence are more likely to produce innovation ideas. This theory would suggest that there is a positive correlation between diversity in teams and team innovation.

Williams and O'Reilly (1998), Webber and Donahue (2001) and Richard and Shelor (2002) have proposed that the relationship between diversity and teamworking might actually have a U-shaped form. This would mean that small increases in diversity would have small positive effects on the overall group problem-solving and innovation, with small impacts on the functioning of the group. However, large levels of diversity would offer little improvements in group problem-solving and innovation, but have a large effect on the functioning of the group. Somewhere in between would offer a balance.

We can understand this theory more clearly by returning to our understanding of social identity and social categorisation theory, and by considering the theory that groups perform better when they have a greater range of knowledge and experience to draw on.

If there are small levels of diversity, the intergroup conflict is low. This is because the people within the team are not from a large range of other groups, and hence have not developed negative attitudes towards each other. However, because the groups that the team has drawn from have similar backgrounds and experiences, the range of knowledge, skills and experiences that can be drawn from in innovation is low. When the team has high levels of diversity, there is increased conflict because people are drawn from a range of different groups, and hence there is increased tension between those groups. To balance this there is a wide range of experience, knowledge and skills to draw on – but if this is not employed effectively because of the intergroup conflict, there will not be effective innovation.

This suggests, therefore, that when composing a team there needs to be careful consideration of the level of diversity within that team. Some diversity will improve the innovation, but too much could be detrimental to performance.

THE IMPACT ON EMPLOYMENT RELATIONS

When employees become part of a group, they might go through a process that results in some of their attitudes and behaviours changing, as we have seen through our look at conformity. There is also the possibility that negative attitudes and behaviours could develop. We have also seen that the way that a group is put together in terms of the diversity of the members can impact on the creativity and success of the group.

The manager, therefore, has a twofold responsibility to the group. There is the responsibility to develop a successful working relationship with the group. There is also the responsibility to ensure that the composition of the group results in the minimum of negative attitudes and behaviours developing, and also the maximum of creativity and success.

In Chapter 6 we shall look at the relationship that management has with a particular group of employees, those in a trade union.

KEY POINTS FROM THIS CHAPTER

- Different subordinates have different styles and personalities.
- The manager needs to understand the personality of the employee in order to develop a successful relationship.
- Employees will be motivated by different things, adding to their individuality.
- Work–life balance is an issue of increasing importance, and also results in very individual needs of employees being demonstrated.

- Many organisations have tried to address the issue of work–life balance through offering flexible working.
- When a new group is formed it goes through a series of stages of development before it is ready to perform at an optimum level.
- Members of a group tend to adopt different roles within the group.
- There is a tendency for group members to conform to the predominant attitudes and beliefs of the group
- One way in which conformity can be demonstrated is through the development of prejudices.
- Institutional racism is an example of how prejudice can be adopted by a group.
- A group needs some level of diversity for optimum performance, but too much diversity can have a negative impact.

EXAMPLES TO WORK THROUGH

1. You have been asked to suggest a number of initiatives that managers could take to improve the motivation of their work-force. Using the motivation theories that we have examined in this chapter suggest three initiatives, using the theory to justify your suggestions.
2. Your managing director has stated that 'Work–life balance is all very well, but if we do not make a profit the employees will have no jobs!' How would you answer this statement?
3. Since moving to teamworking the senior management in your organisation have noted that there has been a significant reduction in the number of suggestions that employees have made about potential improvements to their work. Why might this be? How could you increase the suggestions, whilst still using teamwork?

(Suggestions of answers to the examples can be accessed by tutors at www.cipd.co.uk/tss)

CASE STUDY

DCB Call Centre is a call centre offering call-handling services to a range of customers. It has three main areas of operation:

- taking orders for a retailer selling clothes through a catalogue
- handling calls for an insurance company, relating to reports of motor vehicle accidents
- handling calls for a white goods manufacturer, relating to warranty claims.

The call centre employs 350 call handlers, 78 per cent of whom are female. The call centre operates from 6 am to midnight. It is housed in a new building, with easy transport links to Swindon and Oxford. The call centre has been in operation for eight years.

There is a high rate of turnover of employees, with 65 per cent of the current employees having served less than one year. A series of exit interviews have been carried out, and the top two reasons given for leaving the organisation are hours of work and the pressure of the work.

The work is highly pressurised. All call handlers are given a target number of calls that they should handle each hour, and a target for the maximum length of any one call. There are visual displays in all offices showing who has answered the most calls in the last hour, and who has answered the least. The visual displays also show how many calls are waiting, and how long they have been waiting. If any team lets calls wait for more than 10 seconds, it receives a 'debit mark'. If more than 10 debit marks are given to any team during one week, a fixed amount is debited from its monthly bonus. The monthly bonus is also based on the individual performance of each employee, against his/her targets.

Since the introduction of the Flexible Working Regulations 2002 a number of employees have requested changes to their hours of working. In all cases the requests have been for fewer hours, and also the requests have been to work the more popular hours of the day (primarily 10 am–3 pm). The management took the view that the easiest way to comply with the legislation was to agree to all the requests, and rota the employees who did not have the right to make a request (those who did not have children, or whose children were older than six years) for the remaining hours.

This has led to a very divisive working situation. Those who work the more popular hours are often ignored by the other employees, and this can be to the detriment of the overall performance of the organisation because important product information is sometimes not passed to them.

The number of calls is at its highest during the popular hours of 10 am–3 pm, and then again from 6–8 pm. This means that the employees working during those times typically work in the same section of the call centre every day. They develop a familiarity with the products and hence are able to deal with the calls more quickly. Employees who are required to work during the less busy hours often have to move around all the sections, filling in as necessary. They do not gain the same level of expertise and hence are slower at handling calls. They are penalised through not always achieving the targets required to pay out the monthly bonus.

These difficulties have resulted in a series of problems for the call centre:

- Several employees are complaining that they have no work–life balance because they are always working unsocial hours.
- Clear 'cliques' have developed within the organisation and are disrupting its smooth running.
- A strong dislike of those who have been granted flexible working has developed, to the extent that information is not passed on to them, and some attempts have been made to distort their performance figures.

The management is concerned that these problems are contributing to the high level of employee turnover, and also having an adverse effect on the overall performance of the call centre. Help them address the issues by answering the following questions:

a). Work–life balance is important for all employees, not just parents. How could the organisation address this problem, while still giving an effective service to its customers?

b). Why might 'cliques' have developed? (Use the understanding you have gained of employees within organisations to answer this question.)? How could this problem be resolved?

c). Why might groups of employees develop a dislike of each other? (Again, use the understanding you have gained of employees within organisations to answer this question.) How could this problem be resolved?

Trade Unionism

CHAPTER 6

The objectives of this chapter are to:

- explore the definition and purpose of trade unions
- explore why people choose to join/not join trade unions
- examine data relating to the make-up and size of the trade union movement
- outline the structure of trade unions
- consider the role of the TUC and ETUC
- consider the impact of the Information and Consultation Directive and European Works Councils
- explore the future for the trade union movement.

In Chapter 5 we looked at employees as part of a group. One of the most commonly quoted groupings of employees within the employment relationship is the trade union. In this chapter, therefore, we will give specific attention to the development, role and future of trade unions.

In many ways this chapter provides the link between Chapters 4 and 5, particularly for unionised organisations. The trade union representative is one process of managing the communication and the interaction between management and the employee. In this chapter we shall be considering the benefits and the difficulties of taking this approach.

TRADE UNIONS

Section one of the Trade Union and Labour Relations (Consolidation) Act 1992 (TULRCA) defines a trade union as:

> An organisation consisting wholly or mainly of workers of one or more descriptions and whose principal purposes include the regulation of relations between workers of that description or those descriptions and employers or employee associations.

This legal definition shows that the group of people who wish to be defined as a trade union must be a group of workers whose reason for existence is concerned with relationships with employers. The following example illustrates this point.

ORGANISATION EXAMPLE

Midland Cold Storage v *Turner (1972)*

The employees took industrial action against the employer, instructed by the Joint Shop Stewards Committee (JSSC – the employee representative body within the organisation). The company tried to sue the JSCC because of its actions in threatening drivers who attempted to cross picket lines set up to deter anyone from working during the industrial action. (Section 10 of TULRCA allows for a trade union to be sued.) The courts held that the JSSC was not a trade union, rather it was a pressure group, because it was not primarily concerned with the relationships between workers and employers – hence it could not be sued.

For a trade union to be legally recognised in the UK it must be listed by the certification officer. The post of certification officer was established under Section 7 of the Employment Protection Act 1975. The certification officer is an independent statutory authority appointed by the president of the Board of Trade.

A trade union can be categorised as independent or dependent. The full range of statutory rights that are available to trade unions, their officials and their members are only available to those trade unions that are judged to be independent. These statutory rights include the rights:

- to appoint safety representatives
- to receive information for bargaining purposes
- to be consulted in the situation of redundancies and transfers of undertaking
- to take time off for trade union activities
- not to have action taken against them because of their membership or trade union activities.

(These issues will be explained in more detail in Chapter 11).

The certification officer determines whether the trade union is independent or not. In making that decision the certification officer must consider the definition of independence given in Section 5 of TULRCA:

- The trade union is not controlled or dominated by an employer or a group of employers.
- The trade union cannot be interfered with by an employer or group as a result of the giving of financial or material support or by any other means which could tend towards control.

The process of determining whether a trade union is truly independent was laid down by the Employment Appeals Tribunal (EAT) in the case of *Blue Circle Staff Association* v *Certification Officer (1977)*.

ORGANISATION EXAMPLE

The Blue Circle group of companies formed a staff consultative organisation. Initially it was under the control of the management, and received financial support from the company. The organisation wanted to move away from this control and instituted a new set of rules, and agreed a negotiating procedure with the management in a bid to achieve this independence. Five months after agreeing the rules it applied to the certification officer for a certificate of independence. This was refused on the grounds that there had been no clear move away from the former dependence on the employer.

In giving its judgement the EAT gave some clear guidelines in what issues should be considered when assessing independence. These were:

1. *Finance*: If the organisation is getting any financial help from an employer it is clearly not independent.
2. *Other assistance*: Giving assistance such as free premises from which to operate is likely to rule out independence, although the extent of the support needs to be considered.
3. *Employer interference*: If the organisation gets considerable help from the employer it is unlikely to be independent.
4. *History*: It is quite possible for an organisation to start as dependent, and then to grow into independence. However, the recency of this will be relevant. In the case of Blue Circle the dependence was still very recent.
5. *Rules*: Is there anything in the rulebook of the organisation that allows the employer to interfere with or control it? If so, this is likely to contradict independence.
6. *Single company unions*: Although it is possible to have an independent trade union that is single company, these bodies are more likely to be interfered with than a trade union that represents workers across a range of organisations.
7. *Organisation*: Who is in charge of the group that wants to be recognised as an independent trade union? If it is senior management of the employer it is likely to have more interference.
8. *Attitude*: Is there a record of a robust attitude to negotiation, giving a sign of genuine independence?

Although the legal definition is important in understanding the role of the trade union, it does not allow us to explore the overall purpose of the trade union – particularly in terms of understanding why employees might decide to join. Salamon (2000) suggests that there are six distinct aspects of trade union activities:

- *Power*: The collective strength of the trade union acts as protection and support for the individual, a force to counteract the force of the employer, and a pressure group.
- *Economic regulation*: To ensure that the members of the trade union receive the maximum level of wages and benefits possible.
- *Job regulation*: To have a system of working with the employer to ensure that employees are protected from arbitrary management decisions, and are able to participate in decision-making.
- *Social change*: To develop a society that reflects the social cohesion, aspirations and political ideology of the membership.
- *Member services*: To provide a range of benefits and services for members.
- *Self-fulfilment*: To allow members to work outside of the immediate confines of their job and become involved in decision-making processes.

Gennard and Judge (2005) suggest that the trade union has the primary purpose of protecting and enhancing the living standards of its members. The union achieves this through industrial methods (such as negotiation with the employer) and political methods (such as putting pressure on the government, a process that is usually carried out or co-ordinated by the Trade Union Congress (TUC)).

The many definitions of trade unions that have been given by a number of commentators seem to concentrate primarily on the protection of employees, and on the need to regulate the relationship between the employee and the employer. If we think back to Chapters 4 and 5 in which we looked at the role of the manager and the employee, the suggestion is being made that the two parties need some help, or some representation, in developing a successful working relationship. The means by which this is achieved is through the trade union movement.

ACTIVITIES

Gain a better understanding of the purpose of trade unions. Choose at least three trade unions and access their websites. Browse through the information they give about their history, their aims, the services they provide and the major campaigns that they are running. When you have completed this research write your own definition of a trade union.

STRUCTURE OF TRADE UNIONS

Trade unions traditionally grew up around a trade. The early trade unions in the 1700s had their origins in medieval craft guilds, established to control entry to the crafts and to establish some level of price control (Cannell 2004). In the 1800s further trade unions grew up around specific industries, such as engineering, with the Amalgamated Society of Engineers being established in 1850.

Trade unions today are traditionally classified according to their original basis (Lewis *et al* 2003). The traditional classifications are company unions, craft unions, occupation unions, industry unions and general unions.

Company unions

These are often dependent trade unions, in that they are controlled by the employer. Membership is restricted to those who are employed by the particular company.

Although the control by the employer might be deemed to be negative in some ways, there are advantages of this type of trade union in that all the issues the union addresses are relevant to its members. Trade unions that represent employees from a wide range of organisations are inevitably going to be pulled in different directions, addressing specific needs of their members.

The level of control does not necessarily mean that management has a say in the actual running of the trade union. As we saw in the earlier definition of trade union independence, it could simply mean that the employer gives some financial support to the trade union.

ORGANISATION EXAMPLE

Some examples of company unions were trade unions in the high street banks, such as the Barclays Group Staff Union and the NatWest Staff Association. However, both of these unions merged with BIFU (Banking, Insurance and Finance Union) in 1998 to form UNIFI. (UNIFI went on to merge with Amicus in October 2004.)

Craft unions

Traditionally craft unions were groups of highly skilled workers who had completed apprentice-ships or similar qualifications. The highly skilled workers then passed on their skills to other workers, who were admitted to the trade union when they had learned the same level of skill and were able to be called 'craft workers'.

Many of these traditional crafts have now declined, because technology has replaced many of the skills, resulting in operators with lower levels of skill being able to carry out the same tasks as the previously highly skilled workers.

There are many examples of these smaller craft unions merging with larger trade unions, because there are no longer sufficient members for a specific craft union to be viable. An example is the National Union of Scalemakers, which represented those skilled in producing mechanical scales, which merged with MSF (later to become Amicus) in 1993. The introduction of electronic weighing machines, and the more generic and lower-level skills required to make these products, resulted in the exclusivity of skill represented in the NUS becoming too small for the union to be viable.

Occupation unions

These unions represent employees who do the same job, although they might do it in a range of different organisations. There are still some sizeable trade unions that are occupation-based, such as the National Union of Teachers. A number of trade unions still have names that suggest that they are occupation-based, although they have actually broadened out their membership consid-erably. For example the Transport and General Workers Union (TGWU) was traditionally focused on those working within the transport industry. Today it has five different sectors: food and agri-culture, manufacturing, services, transport, and a sector dedicated to issues particular to women, race and equality.

Occupation unions are effective when there are a significant number of people carrying out a similar job that has very specific issues to address. Hence, the National Union of Teachers: there are a significant number of teachers in the UK, who carry out a similar job and the issues that they need to address are very specific to their profession.

Industry unions

Rather than focusing on the occupation of the employee, an industry union focuses on the type of organisation within which the employee works. Hence, all employees within a particular industry join the same trade union, regardless of the type of work that they do, or the level at which they are working within the organisation.

A good example of this type of trade union is the RMT (National Union of Rail, Maritime and Transport Workers). It has around 70,000 members from all types of transport organisations. The common thread is transport – but the type of work represented within the trade union varies considerably.

General unions

Most general unions that exist today do so as the result of a series of mergers that have diversified their range of representation. Maybe it is inevitable that one of the largest trade unions in the UK is a prime example of a general union.

Amicus has a membership of over one million, and has 22 different sectors. Amicus was initially formed from the merger of the MSF and AEEU trade unions. Since the initial creation of the trade union, there have been further mergers with a range of trade unions. At the time of writing (Autumn 2005) Amicus was in talks with the TGWU and the GMB about a possible merger. If that went ahead the 'super union', as it is being dubbed in the press, would have around 2 million members. Clearly that gives the new union much more weight when interacting at the national level (for example, when negotiating with the government). However, there are also concerns that the needs of the individual could become lost in such a big organisation.

Amicus is a very interesting trade union because of the diversity of its membership. Go to www.amicustheunion.org and find out more about the variety within this trade union.

Single-union agreements

One feature of recognising occupation unions is that an organisation can find itself negotiating and consulting with a wide range of trade unions. This was particularly true before the merger of so many trade unions, and even truer when the craft unions were more prevalent. An organisation that employed a variety of different craft trades on the shop floor, and also had engineers, employees working in finance, administration and general management could be negotiating with 10 or more trade unions. According to the Workplace Employee Relations Survey (1998), one-quarter of unionised workplace with 25 or more employees had four or more unions present.

Clearly this is a time-consuming situation for the organisation when negotiations are taking place, although the overall power of the employees can be diminished, particularly if there is any conflict between the different trade unions.

In the 1980s the use of single-union agreements developed. In such an agreement one trade union represents the needs of all the employees for collective bargaining and representation purposes. Many single-union agreements were associated with the start-up of new organisations, and hence the organisation chose from the start which trade union it was going to work with. However, there were (and still are) instances where an organisation chooses to derecognise some trade unions and recognise just one.

Single-union agreements have often been associated with a more modern and co-operative way of working. Lewis *et al* (2003) list the following as being associated with single-union agreements:

- the trade union expressing support for the goals of the organisation
- single-status employment
- flexible working, including multiskilling and the removal of demarcations between jobs (demarcation of jobs means that employees only do work within their grade of employment, or tasks that are specifically listed on their job description)
- training that supports multiskilling, flexibility and teamworking
- a range of initiatives support the involvement of employees (see Chapter 7)
- a no-strike clause and binding arbitration for the resolution of disputes, generally relying on the principle of pendulum arbitration (where the arbitrator chooses either the management's offer or the employee's claim, rather than seeking a compromise).

Single table bargaining

An alternative to single union agreements is single table bargaining. This is when a range of trade unions are still recognised within the organisation, but they come together to negotiate as one body, rather than in a series of individual negotiations. According to the Workplace Employee Relations Survey 1998, 77 per cent of workplaces that recognised more than one trade union were using single table bargaining.

ORGANISATION EXAMPLE

Honda, based in Swindon, moved towards a single union agreement in 2001. This was initially with the AEEU, but is now with Amicus since the merger of the AEEU and MSF to form Amicus.

The Japanese company opened the site in Swindon in 1985 and initially managed without any trade unions. The decision to recognise the AEEU came following a ballot of employees at the Swindon site.

Workplace representatives

The structure within the trade union will vary depending on its size. However, most trade unions will have some form of hierarchy that starts with workplace representatives.

Workplace representatives are not employees of the trade union. They work within an organisation where the relevant trade union is recognised (see Chapter 11), and are elected by members of the trade union. If the trade union is independent they have the statutory right to take time off to carry out their trade union duties. These duties will typically involve such activities as representing members at disciplinary meetings, representing their members who have raised grievances and negotiating with the employer.

In organisations where there is a large number of trade union members there will be a number of workplace representatives. These will typically be elected to represent different departments within the organisation. If there is a lot of trade union activity it is possible that an employee will be elected as the senior workplace representative (often referred to as a 'convenor') and will work full-time on union business. However, the convenor will remain an employee of the organisation, with continuous service accruing. The trade union and the organisation will come to an agreement over who pays the convenor.

Local branches

The primary unit of the trade union is the local branch. If one organisation has a large number of trade union members there might be just one branch within that organisation. However, most branches cover an area of the country and draw together all the trade union members in that geographical area. The size of the local branch will vary according to local membership, and could be very small or several thousand.

Hyman (1994) points out that, as with many such organisations, low attendance at branch meetings is a common problem. However, Hyman emphasises that without branch attendance it is not possible for the trade union to know whether it is truly representing the issues its members care about. Indeed, if we refer back to the six aspects of trade union activity defined by Salamon, without branch activity there is likely to be less power within the trade union.

Area/regional offices

The trade union is then likely to have a structure involving a series of area or regional offices. These are staffed by employees of the trade union. Within the staffing there will be regional/district officers who support the workplace representatives. If the organisation and the workplace representative are unable to reach an agreement on an issue, it is typical for the regional officer to meet with them to try to assist in reaching a solution.

National executive committee (NEC)

The final level in the hierarchy is the national executive committee (NEC). The responsibility of this committee is to administer and control the trade union. The size of the NEC varies greatly between trade unions. Some trade unions have a small group of full-time employees operating as the NEC, others have a larger group of part-time lay members.

The Trade Union Act (1984) and the Employment Act (1988) imposed a method of electing the NEC members. Prior to 1984 the election was typically carried out at the annual conference of the trade union. However, the legal requirement now is that all members of the executive committee (and particularly the general secretary and the president) must be elected directly by the membership through a secret postal ballot.

TRADE UNION STATISTICS

Trade union membership has declined considerably over the past three decades, although that decline has steadied in recent years. The membership numbers are shown in Table 6.1. In the next section we consider possible reasons for the decline in this membership.

Although there is no question that trade union membership has declined considerably over the past 30 years, the figures also suggest that membership levels have been largely stable over the

Table 6.1 Trade union membership, Great Britain

Year	Membership (millions)
1975	11.7
1980	12.6
1985	10.8
1990	9.8
1995	8.0
2000	7.8
2003	7.7

Source: certification officer reports.

Table 6.2 Number of trade unions in Great Britain

Year	Number of trade unions
1975	446
1980	467
1985	391
1990	306
1995	260
2000	221
2003	213

Source: certification officer reports.

past 10 years. In 2005 the general secretary of the TUC, Brendan Barber, reported that there was an overall increase in trade union membership of 20,000. Although that is not a large increase, the suggestion was that this might be the start of a larger increase. Specifically Barber noted that the Public and Commercial Services Union had grown by 50,000 over the previous 10 years, and the Union of Shop, Distributive and Allied Workers had seen its membership grow by around 60,000 in the same period.

Over the past 30 years the actual number of trade unions has also reduced. This is primarily due to the number of mergers to which we have already made reference.

Of the 7.7 million trade union members reported in the 2003/04 certification officer report, 6.5 million were members of the largest 16 trade unions, representing 84 per cent of all trade union members. Again, this is largely representative of the number of mergers that have taken place. The membership of the 16 largest trade unions was reported as shown in Table 6.3.

It is interesting to note the variety of trade unions that are in this list. There are the big general

Table 6.3 Membership of the largest trade unions in Great Britain

Trade union	Membership
UNISON	1,289,000
Amicus	1,061,551
Transport and General Workers Union	835,351
GMB	703,970
Royal College of Nursing of the UK	359,739
National Union of Teachers	331,910
Union of Shop Distributive and Allied Workers	321,151
Public and Commercial Services Union	285,582
Communication Workers Union	266,067
National Association of Schoolmasters and Union of Women Teachers	265,219
Association of Teachers and Lecturers	202,585
UNIFI	147,607
Union of Construction Allied Trades and Technicians	115,007
British Medical Association	113,711
Prospect	105,480
Graphical Paper and Media Union	102,088
Note: Since this report the Graphical Paper and Media Union merged with Amicus in 2004.	

Source: certification officer reports.

unions (Amicus, TGWU and GMB, for example). However, the largest trade union is actually an industry union, UNISON. UNISON represents workers within the public sector at all levels. As the public sector is such a large employer, and UNISON is the primary union within the public sector, it is probably inevitable that the union has such a large membership.

There are also large occupation unions: the Royal College of Nursing and the National Union of Teachers being good examples. These trade unions represent professions that have a lot of employees within Great Britain, which partly accounts for their size. It is interesting to note that two of other largest unions also represent teachers, the NASUWT and the ATL.

Another union that is specific to a particular occupation is Prospect. This is a trade union representing engineers, scientists, managers and specialists in areas as diverse as agriculture, defence, energy, environment, heritage, shipbuilding and transport. It is the largest union in the UK representing professional engineers.

Another interesting statistic is the distribution of trade unions by size, as shown in Table 6.4.

Table 6.4 Trade unions: distribution by size

Number of members	Number of unions	Membership
Under 100	44	1,125
100-499	40	11,668
500-999	22	16,686
1,000-2,499	23	40,547
2,500-4,999	23	83,842
5,000-9,999	10	72,122
10,000-14,999	7	81,720
15,000-24,999	9	167,808
25,000-49,999	15	517,016
50,000-99,999	4	237,431
100,000-249,999	6	786,478
250,000+	10	5,719,540

Although this shows how the majority of trade union membership is concentrated in the 16 largest trade unions, it also shows that there are still a considerable number of small trade unions.

ACTIVITIES

For a full list of trade unions read the *Certification Officers Annual Report* (the full list is in Appendix 1). Access the report at www.certoffice.org.

The statistics so far have concentrated on the size of the trade unions. It is also important to look at data relating to the composition of the trade union movement. The following statistics all come from *Labour Force Survey* published in 2002.

First, it should be noted that only 29.1 per cent of employees in the UK belong to a trade union.

The proportion of those members by gender is shown in Table 6.5.

In the period 1991–2001 the membership of men within the trade union movement fell by 13 percentage points. In the same period the membership of women fell by 4 percentage points, with the result that there is no significant difference in the membership between genders.

It has been of concern to the trade union movement for some time that young people entering employment are not joining a trade union at the rate that this age group once did. We examine the possible reasons for this in the next section. However, Table 6.6 shows that trade union membership is concentrated among older rather than younger employees.

Table 6.5 Gender split of trade union members

Gender	Percentage of members
Male	53
Female	47

Table 6.6 Age of trade union members

Age	Percentage of members
Under 20	1
20-29	13
30-39	28
40-49	30
50+	27

Table 6.7 Trade union membership according to ethnic origin

Ethnic origin	Percentage of members
White	95
Asian/Asian British	2
Black/Black British	2
Chinese and other	1

Another issue of importance is the representation of different ethnic origins within the trade union movement. The breakdown of membership according to ethnic origin is shown in Table 6.7.

In interpreting these statistics we have to remember that there are significantly more people of white origin in the workplace, and hence it is probably inevitable that there will be more white trade union members. It is important, therefore, to look at the percentage of employees from each ethnic origin that are in a trade union (see Table 6.8). We see here that there is some variation according to ethnic group, but it is of little significance.

A traditional view of trade unions might suppose that the majority of members are unskilled or semi-skilled, with minimal representation of higher qualified employees. However, the statistics showing trade union membership by qualification shown in Table 6.9 do not support this view.

One further classification that is of interest, particularly with the rise in flexible and part-time working, is the work status of trade union members. It is possibly inevitable that more trade union members are full time, rather than part time (see Table 6.10).

The difference between those who work full time and part time is probably less surprising. It is possible that those who work part time are less concerned about issues associated with their employment, because it is not such a large part of their lives. Alternatively, it could be

Table 6.8 Trade union membership within ethnic groups

Ethnic origin	Percentage of ethnic group
White	29
Asian/Asian British	25
Black/Black British	30
Chinese and other	22

Table 6.9 Trade union membership by qualification

Highest qualification	Percentage of members
Degree or equivalent	23
Other higher education	15
A level or equivalent	23
GCSE or equivalent	18
Other	11
No qualifications	9

Table 6.10 Trade union membership by work status

Work status	Percentage of members
Full time	82
Part time	18

that part-time jobs are more typically found in organisations where trade union membership is low.

What these statistics show us is that the trade union membership as a whole is not fully representative of the working population. It is important, therefore, that when promoting the interests of their members trades unions do not unintentionally favour particular groups within society because they are most strongly represented in their movement.

FACTORS INFLUENCING THE DECLINE OF TRADE UNION MEMBERSHIP

As we have seen from the statistics in the previous section, trade union membership has declined significantly over recent decades. Why has this happened?

Psychological contract

We have referred to the psychological contract between the employer and the employee a number of times. This is a very individual and personal contract. If both parties are satisfied with the psychological contract they are unlikely to see the need for the assistance of any other party in managing their relationship. However, Townley (1994) suggests that there is an inevitable gap between what is promised and what is actually realised. Although the psychological contract might exist, it can become obscured by the economic power of the employer, in comparison with the employee. In such a situation the employee might be more likely to turn to a third party, such as a trade union, to assist with the gap that has occurred.

The decline of the manufacturing sector

The manufacturing sector has traditionally had a strong trade union membership. However, this sector has declined significantly and the service sector, which has a traditionally lower trade union membership, has become the dominant sector of employment in the UK. It is logical, therefore, that trade union membership will have declined.

Booth (1989) suggests that over two-fifths of the decline in trade union membership in the 1980s can be attributed to the decline in areas of employment where membership has traditionally been strong.

The attitude of young people towards trade unions

As we saw in the statistics in the previous section, trade union membership is concentrated among the older age groups. This is of concern to trade unions, because the eventual result of this trend is a further significant decline in total membership. It is also an important issue because research by Machin and Blanden (2003) showed that young people are 30 per cent more likely to join a trade union if their father was a trade union member. Given the strength of this family influence, as the generations progress the suggestion is that the decline in membership will grow even more sharply.

In Chapter 5 we looked at the issue of conformity within groups. A few decades ago not belonging to a trade union would have been non-conforming behaviour. In some situations today belonging to a trade union is non-conforming behaviour, and as we saw in Chapter 5, not conforming to the group can be an uncomfortable experience. As young people are being brought up in a generation where trade union membership is less common, it might be seen as non-conforming behaviour to go ahead and join a trade union.

Young people are also entering a workforce that is more protected by employment legislation than ever before. (We look at the extent of this protection in Chapter 12.) Hence, they are likely to see less need for trade union representation.

The age of the workplace

Research by Machin (2003) shows that, in 1998, just over a quarter of workplaces less than 10 years old recognised a trade union – half the corresponding figure of older workplaces. Machin suggests that workplace age is a central factor in explaining the decline of trade union membership. His research also shows that, if a trade union is recognised in a young workplace, union density is around 11 per cent lower than it is in the older workplace.

This also links to the issue about younger workers not joining trade unions, as younger workplaces often attract younger workers.

Increased legislation

As we will see in Chapter 13, there has been a significant growth in employment legislation covering all aspects of employment. Hence, employees have much greater personal protection than people who were in the workplace 20–30 years ago, and might not see the need for the additional protection of the trade union.

The converse of this argument is that there is a greater need for trade union representation because the law has become increasingly complicated, and employees need the experts within the trade union to guide them through it. However, with the increase in use of the Internet employees have access to a very wide range of advice and guidance, which might negate this argument.

Employees' increased knowledge

As we shall see in Chapter 10, employees are increasingly taking their grievances to employment tribunals. There seems to be an increased level of knowledge among employees of the options available to them in dealing with disputes at work. Again, this is partly due to the increased availability of information through the Internet.

The success of the trade union movement

Employees are not going to be attracted to join a movement that never seems to win any battles. Although there is a wide range of disputes where trade unions do achieve what they wanted, there are also some well publicised examples when they seem to lose.

One of the best publicised was clearly the miners' strike of 1984–85, when the National Union of Mineworkers suffered a humiliating defeat. This dispute marked a significant change in the fortunes of trade unions. More recent disputes such as the Fire Brigade Union unsuccessfully seeking a 40 per cent increase in pay in 2003 might have added to the perception that trade unions are not successful in winning the big battles.

In addition, there has been the collapse of MG Rover in 2005, an event that the trade unions were unable to influence in any way. Again, the perception is that the trade union movement is not being successful.

However, in viewing these examples, and many others, it is important to define what success is. Success might not always be about winning the big argument (in the miners' strike, stopping pit closures). Success could also be about raising the profile of a grievance and getting some concessions. For example, in the fire strike of 2002/3 the original request of a 40 per cent pay increase was not achieved. However, an increase well above inflation was achieved, and this might still be perceived as 'success'.

Look at a number of examples of conflict between trade unions and management. For each example, try to identify how 'success' might have been defined by both the management and the trade unions. Do you see many examples of a difference in definition of success?

The state of the economy

The UK has had a considerable period of relative prosperity, and low unemployment. When employees are faced with fewer redundancies, and the ability to find employment relatively easily, they are less likely to think that they need the support of trade unions. In addition,

Metcalf (2005) states that in a unionised workplace employment grows 3 per cent more slowly, or falls 3 per cent more quickly, than it does in a similar non-unionised workplace. This could be the result of change taking place more quickly in a non-unionised workplace, or might be the result of growing competition from non-unionised organisations. Whatever the actual reason, the trend has a serious implication for ongoing union membership.

Style of management

Although there are still many examples of poor management in UK organisations, there is an increased awareness of the need to manage effectively in order for the organisation to achieve maximum success. As a result we see organisations, such as those in the *Sunday Times* survey of 100 best companies to work for, that are working hard to treat their employees well. Again, there is a reduced need for trade union representation.

The increase in flexible working

There has been a marked increase in the number of employees working on part-time and fixed-term contracts. It is possible that employees on such contracts do not have the same motivation as full-time employees to seek the protection that is offered from trade union membership. It is also possible that they do not have the same desire to influence the organisation as full-time employees might have.

Job mobility

Several years ago employees tended to join an organisation and stay with that organisation for all their working life. Nowadays that approach is rare. It can be more difficult for employees to keep changing trade union when they move jobs, and the effort of doing this might lead to a decline in trade union membership.

Roots of union power

Metcalf (2005) suggests that the roots of union power are the closed shop and the strike threat. Closed shops (where it is a requirement of the job that a person joins a trade union) became unlawful as a result of the Employment Act 1980, and there are varied opinions on the actual impact this had on the numbers of trade union members. However, although it might be difficult to determine the actual number of employees who would not have been in a trade union if there had not been a closed shop in place, it is certain that removing this 'requirement' to be in the trade union resulted in a subsequent loss of power.

Against these reasons for the decline in trade union membership, it is important to recall why employees do join trade unions. One of the primary reasons is that the trade union has a duty of care to all its members. Therefore, if the member has any difficulties at work (such as a disciplinary hearing) the trade union has an obligation to advise and represent that member (unless the member has acted in defiance of trade union advice or best practice). For many employees the knowledge that this support is there if needed is very important.

ACTIVITIES

Are you a member of a trade union? Why/why not? Ask a number of friends or colleagues the same question. What are the primary reasons you find for and against trade union membership?

THE IMPACT OF EUROPEAN WORKS COUNCILS AND THE INFORMATION AND CONSULTATION DIRECTIVE

A key role of the trade unions has been to consult and negotiate with employers through elected representatives. In most organisations that recognise trade unions (the definition of recognition will be explored in detail in Chapter 11) there are formalised processes agreed for this negotiation and consultation to take place. In non-unionised organisations there are less likely to be representatives. The number of worker representatives according to union presence is shown in Table 6.11.

As we see from Table 6.11, in 89 per cent of workplaces where there is no union present there is no worker representative. This lack of representation, and the accompanying lack of opportunity for communication between the employer and the employee, have been partly addressed through two pieces of legislation.

The first of these pieces of legislation introduced European Works Councils (EWCs). The European Works Council Directive was implemented in the UK by the Transnational Information and Consultation of Employees Regulations 1999, which came into force on 15 January 2000. The regulations require that a EWC, or an alternative process for consulting and informing employees, is set up for 'community-style undertakings' if a valid request to do so is received. A valid request must include at least 100 employees from at least two member states. A community-style undertaking is defined as an undertaking with at least 1,000 employees within the member states, with at least 150 members in each of at least two of the states.

From 15 January 2000 any undertaking that has not already set up a voluntary EWC must start negotiations about setting up an EWC within six months of receiving a request to do so. If the undertaking refuses to commence negotiations it can be ordered by the EAT to set up a statutory EWC as defined in the regulations.

The purpose of the EWC is for the employees to receive information on, and to consult about, matters that interest the company as a whole. These include issues such as business structure, economic and financial situation, mergers, cutbacks, redundancies, production and sales.

There should be a minimum of three members of an EWC and a maximum of 30, with at least one representative from each member state where there is an undertaking. The EWC is required to

Table 6.11 Worker representatives, by type of union presence (percentage of workplaces)

	No union present	Union present, no negotiation	Recognised unions	All workplaces
Union and non-union rep	-	-	10	4
Workplace union rep	-	-	64	28
External union rep	-	-	8	4
Non-union worker rep	11	19	1	7
No worker rep	89	81	17	56

Source: Workplace Employment Relations Survey 1998.

meet at least once every year. The organisation is required to pay the costs of the EWC, which can include costs relating to travel, accommodation, interpretation and any resources required for members to carry out their duties.

Members of the EWC are entitled to paid time off for the carrying out of their duties. Any dismissal or detriment relating to membership of an EWC will be automatically unfair.

According to the CIPD Factsheet (2005) *European Works Councils* there is little evidence that organisations have used EWCs to develop any transnational bargaining arrangements. Most organisations that have set up EWCs tend to keep their domestic consultation arrangements separate from the EWCs, largely because there are specific issues to be addressed at a domestic level that are not relevant to all member states.

ORGANISATION EXAMPLE

A number of trade unions have worked with organisations in setting up European Works Councils. This is of benefit to both the organisation, in that it is drawing on the experience of the trade union, and to the trade union in that it is influencing the structure and remit of the EWC.

As one of the largest trade unions Amicus has been involved in a wide range of EWCs. To gain an idea of the large number of EWCs that are actually in existence, look at the list at:
www.amicustheunion.co.uk
searching on 'EWC listing'. This is a lengthy and very interesting list.

Clearly the EWC regulations apply only to multinational companies. A further piece of legislation introduced the requirement to set up consultation groups in organisations that operate in just one member state. The Information and Consultation Directive (no 2002/14) addresses the need to establish a general framework for the rights to information and consultation of employees in undertakings in the European Community. As with EWCs there is only the requirement to take action if a valid request is made. In this case to be valid the request must come from at least 10 per cent of the employees (or at least 15 employees if the workforce comprises fewer than 150 staff, or at least 2,500 employees if it comprises more than 25,000 staff).

Legislation in the UK was introduced in April 2005 in the form of the Information and Consultation of Employees Regulations 2004. Initially the directive applies only to businesses with 150 or more employees. The directive will be extended to businesses with 100 or more employees by March 2007, and to all businesses with 50 or more employees by March 2008.

The rights given to employees in the directive are to receive information relating to such issues as activities in the organisation, economic position, the development of employment (particularly when this might involve a threat to employment) and any proposed substantial changes in work organisation or contractual relations. The information must be given in sufficient time to allow the employees to prepare for consultation. Consultation must then be carried out with appropriate timing and content at the relevant level of management. The consultation must involve the employees' representatives having ample opportunity to express their opinions and take place with a view to reach agreement.

The purpose of the EWCs and the Information and Consultation Directive is to ensure that employers and employees enter meaningful discussions about matters that affect both the employees and the organisation. Clearly some organisations already have effective ways of approaching this issue of consultation. Greater consultation should lead to less conflict between the employer and employees, particularly if consultation is entered into with a clear intention to reach agreement. However, some employers might resent the formality of the negotiation and consultation structure that is being imposed on them, and there is the potential that this might actually damage employment relationships.

It is important to note that all employees within an organisation are covered by these directives, and hence, in an organisation that recognises trade unions, there are likely to be employee representatives who have no trade union affiliation as well as the trade union representatives making up any consultation body. In an organisation that has a high percentage of trade union members there is unlikely to be much difference between the trade union negotiating body and the newly formed consultation body.

Younson (2002) suggested that this is a major issue for trade unions to consider, because there might be a situation in which the consultation body reaches an agreement that the trade unions do not support. Potentially, therefore, the impact of the new legislation is such that the power of the trade union is diminished.

It is too early to say what impact the Information and Consultation Directive will have on the consultation bodies that are already established within organisations. As has already been noted, an organisation only has to act in accordance with the directive if there is a request from at least 10 per cent of employees. If the current consultation arrangements in an organisation are already working effectively it could be argued that there is unlikely to be a request for action. However, if there is discontent between trade union and non-trade union members within an organisation, this might be an opportunity to alter the consultation arrangements.

As we shall see when we explore the issue of trade union recognition in Chapter 11, 40 per cent of employees within an identified bargaining unit in an organisation have to support trade union recognition in order for the organisation to be legally obliged to recognise the trade union. This is considerably more than the 10 per cent who are required to request action under the Information and Consultation of Employees Regulations 2004. It might be possible, therefore, that employees who have not got sufficient support to achieve trade union recognition decide to use this route rather than trade union recognition to agree some formal consultation agreement. This could be a further impact on overall trade union membership.

Despite this, it should be noted that the legislation is restricted to organisations with 50 or more employees. According to Lewis and Sargeant (2004) this represents just 3 per cent of all EU companies, but 50 per cent of all employees.

ACTIVITIES

Find out if the organisation in which you work, or an organisation with which you are familiar, has been requested to take any action under the Information and Consultation Directive. If it has, what action has been taken? If there has been no request from employees for any action to be taken, why do you think this is?

THE TUC AND THE ETUC

The Trade Union Congress (TUC)

The Trade Union Congress (TUC) is the body that represents most trade unions in the UK. It has 70 affiliated trade unions, representing around 7 million trade union members. It describes itself as the 'voice of Britain at work', and is primarily involved in campaigning for a fair deal at work and social justice at home and abroad.

According to the TUC website (www.tuc.org.uk), the primary purposes of the TUC are to:

- bring Britain's unions together to draw up common policies
- lobby the government to implement policies that will benefit people at work
- campaign on economic and social issues
- represent working people on public bodies
- represent British workers in international bodies, in the European Union and at the UN employment body, the International Labour Organisation
- carry out research on employment-related issues.
- run an extensive training and education programme for union representatives
- help unions develop new services for their members
- help unions avoid clashes with each other
- build links with other trade union bodies worldwide.

Of the 16 largest trade unions only the Royal College of Nursing and the British Medical Association do not belong to the TUC. In addition, the Police Federation is barred by law from joining the TUC. Although the TUC has, therefore, almost a 'monopoly of representation' (Sinclair 1999) there is debate about the impact that it has. Although trade unions might be affiliated to the TUC they still retain their status as independent trade unions and pursue their own issues. The TUC has some influence over trade unions, but some would argue that it has minimal power.

One power that the TUC does have over its members is the ability to expel any trade union that does not abide by TUC policies, or that is involved in any activities that are of overall detriment to the trade union movement.

 In 1988 the EETPU trade union was expelled from the TUC. The EETPU had reached two single union recognition agreements and these had been referred to the Disputes Committee of the TUC. The Disputes Committee ruled that the two agreements should be terminated, but the EETPU did not abide by the decision of the committee and no alternative form of representation was agreed. As it did not abide by the TUC decision it was expelled.

In 1992 the EETPU merged with the AEU (later to merge with MSF to form Amicus) and was readmitted to the TUC as part of the newly merged trade union.

The policy-making body of the TUC is the annual Congress which meets for four days each year during September. Each affiliated union can send delegates to Congress. The larger the union, the more it can send. At Congress 'motions' (resolutions for debate) are proposed and discussed. These form the basis of the TUC's work for the next year.

In between the annual Congresses, responsibility for the work of the TUC lies with the General Council. Its 56 members meet every two months at Congress House to oversee the TUC's work programme and to agree new policy initiatives. The larger trade unions are automatically represented on the General Council, with up to six members depending on the size of the union (this is calculated on a sliding scale, with six seats being reserved for trade unions with 1.2 million members or more). The smaller unions ballot for a number of reserved places. In addition, there are four seats specifically reserved for women from unions with fewer than 200,000 members, and three seats reserved for black workers (one from a union with more than 200,000 members, one from a union with less than 200,000 members and one woman). There is also a reserved space for one representative for each of the following categories: young workers, workers with disabilities, and lesbian, gay, bisexual and transgender workers.

Since 1994 the TUC has had an Executive Committee. This is appointed each year at the first post-Congress meeting of the General Council from amongst its own members. The Executive Committee meets monthly to implement and develop policy, manage the TUC financial affairs and deal with any urgent business. Also, at the first post-Congress meeting, the General Council elects the TUC president for that Congress year. She or he chairs General Council and Executive meetings and is consulted by the general secretary on all major issues.

The General Council sets up task groups to deal with specific areas of policy such as learning and skills or representation at work. Committees are permanent bodies that link to other parts of the trade union movement. The Women's Committee includes members elected at the annual TUC Women's Conference as well as General Council members. The Race Relations Committee, the Disability Committee and the Lesbian, Gay Bisexual and Transgender Committee have similar links to their own conferences. The Young Members' Forum also reports to the General Council, as does the body representing trades union councils (local trade union bodies).

Go to the TUC website (www.tuc.org.uk) and browse through the various sections to gain a better understanding of the activities of the TUC.

ACTIVITIES

European Trade Union Confederation (ETUC)

The ETUC was set up in 1973 to promote the interests of employees at European level, and to represent them in the various EU institutions. As of 2005 the ETUC had 76 national trade union confederations as members, from 24 European countries, as well as 11 European industry federations, and observer organisations in Macedonia and Serbia. In total, the ETUC is representing a total of around 60 million members. The ETUC is one of the EU's social partners, and is recognised by the European Union, the Council of Europe and by the European Fair Trade Association.

The main aims of the ETUC are to:

- influence decision-making through working with key European institutions
- negotiate with employers at European level
- co-ordinate major campaigns.

The ETUC determines the policies and activities in which it will be involved through elected representatives. There is a Congress which is the overall policy-making body, and this meets every four years. The Congress elects the general secretary. The activities and policies of the ETUC are determined between Congresses by the Executive Committee and the smaller Steering Committee. The day-to-day activities are run by the Brussels-based Secretariat.

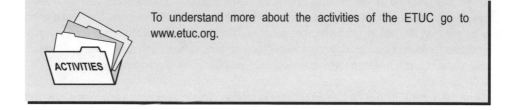

To understand more about the activities of the ETUC go to www.etuc.org.

ACTIVITIES

PARTNERSHIP

Although the traditional, and rather dated, view of the relationship between trade unions and management may be focused on conflict, the TUC has been working for a number of years to move away from this image to an emphasis on the trade union and the employer working together towards common goals. This process is known as working towards partnership.

The TUC General Council in 1999 identified six principles, which underpinned a genuine workplace partnership between unions and management. They are:

- a commitment to the success of the organisation
- a focus on the quality of working life
- a recognition and respect of the legitimate roles of the employer and the trade union
- a commitment to employment security
- openness and transparency
- adding value to all concerned.

In many ways these six principles are describing a collective psychological contract between management and employees. The employer wants a commitment to the success of the organisation, a respect for its legitimate role and the commitment to add value. The employee wants a good quality of working life, a respect for legitimate roles, employment security, and openness and transparency.

In 2001 the TUC went on to form the TUC Partnership Institute. The purpose of this Institute is to help organisations develop progressive employment relationships so that partnership agreements can be entered into.

According to the Institute the benefits for employees include:

- greater job security
- a greater involvement in decision-making
- better quality jobs
- greater investment in skills and training
- greater influence over the organisation and management of working time
- improvements in recognition, membership levels and facilities.

The benefits for employers are:

- less time spent on grievances
- better decision-making
- a higher skilled workforce
- improved morale
- more flexible approach to work organisation
  (source: www.partnership-institute.org.uk)

The TUC Partnership Institute gives a number of case studies illustrating how it has facilitated organisations and trade unions in reaching partnership agreements, and the benefits that have been achieved from this.

One example they give is UNIFI and Barclays Bank. In 1997 there were a series of one-day strikes over pay and grading. Both UNIFI and Barclays saw that the way employment relationships were being conducted was unproductive, and they started on the process of reaching a partnership agreement in 1998. First, they set up a project to develop a process of implementation for the partnership agenda. They then carried out a needs analysis, resulting in a training and organisation development programme. As a result of the changes that were implemented through this programme, they now state that the partnership principles, as outlined by the TUC, are embedded in their culture.

In many ways the partnership route seems the obvious route for trade unions and management, as the benefits to both sides seem clear. However, there are potential difficulties. First, it might not be possible to achieve partnership if the employer is hostile to the presence of a trade union (Kelly 1998). This might be an increasingly relevant issue as some employers are forced into recognising trade unions through the current recognition procedures.

Another potential difficulty can be external pressures on the organisation, which mean the benefits of the partnership agreement for both the employer and the employee do not materialise. This is illustrated in an article by Whitehead (1999):

The Rover Group reached a partnership agreement known as the 'New Deal' in 1992. It was one of the first organisations in the UK to embrace the idea of a partnership agreement, before the setting up of the TUC partnership institute.

Although the New Deal involved considerable detail, the primary issue was that flexible working practices were agreed in exchange for a promise of no compulsory redundancies. However, although the agreement gave the employees some guarantee of job security, in 1998 the new owners BMW called for 1,500 redundancies, followed by a further 2,500 redundancies. In total, 8,000 people took voluntary redundancy over a period of around two years. Although this was all achieved with no compulsory redundancies, there was a serious threat to job security.

Eventually, in 2005, the New Deal lost its relevance due to the collapse of the Rover Group. Although both sides had entered into the partnership agreement in good faith, the external factors pressurising the company proved to be too great.

THE FUTURE FOR TRADE UNIONS

As we have seen, the membership of trade unions has declined over recent decades, although that decline has now steadied. It is very unlikely that the trade union movement will ever disappear, but it is having to address a number of issues in order to maintain its current membership levels. Issues it needs to consider include:

- Trade unions need to have clear processes for recruiting new members. A survey by Heery *et al* (2000) found that most major trade unions have formal recruitment and retention policies. A number of trade unions are also attempting to address specific groups of employees, such as the Scottish Trade Union Congress launching a programme in 2005 to promote trade union membership to school leavers.
- Trade unions are offering a wide range of benefits associated with membership to broaden the attraction of membership. These include discounts on financial products such as insurance and mortgages. Look at any of the websites of the main trade unions to see the benefits that they offer.
- Trade unions need to fight campaigns that are relevant to employees today. For example, in 2005 two of the major campaigns of Amicus related to pensions and the protection of jobs that might be moved offshore. These are issues that are of interest to a significant number of employees across all occupations and industries.
- Trade unions also need to consider the nature of the employment relationship that organisations are developing with their employees, and their role within this. With the change in focus from collective to individual relationships, trade unions need to adjust their role to support this relationship, rather than try to pull it back to the old style of collective relationships.
- Trade unions need to support and train their workplace representatives. Employees are more likely to join a trade union if it is recognised and is active in their place of work. Hence, to survive and to grow trade unions need a network of active and committed workplace representatives. Most trade unions offer a range of training courses for their workplace representatives.

- A trade union is an organisation whose principle purpose is the regulation of relationships between the employer and the employee.
- A trade union can be independent or dependent.
- Trade unions are classified as company, craft, occupation, industry or general.
- A single union agreement is when an organisation recognises just one trade union that represents all employees.
- The structure of a trade union will depend on its size, but will typically include workplace representatives and a national committee.
- Trade union membership has declined significantly over the past 20–30 years.

- 84 per cent of all trade union members in Great Britain are in just 16 unions.
- 29.1 per cent of employees in the UK are members of a trade union.
- The European Works Council Directive and the Information and Consultation Directive have given employees the right to request that formal consultation is set up, if certain prerequisites are met.
- The TUC has 70 affiliated trade unions.
- The ETUC is the voice of trade unionism at a European level.
- Partnership agreements are seen as the way for employers and trade unions to move forward together.

1. Your organisation has worked with trade unions for many years. Recently a workplace representative has resigned and despite numerous requests no employee will volunteer to take her place. Why might this be?
2. Would a partnership agreement be successful in your organisation? Why/why not?
3. Over 10 per cent of the employees in your organisation (which has more than 150 employees) have requested that a consultation body be set up in accordance with the Information and Consultation Directive. How would you address this request so that the result brought the maximum benefits for both the employer and the employee?

(Suggestions of answers to the examples can be accessed by tutors at www.cipd.co.uk/tss).

GFN is a trade union that represents administration, clerical and junior management employees. It has been in existence for almost 70 years. It has a national coverage, and splits its operations into four regions. The four regional officers then report into the National Executive which is based in London.

At its peak in the 1970s GFN had 65,000 members. At present it has around 33,000 members. More worrying, perhaps, in the last year it had only 380 new members, while 650 left, primarily because they had retired from employment.

The National Executive is concerned about the future viability of the trade union, and has met to consider the options for its future. The ideas that have been discussed are:

- *Merge with another trade union.* This is an idea favoured by a number of the Executive members, but met with great resistance by others. There is another trade union that represents similar groups of employees, which also is declining. However, some of the Executive strongly believe that GFN will lost its identity if it merges with another trade union, and that the service offered to its members will suffer.

- *Recruit more members.* This seems to be the obvious answer! So far, a number of advertisements extolling the benefits of joining GFN have been placed in the national press. There seems to have been very little interest generated from this. Existing trade union members have also been asked to encourage their colleagues to join the trade union, with the offer of a discount on membership rates if they are successful. This has generated some interest, but not enough to replace the number who leave the trade union each year.
- *Change the way the trade union operates.* Some of the Executive believe that the message given by the GFN needs to be changed. They believe that the trade union needs to take a more modern and more relevant approach to the world of work. However, others are concerned that this approach would diminish the role of the trade union, and would result in them being little more than employee representatives ignoring their trade union roots.

In deciding which of these three options is the best to pursue the Executive has been trying to understand what the employee of today wants from a trade union. It is concerned that the GFN is portrayed as being old-fashioned and out of date, and hence wants to address this image. However, it is not sure what image it should be promoting, and hence does not know how to proceed.

Questions

1 Take each of the three options that have been proposed by the Executive and analyse the advantages and disadvantages of each.
2 The GFN wants to develop a new image that is attractive to today's employee. Advise it on how it could achieve this.
3 Given the analysis you have undertaken in answering the first two questions, suggest what actions the GFN should now take, and justify your answer.

Employee Involvement and Participation

CHAPTER 7

The objectives of this chapter are to:

- explore the reasons that organisations embrace employee involvement and participation
- outline the difference between employee involvement and participation
- examine different approaches to employee participation
- examine different approaches to employee involvement
- consider the factors that can influence the success of involvement and participation
- analyse the use of involvement and participation in organisations
- consider the impact of the culture of an organisation
- evaluate the link between high performance working and involvement/participation.

In the last three chapters we have focused on understanding the two parties within the employment relationship. We now move on to four chapters looking at some important and specific processes within that employment relationship.

We start in this chapter by looking at the process of employee involvement and participation. We then move on, in Chapter 8, to look at the process of negotiation and bargaining. In Chapter 9 we look at issues associated with resolving individual conflict and finally, in Chapter 10, we look at the processes surrounding the management of employee reward.

THE BACKGROUND TO EMPLOYEE INVOLVEMENT AND PARTICIPATION

As we saw in Chapter 1, management theorists in the late 1800s/early 1900s, such as Taylor (1911), believed that the best approach to ensuring the high performance of organisations was scientific. Hence, Taylor recommended that jobs be reduced to rules, laws and formulae that should be determined by management. The result of this approach was that tasks were broken down into small components, and employees were tasked with doing simple tasks repetitively with minimal opportunity to change or influence procedures.

As we observed, Henry Ford adopted this scientific approach when he developed his first car factories. Ford (1923) noted that some jobs were so boring and monotonous that he could not understand why employees would continue to do the work. However, he found that no discernible harm had been done to any employees through doing such work, and if employees did not want to do the work they could always leave the organisation.

Although the deskilling of jobs started in manufacturing industry, Wilson (2004) reports that it was soon extended to other areas of work, such as clerical jobs. As Braverman (1974) reports, thinking work was removed, resulting in jobs that were largely uninteresting, lacking in opportunity for decision-making and without any variety.

In the 1920s work began to take place to think about how employees' productivity could be improved, and the link between motivation and performance was examined. The first set of studies on this issue were the Hawthorne studies that took place in an organisation called Western Electric between 1924 and 1932 (reported by Roethlisberger and Dickson 1939). The first of these experiments was looking for a link between illumination of work premises and productivity. The expectation was that an increase in illumination would increase productivity. The workers were divided into two groups, with one group being given more light and the other being left with no change to the illumination. It was found that productivity increased regardless of whether the illumination was increased or decreased. A study was also carried out where the workers observed workmen supposedly changing light bulbs, although actually no change was made. Despite there being no change the workers commented favourably on the increased illumination.

Although there were some significant problems with the controls in the Hawthorne experiments, the studies did show that positive treatment of employees increased motivation and productivity. This led to the start of a change in the ways management planned work, although well into the 1950s and 1960s work was still organised in mechanistic and bureaucratic ways.

A big contribution to the change in approaches to planning and organising work came as a result of the growth of Japanese industries following the Second World War. After the war Japan and many European countries had to largely rebuild shattered organisations, economies and infrastructures, which gave the USA many opportunities for market dominance. During this time many organisations became very complacent about quality and costs. Daft (1998) reports that Xerox discovered that it was using 1.3 overhead workers for every direct worker, while its Japanese affiliate needed only 0.6 overhead workers.

After the Second World War a US statistician named W Edwards Deming identified the need to improve quality, and to achieve this by looking at, and eliminating, variation within processes. According to Walton (1992), his fundamental philosophy was that most of the problems relating to productivity and quality are within the systems rather than within the people who operate those systems. Deming's philosophy was largely rejected in the USA – as already noted US companies had market dominance and did not see the need to improve systems – and so Deming went to Japan and carried out a lot of his work with organisations that were rebuilding. They adopted his philosophies, and many today credit Deming's contribution as being key to the success of many Japanese companies.

In the 1980s many UK organisations started to struggle as the economy entered a period of recession. During this period many Japanese organisations began to take significant market share away from UK companies, and there was a growing realisation that the high standards of quality and cost reduction achieved by many Japanese companies had to be matched by UK companies. During this decade most major organisations embarked on 'total quality management' (TQM) programmes with the purpose of involving all employees in significant quality improvements.

The motorcycle industry is an example of a sector that was badly hit by the growth of Japanese competitors and the recession on the 1980s. Prior to the 1980s the UK motorcycle industry was the largest in the world. However, because of the introduction of motorcycle manufacturing in Japan at competitive prices and with high levels of quality, and as a result of internal difficulties, Triumph – the only remaining UK manufacturer of motorcycles – closed in 1983. At this time there was no longer any motorcycle production in the UK. After a series of further developments Triumph was 'reborn' and manufacturing restarted in the 1990s.

A large number of TQM programmes in the 1980s were developed around the principles of Deming, and his 14-point plan for TQM:

1. *Constancy of purpose*: Ensure that there is continual improvement of all products and services.
2. *Adopt the new philosophy*: We can no longer accept delays, mistakes and defective materials.
3. *Cease mass inspection*: Build quality into the process, and do not rely on inspection.
4. *End 'lowest tender' contracts*: Focus on quality rather than just on a price tag.
5. *Constantly improve systems*: Continually identify problems and eliminate them.
6. *Introduce training*: Provide modern methods of training and education for all employees.
7. *Introduce leadership*: Introduce modern methods of leadership that focus on helping people to do a better job.
8. *Drive out fear*: Encourage two-way communication and other ways of driving out fear from the organisation.
9. *Break down barriers*: People must work together, and there should not be barriers between different departments.
10. *Eliminate exhortations*: Stop using slogans and posters to exhort the workforce to work harder and better. Such exhortations create adversarial relationships.
11. *Eliminate targets*: Stop using arbitrary targets that might not be achievable.
12. *Permit pride of workmanship*: Put the emphasis of work performance on quality.
13. *Encourage education*: Put in place a vigorous programme of education and self-improvement for everyone.
14. *Top management's commitment*: Management must be clearly committed to ever-improving quality and productivity.
    (source: www.deming.org.uk)

The adoption of philosophies such as Deming's resulted in a different way of managing employee relations. Gone was the emphasis on quantity, on following instructions and on being exhorted to work harder and faster. This was replaced by an emphasis on quality, on thinking about the work and on working effectively and productively.

An organisation that developed an innovative approach to TQM was Motorola. The initiative known initially as '4 by 94', and nowadays as the Six Sigma programme, started at Motorola in the USA, but was translated to Motorola organisations throughout the world. Six Sigma is a mathematical measure that equates to 3.4 parts per million. The 4 by 94 programme was an initiative to achieve the standard of no more than four defects in every million opportunities to make a defect by the year 1994. Initially the programme was focused on manufacturing activities, but it was extended to cover all employees in Motorola. Today Six Sigma is still a programme that is run by

Motorola University in the USA, with the focus on Six Sigma as a metric, a methodology and a management system.

Source: www.motorola.com.

Whether organisations adopted the Deming approach or another approach, there was a growing realisation that employees had much to offer organisations, and a competitive edge could be gained by involving employees more fully in the organisation. It is this new approach that formed the basis for the growth of employee involvement and participation initiatives in many organisations.

It is also interesting to note that there was a certain level of political influence in encouraging employee involvement. The Companies Act 1989 required directors to include information in their annual reports relating to the involvement of employees in the affairs, policy and performance of the company. Although this does not amount to a requirement to actually involve employees in the organisation, it does highlight the importance of doing so.

ACTIVITIES

Find out whether the organisation you work for, or an organisation with which you are familiar, introduced a TQM programme during the 1980s (or possibly the 1990s). Why did they do this? If they did not, is there a reason why not? Match the 14 Deming principles against your organisation. Do they meet with this standard?

It would be wrong to assume that employee involvement and participation is an approach that has no difficulties. In the 1980s when such programmes were being introduced into organisations there was significant suspicion, especially among employees who saw the initiatives as ways to get more ideas and contributions from them without paying for the effort. Marchington (2001) makes some interesting observations about employee involvement schemes:

1. The process of employee involvement is primarily instigated by management.
2. It is assumed that employees want greater involvement, regardless of the form it might take.
3. It is thought possible to achieve unity of purpose between employees and their managers.
4. It is expected that greater commitment and productivity will result from employee involvement.

Marchington also notes some interesting assumptions that underpin many employee involvement schemes, and questions their accuracy:

1. Line managers will ensure that employee involvement schemes happen in the workplace, and that they are successful.
2. Employee involvement will alter employee attitudes positively, resulting in changed work behaviour that will result in greater commitment and productivity.
3. Trade union representatives (or other employee representatives) will accept the introduction of such schemes, and will accept any sidelining of their role that results.

Despite these concerns, which clearly shed some doubt over the possible success of any employee involvement schemes, most TQM programmes in the 1980s did go ahead with the co-operation of employees, and the fortunes of many organisations were transformed as a result.

The reason for this apparent success can probably be linked back to the psychological contract. It is important to remember that these programmes were largely taking place during the most severe recession in the UK economy for many years. It was a time, therefore, when many employees had very real concerns about their job security. In such a situation the demands and expectations of an employee within the psychological contract are focused primarily on job security, and other demands that might feature at a time of prosperity are put to one side. Hence, if the demands of the employer are for greater involvement in the organisation, or co-operation with initiatives springing from a TQM programme, and if the perceived results of this co-operation is greater job security, employees are likely to meet with the employer's demands in the hope of fulfilment of the psychological contract.

THE RELEVANCE OF EMPLOYEE INVOLVEMENT AND PARTICIPATION TODAY

Now we have seen how the need to involve employees more effectively in the organisation has developed, an important question is whether these approaches are still relevant today.

Today many successful organisations have moved on from looking in isolation at ways of involving employees, and have started to focus more broadly on what are known as 'high-performance work practices' (HPWP). According to a joint CIPD/DTI research document (2004), HPWP are grouped together into three broad areas:

- high employee involvement practices (eg quality circles, self-directed teams)
- human resource practices (eg sophisticated recruitment practices, performance appraisals)
- reward and commitment practices (eg various financial rewards, family friendly policies).

The report found that the number of HPWPs adopted by an organisation was directly linked to the organisational performance. The report also found a link between different areas of HPWP and different types of business outcomes. For example, human resource and reward and commitment practices were better at facilitating better support for staff and enhanced organisational competitiveness than high employee involvement practices.

We see, therefore, a more holistic approach to employee relations from the use of HPWPs, in comparison to focusing only on high employee involvement practices. However, it is very important to note that the high-performing organisations cited in this report are still using employee involvement as a fundamental part of their approach to employee relations. It has not been replaced by anything else.

Other research also suggests that there is a significant link between the use of employee involvement/participation and high-performance organisations. According to the DTI consultation paper *High performance workplaces* (2002), there is no one formula for a successful organisation, but successful organisations have the common characteristic of involving employees and communicating effectively with them. The Engineering Employers' Federation report on US and UK manufacturing productivity (2001) provides clear evidence that new workplace practices incorporating involvement of employees have been a contributing factor to productivity growth in the USA.

It is also important to consider the link between increased employee involvement/participation and partnership deals (which were described in some detail in Chapter 6). Although partnership was described within the context of trade unions – which is essential because this is a funda-mental part of the future vision for trade unions – it is important to note that partnerships can be formed between employers and non-unionised groups of employees. This is increasingly common when employees are involved and participating in the organisation, because there is a sense of partnership in solving problems and in securing the future of the organisation.

In the CIPD/DTI report there are a number of case studies given of organisations that have successfully adopted the HPWP approach. One example is the drinks company Bacardi-Martini. In the grouping of 'high employee involvement' it has initiatives including an 'Agile Team' to encourage innovation, an employee engagement survey and a process of identifying morale indicators. In the grouping of 'HR best practices' it has an appraisal process and a 'Back to the Floor' scheme for managers. In the grouping of 'Reward and commitment practices' it has family-friendly policies and family/spouse-inclusive benefits.

This is an example, therefore, of an organisation that has not just considered the impor-tance of employee involvement in the employee relationship, but has also looked more widely at other management practices.

Another important indicator of today's relevance is the actual usage of employee involvement schemes and related management practices in the UK. The use of schemes in workplaces with more than 25 employees (based on a survey of 1,962 managers) was as listed in Table 7.1. Only 2 per cent of managers reported that none of these practices was used in their organisation.

Although the report shows a relatively high usage of employee involvement schemes, it is inter-esting to note some of the differences of opinions between employees and employers. In the Workplace Employee Relations Survey (WERS) (Cully *et al* 1998), 70 per cent of managers agreed with the statement that 'we do not introduce any changes here without first discussing the implications with employees'. However, 40 per cent of employees stated that their managers were poor or very poor at providing them with the opportunity to comment on proposed workplace changes (compared with 30 per cent who rated them as good or very good).

The implication of the various research quoted in this section, therefore, is that an organisation that does not have HPWPs, or at least some structured approach to employee involvement, will not be successful. Conversely, an organisation that does have HPWPs or a structured approach to employee involvement will be successful. This, however, is far too simplistic a conclusion.

If we look back at Chapters 1 and 2 in this textbook there are a number of external and internal factors that impact on an organisation. The success of an organisation cannot be divorced from these factors. It is possible, therefore, for an organisation to have a number of HPWPs and be rendered unsuccessful by factors largely (or partly) out of its control. (Is this what happened to the MG Rover Group in 2005, when it collapsed? There were clear external pressures on the potential to succeed although a number of HPWPs had been adopted.)

Table 7.1 Use of 'new' management practices and employee involvement schemes

	Percentage of workplaces
Most employees work in formally designated teams	65
Workplace operates a system of team briefing	61
Most non-managerial employees have formal performance appraisal	56
Staff attitude survey conducted in the last five years	45
Problem-solving groups exist	42
Single status between management and non-management	41
Regular meetings of entire workplace	37
Profit-sharing scheme for non-managerial employees	30
Workplace uses a just-in-time process for inventory control	29
Workplace-level joint consultative committee	28
Most supervisors trained in employee relations skills	27
Attitudinal test used before making appointments	22
Employee share ownership scheme for non-managerial employees	15
Guaranteed job security or no compulsory redundancies policy	14
Most employees receive at least 5 days training per year	12
Individual performance-related pay scheme for non-managers	11

Source: Workplace Employee Relations Survey 1988.

The question remains, however: can an organisation that totally ignores HPWPs and employee involvement be truly successful?

ACTIVITIES

Answer the question that was posed in the last sentence. Do you think that an organisation that adopts no HPWPs or employee involvement can be truly successful? What evidence do you have to support your answer?

THE DIFFERENCE BETWEEN EMPLOYEE INVOLVEMENT AND EMPLOYEE PARTICIPATION

Having seen that there is a business case for pursuing HPWPs we now focus on the grouping of employee involvement and participation. We shall start by considering the difference between the two terms, then look at examples of these practices in some detail.

The two terms 'employee involvement' and 'employee participation' are often used interchangeably. However, there are some significant differences that should be noted.

Employee participation focuses on the collective rights of employees to become involved in decision-making in the organisation (Hyman and Mason 1995). However, there is a significant difference between collective bargaining (see Chapter 8) and participation. Collective bargaining typically focuses on areas where employees have traditionally been allowed, or encouraged, to become involved. However, participation is where the involvement of the group of employees is in decision-making that has typically been under the control of management (Wall and Lischeron 1977).

Employee involvement, however, is focused on releasing the full potential of people at work. It is applied more to individuals at work, and processes whereby the creativity and abilities of those employees can be released for the good of the organisation.

Clearly there is a link between employee participation and involvement. Employees who are involved in decision-making as a group are also likely to be encouraged to participate as individuals. However, there is an important distinction between the two terms. As Salamon (2000) notes, involvement is a process of encouraging support and commitment to the objectives and values of the organisation that have been defined by management, whereas participation is the process of influencing and taking part in organisational decision-making.

Another important distinction is that employee involvement is largely task-based whereas employee participation has a wider remit. This links to the definition of employee involvement being focused on the release of individual potential, because the individual is likely to be more focused on specific tasks (Geary 1994).

As we have noted, employee involvement is about releasing the full potential of people at work. This fits well with the unitarism approach to employee relations (see Chapter 1). The key theme of unitarism is harmony between employer and employee and having a common purpose/goal to work towards. Employee involvement is a process by which the achievement of this common purpose/goal can be reached.

When we examined the approach of unitarism in Chapter 1 we also noted the weakness of the theory, in that it presumed that employees and employers have the same goals, and it also presumes that conflict does not occur. We then looked at pluralism as another approach to employee relations – an approach that suggests there are several sectional groups within an organisation that have different goals, and there is a central body that is trying to encourage the sectional groups to work together towards one common goal. Employee participation fits well with the pluralist approach, because there is more emphasis on influencing decision-making, through a collective approach.

The issue of collectivism and individualism (also discussed in Chapter 1) becomes relevant here. The emphasis of employee involvement is on the individual. Although a large number of employee involvement initiatives involve working in teams, the primary emphasis is on releasing the potential of the individual. This is in contrast to employee participation, which is often through the process of employee representation – which links clearly back to collectivism.

An important question to consider, therefore, is whether employees are willing to become involved or to participate in the organisation. If we think back to the different subordinate styles described in Chapter 5 (Belbin 1996), we can see that receptive subordinates might struggle with the demands of involvement and participation because they are more comfortable with following instructions. All the other styles will have some degree of comfort with increased involvement.

It is quite possible that some employees will be more comfortable with the collectivism approach, because it directs the spotlight away from them as individuals and onto the group, where they are likely to feel less exposed. This might partly link to the style of the subordinate, but it could also link to the confidence that employees have in their expertise and skill.

Another interesting consideration is the motivation of employees to become involved, or to participate in decision-making. As we noted in Chapter 5, employees have different motivations for being at work, and different motivators within the workplace. Hence, if employees believe that greater involvement or participation will help to achieve the desired goals they are more likely to co-operate. For example, refer back to Vroom's expectancy theory. If the employee can see how personal involvement can make it more likely that a goal will be achieved, the motivation to achieve that goal will be increased.

When employee involvement and participation was initially introduced to UK organisations there was a lot of initial suspicion. A great fear was that increased efficiency would lead to the loss of jobs, because fewer people would be needed in an organisation. Although that fear was realised in a number of organisations, the alternative view is that the loss of jobs would also have been inevitable if the efficiency improvements had not been met.

ORGANISATION EXAMPLE

We have already used the fire fighters' strike of 2004 as an example of difficulties within the employment relationship. As we have noted, the dispute was eventually resolved with the agreement of a phased pay increase over a three-year period, in return for the fire fighters agreeing to a series of improvements to efficiency.

Since the agreement ending the dispute was reached in 2004 there have been a number of smaller disputes, with industrial action being threatened. On a number of these occasions the issue has been improved efficiencies. For example, in June 2005 the Fire Authority proposed a new rotating 12-hour and eight-hour shift pattern, arguing that this would lead to greater efficiencies. At the time of writing a threat of industrial action still exists, because there is the fear that the proposed efficiencies will lead to job cuts, as well as concern being expressed over the impact that the shifts might have on family life.

Source: www.bbc.co.uk/news, 3 June 2005.

EMPLOYEE INVOLVEMENT

Marchington *et al* (1992) divided employee involvement into two distinct categories, downward involvement and upward involvement. The downward involvement initiatives are processes whereby the employer is sharing information with employees. The upward involvement initiatives are where employees identify and (hopefully) solve problems and issues and communicate their findings to management.

In looking at the issue of employee involvement we shall start by looking at downward involvement. This group of initiatives is primarily related to communicating with employees.

According to WERS 1998, an increasing number of organisations are communicating regularly with their employees. Indeed, as we saw from the earlier list of employee involvement practices, 61 per cent of organisations have a form of team briefing in place.

In communicating to the workforce management are sharing some of the power they have. When we looked at French and Raven's (1958) categorisation of different types of power in Chapter 4, we saw how power can be based on the expertise and knowledge of the employer (expert power). However, we can also see how having more knowledge of the organisation can impact on all the types of power that were categorised. For example, a manager would not be seen as having the power to reward (reward power) or the power to punish (coercive power) if he/she did not have a more senior rank within the organisation hierarchy. It is expected, and is probably inevitable, that as one progresses up the ranks in an organisation one gains more knowledge, because one gets closer to the source of all the organisational knowledge, the most senior executive.

If management are sharing some of the power they have, there has to be a purpose in doing this. It is also important that the process that is used is most effective.

Shaw (1978) investigated five different structures of communication to see which were most effective. All the communication patterns he examined were theoretically effective in passing information to members of the team. However, his focus was on understanding which of the various systems was most effective. The five different structures that he looked at were split into two groups:

The first group is centralised structures. The three structures within this are:

- *Chain*, where information is passed from person to person.
- *Wheel*, where one person at the centre passes information out to all the others.
- *Y*, where information is passed along a chain and then one person at the end of the chain is responsible for passing it to two others.

These forms of communication are illustrated in Figure 7.1.

Shaw found that these centralised networks led to an unequal sharing of information, because all the group members had to go through a central person. Those who were nearest to the central person received most information, meaning that those at the extremes of the network received less information.

An example of how a centralised network is used in organisations is team briefing. The typical approach to team briefing is a cascade of information that comes from top management. Top management brief their direct reports, who brief their direct reports and so on, until the information is passed through the whole organisation. The most typical style, therefore, is the chain.

The main difficulties that are reported with team briefings are that the message can become distorted as it is passed along the chain. There is also the possibility that some briefers might misinterpret information, or forget to communicate all the information. Most organisations try to avoid this problem by having detailed briefing notes, but there is no control over whether the briefing notes are carefully followed.

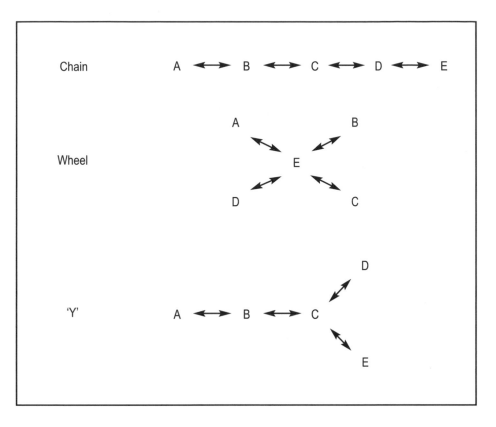

Figure 7.1 Centralised structures

Another difficulty that is shown well in the model by Shaw is the process for the asking and answering questions. If we refer back to Figure 7.1, the only logical way for questions to be answered is for them to be passed back to the central person. Once that has been achieved the answer to the question has to be passed back to the person who asked it. We can see how the process of answering could easily fail.

Despite the difficulties with team briefings they are a popular way of disseminating information quickly to all employees. Organisations have attempted to address some of the common difficulties that occur through the use of technology, showing videos with a message from the central person, or through the use of video conferencing.

Another form of communication that fits this centralised network is the production of newsletters, or communicating online through a company intranet. Again, the information comes from a central person, but because it is written material the message is not distorted. The difficulty with relying on this form of communication is that it presumes that employees will take time to either access the intranet (and have access to a computer to achieve this) or read the written document.

Shaw also identified two forms of decentralised networks:

- *Comcon*: information passes in all directions between different group members
- *Circle*: information passes between the different group members in a more formal structure.

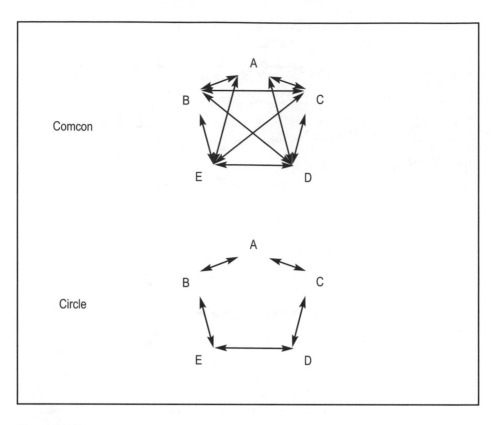

Figure 7.2 Decentralised networks

These forms of communication are illustrated in Figure 7.2.

In a decentralised network the information can flow freely from one person to another without there being a need to go through a central person. This means that all group members have equal access to information.

A form of team briefing does work as an illustration for this decentralised network of communication. A team briefing can be on a purely local basis, with the team leader focusing on local issues, such as the performance against targets the previous day and the targets that have been set for today. This type of team briefing is usually more informal, with everyone communicating and sharing information.

Baron and Greenberg (1990) researched the effectiveness of the two different communication networks. They found that in decentralised networks there was greater equality of decision-making and more equality in status between the different members. In centralised networks the group members at the edges of the group were less powerful than the others, and tended to be left out of decision-making. Those at the centre of the centralised networks had their power enhanced since they were in control of the flow of information. In conclusion, they found that group members in centralised networks reported less satisfaction than those in decentralised networks.

Another important consideration is the content of the communication. Townley (1994) argued that information can be 'educative', with the purpose of educating employees so that their expectations can be shaped by management. A good example of this is an organisation giving information about its financial performance before a pay negotiation takes place, so that employee expectations are shaped by the economic realities. Alternatively, information can be commitment-based, with the purpose of engendering a joint problem-solving approach. An example of this is information about customer feedback surveys, with the purpose of addressing the key concerns jointly.

In the *Sunday Times* survey of 100 best companies to work for there are many examples of organisations that have effective communication processes in place. Indeed, it could be argued that effective communication is a feature of such successful organisations. Examples include the following.

Astra Zeneca has a very thorough intranet system. It has designed an attractive front page that always comes up when an employee logs on to his/her computer in the morning. This reminder of the existence of the intranet, alongside regular updates of news and information, encourages employees to take a look at the intranet at least once a day.

Timpson produce a 36-page newsletter every Wednesday. This is an interesting use of a newsletter because it is a decentralised form of communication, rather than centralised. This is because most of the content is written by staff members, rather than the newsletter being a tool for one central person to give out information. It is also focused on the people in the organisation, rather than being primarily company news.

Although we are examining communication as a process within employee involvement, it has to be noted that it is a key foundation in the process of employee participation. As we shall see in the next section, employee participation focuses largely on representative-based initiatives. A number of these require the giving of information from management so that employees can contribute effectively. In Chapter 6 we looked at the demands placed on organisations by the setting up of European Works Councils and the requirements of the Information and Consultation with Employees Regulations (2004). Compliance with both these pieces of legislation requires the giving of information, and hence a process of effective communication. In a negotiation and bargaining situation there is a legal requirement to reveal a certain amount of information, and we look at this in more detail in Chapter 8.

How does management communicate with employees in the organisation in which you work, or in an organisation with which you are familiar? Find out why that form of communication has been adopted. Is it successful? In answering this question ask some managers what criteria they would use for determining whether communication has been successful.

Having looked at downward involvement, we now move onto upward involvement. As already noted, the emphasis here is on communicating back to management, rather than receiving information.

Again, the centralised and decentralised networks are relevant. In a centralised network information is being fed back to one central person, from one individual. Clearly, the logistics of all employees feeding back to one central person are somewhat complex in a large organisation. Hence, a process that is commonly used is the attitude survey.

Many organisations carry out regular attitude surveys (at least annually) to find out opinions of employees on a wide range of issues. The survey is typically carried out through a written questionnaire. Although some surveys will be circulated to just a sample of employees, most organisations try to cover all employees.

As we saw in the information from WERS 1998, 45 per cent of workplaces in that survey had carried out a staff attitude survey in the past five years, making it one of the more popular methods of employee involvement.

As Hollinshead *et al* (2003) note, once the survey has been conducted the information gathered becomes the property of management, and the process of upward involvement and the associated communication ceases. There is a danger of raising expectations by carrying out a survey. Employees feel that they have been led to believe management will take action as a result of their feedback, and they can become demotivated if they see no action being taken. If this situation occurs, employees will be less motivated to respond to similar surveys in the future.

However, an attitude survey is an excellent way to gather and process a lot of responses, which is probably the reason that so many organisations use them. If used effectively by the organisation, they can be a useful way of identifying areas of dissatisfaction amongst employees, and addressing them. This is particularly relevant for an organisation that is suffering a problem such as high employee turnover.

ACTIVITIES

Does the organisation you work for, or an organisation with which you are familiar, carry out attitude surveys? If so, find an example of the type of questions it has asked. Then talk to someone involved in devising the survey to understand the reasons behind the questions that have been asked. How is the information used once the survey has been completed? What percentage of employees complete the survey? If the survey has been carried out for several years, find out if the number completing the survey has decreased or increased significantly. Why do management think this change might have occurred?

Another form of upward involvement that has had a rather mixed reception from employers is the suggestion scheme. This is also a centralised form of communication, in that an employee passes a suggestion of improvements that could be made to a central person. The suggestion is typically assessed by the central person and some form of reward is offered for it. In some organisations this is a fixed amount for each suggestion, in others it is a percentage of the cost saving that results, or something similar.

Those who do not support the use of suggestion schemes point to the individual nature of the reward, which works against the successful use of teamwork (presuming that teamwork is part of the approach adopted by the organisation). Others would argue that it is part of an employee's job to produce ideas of improvements, and there should be no additional payment for this.

Production at the BMW plant in Oxford in 2002 was 30 per cent more than expected. During this year 10,339 suggestions were received from employees – more than two per worker. This resulted in an overall saving of more than £6 million. Examples of suggestions include changing progress report cards from A3 to A4 (which saved £4,500) and the best idea came from a group who found a way to halve the number of roof soundproofing blocks, resulting in a saving of £115,000. All those who gave a suggestion received a cash reward. During 2003 the system was changed and all employees were entitled to a bonus of £260 if, in addition to meeting quality and output targets, they came up with an average of three ideas bringing savings of £800.

Source: *Financial Times*, 19 March 2003.

On 16 June 2005 the CIPD reported on its website the findings of a survey called 'Ideas at work: the untapped resource', which had been commissioned by Vodafone. The report concluded that employers were missing out on ideas from their workforce because they were failing to capture their ideas and innovations effectively.

The survey found that the most significant factors in encouraging workers to share ideas were financial rewards and personal recognition. The most popular form of encouragement was a pay rise, with 37 per cent of respondents voting for it. The second most popular incentive was personal recognition, with 25 per cent of people voting for it. Of the 2,000 people surveyed, more than half said they were not formally encouraged by their workplace to come up with new ideas.

The survey also found that manual and clerical workers were as likely to come up with new ideas as others, including those at management level, but their ideas were more likely to be ignored. Of the 44 per cent of unskilled manual workers who believe that management did listen to their ideas, 49 per cent never saw their ideas implemented (compared with 19 per cent of all workers).

This is an interesting survey because it identifies that most employees expect some reward for their suggestions, and are dissatisfied when there is no reward. The type of reward is likely to be linked to the reason that the employee gave the suggestion (was the suggestion given as a means of earning extra money?) and to the motivators for that employee. (For instance, an employee who is motivated primarily by job security might expect less personal reward if he/she can just see that the suggestion has helped secure the future of the organisation.)

The last example of upward communication we examine is 'quality circles'. The setting up of quality circles was largely linked to TQM programmes. A quality circle is a group of employees who meet regularly with the purpose of identifying, analysing and improving issues relevant to the organisation. They are typically a work group who already work together, although some organisations form groups to facilitate the sharing of ideas, such as putting together a cross-functional group when employees work in a functional structure (see Chapter 1). Membership of a quality circle is voluntary. Meetings of the group might be during or outside working time.

The quality circle operates without the interference or guidance of management. Hence, it is usual for the group to choose its own leader from among the group and to choose its own issue to tackle. If management are seen to tell the group what to tackle or to guide it towards a particular solution, the whole point of using this as an employee involvement issue (to release the full potential of people at work) can be thwarted. If a quality circle is not allowed to work with a significant amount of freedom it could be questioned whether it is different to any ordinary work team.

Difficulties can occur with this approach, and one key problem can relate to the functioning of the group. As we saw when we looked at the work of Tuckman and Jensen (1977) in Chapter 5, groups go through a series of steps before they operate effectively. Management therefore needs to exercise a certain amount of patience before it sees results from a quality circle.

Although the quality circle needs to operate with a certain amount of freedom to allow the full potential of employees to be released, it is also important that certain parameters are set. For example, if a quality circle worked on an issue and came up with a solution that management chose to reject for some reason, this would be very demotivating for the quality circle and could affect the future success of quality circles. However, the solution of accepting any suggestion from the quality circle, regardless of its feasibility, is clearly not acceptable.

There is also a potential difficulty of membership within the quality circle changing, which could affect the smooth operation of the group. This is particularly relevant in organisations with a high staff turnover.

Naylor (2004) notes that quality circles originated in Japan, where they have been very success-ful. More than 13 million Japanese employees participate in quality circles, always voluntarily and usually outside normal working hours. However, as Naylor notes, quality circles fit well into the Japanese culture, with the emphasis on groups rather than individuals, on lifelong loyalty to an organisation and on a lack of significant demarcation in job roles. Naylor suggests that the differ-ent context of UK organisations makes it difficult for quality circles to operate effectively in the way that they were originally devised, with some of the key principles being eroded.

Another group of involvement initiatives are financial incentives. These include such things as profit-related pay, performance-related pay, employee share schemes and bonus schemes. We examine all of these initiatives when we look at the broader topic of reward in Chapter 9.

EMPLOYEE PARTICIPATION

As we have already noted, employee participation refers to collective representation of employ-ees. Primarily it is linked with state initiatives that promote the right of employees to be involved with decision-making processes in the organisation (Hyman and Mason 1995). However, this focus on the state gives a rather limited view, because many of the recent initiatives are actually at European level, and the initiatives that are put in place as a result of employee pressure cannot be ignored either.

Prior to the growth in employee involvement in the 1980s and onwards, as chronicled earlier in this chapter, most involvement of employees within organisations was on a collective level. However, it is not necessarily true to say that employee participation existed. Most collective involvement related to bargaining, and as we have already noted, that is not involvement in decision-making as defined by employee participation.

The emphasis on employee involvement has partly been driven by the need for organisations to use the full potential of their employees. However, as we noted in Chapter 1, there has also been a significant cultural move towards individualism, and this would suggest more focus on involvement initiatives, rather than participation initiatives.

Indeed, Salamon (2000) suggests that there has been a definite move towards involvement rather than participation, partly driven by the more strategic, integrated and managerial approach to the management of people.

It is interesting, therefore, to see that the two big drivers of employee participation that have come out of Europe are quite recent in origin. As we saw in Chapter 6, organisations legislation relating to European Works Councils (EWCs) became part of UK law in 1999, and legislation requiring employees to provide information and consult with employees or their representatives became part of UK law in 2004. Both of these initiatives are focused on employee participation.

It is too early to determine the impact of the information and consultation with Employees Regulations 2004. However, it is possible to explore whether EWCs have truly met the definition of employee participation.

As explained in Chapter 6, the EWC has between three and 30 members, with at least one representative from each member state where there is an undertaking. Given the range of country-based issues that can therefore be represented at a EWC, it is perhaps inevitable that the emphasis of EWC business is at a corporate level – it is probably the only level at which all the EWC members have a common interest. Cressey (1998) suggests that trade unions are fully aware that the opportunity for real participation (that is, influence on decision-making) when operating at this level is very limited. When one also considers other factors such as the frequency of meeting (the minimum requirement is to meet once a year), the potential language barriers and the possibility of achieving anything when working as a group of 30, there has to be a serious question mark over the EWC being a good example of employee participation.

Ramsay (1997) argues, however, that EWCs can be an important first step towards democracy in the workplace. EWCs do represent the interest of all employees within the organisation, and because of the level at which they operate they do have the opportunity to be involved with strategy at a high level.

However, Ramsay goes on to question whether the involvement of EWCs is actually a process of employees influencing management, or whether it is a process of management doing a very good job of selling the ideas and approaches it has already decided to pursue.

As we have already noted, organisations that meet the numerical requirements of the legislation are required to set up an EWC. However, according to the European Trade Union Confederation (www.etuc.org.uk), 1,800 companies are estimated to be covered by the legislation, but only 36 per cent have EWCs in operation. In total around 60 per cent of workers across Europe are represented by EWCs, because many of the organisations that have put EWCs in place are the larger multinational firms.

The ETUC suggests that the reason that many organisations have not set up an EWC is related to a reluctance to involve employees in decision-making, or not having an active trade union presence. Although the EWC does not have to be composed of trade union representatives, it is often trade union representatives that request management to form an EWC if they have not done so voluntarily.

The ETUC has examined some of the difficulties related to EWCs and suggest both sanctions for organisations that do not comply, and also changes to the EWC Directive. Relating to sanctions it suggests that:

- member states identify sanctions that vary in proportion but are sufficient to dissuade non-compliance
- if organisations make decisions that have a substantial impact on workers without taking part in consultation, the decisions would be legally invalid or the employer should have to make special compensation.

Clearly sanctions can work to ensure that an organisation complies with legislation. However, it is debatable whether sanctions can really make organisations involve employees in decision-making. If organisations are operating because of a threat of sanctions, one could question whether Ramsay's concerns of management 'selling ideas well' instead of really welcoming participation will be realised.

The ETUC also suggests a number of changes that should take place. These include:

- EWCs setting up a number of smaller steering committees that can meet at short notice. At present such committees exist in around 50 per cent of all EWCs.
- Providing more training to EWC members so that they can perform their role effectively (at present this is paid for by around 40 per cent of all companies). The training would cover languages and economic, financial and social affairs.
- Giving a clearer definition of information and consultation in the directive.
- Redefining confidentiality. At present it is possible that EWC members are restricted from sharing important information with their trade union colleagues or employee representatives at a local level.
- Having better access to expert advice.
- The right to hold preparatory and follow-up meetings.
- A reduction in the period allowed for negotiating agreements, from the current three years to one year.
- The right for EWC members to enter company sites.

Nearly all these proposals would enhance the influence of EWCs. However, the question remains whether senior management can really be influenced in their decision-making if they do not want to be influenced.

ACTIVITIES

Research an organisation that has an EWC. (Examples include most multinationals. Some names to start your search are Glaxo Wellcome, IBM, United Biscuits, Honda.) Try to find out how the EWC operates. If you can speak to someone involved in the EWC, try to find out whether the EWC is seen as successful or not. Why is this?

Another form of participation that has become part of a number of European countries is participation at board level, known as 'worker directors'. At present the requirement to establish worker directors is not part of UK law.

Interestingly, the debate on what is often seen as a relatively modern initiative began in the UK as a result of the Bullock Committee of Inquiry on Industrial Democracy (1977). Bullock's brief was to consider how industrial democracy could be extended through employee representation at board level. The terms of reference for the committee demonstrated significant support for employee participation from the then Labour government.

The actual terms of reference given to the committee caused a certain amount of controversy, and this resulted in the committee finally producing two reports. One of these reports was from the trade union and academic members, and they recommended the introduction of employee representatives at board level. The other report was from the employer representatives, and this argued strongly against the terms of reference stating that such an approach to democracy should not be forced on any organisation that was not willing to accept it.

An important factor was the board structure within the UK. Most organisations in the UK have a unitary (single) board, whereas organisations in some other European countries (Germany, for example) have a two-tier board. In the two-tier system one tier deals with detailed decision-making, and the other level is more concerned with company performance and the quality of the management. In Germany worker directors are appointed to the lower level of the two tiers (known as the supervisory board) rather than the higher level (known as the executive tier).

However, the Bullock Committee was recommending that the single board structure in the UK should remain. Indeed, their argument made good sense: if the purpose of the initiative was to involve employees in decision-making and the decision-making only took place at the higher level, surely employees would have to be involved at that higher tier. The proposal to split into two tiers, and only have employees as part of the non-decision-making tier, worked against the aims of increasing employee participation.

No action ever resulted from the Bullock Committee despite a white paper on industrial democracy being produced in 1978, based on the proposals of the main report. The Conservative government returned to power in 1979 and saw participation as something for organisations to resolve on their own, and hence the idea of worker directors was not pursued.

At present there are no proposals to revive the proposals relating to worker directors. It is interesting to consider whether the proposals are still relevant nearly 30 years after they were first made. Since that time, as we have seen, there has been a significant increase in employee involvement and a shift away from collectivism to individualism. There has also been a significant decline in trade union membership. Although it would be quite possible to have non-trade-union members as worker directors, much of the impetus for representation at board level originally came from trade unions.

It is probably the growth in employee involvement that is most relevant here. If employees feel that they are more involved in the organisation through these processes, it is possible that they will not see the need for the more formal route offered by such schemes as worker directors.

FACTORS AFFECTING THE SUCCESS OF EMPLOYEE INVOLVEMENT AND PARTICIPATION

In this chapter we have looked at a range of different initiatives relating to employee involvement and participation. However, not all organisations that pursue such initiatives find them to work effectively. What factors impact on the success?

Organisation structure

In Chapter 1 we looked at a range of different organisation structures and saw the difficulties and benefits associated with each one. As Daft (1998) explains, the type of structure within the organisation helps to determine where the control is. So, for example, in the matrix structure the control is spread out amongst the different functional and project groups. However, in a more traditional functional structure the control is clearly located at the top of the organisation. If employee involvement and participation is going to be successful the nature of that control must not be such that all the involvement is downward, and upward involvement is either discouraged or is lost in the process of moving up through the levels of the organisation.

Leadership

As we saw in Chapter 4, there are a variety of different styles of leadership. Certain styles are likely to be more receptive to the involvement of employees, both individually and collectively. For example, an authoritarian leader is likely to find it more difficult to accept and promote involvement than a democratic leader.

Employee style

In the same way that different leadership styles can impact on the success of involvement, so can different employee styles. As we saw in Chapter 5, Belbin (1996) identified a range of different styles. For example, those with a receptive style are likely to find it more difficult to become involved in the initiatives we have explored compared with those who are self-reliant or collaborative.

Power

Introducing any form of employee involvement means the delegation of some amount of power. Some managers and leaders are reluctant to do this.

KEY POINTS FROM THIS CHAPTER

- Management theorists in the late 1800s/early 1900s largely adopted the scientific approach to management.
- After the Second World War Deming was very influential in the successful rebirth of Japanese industries.
- The TQM movement grew in the UK in the 1980s.
- Today, emphasis is on high-performance work practices, which are grouped into high employee involvement practices, human resource practices and reward and commitment practices.
- Employee involvement involves the releasing of the full potential of people at work.
- Employee participation involves the collective involvement of employees in the decision-making process in an organisation.
- Employee involvement largely fits with the unitarism theory.
- Employee participation largely fits with the pluralist theory.
- Employee involvement initiatives are divided into downward and upward initiatives.
- Communication can be centralised or decentralised.
- Upward involvement is communicating back to the senior management, through initiatives such as suggestion schemes, attitude surveys and quality circles.

- Examples of employee participation include European Works Councils and worker directors.
- The success of employee involvement and participation initiatives is partly down to factors such as the organisation structure, leadership, employee style and the delegation of power.

EXAMPLES TO WORK THROUGH

1. For about five years your organisation has operated a system of quality circles. You are the HR manager and you have been asked to assist a quality circle that has become increasingly demotivated and frustrated. Your first task is to understand what has gone wrong. What issues will you explore in determining this?

2. Do you think that worker directors will ever be introduced successfully into the UK? Why/why not?

3. The organisation you work for, or an organisation with which you are familiar, wants to apply to become one of the companies listed in the *Sunday Times* survey of 100 best companies to work for. What factors do you think would stop it being successful in this attempt, and what factors would support it? Could any of the issues be addressed through increased employee involvement or participation?

   If the organisation you work for is already listed as one of the 100 companies, identify which factors you think have made it most successful in its listing. Has employee involvement and participation been an influence on the success? If so, how?

CASE STUDY

You are the HR manager at Stoneleys, a nationwide retail organisation. Stoneleys has 135 branches across the UK, with the highest concentration being in the south-east of England. Stoneleys sells ladies', men's and children's fashion, as well as a range of homeware products. It has been in operation for 45 years, and is a well-established player on the high street.

Stoneleys has around 20,000 employees across the country. The actual number working in any one store depends on the size of the store, and varies from 50 to 250. Around 65 per cent of the employees are female, and 55 per cent of all employees work part-time. Employee turnover runs at around 35 per cent per year, although there are a lot of long-serving staff as well.

In the same way as many organisations, Stoneleys introduced a TQM programme at the start of the 1990s. This included a training programme for all staff, with particular focus on customer service. Today, new staff still receive part of this training during their induction programme. The managing director of Stoneleys strongly believes that customer service is the element that separates out one retailer from another, and hence much emphasis is placed on this.

As a result of the TQM programme a comprehensive communication programme was introduced. This started nearly 12 years ago, and still runs successfully. There are daily team briefings, monthly videos circulated with a message from the managing director, and every two months an employee newsletter is produced. Employees typically report that they understand what is happening in the organisation.

Despite this successful communication the managing director is concerned that employees are becoming less and less willing to share their ideas of how Stoneleys can be improved. She believes strongly that the store employees have the best access to the customers, and hence hear more about what the customers want and don't want than she does! However, the suggestion scheme that was introduced seven years ago is now rarely used, and she feels that employees have stopped thinking about how Stoneleys can be improved.

During the TQM programme one initiative that Stoneleys decided not to introduce was quality circles. At the time it was felt that it was too difficult to operate them because so many employees worked differing shifts, and the stores needed all employees to be out in the store, and not sitting in meetings. However, the managing director has begun to consider whether quality circles should now be introduced to encourage employees to contribute their ideas again.

She recently met with a colleague who works at a senior level in the retail sector, and has had great success with using quality circles. As a result of this discussion she is convinced that Stoneleys could make them work. However, at today's management meeting she has met with a lack of enthusiasm from her senior managers. They do not believe that the introduction of quality circles is worth the disruption to usual store duties, and are reluctant to pursue the idea. They do, however, agree that the flow of ideas that used to come from store employees has stopped – and they agree that this is to the detriment of Stoneleys overall.

Questions:

1 Explore the advantages and disadvantages for Stoneleys in introducing quality circles. As a result of your considerations recommend whether they should pursue this idea or not.
2 Suggest one alternative way that Stoneleys could encourage the contribution of ideas from the store employees. Explain how this would work, and suggest whether it is a better idea than quality circles or not.
3 Why do you think that the use of the suggestion scheme ceased? Do you think it would be a good idea to reintroduce the scheme? Why/why not?

Collective Bargaining and Negotiation

CHAPTER 8

The objectives of this chapter are to:

- outline the definition and function of collective bargaining
- explore the context within which collective bargaining takes place
- consider the purpose of collective bargaining
- outline the differing structures of collective bargaining
- explore the process of negotiation
- analyse why collective bargaining can end in conflict.

In this chapter we look at another process in employee relations, the process of collective bargaining. Within this we look at the skill that is most commonly used within collective bargaining, that of negotiation.

In considering collective bargaining we shall draw specifically on the knowledge we gained in Chapters 4 and 5 about the two main parties to the employment relationship, management and employees. It is important to realise that collective bargaining is not just about trade unions, but we shall look at the role of trade unions within this process, and hence draw on knowledge we gained in Chapter 6.

ACTIVITIES

It is important that, as part of your studies, you learn about collective bargaining. That learning will be greatly enriched if you are able to observe or be part of a collective bargaining process. If you are currently working in an organisation, ask the head of HR if you can be involved in any collective bargaining that takes place (as an observer, or as part of the bargaining team). If you are not currently working in an organisation, try to find someone who has been involved in collective bargaining – from either side – and ask him or her what it was really like!

WHAT IS COLLECTIVE BARGAINING?

Collective bargaining is a process that has been part of employment relationships for many decades. Indeed, the first theoretical approach to collective bargaining was identified by Webb and Webb (1902). At the time of the development of this theory, the trade union played an important role in collective bargaining. Indeed, that role grew to be stronger as decades passed. We start by examining Webb and Webb's theory, but it is important to remember the changing role of the trade unions, as we have already examined in Chapter 6.

Webb and Webb saw collective bargaining as one of the three methods used by trade unions to reach their goals of preserving and improving benefits for their members. The other two methods were:

- mutual insurance, which was the provision of benefit payments to members affected by sickness, strikes or unemployment
- legal enactment, which was lobbying for improvements in the legislation that protected their members.

Webb and Webb did not give a clear definition of collective bargaining, rather they described it. They described how an individual employee applies for a job and talks directly to the employer about the proposed terms and conditions of employment. The individual employee then decides whether to accept or refuse those terms, without any reference to any other employees. Hence, an individual bargain is formed.

However, if a group of employees bargain with the employer (typically through representatives), then rather than an individual contract being formed, a single agreement is reached which affects all employees. Hence, collective bargaining is simply the collective equivalent of individual bargaining.

Flanders (1968) criticised the view of Webb and Webb, primarily because he did not agree that it was possible to draw parallels between the process of individual and collective bargaining in the way that they had proposed.

First, Webb and Webb started their comparison by looking at the process of determining an individual contract of hiring labour. Flanders observed that this typically led to a legal contract between the employer and the employee. However, the process of collective bargaining is not related to this determination of a legal contract, rather it is determining a set of rules by which the employment relationship will be governed. Flanders argued, therefore, that collective bargaining was actually a process of regulating the individual bargaining process, rather than replacing it.

Flanders' definition of collective bargaining is, therefore, a process that involves the joint making of procedural rules. Flanders extended the definition of collective bargaining from the hiring of labour, as proposed by Webb and Webb, and saw it as involving everything that is part of avoiding or resolving conflict. The purpose of collective bargaining is to have rules that define the rights of employees in a range of situations including discipline, reward and training. Collective bargaining results in rules that protect employees from discrimination, favouritism and arbitrary decision-making.

The theory proposed by Webb and Webb saw collective bargaining as an economic institution, which Flanders saw as a limited definition. Flanders proposed that collective bargaining is actually a political institution, determining rules to govern the relationship between management and employees.

Blyton and Turnbull (2004) suggest that collective bargaining can be seen as a means of management control. This definition does not seem to fit with the concept of 'collective' bargaining, which suggests some element of joint control. However, as Blyton and Turnbull observe, if the employees refuse to participate in collective bargaining, terms of employment will simply be set unilaterally by the management, hence giving them control of the employment relationship.

A clear and succinct definition of collective bargaining is quoted by Blyton and Turnbull (Goodman 1984):

A process through which representatives of employers and employee organisations act as the joint creators of the substantive and procedural rules regulating employment.

This clear definition draws on the theory proposed by Flanders of agreeing procedural rules, and also emphasises the joint nature of the bargaining process.

This definition leads us on to consider the function of collective bargaining. Chamberlain and Kuhn (1965) list three functions of collective bargaining:

Market or economic function

This is the process of agreeing a price at which labour will be supplied to the organisation, and it affects both present and future employees.

This function of collective bargaining is probably the one that we hear of most in the press. This is because it relates to disputes over pay that are often well reported.

An example we have already cited earlier in this book is that of the Fire Brigades Union seeking a 40 per cent pay increase, which led to industrial action in 2003. The industrial action was a result of the process of collective bargaining breaking down – something we examine further later in this chapter.

Governmental function

This function is the political process in which the agreements that are reached are the rules and laws agreed by the management and employees. Within this function is the grievance process, whereby any differences of interpretation of the rules can be considered, as well as any potential breaches of the rules.

Rules and laws can be interpreted quite widely. For example, the miners' strike of 1984 was primarily about the way in which the mining industry was to be restructured, and hence the bargaining was about the process (the rules) that would be followed to achieve this restructuring.

A more recent example has been seen in the BBC, where there was a day of industrial action in May 2005. This industrial action was a protest against the proposals to cut 3,780 jobs and the associated restructuring of BBC departments.

Decision-making function

This function is the process by which employees (through their representatives) can be involved in making decisions that affect their working lives. This restrains managers from imposing terms unilaterally upon employees.

An example of collective bargaining as a decision-making function is the proposal, made in 2004, to raise the pensionable age of public sector workers from 60 to 65 years, and to base the pension on average earnings during employment within the public sector, rather than on final salary as it currently is calculated.

As we noted in Chapter 3, these proposals resulted in plans for a day of industrial action in March 2005. However the industrial action never occurred because the changes were not implemented as proposed and they were withdrawn for further review.

Try to think of at least one further example of each of the three functions of collective bargaining as defined by Chamberlain and Kuhn.

The definitions of collective bargaining that we have explored so far have all indicated that the final result is agreement. However, it would be wrong to presume that this is a straightforward process. Chamberlain and Kuhn recognised this, and identified two different models of collective bargaining:

Conjunctive bargaining

Conjunctive bargaining is when the two parties reach a final agreement as a result of mutual coercion, and arrive at this final result only because they are indispensable to each other. Chamberlain and Kuhn suggested that in this model, coercion is a dominant feature, and the outcome of the bargaining is a factor of the bargaining power of each party.

Coercion from the side of the employee is likely to be best illustrated by the employees taking industrial action. We explore this more in Chapter 11. Coercion from the side of the employer can be more varied, and can be somewhat subtle (for example withdrawing intangible benefits such as open communication) or quite draconian (for example, threatening significant redundancies if a pay offer is not accepted).

Look through newspapers and websites for examples of coercive bargaining (a good source to try is www.bbc.co.uk/news). At any one time there are usually examples being reported. The examples that you will find are likely to be mostly threats of or actual industrial action, rather than coercion from employers. Why do you think that is?

Co-operative bargaining

Chamberlain and Kuhn suggested that collective bargaining cannot reach the level of co-operative bargaining unless both parties accept that neither will gain further advantages unless the other side gains too. Hence, the central theme of this model of bargaining is the willingness to make concessions. This does not mean that both parties are working towards a common goal, rather they have realised that they will not reach their desired goal unless there is some concession to the demands of the other party.

An excellent example of co-operative bargaining is the conclusion to the industrial action taken by the Fire Brigades Union (FBU) in 2003. As we have already noted, the industrial action occurred after the employers rejected a 40 per cent pay claim from the FBU.

However, the employers wanted something – and that was the modernisation of the fire service. A report was commissioned (known as the Bains Report) which identified many areas of modernisation that needed addressing. Although the FBU largely did not want the modernisation that was proposed, it realised that it would not achieve what it wanted (a significant pay increase) unless it made concessions over the modernisation proposals.

The eventual settlement of the situation was an agreement that involved a 14 per cent pay increase phased over three years, in return for co-operation with a series of modernisation initiatives. At the time when each phase of the pay increase was due, a review took place to consider whether co-operation had taken place – whether the planned modernisation had happened. If it had not, that particular phase of the pay increase was not awarded. Although the employer did not want to give a high pay increase, and the FBU did not want modernisation, the only way that either party was to reach the overall goal was through co-operative bargaining.

THE AIM OF COLLECTIVE BARGAINING

In understanding collective bargaining we have identified that there is some topic that is being discussed by both parties. The topics covered by collective bargaining can be broken down into two main areas, substantive terms and procedural terms.

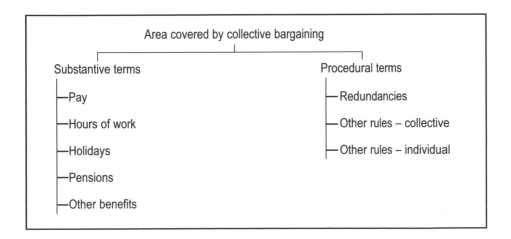

Figure 8.1 The areas covered by collective bargaining

Substantive terms

Substantive terms are possibly the focus of collective bargaining that we would most readily recognise. They are terms that are concerned with the economic terms of the employment relationship. Primarily they are concerned with pay and benefits, and they include bargaining in the following areas:

Pay

This has to be the area of collective bargaining most readily associated with collective bargaining. However, as we shall see in Chapter 9, issues concerning pay are not just about an annual increment to a basic rate. There are also issues such as bonuses, overtime, shift premium, guaranteed payments and so on.

Many organisations participate in bargaining over pay on an annual basis. This is because pay rates are linked to such things as the annual rate of inflation and the performance of the organisation. Both of these factors are not items that can be predicted in the long term. However, entering into pay discussions on an annual basis can be a time-consuming process, and some organisations have entered into longer pay deals in a bid to reduce the time and disruption of annual bargaining.

In October 2004 the workers at Jaguar accepted a pay deal of 6.5 per cent to be paid over two years. This was recommended by the trade union Amicus, as a good deal in the light of impending site closures and associated redundancies.

Another example of a pay deal agreed over a period of time is the deal to settle the fire fighters' strike of 2003. However, the reason for this was quite specific (as detailed earlier in this chapter) – to tie in modernisation progress with increased reward.

Hours of work

In the 1980s the trade union movement ran a general campaign to reduce the working week for manual workers from the typical average at the time of 40 hours to 37 hours per week. The primary reason for this campaign was that non-manual workers typically worked 37 hours per week, and this was part of the overall strategy for harmonisation between the terms of white and blue collar workers. Although a significant amount of harmonisation has been achieved, a survey by *IRS Employment Review* (2004) found that disparities still exist.

The survey found that median working hours are the same for blue and white-collar workers in chemicals, finance, general services, paper and printing, retail and wholesale, and transport and communications. However, there are differences in construction, engineering and metals, food, drink and tobacco, and general manufacturing. The differences are largely small: only in the food sector does the difference amount to more than one hour per week.

The Working Time Regulations 1998 (which we look at in more detail in Chapter 13) gave a maximum working week of 48 hours. However, UK employees are allowed to sign an opt-out from this, hence working more than 48 hours. It is interesting to note that hours of work are still an issue of some contention, despite this legislation. According to the *IRS Employment Review* report, Acas dealt with more than 7,500 disputes relating to working time in the 2003/04 period.

Holidays

The Working Time Regulations 1998 also introduced legislation relating to holidays. All employees are entitled to four weeks' paid annual holiday (which can include statutory holidays). However, in organisations where the annual holiday allowance is at the legal minimum, there could be pressure from employees to bargain for an increase.

Pensions

This is becoming an increasingly relevant issue. Pension funds are governed by strict rules, and it is unlikely that any of these rules could be altered even if both the employer and the employee wanted this to happen. Hence, any bargaining is more likely to be about any proposed alterations to the way that final payments are calculated. (The main difference is between final salary schemes, which are calculated as a percentage of final pay, giving a guaranteed income to employees, and money purchase schemes, which are based on the investment of contributions, and do not give a guaranteed pension income. Final salary schemes are more expensive for employers to run, and there has been a general trend away from them in recent years.) With people living longer the monies taken from pension funds have increased, leading to great concerns over the level of funds in some pension schemes.

ORGANISATION EXAMPLE

In late 2005/early 2006 a number of organisations announced decisions to close final pension schemes. These included Rentokil, the Co-operative Society and Harrods.

Other benefits

Although we have looked at the substantive terms and conditions that are most likely to be the topic of collective bargaining, there are other issues that could be raised. These include all benefits, including issues such as health and safety, sick pay, private medical facilities, leisure benefits (eg gym membership), provision of crèches, company cars and cheap loans.

Procedural terms

Procedural terms are the rules that regulate the employment relationship. It is likely that the rules will be agreed between the employees and employer in the form of a collective agreement (see later in this section) and any attempt to act in variation of these rules is likely to cause conflict. The main issues covered by procedural terms are discussed below.

Redundancies

As we shall explore in Chapter 10, there is detailed legislation governing how redundancies should be handled. However, many organisations also have their own redundancy agreements which add further detail to the basic legal requirements. This might include enhanced benefits to employees affected by redundancies, such as enhanced compensatory pay.

However, most of the disputes that are reported in relation to redundancies are over whether the redundancies should actually take place, rather than the precise handling of the redundancies.

As we noted earlier, in May 2005 employees of the BBC took industrial action over plans to remove 3,780 jobs and over proposals to privatise part of the corporation. The issue here was not over the process of handling redundancies; rather it was over the proposals to make such large numbers of employees redundant.

Other rules – collective

The remainder of the procedural rules can be divided into those that affect individuals, and those that affect employees collectively. Examples of rules that affect the collective group include processes for negotiation and consultation, and processes such as recruitment and selection.

Other rules – individual

The procedural rules that affect the individual include such things as individual grievances, disciplinary proceedings and equal opportunities. On most occasions an individual grievance will not result in any collective action. This is primarily because there is cost involved to individuals of taking industrial action (loss of pay as a minimum) and people will generally be reluctant to take a personal loss over a situation in which they are not personally involved. However, there are occasions when the employees are sufficiently enraged by the actions of the employer against an individual that they will take action.

In November 2003 an employee (who was also a trade union official) working on the London Underground was dismissed after being seen coming out of a squash club. At the time he was absent from work because of a sprained ankle. He appealed against the dismissal, but it was upheld. As a result of this about 100 members of the Rail, Maritime and Transport Union held a 24-hour strike, disrupting part of the London Underground.

COLLECTIVE AGREEMENTS

The agreement that is finally reached through the process of collective bargaining is known as a collective agreement. However, unlike the result of individual bargaining as described by Webb and Webb (an individual contract of employment), a collective agreement is not legally enforceable.

An agreement that is reached at the end of the bargaining process might be confirmed in writing, or it might be verbal. Having the agreement in writing does not affect its legal enforceability.

Although it is true that a collective agreement is not legally enforceable, if terms of employment flow from the agreement and become part of the individual's contract of employment they do become enforceable.

A collective agreement can be incorporated (become part of) a contract of employment by express incorporation or implied incorporation.

Express incorporation

Here there is a clear statement that the employer and employee agree to be bound by a collective agreement. This is typically a statement in the collective agreement that expressly incorporates the collective agreement into the contract of employment. An example of express incorporation is found in the following case.

NCB v Galley (1958)

The pit deputies working for the National Coal Board had contracts of employment that stated that they were regulated by any relevant national agreements. After negotiation with the trade unions a national agreement was revised, and a clause was inserted requiring pit deputies to work on such days as reasonably practicable. This could potentially involve working on Saturdays. Galley refused to work on Saturdays and was held to be in breach of his contract. This was because his contract of employment stated that his employment was governed by national agreements, and hence the revised collective agreement had been expressly incorporated into his contract.

Implied corporation

If there is no express term an alternative is to claim that the collective agreement has been incorporated into a contract of employment by 'implication'. If the employer and employee have always conducted the employment relationship in accordance with the collective agreement, it could be thought to be implied that they have agreed to be bound by that agreement. However, this is less certain than a term that has been expressly incorporated, as the intention to be bound by an agreement can always be challenged.

Campbell v Union Carbide (2002)

Campbell was employed as a chemical plant operator, initially with ICI. ICI entered into a collective agreement with the recognised trade union, which included a clause covering redundancy payments (and was stated to be legally binding) and another clause headed 'discretionary severance in non-redundancy cases'. The part of ICI in which Campbell worked was transferred to Union Carbide Ltd, along with all terms and conditions of employment. After a period of time Campbell was given notice of termination on the grounds of ill health. He claimed that he was entitled to payments under the 'discretionary severance in non-redundancy cases' clause because these payments had been made by the organisation in all previous cases when an employee had been terminated following a lengthy period of sickness absence. Union Carbide refused to make the payment, stressing that the payments were classed as 'discretionary'.

The Employment Appeals Tribunal ruled that, although the payments had always been made, this did not give rise to incorporation by implication or evidence of a contractual term. The important question was whether there was evidence that both parties intended

> the payments to form a term of the contract. Because the payments had specifically been called 'discretionary' payments it ruled that the employer had indicated there was no intention for the payments to be contractual, and hence there was no requirement to make the payments.
>
> The suggestion is, therefore, that if the payments had not been specifically stated as being discretionary, and had always been paid in such circumstances, the terms of the collective agreement could have been seen to become part of the contract of employment through implication.

Given that there is no guarantee that the terms of a collective agreement can be enforced, one has to question why it is worth going through the process of collective bargaining to reach an agreement. In answering this there has to be an evaluation of the alternatives. Hollinshead and Leat (1995) report that in many other countries collective agreements are enforceable, with penalties being imposed if either side reneges on the deal. However, as Lewis *et al* (2003) note, the topics covered by collective agreements usually relate to dynamic and continuous processes. If no lifetime was fixed on a collective agreement (as would surely be required if the agreement was being legally imposed), then there could be less responsiveness to change in the organisation, or the parties will be forced to renegotiate an agreement that is still fit for purpose. Given this, some would argue that the current situation of collective agreements being legally unenforceable actually has advantages.

It is also relevant to refer back to the two models of bargaining defined by Chamberlain and Kuhn (1965), coercive and co-operative. If one party reneges on a deal the other party still has the sanction of coercion, however that might be applied. Alternatively, if both parties have identified mutual gains from reaching agreement, one could argue that they are unlikely to renege on any resulting collective agreement.

THE STRUCTURE OF COLLECTIVE BARGAINING

The structure that is applied to collective bargaining will affect the remit of the bargaining, and will also help determine which bargaining process affects which employees. In looking at the structure we need to consider several aspects.

Scope

As we shall see in Chapter 11, there is a process defined in law through which trade union representatives and employers must proceed in order for a trade union to be recognised for bargaining purposes. Once that recognition has been achieved, a further decision is the scope of the issues that will be covered by the bargaining process. It is incorrect to presume that once a recognition agreement has been reached, the trade union representatives have the right to bargain on any issue. Some agreements will be focused on just one issue, such as pay, although most will have a much broader remit.

Units

Once the topics that will be covered by the bargaining process have been identified, the next stage is to identify which employees the bargaining process covers. As we shall see in Chapter 11, an important part of the recognition process is identifying which employees form part of a 'bargaining unit'.

In some organisations, particularly those with diverse ranges of skills and employment groups, there could be a large number of bargaining units. Bargaining units will usually fit around logical differences in the terms and conditions of employment for employees. For example, if an organisation employs manual workers on a productivity-related bonus scheme there are likely to be different issues to be discussed within the bargaining process compared with white-collar workers paid according to salary bands. However, this demarcation between working groups has declined as a result of the harmonisation of terms and conditions between management and non-management employees. As a result of this harmonisation many of the issues that previously related to just one employment group can now be applied to all employment groups in an organisation. According to WERS 1998 only 28 per cent of the 45 per cent of workplaces that recognised trade unions for collective bargaining conducted negotiations with more than one bargaining unit.

Representation

The number of bargaining units in organisations has also been affected by the merger of trade unions. In organisations where there have traditionally been a number of craft unions representing specific areas of employment, there has been a merger of bargaining units as trade unions have merged.

However, it should not be presumed that large organisations are increasingly negotiating with just one trade union. Indeed, according to Burchill (1997), there are over 40 trade unions in the NHS.

Levels

Collective bargaining can be carried out at a number of different levels, from multi-employer down to organisational level. We shall explore the various levels:

Multi-employer
Multi-employer bargaining, also known as industry-wide or national bargaining, is where the agreement is negotiated between trade unions at a national level and employers' associations.

ORGANISATION EXAMPLE

In May 2005 it was reported that UK higher education employers had offered an annual pay increase of 3 per cent to all staff. This offer was made by the Universities and Colleges Employers Association to a group of three trade unions which were working together representing the higher education employees (Natfhe, the National Association of Teachers in Further and Higher Education, AUT, the Association of University Teachers, and the Educational Institute of Scotland).

The pay offer was initially rejected, although agreement was finally reached. However, the point being illustrated here is the level of bargaining, between an employers' association, and a group of trade unions operating at national level.

The advantages to the employer of operating multi-level bargaining are:

- There is a sharing of the resources required to go through the bargaining process.
- It gives standard minimum terms and conditions to employees in a particular sector.
- It leaves local management free to address local business issues.

The advantages to employees of operating multi-level bargaining are:

- They are also able to share the required resources for the bargaining process.
- It gives fairer treatment of employees throughout the particular sector. (Employers have to provide the minimum terms and conditions. However there can be a perception of unfairness if some employers choose to operate above the minimum while others do not.)
- It provides a 'safety net'. Elliott (1981) notes that it gives a minimum level of terms and conditions below which no employee should fall.
- They have more force if negotiating as one large body.

However, there are also significant disadvantages. For employers:

- They might have to pay more as a result of national negotiations than if they had bargained at a local level.
- Some employers could be forced to pay more than they can really afford.
- It ignores the local labour markets.

For employees:

- There is less opportunity to focus on local issues.

According to the *Workplace Employee Relations Survey 1998* in 1980 multi-employer bargaining affected 43 per cent of all workplaces. By 1998 just 14 per cent of workplaces were affected by multi-employer bargaining. Within the private sector just 4 per cent of workplaces were covered by multi-employer bargaining.

It can be concluded, therefore, that most of the multi-employer bargaining that does still exist occurs within the public sector. Sectors such as the banking industry and the transport industry that did negotiate at multi-employer level in the past have now moved to single employer bargaining, because of increased competition and deregulation.

Single-employer

Single-employer bargaining, or company bargaining, is where all pay and conditions are negotiated at employer level, in either single-site or multisite organisations (Farnham 2000). Although single-employer bargaining might appear to exist in an organisation, there is the possibility that there is actually split-level bargaining. For example, issues such as policy on benefits (eg pensions, company cars, medical insurance) might be decided at the employer level. However, issues such as pay, shift patterns and similar matters might be decided at site level.

As Salamon (2000) notes, a big advantage of single-employer bargaining is that the terms and conditions are decided by people at the local level, rather than those who are remote from the situation. This results in management and employees becoming more committed to and responsible for the agreements that they reach.

However, if there is some bargaining happening at employer level and some at site level, there can be fragmentation and it can result in something of a lottery for the employees. Their terms and conditions of employment can become affected by the ability of their representatives to bargain, rather than be governed in accordance to overall company policy.

Workplace bargaining

This is where bargaining takes place at the most local level, typically the site at where each group of employees is based. Workplace bargaining is either autonomous or co-ordinated. Autonomous bargaining is where the site has total freedom to reach an agreement on terms and conditions, without referral to any higher level. Co-ordinated bargaining is where the workplace bargaining is restricted to limits that have been set at a higher level.

The advantages of workplace bargaining are that it is typically much more transparent to the employees. There is much more ability to understand what has taken place and why. It also allows management to respond to local situations, and to react flexibly. Because of the personal involvement of local representatives and local management, there is likely to be much more commitment to the final agreement that is reached.

The disadvantages are that it presumes that the representatives and management at local level have the necessary skills to successfully carry out the bargaining process. It can be more difficult to control the overall costs, especially during pay negotiations if there are claims for pay parity with other groups of employees.

As we have already noted, sectors such as banking once conducted collective bargaining at multi-employer level, but now operate at single-employer level. This removal of bargaining to a more local level is known as decentralisation. As Bridgford and Stirling (1994) note, decentralisation is not just specific to the move from multi to single-employer-level bargaining. It is moving from any broader bargaining group to a narrower group. So, for example, moving from single-employer bargaining to workplace bargaining is also a process of decentralisation.

Decentralisation in the UK was encouraged by the Conservative government of 1979–97, which was strongly committed to the concept of a free market. It saw, therefore, that multi-employer-level bargaining was actually a way of interfering with the freedom of organisations to make decisions (Fatchett 1989).

It is certainly true that employers have been keen to pursue decentralisation of bargaining, whereas trade unions have often been reluctant. To understand this we can refer back to the advantages and disadvantages of multi-employer bargaining. Here we can see that the advantage to the trade unions of having more force through negotiating as one group is taken away by decentralisation. This gives a clear indication of their potential disquiet with decentralisation, and also suggests why the employer might be keen to pursue it.

ACTIVITIES

Find out how bargaining is conducted in the organisation in which you work, or an organisation with which you are familiar. Has this process of bargaining been used for many years? If so, what are the advantages of the approach? If it has changed, what were the reasons for that change?

THE USE OF COLLECTIVE BARGAINING

As we noted in Chapter 6, trade union membership in the UK has declined steadily since the 1970s. Collective bargaining is primarily related to bargaining between trade unions and employers, and hence it is logical that collective bargaining has declined alongside trade union membership.

Table 8.1 Overall collective bargaining coverage, by broad sector and union recognition 1984–98

	Percentage of employees covered by collective bargaining			Percentage rate of decline per annum	
	1984	1990	1998	1984–90	1990–8
All workplaces	70	54	40	-2.9	-3.3
Broad sector:					
Private manufacturing	64	51	46	-2.6	-1.3
Private services	40	33	21	-2.3	-4.7
Public sector	95	78	62	-2.3	-2.6

Source: Gennard and Judge (2005).

Table 8.1 demonstrates this decline in collective bargaining.

As Table 8.1 shows, the area with the highest coverage of employees by collective bargaining is the public sector. The private sector is the area with the lowest coverage. This broadly relates to trade union membership patterns.

Although Table 8.1 shows the percentage of employees covered by collective bargaining, it is wrong to assume that the primary activities of trade union representatives are collective bargaining. WERS 1998 asked trade union representatives which of six duties they spent most time on, and which they considered to be most important. Tables 8.2 and 8.3 shows the results.

It is interesting to note that, although substantive terms might be presumed to be the primary concern of trade union representatives, they actually spend more time on other issues, and identified other issues as being more important.

Table 8.2 Activities judged by trade union representatives to be most important

Maintaining wages and benefits	20%
Job security	23%
Treatment of employees by management	27%
Health and safety	21%
Resolving disputes	6%
Improving workplace performance	4%

Table 8.3 Activities that trade union representatives had spent any time on during the past 12 months

Maintaining wages and benefits	48%
Job security	48%
Treatment of employees by management	63%
Health and safety	64%
Resolving disputes	44%
Improving workplace performance	37%
None of these	13%

ACTIVITIES

Try to find a trade union representative who is willing to talk about his/her activities. Ask the representative what s/he spends most time on, and what issues are seen to be most important. Try to understand why certain issues are deemed to be so important.

NEGOTIATION

The primary skill within collective bargaining is negotiation. Salamon (2000) suggests that there are four essential characteristics of negotiation:

- It is an explicit and deliberate event.
- It is conducted by representatives on behalf of those that they represent.
- The purpose of the process is to reconcile the differences between the parties involved.
- The outcome is dependent, at least in part, on the perceived balance of power in the relationship between the two parties.

Gennard and Judge (2005) identify some specific features of negotiation that are relevant to the employee relations situation:

- The negotiations involve an ongoing relationship. In a commercial negotiation the relationship might only last for the period of agreeing the sale (although with large accounts an ongoing relationship is developed). However, within employee relationships the people who are negotiating also have to work together each day once the negotiations are over. This can act as a restraining influence on both the style and the content of the negotiations.
- The negotiations are always carried out by representatives. This can add some element of difficulty, particularly if there is a suspicion that the representative is pursuing a personal objective, rather than giving a true representation of the views of the group.
- The negotiations are carried out on a face-to-face basis. In many commercial relationships part, or even all, of the negotiation process is conducted over the telephone or

through other communication methods. The face-to-face element of employee relations bargaining makes it much more personal, and engenders a greater sense of personal responsibility for the outcomes. As a result of this face-to-face approach employee relations negotiating typically involves more adjournments for the negotiating party to discuss the progress of the negotiations.

■ The negotiations do not result in legally enforceable contracts. As we have already noted, the collective agreement that is the usual end of the collective bargaining process is not legally enforceable. Hence, there is a need for a significant amount of trust between the two parties that the agreement will be honoured. This is different from commercial negotiations where the detailed agreements are usually written as part of a legally enforceable contract.

■ The negotiations have to end in an agreement. If there is a commercial negotiation, maybe about buying or selling a product, the negotiations can end without an agreement if a price cannot be agreed. However, in an employee relations negotiation it is not possible to walk away from something such as a pay negotiation just because an agreement has not been reached. There has to be a conclusion to the discussions.

Gennard and Judge (2005) suggest that there is a five-stage process that needs to be worked through for a successful negotiation to take place. In explaining the process of negotiation we shall work through those five stages, and to illustrate the process we shall apply each stage to a pay negotiation:

■ preparation and analysis
■ presentation
■ searching for and identifying common ground
■ concluding the agreement
■ writing up the agreement.

Preparation and analysis

Of all the stages in the negotiation this stage is probably the most crucial. Part of the process of preparation is to research the situation so that clear facts are available to the negotiating team. However, it is also important to think about the likely response of the other party, and how this will be addressed. Torrington (1972) suggested that there is a need to think about counter-attack and attack, defence as well as initiative.

A crucial part of this presentation is determining, with the co-operation of the other party, the topic of the bargaining. This is typically achieved through the process of agreeing an agenda of the topics to discuss. This is an important process because the negotiation will progress much more smoothly if both parties are focusing on the same issues.

Within the preparation process it is also important to determine who should be in the negotiating group. It is usual to have an odd number of negotiators, because then there will always be a majority vote if there is disagreement. It is also important to determine the leader of the group, and to decide whether the other group members will actually speak in the negotiations – and if they are to speak how any disagreement between the members will be handled.

In thinking about the composition of the group it is useful to refer back to the team types that were identified by Belbin (1981) – see Chapter 5. It is important that someone is identified to be the leader, someone is identified to take notes and someone is identified to research the issues. If these roles are not clearly identified there is the danger that some tasks within the negotiation process can be ignored.

It is important to gather information to support the negotiation process. In a pay negotiation the type of information that is required is:

- the rate of inflation
- the rate at which recent pay claims have been settled, compared with the rate of inflation
- salary survey information giving data relating to pay rates for similar jobs in the locality
- the budget that has been allowed for these negotiations, and the degree of flexibility that exists in operating this budget
- any information that has been gleaned about the realistic expectations of employees
- other issues that could be used as part of the negotiation (for example, instead of giving the pay increase that is requested, would employees be satisfied to achieve a lower pay increase with a reduction in working hours, or the introduction of a different shift pattern?)
- profitability of the organisation, which will partly determine the ability of the organisation to meet an increased pay demand
- predictions of future performance of the organisation (if a high pay increase is agreed, will the organisation be able to meet this cost on a longer-term basis?).

Once the information has been gathered the next stage is to analyse this data and to use it to plan the negotiations. Salamon (2000) sees a crucial part of this process as identifying the bargaining zone, the difference between the pay increase the management want to achieve and the maximum pay increase they are prepared to consider.

The information should also be used to determine the minimum offer. The negotiations can be soured by the employer starting with a pay offer that is seen as derisory. All offers must be realistic to both sides of the negotiation.

An important part of this analytical process is trying to identify the issues that are really part of the negotiation, and their importance to both parties. One structured way of achieving this analysis is through the use of an aspiration grid. An example of an aspiration grid is given in Table 8.4.

Table 8.4 Aspiration grid

Items for negotiation	Management			Employees		
	Ideal	Real	Fallback	Fallback	Real	Ideal
Basic rate increase of 2.5 per cent	X	X	X	O	O	X
Introduction of productivity bonus	X	X	O	X	X	X
Increase in holiday entitlement	X	O	O	X	X	X
Changes to parental leave	X	O	O	O	O	X
Retention of no-strike clause	X	X	X	O	X	X

Source: Gennard and Judge (2005).

In devising an aspiration grid the first stage is to identify all the issues that are part of the negotiation, and list them down the left-hand side. The next step is to consider whether either party is prepared to 'trade' that item. An 'X' denotes that the party is not prepared to trade, and an 'O' denotes that the party is prepared to trade.

The next step is to identify at which stage the trade might take place. This is divided into ideal, real and fallback.

Hence, the first line of the aspiration grid shown above shows that management will not trade on a basic rate increase of 2.5 per cent. The employees ideally will not trade on a basic rate increase of 2.5 per cent, but realistically they will trade – and they will also trade as a fallback position. This suggests that management will not give more than a 2.5 per cent pay increase whatever the pressure. Ideally the employees want to trade on this and achieve a higher pay increase. However, realistically they realise that they will not achieve more than a 2.5 per cent increase and they will accept it.

The third line of the aspiration grid shows us that management will not trade on an increase in holiday entitlement in an ideal situation. However, both realistically and as a fallback position they will trade on an increase in holiday entitlement. The employees will not trade on an increase in holiday entitlement in any situation. This suggests that the employees are determined to achieve an increase in holiday entitlement. Ideally the management would not give an increase in holiday entitlement, but they accept that realistically they will have to.

It is difficult to draw up an aspiration grid because it is not known what items the other party are prepared to trade, and at what level. However, the rigour of completing an aspiration grid does mean that all of the negotiating group have a clear understanding of their own position, and it forces them to think carefully about the expectations of the other party. In doing this there is a better opportunity to plan the attack, counter-attack, defence and initiative as suggested by Torrington.

Presentation

Once the parties have researched the information they need to prepare for the negotiations, the next stage is to meet together and make initial presentations. It is usual for the party requesting the negotiations to give a presentation first. In the case of a pay negotiation it is likely that this will be the trade union representatives, because they will have made a pay claim.

The primary objective of this stage is to set out the key issues and to try to understand the key issues as the other party sees them. An important part of the tactical positioning is deciding how much to say. If one gives too much detail it is possible that the negotiating position will be compromised. However, if too little is said it could just be a source of irritation to the other party, and could result in the negotiations starting with a negative attitude.

Torrington and Hall (2002) suggest that negative attitudes can be increased if there is a greater differential between the power bases of the two parties. Power does, indeed, have an important impact on the negotiation process.

If we refer back to the types of power (see Chapter 4) that were identified by French and Raven (1958) we can see how power will impact on the process. If there is a perception from the employees that the management negotiators have reward power, they are more likely to believe the negotiation process has a purpose. If they do not believe the negotiators have the power to determine reward, they will not see that they are negotiating with people who truly have any influence.

ORGANISATION
EXAMPLE

We have already seen how this can confuse a negotiation when we looked at the fire strike of 2003. As we have already noted, at one stage a deal was agreed between the Fire Brigades Union and the local employers, but it was vetoed by the deputy prime minister (acting as the government representative). This then damaged the further negotiations because the FBU no longer believed that the negotiating team had any reward power, and hence saw the negotiations as relatively pointless.

If the management are seen to have legitimate power, the employee negotiating group might be reluctant to argue strongly during the negotiation process. This is because there is the perception that those with legitimate power have the right to make decisions, even if they are disliked. Hence, if a pay offer is made that is not what is wanted, the employees might be reluctant to argue because of the perceived legitimate power. In the same way, they might be reluctant to argue if they perceive that the management have some form of expert power, and believe that they are in no position to argue with the management.

If the perception is that management have referent power, the employees might find themselves agreeing with the management's point of view because the leader is particularly persuasive and is able to influence them easily. Alternatively, they might perceive that management have coercive power and might be fearful of arguing too strongly because of potential repercussions on them.

Hence, although the presentation stage is partly about tactics we also see how the relative power bases of the two parties can have a significant effect on how the negotiations proceed.

Identifying common ground

Once the initial positions have been shared the next stage is to try to identify common ground. In understanding how this can be achieved we can refer back to the aspiration grid. In the preparation stage the two parties have tried to guess the negotiating stance of the other side. As the negotiations proceed they start to have a clearer idea of the negotiating stance, and might need to revise their completion of the grid.

An important part of this is to identify if there are any issues that are not worth discussing, because neither party is willing to 'trade' them. Hence, any item that has an 'X' in the fallback column for both the employees and the management is not worth pursuing, because what the grid is illustrating is that neither party is prepared to move on that issue.

Gennard and Judge (2005) define negotiation as involving purposeful persuasion and constructive compromise. In searching for the common ground it is these two processes that are being enacted.

It is also important to remember one of the features of employee relations negotiations that we identified at the start of this process: the negotiation has to result in some form of agreement. Hence, it is important that both parties accept that there is likely to be the need for some level of compromise in order for an agreement to be reached.

ORGANISATION EXAMPLE

As we have already noted, in 2004 the government announced proposals to raise the pensionable age of public sector workers from 60 to 65 years, and to base the pension on average earnings during employment within the public sector, rather than on final salary as it currently is calculated. The government said that this approach was fairer for the lower-paid employees, and not a cost saving measure.

The trade unions involved (PCS, Amicus, UNISON and TGWU) all reacted strongly against these proposals and planned a day of strike action. However, because of the sensitive timing (the day of strike action would have been just before the General Election) and the strength of feeling, the proposals were withdrawn and further talks were planned.

Here we see a situation where the trade unions were faced with an issue over which they were not prepared to compromise. Compromising within employee relations typically involves both parties giving way on something. The unions were not being offered anything in return for the changes to the pension system, and hence they did not see that they were gaining anything from the proposals. If they had agreed to the proposals they would have seen it as giving in rather than compromising.

The strategy adopted by the two parties will also influence how successful they are in reaching the common ground. If both parties adopt a 'win-win' strategy the process is likely to be more successful. A 'win-win' strategy is when both parties adopt a positive attitude and look to resolve the conflict in a way that will benefit both parties (Greenhalgh 1986). Alternatively, there can be the adoption of a 'win-lose' strategy where the focus is on winning through the process of defeating the other party. Adopting a 'win-win' strategy will lead to more positive long-term employment relationships, because whatever the parties achieve in the negotiating process, there is a greater perception that it has been fair and constructive.

Daft (1998) also identifies the relevance of superordinate goals. A superordinate goal is the overall goal of the organisation, and it requires the co-operation of all groups of employees in order to achieve it. Hence, in thinking about the position of each side in the negotiation it is also for each side to think about how their position affects the overall success (even survival) of the organisation. Employees might want a significantly higher pay increase, but if the result of the increased cost to the organisation is that its survival is threatened, the pursuit of the individual goals might actually result in an overall negative result.

Concluding an agreement

At some stage one of the parties has to say that it is not prepared to negotiate any more, that it has reached its final offer, or has reached the final proposal it is prepared to accept. If it is management that is taking that stance, it is very important to judge the situation carefully. If management says it is making a final pay offer, and then increases it a short time later when faced with the threat of a ballot for industrial action, there is the very real possibility that the trade unions will sense that there is yet more to achieve, and hence will continue the pressure for an increased offer.

We explore the issue of industrial action and the associated legislation in detail in Chapter 11.

However, it is important to note at this stage that, if the employee representatives are not content with the final offer that has been made, this is an option that is open to them. As we shall see in Chapter 11, before any industrial action can take place there must be a ballot of all the employees who are affected. In many cases the management will wait for the results of that ballot before it considers whether it is prepared to reconsider the final offer. Of course, it is always possible that the employees will vote to accept the offer that has been made, despite the recommendations of their representatives – and it is also possible that there will be only a very small minority in favour of industrial action, which reduces the power of the representatives significantly.

Writing up the agreement

Although we have already noted that a collective agreement is not legally enforceable, the last stage of writing the agreement is important, so that both parties understand what has been agreed. Even when both sides believe that they have reached an agreement, there is the potential for there to be misunderstandings over the detail within it.

ACTIVITIES

We all negotiate. Some of us who work in a sales environment are negotiating on a regular basis. Think of a situation you have negotiated – over the price of an item, where to take your holidays, what to do at the weekend. What approach have you taken to the negotiation? What power bases were evident in the negotiation? Did you adopt a 'win-win' strategy or a 'win-lose' strategy? How could you improve your approach to negotiation?

WHY ARE AGREEMENTS NOT ALWAYS REACHED WITHOUT CONFLICT?

Although we have already acknowledged that an agreement has to be reached, there are a number of occasions when the agreement is not reached before some sort of conflict is encountered. What factors might mean that the negotiation process does not run smoothly?

Abuse of power

We have already revised the types of power as identified by French and Raven (1958). If management abuses that power and uses it to stifle the negotiations there is the possibility that an agreement is not reached because the discussions are not full and frank.

Goal incompatibility

Daft (1998) suggests that goal incompatibility is probably the greatest cause of conflict between groups in the negotiation process. If the overall goal of management is to cut costs, and the overall goal of the employees is to achieve an increase in pay, the two goals are incompatible. Hence, other routes need to be considered to achieve the goals of both parties. Is there a way that the pay increase can be paid for by productivity increases, or can costs be cut elsewhere?

External factors

As we saw in Chapter 2, employment relationships do not exist in a vacuum, they are affected by the external environment. For example, following the tragic events of 9/11 2001 any negotiations between employees and management of airline companies had to change focus to become about survival, rather than about increased benefits.

No clear decision-maker

As we have already noted, in the case of the 2003 fire fighters' strike the negotiations ran into difficulties because it was not clear who, on the side of management, was actually making the decisions. If one party perceives that it is not talking to the actual decision-maker it might not see the point of continuing with the negotiations.

Unreasonable expectations

Many would point to the claim of the FBU, which precipitated the 2003 fire fighters' strike, as being an example of unreasonable expectations. The initial pay claim of 40 per cent was seen by many as being completely unreasonable. However, one could question whether the FBU ever really expected to achieve anything near 40 per cent. Arguably it considered that it needed to start with an excessively high claim to indicate its seriousness about achieving a settlement that was much higher than inflation.

Psychological contract breached

If the employees perceive that management has breached the psychological contract, there is a possibility that the basic trust within the relationship has broken down. If trust has broken down, negotiations are unlikely to be successful, particularly in the stage of identifying the common ground, because each party is less likely to trust the information it is receiving from the other side.

Rogue leaders

There are occasions when either party might have a leader to the negotiations who is not truly representing the views of the party. If the leader is pursuing a personal agenda, the negotiations are likely to break down.

Management style

If we look back to the management styles that we explored in Chapter 4, we can see how the democratic and laissez-faire styles of management might lead to more successful negotiations than the authoritarian style.

Subordinate style

If we look back to the subordinate styles that we explored in Chapter 5, we can see how the reciprocating and self-reliant style might find negotiating with management an easier process than would informative, collaborative and receptive employees.

KEY POINTS FROM THIS CHAPTER

- Collective bargaining is a process through which representatives of employers and employee organisations act as the joint creators of the substantive and procedural rules regulating employment.
- The three functions of collective bargaining are market/economic, governmental and decision-making.

- Conjunctive bargaining is when the end result is determined by the parties being indispensable to each other.
- Co-operative bargaining is characterised by compromise on both sides.
- Substantive terms are the economic terms of the employment relationship.
- Procedural terms are the rules that regulate the employment relationship.
- Collective agreements are not legally enforceable, unless they become incorporated into the contract of employment.
- The structure of collective bargaining is affected by the scope of the bargaining, the definition of the bargaining units and the nature of the representation.
- Bargaining can take place at different levels: multi-employer, single employer and workplace negotiations.
- Negotiation is explicit and deliberate, is conducted through representatives and has the purpose of resolving conflict.
- Negotiation is a process with a number of stages: preparation and analysis, presentation, identifying common ground, concluding the agreement and writing the agreement.
- Negotiation can fail through abuse of power, goal incompatibility, external factors, there being no decision-maker, unreasonable expectations, the psychological contract being breached, rogue leaders, management styles and subordinate styles.

EXAMPLES TO WORK THROUGH

1. Search in the newspapers or on the Internet for two recent examples of collective bargaining. Research the situation to understand how it has arisen, and why collective bargaining is being used. At what level is collective bargaining taking place? What is the scope of the bargaining?
2. For the two examples of collective bargaining that you researched in response to the last question, try to write an aspiration grid summarising the negotiating stance of each of the parties.
3. Prepare for a pay claim that has been made by the employee representatives in your organisation. Identify the information that you will need, and where possible source this information.

(Suggestions of answers to the examples can be accessed by tutors at www.cipd.co.uk/tss)

CASE STUDY

PCB Ltd is a manufacturing organisation based in the Greater Manchester area. Its primary operation is the manufacture of electronic products, mainly printed circuit boards. The products it makes are used by a range of white goods manufacturers.

PCB Ltd has 2,500 employees, 78 per cent of whom are in a trade union. The trade union is recognised for collective bargaining purposes. The organisation has recently been involved in the annual pay negotiations, and has now reached stalemate. The trade unions do not think that a fair offer has been made, and the organisation is not prepared to offer any more.

The current situation is that PCB Ltd has offered:

- 3 per cent increase on base pay
- 1 per cent to be distributed in performance-related pay
- a 38-hour week.

However, the trade union is requesting:

- 8 per cent increase on base pay
- no bonus schemes of any sort
- 37-hour week (to finish at 1 pm on a Friday)
- review of holiday allowance.

The following are important statistics that have been agreed by both parties:

- The current pay bill is £50 million.
- The anniversary date for pay reviews is 1 April each year.
- The current levels of pay are equal to the local median.
- Inflation is currently 3 per cent.
- Past increases have been:
  - 2004 = 4 per cent (inflation = 3.5 per cent)
  - 2003 = 2 per cent (inflation = 2.2 per cent)
  - 2002 = 3 per cent (inflation = 3.0 per cent)
- The terms and conditions at PCB Ltd are fully harmonised.
- There are 25 days' holiday per year, plus 8 bank holidays.
- Sick pay is paid in full for six months after three years' service.
- There is no company maternity/paternity pay.
- The standard hours are 39 per week.
- There is no bonus system.
- The weekly working pattern is:
  - Monday–Thursday 7.30 am–12 noon; 12.30 pm–4 pm
  - Friday 7.30 am–12 noon; 12.30 pm–3 pm.
- The average age of the employees is 33 years.
- The average length of service for the employees is 7.8 years.
- The male:female ratio is 61:39.
- Staff turnover is 5 per cent.
- Recruitment is reasonably easy, apart from some key skills.

Questions

a) Draw up an aspiration grid showing the expectations of either side.
b) Explain what the aspiration grid tells you about the best way to try to resolve the negotiations.

c) You are the manager leading the negotiation team for PCB Ltd. You have been told very clearly that the value of your current offer must not be exceeded. Suggest a number of different ways that you could spend the money, which might come closer to meeting the requirements of the employees.

(Note: If you are studying employee relations with a number of fellow students you might find it interesting to carry out this case study as a role play. Divide into two groups – trade union representatives and management representatives – and carry out the negotiation!)

Resolving Individual Grievances

CHAPTER 9

> The objectives of this chapter are to:
>
> - explore why individual grievances occur in organisations
> - consider the most common types of grievances that occur
> - outline the requirements of the Statutory Grievance Procedure
> - consider the specific issues of harassment and bullying
> - analyse the history of employment tribunals
> - consider the impact of employment tribunals on the employment relationship
> - consider the future of employment tribunals.

At the end of Chapter 8 we considered why the process of collective bargaining and negotiation sometimes ends in conflict. In this chapter we look at this issue in more detail, with particular focus on conflicts between the organisation and the individual employee. In the second half of this chapter we examine the particular role of the employment tribunal in resolving conflicts between employees and the employer.

GRIEVANCES IN THE EMPLOYMENT RELATIONSHIP

In Chapter 8, when we looked at the issues associated with collective bargaining, we were focusing on conflict between groups of employees and the employer. However, not all conflict in the organisation involves groups of employees. There are also situations where individual employees experience conflict with the employer.

An employee can express conflict in a number of ways. According to Gennard and Judge (2005), the impact of conflict can be shown in the following ways:

- employee frustration
- deteriorating interpersonal relationships
- low morale
- poor performance, resulting in lower productivity and/or a poorer quality to output or service
- disciplinary problems, including poor performance by employees
- resignation and loss of good staff
- increased employee absenteeism
- withdrawal of employee goodwill
- resistance to change.

All these factors have a negative impact on the employment relationship, and hence there is a clear business case for trying to resolve such conflict quickly.

The top 10 grievances that were raised by employees, according to the Industrial Relations Services 2002 survey, are listed in Table 9.1.

Table 9.1 Top 10 grievances

Complaint	Percentage of employees making complaint
Harassment/bullying	45
Discipline	27
New working practices	23
Grading	22
Discrimination	18
Work allocation/staffing levels	17
Non-pay terms and conditions	17
Pay	15
Health and safety	2
Miscellaneous	18

ACTIVITIES

Find out what issues have been raised as grievances in the organisation in which you work, or an organisation with which you are familiar. Why do you think that these issues have been of particular concern in that organisation?

It is too simplistic, however, to suggest that addressing the issues listed above will lead directly to a reduction in the negative impacts on the employment relationship that we listed earlier. It is quite possible that the grievance that is being expressed is the main concern, or the concern that is at the forefront of the mind at that particular time. However, the negative impacts on the employment relationship are likely to be attributed to a much broader negative attitude to the organisation.

Attitudes are behavioural and cognitive tendencies expressed by evaluating particular people, places or things with favour or disfavour (Eagly and Chaiken 1993). Hence, if the employee evaluates a specific aspect of the workplace and comes up with an overall negative impression, there will be a negative reaction to the organisation.

Eagly and Chaiken went on to find that the link between attitudes and behaviours is not always predictable. The link depends on the strength of the attitudes. Hence, if we go back to our list of grievances above, if an employee feels very strongly that new working practices are unfair he/she is more likely to exhibit the negative behaviours listed at the start of this section, than if he/she just finds the new working practices mildly inconvenient.

Hence, in resolving grievances within the workplace there are two approaches that the employer needs to take. In some cases there is the need to eliminate the issue (for example, with bullying and harassment). However in other cases it will not be feasible to eliminate the issue (for example, new working practices), and in this case it is important to attempt to change the attitude.

One way in which employers can attempt to do this is through linking the source of the negative attitudes with positive stimuli. Lohr and Staats (1973) showed that the words used when communicating could influence attitudes. Presenting new working practices in a positive way, emphasising the benefits that they will bring, is more likely to foster positive attitudes towards the change than just presenting the facts.

Research has also shown that the nature of the communicator can have an impact. If the person communicating the news about new working practices is characterised by trustworthiness, expertise, attractiveness or similarity to those who are listening to the message, the audience is more likely to be persuaded that the proposals are acceptable (Wilder 1990).

As we saw earlier, employees are likely to conform to group norms. Hence, if one employee has a negative reaction to something it could be effective to group that employee with others who are positive about the proposal. Not only is this likely to help change the attitude, but some of the positive aspects of the proposals could be communicated.

However, despite attempts to change attitudes there will still be occasions when employees feel sufficiently strongly about a situation that they will decide to raise a grievance.

The general attitude to work is typically measured through looking at job satisfaction. Although it cannot be said that all those who are satisfied have no grievances, it is likely that there is some link between having no grievances and an overall feeling of job satisfaction.

In the Workplace Employment Relations Survey (WERS) 1998, 60 per cent of employees surveyed expressed themselves as being satisfied in their jobs. There were significant differences in levels of job satisfaction in relation to the employees' ages, the hours they worked and their occupations. Job satisfaction increased with age, with 73 per cent of those aged 60 years and over expressing satisfaction, compared with just half of those aged less than 20.

Of part-time workers, 62 per cent expressed satisfaction, compared with 51 per cent of full-time workers. The most satisfied group were those working less than 10 hours per week. One reason for this is that the job is a smaller part of life for those working shorter hours, and hence issues do not reach the same level of dissatisfaction as they do for those whose job is a major part of their life.

In the case of managers, 71 per cent were satisfied, which was higher than other occupational groups. The lowest was those working in operative and assembly jobs, where satisfaction was only 40 per cent. This might be because the lower individuals are in the organisation, the less they feel that they have personal control over what is happening, and the less ability they have to change things that are causing them dissatisfaction.

It is also interesting to note the link between job satisfaction and elements of the employment relationship. The two most significant indicators were the level of commitment: 73 per cent of those who were satisfied had a high level of commitment to the organisation. Also, 90 per cent of those who were satisfied considered that they were consulted about changes in the workplace. This suggests that those who have grievances are likely to be less committed to the organisation, and also suggests that consulting with employees will help to stop grievances developing.

Given this link between satisfaction and elements of the employment relationship it is interesting to look in more detail at particular aspects of the relationship. Guest and Conway (2004) carried out a survey into employee well-being and the psychological contract. Among their findings were the following:

- 26 per cent stated that they receive little support from their supervisor.
- 11 per cent said they received little support from their colleagues.
- Only 2 per cent said that relationships with their colleagues were not good.
- 13 per cent had experienced bullying or harassment in the past year.
- 4 per cent are unclear about their duties and responsibilities.
- 45 per cent said they had to do things one way when they believe they should be done differently.
- 17 per cent said they were unable to participate in or contribute to changes at work that affect them.

The analysis of the survey went on to look at the links between these factors and stress in the work-place. However, what is of interest to us here is the potential dissatisfaction that employees might experience as a result of these factors. As we have already noted, if employees are dissatisfied they are more likely to raise grievances in the workplace.

To understand the levels of satisfaction among employees a lot of organisations carry out regu-lar (typically annual) attitude surveys. By identifying the key areas of dissatisfaction they can try to improve these areas and hence attempt to make attitudes at work more positive. However, if organisations carry out attitude surveys and do not take any action as a result of the findings, they are likely to increase dissatisfaction, because they have raised employees' expectations by carrying out the survey.

The likelihood of employees having a negative attitude to work is also influenced by their expectations of work, and what they want from the work experience. This was illustrated by the work of Goldthorpe *et al* (1969), who examined the attitude and behaviour of assembly line workers at the Vauxhall car manufacturing plant in Luton. They concluded that there were three different orientations to work:

- *An instrumental approach to work*: Work is a means to an end outside of the work situation. Work is a means of acquiring the income to support a valued way of life.
- *A bureaucratic orientation*: Describes people who sought to give services to a company over a long time in return for a career that sees some promotion and increases in salary, security and pay.
- *A solidaristic orientation*: Characterises those people who, in addition to an economic orientation, also value group loyalty.

This research suggests that different people are seeking different things from the work experi-ence, and hence there is no one determinant that will indicate whether they will have an overall positive or negative attitude to work. This links back to the individual concept of the psychological contract, and the personal expectations that each employee has of the employer.

As Torrington and Hall (1998) note, raising a grievance is a relatively drastic step. It moves away from 'grumbling' and general discontent, and results in the grievance being made formal. They suggest that raising a grievance is the top level of three tiers of dissatisfaction:

- *Dissatisfaction* This is the level at which employees are generally unhappy, but might not express the unhappiness.

用言语表述

- *Complaints* This is the level at which employees verbalise their specific dissatisfaction.
- *Grievances* This is the top level at which employees make a formal complaint that is then addressed through a recognised procedure.

The correctness of Torrington and Hall's judgement that raising a grievance is a drastic step can be seen by referring back to the experiments of Asch (1955) which we looked at in Chapter 5. Employees find it more comfortable to conform to the decisions of the rest of the group. If an employee is raising an individual grievance he or she is often acting without the support of the rest of the group, and sometimes contrary to the decision of that group – and this can be a very lonely experience.

According to the CIPD survey *Managing conflict at work* (2004), grievance procedures are not used frequently in organisations. Of the organisations surveyed the average number of grievances raised each year was nine. This was broken down by sector as shown in Table 9.2.

Table 9.2 Use of grievance procedures

	All respondents	Manufacturing, production	Voluntary, community, not for profit	Private sector	Public sector
Average number of grievances raised	9	4	3	15	7

Raising a grievance can make the employee unpopular with colleagues and management, particularly if the grievance is directed at them in some way. This has been demonstrated in a number of cases that have been taken by women working in city firms. There are allegations of a 'laddish culture' which makes it difficult for a woman to progress to senior positions, and also can result in behaviour that some women find offensive.

This is illustrated in the case of Stephanie Villalba, who made a high-profile claim against the bankers Merrill Lynch. She claimed unfair dismissal, sex discrimination and that her pay and benefits were not comparable with men doing similar jobs. She won her case on the unfair dismissal and equal pay claims, but not on the sex discrimination.

The employment tribunal found that there was no evidence of the laddish culture that she alleged existed. She had complained of bullying behaviour directed at her because of her gender. However, these complaints were dismissed.

In this case Ms Villalba had actually been dismissed from the organisation when she voiced her grievance. However, it can be seen how the working relationships would have become very difficult if she had voiced her grievance while still working in the team. Because part of her grievance was about the very culture in which she operated it was, indirectly, directed at a number of her peers as well as management.

GRIEVANCE PROCEDURES

The *Acas Code of practice on disciplinary and grievance procedures* (2004) advises that employees should, in the first instance, attempt to resolve any grievances with the employer informally. It states that the reason for this is that it helps to maintain good relationships between the employee and the employer, and also that problems are more likely to be solved quickly if an informal approach is taken. When it is not possible to resolve the issue, a formal grievance procedure should be used.

The Employment Act 2002 introduced Statutory Grievance Procedures through the Employment Act 2002 (Dispute Resolution) Regulations 2004. The requirement to follow the statutory procedures became law in the UK in October 2004.

The requirement to use the Statutory Grievance Procedure is binding on all employers and employees, irrespective of the size of the organisation. The statutory procedure was introduced to try to ensure that employees' concerns are dealt with in the workplace and hopefully resolved there, without the need for the intervention of an employment tribunal. If an employee has a grievance, he or she must use the statutory procedures before making a claim to an employment tribunal. If at least 28 days have not elapsed since a written complaint was sent to an employer, the tribunal will refuse to hear the complaint.

The exceptions to this rule are when raising a complaint through the statutory procedures might result in a significant threat to a person, where the issue is harassment and there is a reasonable belief that taking a claim through the statutory procedures would increase the harassment.

The statutory procedures are set out as a minimum standard. Organisations can operate a more detailed procedure, as long as they meet this basic minimum standard.

In the same way as the Statutory Disciplinary Procedure (which we shall examine in Chapter 11), the 2002 Act sets out two statutory procedures, a standard procedure and a modified procedure.

Standard procedure

The standard procedure has three steps:

1. The employee must set out the 'statement of grievance'. This involves setting out the grievance in writing, and sending a copy of the statement to the employer.
2. Once the employer has received a copy of the written statement of grievance, the employer must invite the employee to attend a meeting to discuss the grievance. The meeting must not take place unless the employee has made it clear what the basis for the grievance is, and until the employer has had a reasonable period of time to consider the response to the statement. 'Reasonable period of time' is not defined in the legislation, and it is expected it will vary in accordance with the complexity of the grievance that has been raised. The employee must take all reasonable steps to attend the meeting. After the meeting the employer is required to inform the employee of the response to the grievance. The employer must also make the employee aware that there is the right of appeal if there is not satisfaction with the response that has been given.
3. If the employee wishes to appeal against the response given, s/he must inform the employer. On receiving notice of the appeal the employer must invite the employee to attend a further meeting. The employee must take all reasonable steps to attend the meeting. After the appeal meeting the employer must inform the employee of the final decision.

The 2002 Act also allows for a modified procedure to be used when a dismissal has already occurred. If the employee is aggrieved by the dismissal, or by some outstanding issue (such as payment of outstanding wages), there is the requirement to only follow the two-step procedure:

1. The employee must set out the grievance in writing and send a copy of the statement to the employer.
2. The employer must set out the response in writing and send a copy of this response to the employee.

At all stages of the statutory procedures employers should take action without unreasonable delay. The timing and locations of meetings should be reasonable, so that employees can easily attend. The meetings must be conducted so that both the employer and the employee have sufficient time to explain their cases. Wherever practicable, an appeal should be heard by a more senior manager than the manager who conducted the meeting in step 2.

There is no express mention of the right to be accompanied at a grievance hearing in the Employment Act 2002. However, the Employment Relations Act 1999 gives workers a statutory right to be accompanied by a trade union representative or a fellow worker when attending a grievance hearing.

ACTIVITIES

Find out if your organisation, or an organisation with which you are familiar, has a grievance procedure. Does it meet the statutory requirements? Can you identify any ways in which the procedure can be improved?

Although it is essential that employers follow the statutory procedure, it is important to emphasise the role of managers and leaders in intervening before a grievance reaches a formal stage. In Chapter 4 we examined the role of the manager and leader, and it could be argued that if these roles are carried out effectively the instances of formal grievances should be minimal. This is because employees should have a relationship built on respect and trust which allows for issues to be discussed openly as they occur. This does not mean that grievances will never occur, rather that early intervention addresses issues which need never escalate into formal grievances.

Although we have emphasised the importance of effective management and leadership, it cannot be ignored that employees have different perceptions of fairness and justice (as illustrated in the equity theory of motivation, explained in Chapter 4). Hence, management might make an early intervention in a bid to stop a grievance developing, but be unsuccessful because of the perceptions of the individual employee.

As well as following a procedure that meets at least the minimum requirements of the statutory procedure, it is also important that the employer handles claims effectively and sensitively. As we have already seen, there can be negative behaviours resulting from dissatisfaction, and those behaviours are likely to increase if there is the perception that grievances are not being handled fairly.

Gennard and Judge (2005) suggest that there are a number of stages that management should work through in addressing a grievance effectively. These are:

- receiving the grievance
- preparing for a meeting with the employee (and a representative if applicable)
- meeting with the employee (and representative)
- confirming the common ground between the employee and the employer
- resolving the grievance
- reporting the outcome.

The process for handling the grievance, therefore, mirrors the process for negotiation.

Hearing the grievance

As we have already noted, the employee will have written down a statement of the grievance to start the grievance procedure. Hence this stage will be the receipt of the written statement by the employee's manager.

It is important that the manager does not make an immediate reaction, such as going into an open-plan office and discussing it with the employee in front of other colleagues. It is also important that the manager thinks carefully about who else should be made aware of the grievance (if anyone). Confidentiality needs to be preserved, but it might be appropriate to make a more senior manager or the HR department aware of the complaint.

Preparing for the meeting

The manager then needs to investigate the allegations that have been made. This might involve asking questions of other people (for example, if the complaint is about arguments between colleagues). It might require some research (for example, if the complaint is about working practices and the hours worked under a new scheme).

It is important that the research is carried out with the attitude that the grievance needs to be addressed fully and effectively. If the attitude is that the grievance is unfounded, it is likely that any information that is gathered will be interpreted in this negative way.

Meeting with the employee

The basis for the grievance has already been explained. The purpose of the meeting is to gain clarification of any issues that are not clear, and also to allow the employee the chance to air the grievance. Hence, it is important that the employee is allowed adequate time to express the grievance, so that s/he is comfortable that all the facts have been presented.

It is also the opportunity for the manager to present the facts that have been gathered, whether or not they support the grievance that has been raised. Rather than the employee just being given a final opinion, it is important that he or she understands the facts that have been used in reaching the conclusion.

Confirming the common ground

Many grievances are somewhat complex, and hence it is important to separate out the different issues and address each one. In doing this it might be possible to identify some common ground. It can perhaps be concluded that there is agreement on some points, leaving the areas where there is disagreement for further consideration.

This is important, not only as a means to reach a final solution, but also because having some areas of agreement gives a more positive feel to the proceedings. If everything revolves around disagreement, the meeting will have a much more negative feeling.

Resolving the grievance

The best solution is that the manager and the employee agree on the outcome. It might not be the outcome that the employee originally wanted, but through understanding the facts from the manager the employee might come to accept a compromise position.

If it is found that the grievance was real, the resolution has to be about removing that grievance. If it is found that there was no substance to the grievance, the manager needs to ensure that the employee understands why this conclusion has been reached. If the employee does not, all the negative manifestations of the grievance will remain.

Reporting the outcome

As we have already seen, the manager has a legal obligation to report the final outcome of the grievance to the employee. However, it might also be appropriate to report the findings more widely, especially if other members of the organisation are affected by the outcome.

It might also be necessary to arrange training for employees to ensure that similar problems do not arise in future, or even to take disciplinary action against an employee who has been acting improperly and has contributed to the grievance.

Once the grievance has been resolved it is important for the manager to monitor the situation to ensure that the employee is satisfied with the solution. This is particularly important if any negative behaviours have been demonstrated as a result of the grievance.

HARASSMENT AND BULLYING

A specific type of grievance that can be difficult for both the employee and the organisation to manage is harassment and bullying. The CIPD define bullying as:

> persistent behaviour against an individual that is intimidating, degrading, offensive or malicious and undermines the confidence and self-esteem of the recipient.

The CIPD defines harassment as:

> unwanted behaviour that may be related to age, sex, race, disability, religion, sexuality or any personal characteristic of the individual. It may be persistent or an isolated incident.

In the CIPD *Employee well-being and psychological contract survey* (2001), 13 per cent of respondents reported experiencing bullying or harassment in the past 12 months. The survey reports one estimate that bullying costs employers 80 million lost working days and up to £2 billion in lost revenue each year. It is thought to account for up to 50 per cent of stress-related workplace illnesses.

As can be seen from Table 9.3 (taken from the CIPD survey *Managing conflict at work* (2004)), a large number of allegations of bullying are against management. These are the very people that the employee is expected to bring a grievance to, which can deter employees from making a formal complaint.

Table 9.3 Job roles of employees accused of bullying

	All	Manufacturing, production	Voluntary, community, not for profit	Private sector	Public sector
Line manager	38	29	33	33	53
Peer colleague	7	39	28	31	47
Department manager	22	15	16	20	31
Subordinate	12	10	7	11	20
Director	9	6	13	6	13
HR	2	1	2	1	5

ORGANISATION EXAMPLE

Driskel v *Peninsula Business Services (2000)*

Driskel worked for Huss, and during the time that she worked for him was subjected to a lot of sexual repartee. She applied for a promotion, and he was to be the interviewer. The night before the interview he told her to wear a short skirt and a see-through blouse showing a lot of cleavage to the interview. She ignored the comment, just pointing out the next day that she had not done as he had asked. She subsequently made a complaint of sex discrimination. There was a rather prolonged investigation and eventually Driskel told the employer that she would only work if Huss were moved elsewhere. She was told that this was impractical and she would be dismissed if she did not work with her department head. This happened, and Driskel successfully claimed unfair dismissal and sex discrimination

In this case, the difficulty was not only to whom she could make the complaint, but the concern expressed by Driskel that the relationship had deteriorated to the extent that she was no longer prepared to work with Huss. It has to be realised that the process of hearing a grievance can result in employment relationships that are damaged to the extent that working together is no longer viable.

It is important to note that bullying and harassment are behaviour that employees find unacceptable. Workplace banter might be totally acceptable to most of the employees, but if one employee finds it unacceptable it should be stopped. It is also important to note that one isolated incident can be classed as harassment or bullying.

ORGANISATION EXAMPLE

Bracebridge Engineering Ltd v *Darby (1989)*

On one occasion two male supervisors stopped Darby as she went to wash her hands. She had been criticised on a number of occasions for leaving early, and it was thought that she was again attempting to leave early. They carried her forcefully into a darkened room where they sexually assaulted her and made lewd comments to her. She complained to a manager, but it was decided to take no action against the supervisors. She resigned and claimed sexual discrimination and harassment. The employers argued that the incident was an isolated event and hence it could not constitute harassment. However, the EAT determined that a single event could constitute harassment if, as in this case, it had been sufficiently serious. It was also found that the treatment Darby suffered would not have been suffered by a man, and hence this was an incident of sexual discrimination and harassment.

Legislation relating to harassment is found within discrimination legislation (hence, sexual harassment is seen as sex discrimination, racial harassment as race discrimination and so on). However, harassment and bullying are also subject to criminal law.

The Criminal Justice and Public Order Act 1994 in England and Wales made it a criminal offence for an individual to commit an act of deliberate harassment against another person. This Act does not apply in Scotland. To be covered by the Act, however, the harassment must be shown to have been intentional. This contrasts with the discrimination laws, under which a claim can be made out irrespective of whether there was a deliberate intention to harass the victim.

Another criminal law governing harassment which applies throughout the UK is the Protection from Harassment Act 1997. This Act makes it a criminal offence to pursue a course of conduct that amounts to harassment, or which causes a person to fear that violence will be used against them, on at least two occasions. The principal objective of this Act was to provide protection to individuals who were the victims of stalking. There is no requirement under this Act for the behaviour in question to be intentional for it to be an offence.

Furthermore, the Anti-terrorism, Crime and Security Act 2001 created an offence of religiously aggravated harassment. The Act amended the Crime and Disorder Act to include a new category of 'religiously aggravated criminal offences'. Thus, harassment or hostility at work based on a person's membership of a religious group could be a criminal offence, as well as affording the victim the opportunity to bring a claim against the employer for unlawful harassment.

Given the legal requirements to manage harassment and bullying effectively, as well as the business case for addressing all grievances, it is unsurprising that, according to the CIPD survey *Managing conflict at work* (2004), 83 per cent of the organisations surveyed had a bullying/harassment policy.

As we have noted, different employees will have different interpretations of what constitutes bullying and harassment. A number of organisations have put in place initiatives to try to reduce unacceptable behaviour in the workplace, and make employees aware of what is and is not acceptable.

As can be seen from Table 9.4, the most effective ways of managing the issue have been through changes in behaviour, rather than through formal responses through a grievance procedure.

The CIPD survey also considered the question of who the bullies are within the workplace. We have already looked at the statistics relating to job role. It is also interesting to note that 60 per cent of complaints were about men acting as bullies, compared with 43 per cent of complaints about women acting as bullies.

Table 9.4 Success factors in tackling bullying/harassment at work for organisations in the UK

Factor	Employees citing factor as most significant (%)
Line manager behaviour	39
Quick response to problem	16
Top team behaviour	13
Support to help individuals feel confident about raising issues	8
Training	4
Informal response to problem	3
Other staff behaviour	3
Individual champions	0.8
Formal response to problem	0.8
Legal advice available	0.7
Trade union/employee representative behaviour	0.5

Source: CIPD (2004).

It is also suggested that organisational cultures can create and sustain institutionalised bullying. This can be the result of autocratic management styles, which result in individuals being over-loaded with work, having a blame culture, tolerating or promoting aggressive behaviour and not training people in identifying, challenging and changing bullying behaviours. In certain organisational cultures behaving like a bully can be seen as a way to improve career prospects. This is particularly true if the bullying results in high-level results and performance.

EMPLOYMENT TRIBUNALS

If a grievance cannot be resolved within the workplace the employee can take the claim to an employment tribunal.

Employment tribunals were created by the Industrial Training Act 1964 (and at this stage were named industrial tribunals). They were initially created to hear appeals relating to the assessment of training levies under this 1964 Act. Over the next three years their brief was extended to include such things as the determination of the right to a redundancy payment and issues surrounding the lack of, or inaccuracy of, a written statement of terms and conditions of employment.

In the mid-1960s the government became concerned about the number of unofficial strikes, wage inflation and the general existence of restrictive practices in industry. It commissioned Lord Donovan to lead an investigation into these issues. As a result of the investigation the Donovan Report was published in 1968 and gave a comprehensive overview of industrial relations at the time. In particular the report observed two systems of industrial relations that had developed. There was the formal system of negotiation at industry level, and the informal level happening more locally within the organisation. Donovan suggested that many of the problems identified by the government were caused by conflict between these two systems. His main recommendation was the formalisation of industrial relations systems at organisational and industry level.

As part of those recommendations Donovan saw the need for an industrial tribunal system to which employees could bring their grievances. He described this system as needing to be easily accessible, informal, speedy and inexpensive. The idea was that employees with a grievance could go to a body that would give an impartial judgement on whether they had been treated unfairly. Given the very little legislation at the time that offered the individual employee any protection, the introduction of such a system was a big step forward for individualism.

At first the industrial tribunal system was just this. However, over the years the workload of the tribunals has increased significantly, and many believe the system has moved far from the ideal that Donovan initially described.

It is easy to see some of the key reasons that the workload increased so dramatically. When the Donovan Report was published there was no legislation relating to unfair dismissal (introduced in 1971); sex discrimination (1975) and race discrimination (1976). Today more than half of the claims to the employment tribunals relate to these areas of legislation.

Despite this increasing workload it was still hoped that the employment tribunals system could meet Donovan's ideal. The idea was that an employee who felt he/she had been badly treated by an employer should have the means to get an independent judgement on the issue, quickly and without cost. How are those criteria met today?

Accessibility

The Donovan Report suggested that there should be employment tribunals operating in all major industrial centres, making them easily accessible. In 1971 employment tribunals were heard in 84 locations. Today there are 31 permanent centres at which employment tribunals are heard. In addition to this there are a number of hearings that take place at non-permanent centres. There is also the ability to hear cases almost anywhere if people have particular needs (eg disability) that make it difficult to attend a permanent centre. It is difficult, therefore, to give a specific number of centres, but the system is certainly still very accessible to those who want to use it.

Accessibility can also refer to the ease of registering a claim with the employment tribunal. The system is open to everyone, and the actual process of registering a claim is relatively straightforward. Forms to apply to employment tribunals (ET1) are readily available at places such as the Citizens Advice Bureau. It is also possible to complete the ET1 on line through the Employment Tribunals' website (www.ets.gov.uk).

Informality

This is perhaps now the area which least meets the original Donovan ideal. There are definitely ways in which the employment tribunals system is much less formal than other court systems. There are no wigs and gowns, and the hearing rooms are less imposing than many courtrooms. In higher courts the parties are expected to present their case, and challenge the case of the opposite side. An unrepresented applicant who is struggling to explain his or her case in the employment tribunal will usually be given some assistance by the chairperson to make sure all facts are communicated.

However, it is widely accepted that the employment tribunals have moved away from the picture of the potentially wronged employee presenting his or her grievance in a simple manner, with the employer responding to the accusations. It is now very common for one or both parties to be represented by solicitors or barristers, and the simple arguments are often weighed down by substantial legal arguments. This has impacted on the aspect of informality, but is probably inevitable given the growing amount of legislation relating to employment issues.

Speed

The original Donovan ideal was of a very quick resolution to the grievance. This allowed the employee and employer to put the issue behind them and continue with a good working relationship or, if the employee had left the employer, allowed the employee to leave the issue and move on to find new employment.

All the employment tribunals have targets to hear claims speedily (the current target nationally is to hear 75 per cent of all claims within 26 weeks of them being presented). However, typically many months elapse between the application to an employment tribunal and the hearing. The actual time lapse will depend on the area of the country where the application is lodged and the expected length of the hearing. There are simply too many applications for the process to work any quicker. In the late 1960s there were around 9,500 applications registered at employment tribunals each year. In the year 2003–04 the applications received reached the total of 115,042, although this reduced in 2004–05 to 86,181. The large total in 2003–04 was partly influenced by a number of multiple claims, where groups of claims from a number of employees are brought against an employer. The reduction in 2004–05 is primarily attributed to the reduction in multiple cases.

Inexpensiveness

There is currently no charge for bringing an application to the employment tribunals, although we shall see when we review the future of the employment tribunals that this might change in the future.

If an employee chooses to represent him or herself, and many do, there are obviously no legal costs. If the employee chooses to seek legal representation, legal aid is not available, and the employee must meet those costs. If the employee is a member of a trade union, that union will typically represent the employee, presuming that the union does not feel the case is totally unfounded. In some cases the employee might get representation or support from a body such as the Equal Opportunities Commission or the Disability Rights Commission.

In many courts the unsuccessful party has to meet all or part of the costs of the opposing side. In employment tribunals this is unusual, although the practice is increasing. In 2004–05 costs were awarded in just 1,036 cases (281 times to applicants and 755 times to respondents). The average amount of costs awarded was £1,828.

Although the cost of the system to the employee might not be huge, it should be noted that the overall cost of running the employment tribunal system in 2004–05 was £69,770,000. This is equivalent to £809 for each application lodged.

We can see, therefore, that there are ways in which the 'Donovan ideal' is far from the reality of today. However, the employment tribunals are still a court at the lowest rung of the court hierarchy, and there is still a desire to ensure that the employee is able to bring a case and present it in a simple format.

The process of employment tribunals

An employment tribunal consists of a chairperson and two lay members. The chairperson is a fully qualified lawyer, who either works full time as a chairperson, or who practises law part time. The lay members are appointed by the secretary of state for trade and industry. They have extensive experience and knowledge of employment issues. In each employment tribunal one lay member will come from an 'employee' background (eg a trade union official) and one from an 'employer' background (eg a personnel manager). The three members of the employment tribunal have an equal vote in deciding the outcome of each case.

The purpose of having lay members from different backgrounds is so that there is a full understanding of the issues from both the employer's and the employee's perspective. This helps to ensure a lack of bias in any decision-making, but also helps to put the application of the law into context.

The employment tribunals have jurisdiction to hear cases relating to over 80 different pieces of legislation. In the 2004–05 Employment Tribunals Service's Annual Report the most common types of claims were as shown in Table 9.5.

Settlement prior to the hearing

In most employment law cases Acas has a statutory duty to contact both parties and try to reach a conciliated settlement. Settlements of claims through Acas in 2003–04 were as shown in Table 9.6.

It is usual for the conciliation to involve a payment of some financial sum, although reinstatement or re-engagement can occur in some cases. The purpose of using Acas is, again, partly to reduce the workload of the employment tribunal service. However, some of the acrimony that can occur in the actual hearing is avoided by a settlement prior to the hearing. Although in most cases the employment relationship has already been terminated, it is not uncommon for existing employees

Table 9.5 Employment tribunals service: most common types of claims 2004–05

Claim	Number of claims (total 156,081*)
Unfair dismissal	39,727
Wages Act	37,470
Breach of contract	22,788
Sex discrimination	11,726
Equal pay	8,229
Redundancy pay	6,877
Disability discrimination	4,942
Redundancy – failure to inform and consult	3,664
Race discrimination	3,317
Working Time Directive	3,223
Others	14,118

* This total represents all the areas against which claims were made, rather than the total number of claims made. For example, it is not at all uncommon for someone to claim unfair dismissal, sex discrimination and unfair deduction of wages in one claim. This would count as one claim, but three areas against which a claim has been made.

Table 9.6 Settlement of claims through Acas 2003–04

Claim	Percentage of claims settled
Unfair dismissal	48
Disability discrimination	51
Breach of contract	39
Race discrimination	42
Wages Act	38
Working time	46
National minimum wage	45
Sex discrimination	52
Redundancy pay	17
Equal pay	38
Others	23

Source: Acas Annual Report 2003-04.

to be called as witnesses, or to attend to support former colleagues. Hence, the employment tribunal hearing can be damaging to the employment relationships of other employees who still work within the organisation.

In addition, the applicant can withdraw his/her application at any stage. In 2004–05, 74 per cent of cases lodged with employment tribunals were withdrawn or settled before the full hearing.

Remedies

In cases such as unfair dismissal and discrimination (when employment has ended) there are three options available to the employment tribunal:

1. *Reinstatement*: the employee returns to the job he/she had.
2. *Re-engagement*: the employee returns to the company, but in a different role.

Both of these are rare remedies because the relationship between the employee and the previous management is usually too badly damaged for a working relationship to be resumed. In addition, it is quite possible that the employee has gone on to find new employment while waiting for the hearing. In 2004–05 reinstatement or re-engagement was offered in just 0.2 per cent of cases when an unfair dismissal was found.

3. Compensation: the company is ordered to pay an amount of money to the employee. This was awarded in 31.6 per cent of unfair dismissal cases in 2004–05.

Compensation awards for unfair dismissal are currently capped at £56,800 – this figure is reviewed annually. There is no maximum compensation for a successful discrimination claim. However, large awards are still relatively rare. In 2004–05 average awards of compensation were as shown in Table 9.7.

Table 9.7 Average awards of compensation 2004–05

Claim	£
Unfair dismissal	7,303
Sex discrimination	6,235
Race discrimination	6,699
Disability discrimination	7,500

Given the low levels of compensation it is justifiable to ask why anyone would want to go to an employment tribunal. It is often more about resolving the conflict and finding out which of the employer and employee was legally right, than the amount of compensation that is awarded. This is particularly true for employees who have been dismissed, and then have to declare this on application forms to all future employers. There is often a desire to regain a clean record.

ACTIVITIES

Attend a local employment tribunal. Hearings typically start at 10 am, so arrive at least 15 minutes before. Explain to the clerk the purpose of your visit, and ask advice for a suitable hearing to watch. Try to attend the full hearing, and (if the decision is given that day) stay to hear the decision.

As we noted earlier in the chapter, claims to employment tribunals have grown sharply over the years. Initially it seemed the level of growth had reached a peak in 2000–01, with the number of applications falling in 2001–02, and then falling further in 2002–03. However, in 2003–04 the number rose again to 115,042 before falling in 2004–05 to 86,181. Before trying to understand the reason for the recent drop in claims, it is important to understand why the number of claims rose steadily for several years:

1. *Every time new legislation is introduced there are new claims that can be brought to an employment tribunal.* As we shall see in Chapter 13, there is a wide range of legislation protecting the individual. Every time another piece of legislation is introduced the potential workload of employment tribunals increases.
2. *More people can bring claims to employment tribunals.* Until February 1995 part-time employees had to have five years' continuous service before they could bring a claim for unfair dismissal to an employment tribunal, and full-time employees had to have two years' continuous service. However, from 1999 all employees have only been required to have one year's continuous service.
3. *Employees are more aware of their rights.* It is certainly true that employees are more aware of their rights. They might not be certain exactly what those rights are, but they know enough to be prompted to go and find out more. It is more likely, therefore, that employees will think about the possibility of bringing a claim.

RESOLVING CONFLICT OUTSIDE THE EMPLOYMENT TRIBUNAL

As we have already noted, taking a conflict to an employment tribunal is a procedure that determines legally the rights and wrongs of what has taken place. However, the process in itself does little to mend the damage that has been caused to the employment relationship. Recognising this, and the need to reduce the costs of running the Employment Tribunals Service, there have been a number of initiatives to encourage the resolution of individual conflicts in other ways:

Acas Arbitration Scheme

The Employment Rights (Dispute Resolution) Act 1998 introduced a new scheme to try to reduce the pressure on the employment tribunals system. It is known as the Acas Arbitration Scheme. The scheme was launched in May 2001 and it was hoped that this would take the strain off the Employment Tribunals system. In reality it has had little impact, indeed it only received 13 applications in 2001–02, 23 applications in 2002–03 and 7 applications in 2003–04.

The Acas Arbitration Scheme only addresses unfair dismissal cases (a further scheme has been added to hear complaints relating to flexible working). Although that limits its jurisdiction, we must remember that nearly half of all claims to the employment tribunals do relate to unfair dismissal. The main advantage of the scheme is that it will hear claims quickly, it will be informal and it will be speedy, maybe going back to the Donovan ideal we examined at the start of this section.

The initial lodging of the claim is still to the Employment Tribunals Service. However, if both parties agree, the claim may then be taken out of the employment tribunals process and directed to the Acas arbitration process. At that stage an Acas arbitrator (not an Acas member of staff, but an independent person appointed by Acas who is deemed to have specialist relevant knowledge) is appointed to the case. The Acas arbitrator then arranges a time for the hearing as quickly as possible, with a target of being heard within a period of two months.

The hearings are conducted informally, and as locally as possible to the parties. There is no cross-examination of witnesses (witness statements may be presented, but the witnesses are not questioned), no formal pleadings and the proceedings are confidential. The two parties simply explain their side of the case to the Acas arbitrator, bringing his/her attention to any relevant documents. Each party is also allowed the opportunity to comment on the other party's written submission. The Acas arbitrator then questions both parties and also seeks views on any remedy that might be awarded. Both parties are then invited to make closing statements. The Acas arbitrator determines whether the dismissal was fair or unfair, and if the dismissal is deemed to be unfair, determines remedies. The decision is not given at the hearing, but is communicated to both parties in writing after the hearing.

The decision of the Acas arbitrator is final. There is no route of appeal unless there is a challenge on the grounds of substantive jurisdiction, or on grounds of serious irregularity. The whole process is relatively informal and hence there is the potential for there to be less negative effects on the employment relationship. However, the very minimal usage of the scheme has meant it has had little impact on the resolution of individual conflict. The minimal usage can be put down to:

1. The limited focus of jurisdiction can be a problem. It is not unusual for a claim to relate to more than one area of legislation. For example, there could be a claim for unfair dismissal and unlawful deduction of wages. If such a claim went through the Acas arbitration route only the part relating to unfair dismissal could be heard. The matter relating to unlawful deduction of wages would have to be referred to an employment tribunal, meaning that the parties would need to attend two hearings. This is unlikely to be popular with applicants or respondents.
2. In addition, if there are any disputes relating to the claim – for instance, was the applicant

actually dismissed? Was the application to the employment tribunal made in time? – the Acas arbitrator cannot hear the claim. Again, it is not unusual for these types of issue to accompany a claim for unfair dismissal.

3. There is no right of appeal. Although this means the claim is finalised more quickly, people might be apprehensive about committing themselves to a scheme where there is no appeal, especially as there is an alternative (the employment tribunal) where there is the right of appeal.

4. The hearings are in private and hence representatives are not able to assess how effective the process is and decide if they want to use this route. In reality this is a small issue, as there have been so few hearings. However, a representative has a responsibility to give the best advice possible to his/her client. Hence, a representative might find it difficult to recommend a process he/she has never seen in operation and knows relatively little about.

5. The Acas arbitrator is not required to be legally qualified. Although the Acas arbitrator will be thoroughly trained, and will have been selected for his/her depth of knowledge and experience, some applicants or respondents might feel uncomfortable that no formal legal qualification is required.

In its Annual Report 2001–02, Acas commented that the reason the scheme has been so little used is that people do not understand the benefits of the scheme, or have not appreciated that the outcome is likely to be the same as going through the employment tribunal scheme. Whatever the reasons for the poor uptake, the scheme is currently under review. There could be alterations made to it, or it could simply be relaunched with more publicity and more explanation.

ACTIVITIES

Would you be willing to have a claim that you made to an employment tribunal heard through the Acas Arbitration Scheme? Why/why not? What would you do to the scheme to make it more attractive?

Costs

Awarding costs to one of the parties was introduced to try to address the issue of costs incurred by parties in fighting unmeritorious claims. The regulations broadened the range of situations in which costs can be awarded. Those who bring misconceived cases will mostly be employees who are not represented who have a real (but misplaced) belief that the employer has acted in some illegal manner. The potential for costs to be awarded should encourage employees to seek more advice before pursuing a claim. However, this does presume that employees realise they might have a weak case, and that they need that advice. It could be argued that if they realised they had such a weak case they might never have considered a claim in the first place!

The awarding of costs against the unrepresented employee does require a change of attitude of the employment tribunals. Although the 'Donovan ideal' might be very distant from today's reality, there is still the underlying idea that tribunals are there for the employee to bring a case against the employer in a simple way, looking for an independent judgement on the issue. Awarding costs might deter the employee who has genuinely been treated badly, going against the whole philosophy of the employment tribunals.

Although the average costs awarded in 2004–05 was only £1,828 the employment tribunal does have the power to award costs up to a maximum of £10,000.

Deposit

Employment tribunals can require an applicant to pay a deposit, following a review of the case at a pre-hearing review. The maximum deposit that can be awarded is £500, although this measure is rarely used.

Strike out

An employment tribunal can strike out a case that is seen to be misconceived, and hence have no reasonable prospect of success. However, most employment tribunals are reluctant to judge a case before all the facts have been presented, and the strike-out could be challenged under the Human Right Acts 1998, specifically the right to a fair trial.

Statutory grievance procedures

As we have already seen, there is now a requirement to try to resolve a grievance within the workplace before bringing it to an employment tribunal. This is hoped to reduce the number of claims to the tribunals.

As we have already noted, the number of claims being brought to employment tribunals has dropped in recent years. However, according to a CBI report (*CBI/Pertemps Employment Trends Survey*) published in September 2005, there is still a lot of concern among employers about the employment tribunal system. Specific findings of the survey were:

- 100 per cent of firms with fewer than 50 staff settled every claim despite advice they would win almost half the cases, and 26 per cent of all firms settled even if they felt the claims lacked merit. This was because many employers feared the costs of fighting a case in an employment tribunal.
- 45 per cent of employers believe the system is ineffective and 50 per cent reported a rise in weak and vexatious claims in the last 12 months despite the reforms.
- 76 per cent have encountered extra red tape because of the new reforms and 26 per cent said the overall system is too costly. Each claim costs a business £4,360 in legal fees alone, on average, on top of management time and stress.
- 55 per cent say the tribunal system has become too adversarial. A further 19 per cent believe it damages rather than helps employee relations.

As a result of the survey the CBI called for employment tribunals to strike out more weak cases and to make more use of costs in deterring employees from bringing weak cases.

KEY POINTS FROM THIS CHAPTER

- The various behaviours that demonstrate dissatisfaction can be damaging to the organisation.
- There is a link between attitudes and behaviour, particularly if the attitudes are strong.
- Raising a grievance is a drastic step for the employee.
- The Statutory Grievance Procedure is a three-step procedure. There is also a modified two-step procedure.

- Bullying is persistent behaviour against an individual that is intimidating, degrading, offensive or malicious, and undermines the confidence and self-esteem of the recipient.
- Harassment is unwanted behaviour that may be related to age, sex, race, disability, religion, sexuality or any personal characteristic of the individual. It may be persistent or an isolated incident.
- Most bullying is carried out by peers or line management.
- Institutionalised bullying is where there is a culture where bullying is acceptable.
- The employment tribunals system was originally intended to be easily accessible, informal, speedy and inexpensive.
- There has been a significant increase in the number of cases coming to employment tribunals, but this did drop in 2004–05.
- The Acas Arbitration Scheme was introduced to reduce the number of claims being heard by employment tribunals, focusing only on unfair dismissal claims.

EXAMPLES TO WORK THROUGH

1. Productivity has been falling in your organisation, and a recent attitude survey within the organisation has identified low morale and general dissatisfaction. How would you explore the reasons for this problem having developed, and how might you address the problems?

2. An employee has informed the HR department that she has been subjected to sexual harassment by a number of colleagues. Your initial investigations have found that other colleagues accuse her of being a bully, and deny that any harassment has taken place. How would you proceed with this case?

3. Employment tribunals were created 40 years ago. Do you think that they still have a role today? What should that role be?

(Suggestions of answers to the examples can be accessed by tutors at www.cipd.co.uk/tss)

CASE STUDY

Eight months ago you joined the ABC charity as a fundraiser. This is a paid position, and you are based at the charity headquarters in Glasgow. There are 33 employees working at the headquarters, in a variety of support functions. The charity has a number of regional branches at which the actual charity workers are based.

You report directly to the general manager, and have one assistant. You work in an open-plan office, alongside the administration and finance teams. On your first day you were very surprised to see a calendar in the general manager's office featuring a topless woman. Although you did not find it personally offensive you did think it was very inappropriate. However, you decided to make no comment.

As time progressed you became very concerned about the sexist attitude of the general manager. He often asks the women in the office about their relationships with their partners, usually making some sexual innuendo. He also makes a number of comments about a 'woman's place' and refuses to let the men take their turn in such things as making the coffees, saying that is a 'woman's job'.

Two days ago you noticed that one of the women in the office had been crying, and when there was a suitable opportunity you asked her what was wrong. She told you, in complete confidence, that the general manager had touched her inappropriately. When she told him to 'get off' he had retorted that he was in charge and if she wanted a job she would not speak like that to him again. She does not want to lose her job, she desperately needs the money and has been out of work for a lengthy period before. However, she hates working in the office and says that the attitude of the general manager is starting to affect her health.

You remembered that there is a grievance procedure within the organisation, and you suggested to her that she raise a grievance following the formal procedure. She laughed when you suggested that, and told you to read the procedure carefully. You have just done that and you have discovered that the procedure clearly states that all grievances should be addressed to the general manager. Clearly, this is not an acceptable course of action for this woman.

What can you do? It seems unfair and unjust that the general manager can behave in this way, and not be stopped. However, you cannot see a way forward. Having thought it through you can see three options:

1. Talk to the general manager yourself and explain that you find his behaviour unacceptable. In doing this you hope that you could encourage him to change his behaviour.
2. Talk discreetly to all the female employees and see if others also have complaints. If there are a number that do, suggest that they meet with the general manager as a group to discuss the problems. This might be easier than one employee talking to the general manager on his/her own.
3. Talk to one of the other senior managers and ask if s/he is prepared to hear a formal grievance about the general manager.

Questions

1 Consider the advantages and disadvantages of each of these approaches.
2 Suggest at least one other approach that could be taken to resolving this problem.
3 Given your answers to the previous two questions, recommend a course of action.

Reward and the Employment Relationship

CHAPTER 10

The objectives of this chapter are to:

- explore the relevance of reward to the employment relationship
- examine the relationship between reward and the psychological contract
- outline different approaches to reward, and consider their impact on the employment relationship
- consider the different impacts of individual and team-based pay
- examine how inequality in pay arises and the impacts of this
- consider the importance of non-financial rewards within the context of total reward.

This chapter is the last of four chapters looking at processes within the employment relationship. Reward has a dual role within the employment relationship: it is a way of encouraging and reinforcing behaviours that are wanted within that relationship, and it is also a way of motivating a change in behaviour to meet the required standards.

In Chapter 11, when we start to focus on the legislation that impacts on the employment relationship, we examine the reverse of reward: punishment in the form of the disciplinary process.

THE RELEVANCE OF REWARD

Armstrong (2002) defines reward as being:

> About how people are rewarded in accordance with their value to an organisation. It is concerned with both financial and non-financial reward and embraces the philosophies, strategies, policies, plans and processes used by organisations to develop and maintain reward systems.

An interesting part of the definition from Armstrong is the statement that reward relates to the employee's value to the organisation. The statement implies that there is a difference in the value of different employees. Indeed, this differing level of value is supported by Schuster and Zingheim (1992), who state that competitive pay should reflect the quality, performance or productivity that deserves a certain level of pay – clearly suggesting that different employees will achieve differing levels of quality, performance and productivity and should be rewarded accordingly.

Although we might accept that employees do have differing levels of contribution to the organisation, we also have to accept that the employees themselves might not have the same perception regarding the levels of contribution. Lawler (1990) states that employees' feelings about the adequacy of their pay is directly affected by the comparisons that they make between their own pay and pay of others. If they perceive there to be an unfair difference they are likely to be dissatisfied, which will have a negative impact on the employment relationship.

However, as Lawler went on to state, one of the difficulties is that employees do not always make relevant comparisons when determining whether their reward is favourable. He suggests that employees will start by making external comparisons with their own pay, and if they are favourable they will then look internally. In short, employees will always find some comparator so that they can conclude that their reward is unfair.

This approach might appear to be very negative, but it is a key issue to address when looking at the impact of reward on employment relationships. It could be argued that if the employee has a fundamental feeling of the reward being unfair, the relationship will not be fully successful, because the dissatisfaction remains and sours the relationship. Indeed, according to Davies (1998), pay is the most frequently cited reason for employee relations disputes in the UK. Hence, we see the relevance of reward in the employment relationship.

Have you ever been in the situation when you have felt your reward in a job is unfair? How did you react? What impact did this have on your relationships at work? Ask at least five other people the same questions, and identify different reactions that people have to the situation.

Bratton and Gold (2003) emphasise the core role of reward in the employment relationship. They define the reward system as being an economic exchange. The employee contributes effort and obeys the instructions of others, and in return receives a level of reward. They go on to suggest that any reward system within an organisation has three objectives:

- to recruit and retain a sufficient number of qualified workers
- to motivate employees to perform to the fullest extent of their capabilities
- to encourage employees to follow workplace rules and undertake special behaviour of benefit to the organisation, without any direct supervision or instructions.

Recruit and retain

Although the levels of reward influence people in their decisions whether to join an organisation, and whether to stay with an organisation, it would be wrong to assume that pay is the primary concern.

According to the 2005 CIPD survey on *Recruitment, Retention and Turnover* the reasons that people leave organisations are shown in Table 10.1. Although we see that pay is not the top issue, we do see that it is a reason cited by 37 per cent of the respondents, which is a significant percentage.

We can also see that turnover of employees is highest in the hotel, leisure and catering sector (64.7 per cent) which is a traditionally poorly paid sector. However, it is also the sector that attracts a lot of people looking for short-term work (eg students working in holidays) and the figures have to be interpreted with that in mind.

Leaving an organisation is clearly the termination of an employment relationship, and hence it is often the ultimate expression of dissatisfaction. The figures from this survey suggest that dissatisfaction with reward can be a significant reason for people deciding to terminate the employment relationship.

Table 10.1 Reasons why people leave organisations given by people surveyed (percentage)

Promotion outside the organisation	53
Lack of development or career opportunities	42
Change of career	41
Level of pay	37
Retirement	20
Redundancy	19
Level of workload	11
Childcare issues	11
Lack of support from line managers	10
Level of working hours	9
Ill health (other than stress)	7
Stress of job/role	6
Leaving to look after family members (not children)	4
Relocation	3
Other	11

Note: people surveyed could give more than one answer.

Table 10.2 Reasons for difficulties in recruiting staff (percentage)

Lack of required specialist skills	63
Lack of required experience	59
Wanted more pay than could be offered	47
No applicants	29
Image of sector/organisation	16
Lack of interpersonal skills	12
High cost of living in the area	9
Lack of required formal qualifications	7

The same CIPD survey also looked at issues relating to recruitment, and asked the survey respondents about the reasons that they might have experienced difficulties in recruiting new employees. The results are shown in Table 10.2. Again, we see that pay/reward is not the most important issue, but it is definitely a significant issue.

The same organisations were asked what actions they have taken to try to attract more applicants. In 37 per cent of cases organisations stated that they had responded by increasing the starting salaries or benefits package.

Some organisations have found it increasingly difficult to attract people to lower-paid jobs, especially in areas of relatively high employment. A number of organisations have addressed this by looking to recruit overseas, and particularly to Eastern Europe where the comparative salaries make working in the UK very attractive.

For example, in June 2005 an Oxford Tesco store recruited a number of workers from Poland after it found difficulty in recruiting locally. In March 2005 Arriva buses in Gwynedd recruited bus drivers from Poland after it also found it difficult to attract employees locally.

Why did you leave all the previous organisations that you have worked for? If money was not the primary reason, did it have any influence on your decision at all? Why did you decide to join each of the organisations that you have worked for? How influential was the financial package when you made your decision?

Motivate performance

There is a difficulty in making a direct link between motivation and pay. On the one hand, people need money and hence work to earn money. On the other hand, there is little evidence that money is a direct motivator at work. Indeed Kohn (1998) (quoted by Armstrong (2002)) states that 'no controlled scientific study has ever found a long-term enhancement of the quality of work as a result of any reward system'. He goes on to say that:

> when you look at how people are motivated it becomes disturbingly clear that the more you use rewards to 'motivate' people, the more they tend to lose interest in whatever they had to do to get the rewards.

Pfeffer (1998) supports this view, stating that people do work for money – but they work even more for having meaning in their lives. Primarily, they work to have fun. He suggests that companies that ignore this fact are essentially bribing their employees and will pay the price in lack of loyalty and commitment.

This approach is refuted by Gupta and Shaw (1998), who identify the instrumental and symbolic meaning of money. The instrumental meaning is what we get from it: better houses, clothes, holidays, cars and so on. The symbolic meaning is how it is viewed by ourselves and others: money signals our status and our worth to society. They suggest that when certain behaviours are followed by money, they are more likely to be repeated. Hence, employees will do the things for which they are rewarded and will ignore the things for which they are not rewarded.

In Chapter 5 we looked at a number of different motivation theories. If we return to those theories we can see how they might support the idea that reward can motivate enhanced performance.

The 'needs theories' of Maslow and Herzberg suggest that unsatisfied needs create tension and dissatisfaction. Hence, with Maslow's (1954) theory, if a lack of money meant that employees could not move up the hierarchy of needs they are likely to become dissatisfied. They will also be motivated to meet their needs, and that could mean fulfilling the need by terminating the employment relationship and taking higher paid employment elsewhere (if this opportunity arose). If there is no opportunity to meet their needs, the tension and dissatisfaction will be exacerbated.

Herzberg's (1957) theory suggests that there are hygiene factors which do not create satisfaction, but can cause demotivation. This suggests that if there is dissatisfaction with reward employees will be demotivated. However, if the reward is perceived to be satisfactory it will not be a motivator – it will simply have no impact at all.

The 'cognitive theories' emphasise the psychological processes that affect motivation, as well as identifying the relevance of meeting basic needs.

Adams' (1965) 'equity theory' suggests that employees will be demotivated if they perceive that their reward is unfair.

Vroom's (1964) 'expectancy theory' suggests that reward will only be motivating if it is both desired, and if there is the belief that it will actually happen. Hence, if employees are part of a bonus scheme that gives a low level of payment its desirability will be low, and hence it will not be a strong motivator. Alternatively, if there is a perception that the bonus targets are so high that the bonus will never be paid out, the bonus will not be a strong motivator.

Latham and Locke's (1979) 'goal theory' suggests that motivation and performance are higher when employees are set specific goals. Hence, if they have specific goals to achieve in order to earn a certain level of reward, they will be more motivated to achieve that specific goal.

All these motivation theories indicate in different ways that reward can be a motivator and a demotivator. Despite the arguments against the linkage between reward and motivation a large number of organisations work on the basis that reward does have a significant impact if it relates to something that the employee is required to do – hence the various approaches to contingent pay, which we examine later in this chapter.

Clearly, one difficulty with identifying the relationship between pay and motivation is the individual nature of employees. There are some people who are very motivated by money, and who will always work harder if they perceive a monetary benefit will be the result. Indeed, this is the basis on which most pay systems for employees involved in sales have been developed – presuming that the linking higher rewards to higher sales will motivate increased sales activity.

In contrast, there are employees who are not motivated by money. Maybe their personal needs are such that they have already reached the self-actualisation of Maslow's hierarchy, or maybe they just have a low level of expectation and demands. It is quite possible that these employees will not be motivated by increased reward.

ORGANISATION
EXAMPLE

In most pay disputes the result of the ballot for industrial action is not 100 per cent in favour of taking action. In the FBU strike of 2002/3, 87 per cent of those balloted were in favour of strike action. The remaining 13 per cent might have been against strike action for a variety of reasons. One of those reasons could have been that the individual fire fighters were not interested in getting a massive pay increase – they were satisfied with their pay as it was.

How much does money motivate you? Try to link your own attitude to money to one of the motivation theories that we have examined. Looking back over your career, can you identify different times when money has been a greater and smaller motivator?

Commitment to rules and behaviours

The third purpose of reward as identified by Bratton and Gold suggests that reward can be used to encourage employees to conform to the rules and culture of the organisation, and can encourage commitment.

The early research of behaviourist psychologists would support this view. Pavlov (1927) found that responses to stimuli can be conditioned by linking them to a second stimulus. Hence, in the example of reward, responses to rules or cultural demands can be conditioned by linking them to the second stimulus of reward. If employees do as required by the organisation they are rewarded, and they are more likely to give the same response next time.

This might seem like a very mechanistic explanation of reward, but it can explain the basis of many bonus systems. For example, if an employee is being paid according to the quality of work that is produced, the idea behind the bonus systems is that the motivation to produce that quality should be improved if payment is made directly for the required output. The difficulty comes if, at some time in the future, the bonus system is removed. Will the required quality of work be sustained, or will it diminish without the associated reinforcement?

Cognitive psychologists would argue that this approach is too simplistic, because it is presuming that people operate like machines, without taking any account of their likes and dislikes, and their personal motivations. Although this is a valid criticism, it is still a fact that most bonus schemes are quite mechanistic in their approach.

REWARD AND THE PSYCHOLOGICAL CONTRACT

At the start of this chapter we noted that different employees might have a different value to the organisation. We also noted that employees make comparisons with other employees when considering their reward and, if they perceive that they are being treated unfairly, the employment relationship is likely to be damaged.

This perception of fairness has a fundamental impact on the psychological contract. Employers will expect the employees to do their best for the organisation, even to 'put themselves out' for the organisation. In return for doing this employees will have some expectation of the level of reward that they should receive. If this level of reward is not received, there will be tension within the psychological contract, which could ultimately lead to the termination of the employment relationship.

Spindler (1994) identifies a difficulty with the role of the psychological contract. He notes that in the psychological contract, by its very nature, the rights and obligations of the parties have not been discussed – and therefore they have not been agreed. If employees have not identified what level of reward they expect in return for their efforts it is difficult for the employer to meet those expectations. Indeed, Spindler goes on to comment that some employees will not even be able to express what reward they expect, they simply know that they are dissatisfied with what they have received.

This lack of ability to express expectations clearly gives the employer a very difficult task. Guest *et al* (1996) would suggest that this is largely because of the changing nature of the psychological contract. They suggest that employees might still want what they have always wanted – job security, a career, fair rewards, interesting work and so on. However, employers no longer feel able or obliged to provide this, and are actually demanding more of employees while providing less in return.

Many would refute this argument, particularly in the current times when unemployment is relatively low, and hence it is more of an employees' market rather than an employers' market. If employees are dissatisfied they find it relatively easy to move on to another job. Therefore, it could be argued that employers actually need to provide more in order to retain employees.

Hiltrop (1995) answers this dilemma by suggesting that a new type of psychological contract is developing. He suggests that the new form of contract is much more short-term and situational, and hence focused on immediate issues rather than the longer term issues of security and career growth. As quoted by Armstrong (2002), he says:

> There is no job security. The employee will be employed as long as he or she adds value to the organisation, and is personally responsible for finding new ways to add value. In return, the employee has the right to demand interesting and important work, has the freedom and resources to perform it well, receives pay that reflects his or her contribution, and gets the experience and training needed to be employable here or elsewhere.

However, this explanation of the psychological contract gives a rather unbalanced view, because it suggests that the employee can demand a range of things in return for adding value to the organisation. In reality, Mant (1996) suggests, this short termism actually results in employees being regarded as little more than resources that can be discarded when they have completed their tasks, and needing to meet the demands of the employer whatever they might be.

Whatever the reality of the content of the psychological contract most commentators agree that, if the contract is damaged, the employment relationship will suffer – ultimately to the extent that one party will terminate the contract. Although this might lead to a view that employees in general are suffering from very negative psychological contracts, this is not supported by recent research.

Guest and Conway (2004) found, in their research, that 40 per cent of the sample did not consider that they were fairly paid, whilst 31 per cent considered that their rewards were unfair when compared with other workers doing similar jobs. This could contribute to the finding that 49 per cent of workers surveyed considered that the employer had only partly kept the promises it had made, and 9 per cent considered that the promises had not been kept at all. The perception that the employer has not kept promises, or is not giving a fair reward for work done, will have a negative impact on the psychological contract.

CONTINGENCY-BASED PAY

At the start of this chapter we noted that employees are likely to be rewarded in accordance with their value to the organisation. A large number of organisations have taken this attitude to reward,

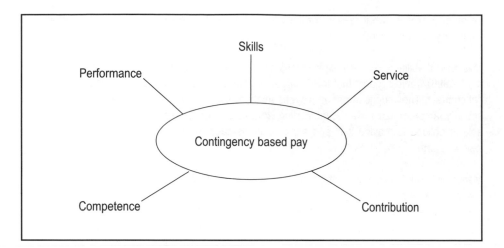

Figure 10.1 Approaches to contingency based pay

and are using a wide variety of approaches under the umbrella heading of 'contingency-based pay'. Contingency-based pay means that an element of the reward package is contingent on factors other than the basic rate for the job. In this section we are going to look at a range of approaches to contingency-based pay, and consider the impacts they might have on employment relations.

Is any element of your reward package contingent on specific factors? If so, do you perceive that this is fair? Talk to the person responsible for reward in your organisation and try to understand why the reward packages have been designed in this particular way.

According to the CIPD survey into *Reward management* (2005), the uses of different criteria to manage pay progression within organisations in the UK are shown in Table 10.3.

Performance related pay

As we can see from Table 10.3, having some element of pay related to performance (either individual or organisational) is a popular way of managing reward. We look at the issue of organisational performance later in this chapter, and here we focus solely on individual performance.

According to Armstrong (2002), performance-related pay (PRP) provides employees with financial rewards (in the form of increases to base pay, or in the form of bonuses) based on an assessment of performance. This assessment is usually made in relation to agreed objectives.

This links back with our initial definition of reward: that the reward reflects the value of employees. It is presumed that employees who perform at higher levels are of more value to the organisation.

There has been much research on the benefits of PRP, with studies both supporting and refuting that there is a link between the introduction of such schemes and increased levels of performance.

Table 10.3 Use of pay criteria to manage pay progression in UK organisations (percentage)

	Manufacturing, production	Private sector	Voluntary sector	Public sector
Performance and skills competency	67	63	39	46
Market rates	46	54	49	21
Organisational performance	44	40	21	20
Wholly on individual performance	30	31	18	26
Team profit/performance	12	12	5	5
Service-related increments	9	8	49	58
Wholly on competencies	6	6	-	4
Wholly on skills	11	5	3	3

Note: more than one method could be identified.

Marsden and Richardson (1994) conducted research into the effects of merit pay in the Inland Revenue. They concluded that the system had, at most, only a small motivational effect on employees. They conducted a follow-up study in 1997 and found that, despite changes that had been made to the scheme by the Inland Revenue, staff tended not to trust the system. Thompson (1992) reported that one-third of employees he surveyed reported that personal satisfaction with their work was sufficient incentive, compared with nearly two-thirds five years previously.

However, a survey carried out by Thompson (1992) of 400 companies in the aerospace sector found that nearly double the number of high-value-added companies (as opposed to low-value-added) applied PRP to more than two-thirds of their staff.

Clearly there is a mixed view of whether PRP is an effective means of approaching reward. However, what is evident is that it is still widely used. The main benefits of PRP to the employment relationship are:

- It does motivate some people. As we have already noted, people are motivated by different things. For those motivated by financial reward there is the potential for PRP to motivate increased levels of performance.
- It does explain what an organisation values as important. This is very important if the organisation is trying to promote particular cultural values, or levels of quality and customer service.
- It gives an explanation to the employee about the way in which employees are valued. Hence, the dissatisfaction that can be felt from making unfavourable comparisons with the reward given to other employees should be reduced or eliminated, because employees should be able to have a rational explanation for the differences that they see.

The main problems with PRP in respect of the employment relationship are:

- It can be very difficult to measure performance. This is demonstrated by the difficulties there have been in introducing PRP to the public sector.

As we saw in Chapter 3, it is difficult to set targets and to measure performance in some jobs. Take, for example, the teaching profession. If teachers are rewarded on the basis of the examination results of their pupils, there are some inequities that have to be addressed. Clearly, some schools have pupils who enter the school with more academic abilities than in other schools. Achieving the same level of examination results in both schools would require very differing amounts of effort from teachers and pupils (and might not be possible in very poor areas of the country). Hence, rewarding on the basis of examination results would be perceived to be unfair. There are currently moves to reward teachers on the basis of the progress of the children in the school, by working out, through a series of tests, the 'added value' that the school adds to each child. Although this also brings concerns (are all children able to progress at the same rate?) it is definitely seen as fairer than rewarding solely on the end results.

- The employee does not always have full control over his/her performance. For example, if an employee is targeted to complete a contract with a customer, and that customer withdraws the contract for no reason that relates to the employee, this will have a direct impact on the employee's measure of performance. However, if the employee cannot affect the measure it is seen as unfair to reward in this way.
- Any individual PRP scheme can inhibit teamwork. This has the potential to damage relationships within a work team.
- There is the potential that employees focus on quantity rather than quality in order to reach the targets. This could work against any cultural values that are being instilled by the use of the PRP scheme.
- Although there is a clearer explanation of what the organisation is valuing in employees, this might not be perceived to be fair. This could be particularly true if there is the perception that some employees are given targets that are easier to achieve than others.
- In many cases the assessment of whether the target has been achieved will have an element of subjectivity. Whenever subjectivity is linked to reward there is likely to be disagreement, and this could have a negative effect on the employment relationship. This could have a particular negative impact on the psychological contract. If the employee perceives that he or she has put in all the effort required, and the employer is not seen to give the expected response (pay the PRP element), he or she will perceive that the psychological contract has been breached.

Competence-related pay

Given the dissatisfaction that started to grow with PRP, organisations started to look for alternative ways of rewarding employees. One alternative that has been developed is competence-related pay. However, as we see from Table 10.3, from the CIPD survey into *Reward management* (2005) it is still not a very popular approach to contingency-related pay.

A competency is defined by Boyatzis (1982) as 'an underlying characteristic of an individual which is causally related to effective or superior performance'. Woodruffe (1991) breaks this definition down into two separate components:

- *competence*: which refers to areas of work in which the employee is competent
- *competency*: which refers to the dimensions of behaviour lying behind competent performance.

When devising a competence-related pay scheme the organisation needs to determine which component of competence it is assessing, or whether it intends to assess both.

A competence-related pay scheme works by identifying the competencies that are required in a job, and the levels of that competency that are required. There is then an assessment of whether the individual employee has met the required level of the competency, and reward is allocated accordingly.

The benefits of competence-related pay to the employment relationship are:

- The scheme is clear to the employee – the employee knows what is valued by the organisation, and hence knows what will be rewarded.
- The scheme allows the employer to make a clear statement about what factors are most important to the organisation, and to direct the development of the employee towards those factors.

The disadvantages to the employment relationship are:

- Competence-related pay is largely seen as much more subjective than the assessment of performance targets. As we have already noted, any amount of subjectivity within the process of determining reward can lead to dissatisfaction and therefore to damage of the employment relationship.
- Not only can there be differences of opinion over whether the required levels of competence have been reached, there can also be differences of opinion between the employer and the employee over what levels of competence are required for the job. If there is a difference of opinion over this, the whole basis of the approach to reward causes dissatisfaction, however well it is applied.

It should also be noted that one of the reasons that this approach to contingency-related pay is not popular is that it is very difficult for employers to maintain. There is a huge amount of work involved in identifying competencies required for each job in an organisation, and the list needs to be maintained constantly. This factor alone has caused many organisations to be reluctant to pursue this approach to reward.

Skills-related pay

Like competence-related pay, skills-related pay concentrates on the inputs that employees bring to the job, rather than on the outputs. In a similar way to competence-related pay, the skills required to do each job and the level of skill required are determined and the employees are assessed against these levels of skill.

As we see from the CIPD 2005 survey into *Reward management,* skills-related pay is not very popular, although it is marginally more popular than competence-related pay. The advantages of skills-related pay for the employment relationship are:

- Again, the employee is able to clearly identify what is valued by the employer, and hence there should be less dissatisfaction when different levels of reward between employees are identified.
- The employer also has the ability to clearly identify what skills are important, both now and for the future.

Disadvantages of skills-related pay to the employment relationship are:

- Again, there is an element of subjectivity that can always be damaging to the employment relationship.
- Again, there can be disagreement over the level of skill that is both required and has been reached, which can have very negative consequences.

Contribution-related pay

As we have seen, there are both benefits and difficulties with performance-related pay, competence-related pay and skill-related pay. A further approach to contingent reward brings the approaches together, with the aim of getting the advantages from each, and the difficulties from none.

As we see in Table 10.3 from the CIPD 2005 survey into *Reward management,* this approach of combining elements of competence/skill and performance was the most popular approach of the organisations surveyed.

Contribution-related pay, therefore, rewards employees for both their input (competencies or skills) and their output (performance). However, although this approach takes a more rounded view of the value of employees, it does not take away some of the difficulties that exist with the two individual schemes: Advantages of contribution-related pay to the employment relationship are:

- It allows employees to understand what is valued by the employer, and the basis on which employees might receive differing rewards.
- It allows the employer to promote the cultural values and behaviours that are most important to the organisation.

The difficulties of contribution related pay to the employment relationship are:

- The issue of subjectivity remains. As already noted, this can damage the employment relationship.
- The difficulties that can exist in achieving performance targets are still relevant. However, in a contribution-related pay scheme it would still be possible to earn an element of the bonus or pay increase, because of the competence element.

Service-related pay

An approach to reward that is still very popular in the voluntary and public sectors is service-related pay. Service-related pay gives an increment in pay, usually annually, to reward long service with the organisation. The logic behind this is that, as people stay longer with the organisation, they gain experience and hence are of more value to the organisation. It is that increased value which is being rewarded. In some organisations the annual increment will be withheld if there has been unacceptable performance.

ORGANISATION
EXAMPLE

Service-related pay is largely associated with the public sector, with teaching and the civil service being two often-quoted examples. However, as we noted in Chapter 3, for many years the public sector has been moving away from rewarding purely on length of service, and has been moving towards rewarding for performance (see later). Most of the difficulties with this change have not been in removing service-related pay, but in the difficulty of measuring performance.

The advantages of this approach to contingency-based pay are that it is easily calculated, and it is based on objective fact (rather than subjective assessment) and hence there can be no argument over whether it has been applied fairly. The result of this is presumed to be that employees will see that the system of reward is fair, and hence there will be no dissatisfaction.

However, this ignores some of the basic principles of reward that we have already examined. If reward has a function of motivating employees, as we have suggested, then employees will not be motivated by a scheme that is based on a factor they cannot influence apart from through the process of turning up at work. The quality and quantity of their work will not impact on their reward, and hence the reward system will not motivate them to work better or harder. There is also the possibility of significant frustration as employees see longer-serving colleagues being paid more, particularly if there is the perception that those colleagues are performing less effectively than themselves.

As we will see when we look at inequality in pay later in this chapter, service-related pay serves to potentially add to inequalities. This is particularly true when considering differences in reward between genders, as women are more likely than men to break their service because of childcare requirements.

ACTIVITIES

Think back through the different approaches to contingency-related pay that have been considered in this section. Regardless of any current pay schemes that exist in your organisation (or an organisation with which you are familiar), which scheme do you think would best support good relationships between employees and the employer in your organisation? Why?

INDIVIDUAL VERSUS TEAM PAY

All of the contingency-based approaches to reward that we looked at in the last section related to individual pay. That, in itself, can cause damage to the employment relationship. As we noted at the start of this book, the employment relationship has a number of different facets to it – it is not just about the relationship between the employer and the employee. If there are negative relationships between team members this can result in overall demotivation.

Thompson (1992) found that the most common method of rewarding a team is to distribute a cash sum that relates to overall team performance among the team members. Different organisations use different approaches to determining how the money should be shared out.

In order for such an approach to team reward to work, there must be a clearly defined team that is working towards a common goal. If team members keep changing, or if a team only works together on a limited number of issues, the reward is likely to be less effective because it is not impacting on all team members equally.

However, as Armstrong (2002) notes, it cannot be ignored that it is individuals within the teams who are receiving the rewards. Hence, the reward system must motivate the individuals, and meet their needs, as well as motivating the team.

A big difficulty with team-based reward is the perception of fairness. It is very rare for all members of a team to expend equal effort, and hence those who have worked hardest are likely to perceive it as unfair that those who have put in least effort get the same reward as them. However, if the organisation wants a culture of teamwork, rather than employees working alone as individuals, rewarding on an individual basis will not support the culture of the organisation.

An increasingly common approach to rewarding employees with a bonus payment is to base the payment on the overall performance of the organisation, the full team of all employees. Such schemes are more common in private sector companies (69 per cent of all organisations surveyed in the CIPD 2005 survey into *Reward management* compared with public sector organisations (22 per cent) and the voluntary sector (23 per cent)).

The prevalence of bonuses based on overall organisation performance, according to the CIPD survey, is given in Table 10.4.

The difficulty with organisation-based bonus schemes is that employees can find it difficult to comprehend what impact they can personally have on the organisation's performance. This is particularly true for employees who work in large organisations. Although the bonus payment is welcome when it comes, and might bring with it some general motivation to perform well, the specific motivation of a particular scheme to influence individual employees is likely to be small.

Scheme driven by business results

Organisations identify particular targets that they want to achieve, and all employees work together to achieve those targets. Although the targets might include financial performance

Table 10.4 Prevalence of bonuses based on overall organisation performance (percentage)

Scheme driven by business results	65
SAYE (save as you earn)	47
Share incentive plans	33
Profit share	14
Gainsharing	2

Note: organisations might have more than one bonus.

they could equally cover a much wider range of issues including customer service, quality, achievement of deadlines or reaching certain levels of innovation.

Save As You Earn (SAYE)

In Save As You Earn (SAYE) schemes, employees save a regular amount each month over a specified period of three, five or seven years. At the end of the savings period employees can buy shares in the organisation with the fund that has accumulated. The shares are bought at the price that they were at the start of the savings period, or at a discount agreed at the start of the savings period. Tax relief is given on the shares that are bought.

Such a scheme has a number of purposes. First, it encourages employees to take an interest in the share price of the organisation – and hence in the overall performance of the organisation. Second, it encourages employees to remain with the organisation on a relatively long-term basis, reducing the costs of employee turnover. Third, presuming that the share price has gone up over the relevant period, employees should receive a good bonus when they purchase the shares (many sell them immediately to get an instant financial gain). However, share prices seem a very remote issue to many employees, and hence the actual link between such a scheme and performance can appear rather vague.

Share incentive plans

Share incentive plans include a range of schemes, from employers giving free shares to employees (up to a value of £3,000 in any one tax year) to an employer matching the shares bought by an employee (ie an employee buys 100 shares, and the employer gives 100 shares to the employee).

If an employee keeps the shares for at least five years no tax or national insurance is paid on the shares. The purpose of share incentive plans is very similar to a SAYE scheme. They encourage employees to stay longer with an organisation, and they promote interest in the performance of the organisation as indicated by the share price.

Profit share

These are also schemes driven by business results, but concentrate solely on profits. Once profits go over a certain level all employees receive a certain percentage of a pool of money that is determined by the size of the profit. This pool might be shared out equally (ie all employees get exactly the same amount of money, irrespective of their status or salary) or the payment might be related in percentage terms to the employees' salaries.

According to Armstrong (2002), in British Gas a set percentage of 3 per cent of group profits is paid to employees, once the required threshold of profits has been achieved. The Bank of Scotland gives employees a minimum of 2 per cent of pre-tax profits and a maximum of 6 per cent. Some organisations do not give an automatic payout to employees. For example, in both Norwich Union and Thomas Cook employees with low performance ratings get no payment.

Gainsharing

As can be seen from the CIPD survey into *Reward management* (2005), gainsharing is not a particularly popular approach to reward in the UK (it is much more popular in the USA). Gain-sharing is where employees share the financial results of improvements in productivity and quality and cost reductions. The payment that is given to employees is taken from the costs savings that result from the improvements.

The advantage of this scheme, over the others we have looked at in this section, is that employees have a clear understanding of what they must do to achieve the bonus. As not all the targets are linked to financial performance, employees are also more likely to have an understanding of how they can personally impact on the improvements. However, the schemes are quite complex to devise, and it is primarily this reason that has made them unpopular.

INEQUALITIES IN PAY

In 1970, when the Equal Pay Act was introduced, there was a gap of 30 per cent between the pay of men and women (according to the Women and Equality Unit). By 2005 that gap had reduced to 18 per cent. This means that women working full-time are currently paid, on average, 82 per cent of men's hourly pay. In *The gender pay gap* – a publication from the government in 2001 – a number of reasons for this gap were suggested:

- *Differences in educational levels and work experience* Historically men had greater educational opportunities than women. Although this is no longer the case in the majority of instances, there might still be some impact of this amongst the older workforce. In addition, women are more likely to take career breaks for childcare reasons and this means that they have less opportunity to accrue work experience.
- *Part-time working* Although the statistical comparisons between pay allow for the differences in hours, part-time working still has an impact. This is because more women than men work part time, and part-time jobs are often concentrated in lower-paid areas of employment.
- *Travel patterns* Women are likely to be able to spend less time than men commuting (because of childcare and other caring responsibilities). Hence, women have a smaller pool of jobs to choose from, and there can be areas where there is a concentration of women looking for work that could push job rates down.
- *Occupational segregation* 60 per cent of working women work in just 10 classifications of jobs. Typically jobs that are held primarily by women are relatively low-paid. Women are still under-represented in higher-paid jobs.
- *Workplace segregation* Within the workplace it is often found that the majority of women are concentrated in the lower-paid jobs.

In 2001 Denise Kingsmill was appointed by the government to investigate the differences in pay between men and women. The Kingsmill Review made a series of 14 recommendations, under the following five headings:

1. Improve the level of information available relating to the pay of women.
2. Improve the level of reporting of relevant information.
3. Increased research, particularly in the best use of women's skills.
4. The use of tax credits to encourage employers to recruit women, particularly to areas where women are under-represented.
5. Improved rights of disclosure so that women can determine whether they are being paid fairly.

Read more about the Kingsmill Review. Details can be found on the Women and Equality Unit website
www.womenandequalityunit.gov.uk
or the Kingsmill Review website
www.kingsmillreview.gov.uk

ACTIVITIES

The government has recommended that organisations carry out regular pay audits. It is not uncommon for inequalities in pay to exist between men and women, but for the organisation to be unaware that the inequalities exist. However, despite the protestations from many trade unions, the requirement to carry out an equal pay audit is not currently compulsory.

Although the primary purpose of an equal pay audit is to identify any areas of inequality, there is also the secondary purpose of showing employees that every effort is being made to remove any inequalities. This should help to address any dissatisfaction with reward that might be damaging the psychological contract.

The Equal Pay Act 1970 was the first piece of legislation in the UK specifically directed at discrimination. It requires equality of treatment in pay and contractual terms (including pension benefits) between men and women doing 'like work', work rated as equivalent, or work of equal value. It should be noted that the Act cannot be used to found claims of unequal pay based on comparisons between employees of the same sex. It is also important to note that the Act only applies to perceived inequalities between men and women – it does not cover any perceived inequalities that have arisen on the grounds of such factors as race or disability. However, if there were such perceived inequalities they could be covered under legislation such as the Race Relations Act 1976 or the Disability Discrimination Act 1995, as an occurrence of treating one group of people less favourably than another.

The Equal Pay Act allows a claim to be brought to an employment tribunal if the man and woman (the claimant and the comparator) are employed on one of the following:

- like work
- work rated as equivalent
- work of equal value.

Like work

The legislation defines this as 'work of the same or a broadly similar nature'. Generally speaking employment tribunals will not be looking for work that is exactly the same, rather they will be looking for a broad similarity. The tribunal will also be looking at the typical tasks in the job, rather than incidental examples of similar tasks. The following case was brought on the basis of like work:

ORGANISATION EXAMPLE

Capper Pass v Lawton (1977)

Lawton was a cook working 40 hours a week and preparing daily lunches for directors and their guests. She compared herself with two male assistant chefs who worked 40 hours per week with 5.5 hours of regular weekly overtime. They were responsible for cooking 350 meals per day for the employees, in two sittings. The tribunal held that the skills and experiences required to do the two jobs were broadly similar, and the type of work carried out was also broadly similar. On this basis they decided that Lawton did similar work to the assistant chefs and allowed her claim.

Work rated as equivalent

If the organisation has an analytical job evaluation scheme then the approach of 'work rated as equivalent' can be used. An analytical scheme breaks jobs down into component parts and either gives jobs a 'value' by awarding points for the component parts, or makes comparisons between jobs. On this basis jobs can be graded. If an employee can show that his/her job has been graded as equivalent to another job, he/she can potentially bring a claim of equal value, although the actual jobs are very different:

ORGANISATION EXAMPLE

Springboard Sunderland Trust v *Robson (1992)*

Robson compared her job of team leader to the job of a male induction officer. Robson's job had been evaluated at 410 points following a job evaluation process, and the induction officer's job had been evaluated at 428 points. The company grading scheme put all jobs between 360 and 409 points in grade three, and all jobs between 410 and 439 points in grade four. Despite this, Robson was treated as a grade three and the induction officer was rated as grade four. The Employment Appeals Tribunal (EAT) and the employment tribunal found that Robson's comparison was allowed because the two jobs were 'work rated as equivalent'.

Work of equal value

The concept of work of equal value was added to the legislation by the Equal Pay (Amendment) Regulations 1983. This was done to bring the legislation in line with the EC Equal Pay Directive. It is much more difficult to show that there is work of equal value. Typically an employment tribunal will appoint an independent expert to examine any claim brought under this concept.

One way to obtain information from the employer in order to examine the claim of work of equal value is to issue an equal pay questionnaire. Prior to the Employment Act 2002 employees could only issue such questionnaires once they had made an application to an employment tribunal. However, as a result of the Employment Act 2002 employees can issue questionnaires prior to bringing a claim. A sample questionnaire has been produced by the Women and Equality Unit (www.womenandequalityunit.gov.uk). The employer is required to respond to the questionnaire within eight weeks.

One example of work that was judged to be of equal value is shown in the following case:

Hayward v *Cammell Laird (1984)*

Hayward, a cook in the Cammell Laird shipyard, claimed her work was of equal value to painters, insulations engineers and joiners working on the same site. An independent expert was appointed by the tribunal and investigated the claim. His conclusion was that there was evidence of work of equal value, and hence the claim was allowed.

At the start of this chapter we considered the issue of different employees having differing values to the organisation. We also identified how this difference can lead to perceptions of unfairness, and can ultimately lead to the termination of the employment relationship.

The Equal Pay Act 1970 attempts to legislate against this unfairness, albeit with a remit that is only focused on gender differences. Hence, if employees are aware that they are receiving differing levels of reward they should be able to identify justifiable reasons for the differences.

The legislation does not mean that all employees have to be paid identically. Indeed, an employer can defend a claim for equal pay by showing that there was a reason for the difference between the pay package of the man and the woman which represented a 'genuine material factor' unconnected with sex. The word 'material' in this context has been held to mean 'significant and relevant'. Factors such as qualifications, experience, performance and in some instances market forces may justify pay differences between a male and female employee. The employer will not, however, be able to defend an equal pay claim solely on the grounds that the company cannot afford to pay the complainant more.

If the reason for an employee's lower level of pay is that he or she has shorter service than the chosen comparator, the employer must be in a position to justify operating a pay scheme based on length of service. To do this, the employer will need to demonstrate that length of experience in the particular job under review actually enables the employee to do the job more effectively. Hence, the employee should be able to understand the differing values that are put on differing levels of experience.

The following cases give examples of defences that might be allowed and disallowed by employment tribunals:

Different negotiating groups: *Enderby* v *Frenchay Health Authority (1993)*

In this case the health authority relied on the defence that the differences in the jobs that had been identified were as a result of the rates of pay being determined by different negotiating bodies. Enderby was a senior speech therapist, and she claimed her work was of equal value to that of male principal-grade pharmacists and clinical psychologists. The European Court of Justice ruled that it was insufficient to rely on the differences resulting from different negotiating groups, and justifications for the actual differences had to be given.

Experience: *Arw Transformers* v *Cupples (1977)*

Cupples was aged 27 years and paid £40.75 per week. She compared herself with a male colleague doing the same work (work study engineer) who was aged 53 years and paid £60 per week. It was ruled that, although her colleague had more experience than Cupples, the work that they were doing was the same and hence the differing level of experience was not a defence to the differences in pay.

Red-circling: *Outlook Supplies* v *Parry (1978)*

If an employee is moved to a job of a lower level, organisations often 'red circle' the rate of pay. This means that the pay is not reduced, but no increases are given until people doing the same work have reached the same level of pay.

Parry was an accounts supervisor and she compared her pay to a male colleague who was also an accounts supervisor, but previously had been an accounts supervisor along-side being an assistant accountant. Because of ill health the assistant accountant part of the role had been dropped and his pay had been red-circled. However, this had happened two and a half years earlier, and the tribunal ruled that red-circling was not a defence because it had gone on too long. Although the EAT agreed that red-circling should not go on for a prolonged period, it did not judge that two and a half years was too long and hence the employer's appeal was allowed.

Location: *Navy, Army and Air Force Institutes* v *Varley (1976)*

Varley worked as a clerk in Nottingham, working a 37-hour week. Colleagues doing the same work in London worked a 36.5-hour week. Varley argued that her hours should be the same as a male clerk working in London. However, she lost her claim because it was held that the difference was owing to the location and not as a result of sex discrimination.

The national minimum wage (NMW) was introduced in the UK in 1999. Although the primary purpose of the NMW was to legislate against the employers who persisted in paying employees at unacceptably low levels of pay, it was also hoped that it would have an impact on the imbalance of pay between men and women. There is no significant evidence that it has had this impact. We look in more detail at the NMW in Chapter 12.

TOTAL REWARD

All of our focus on reward so far in this chapter has been on financial reward. However, it would be an incomplete picture if we did not also consider the role of non-financial rewards. As we noted earlier in this chapter, money does not motivate all employees. A more recent way of approaching reward, therefore, has been through the concept of total reward.

Manus and Graham (2002) define total reward as including all types of reward: base pay, contingency-related pay, employee benefits and non-financial rewards. This approach is holistic. The reward package does not rely on reward mechanisms operating in isolation, rather account is taken of the variety of ways in which employees can be rewarded and can gain job satisfaction, and the holistic reward package attempts to address all of those.

According to Armstrong and Stephens (2005) the components of total reward are split into two groups:

- *Transactional rewards* are those resulting from transactions between the employer and the employee, and include base pay, contingent pay and employee benefits.
- *Relational rewards* are non-financial rewards, which are concerned with learning and development and the experience of work. Hence, issues such as achievement, recognition, responsibility, autonomy and growth are all included in this group.

Non-financial rewards, as can be seen from the list above, focus on human needs. However, they tend to be used on a more individual basis than financial rewards. This is primarily because the needs of employees are very individual, and what might motivate one employee could potentially demotivate another employee. For example, promotion and increased responsibility could bring a lot of satisfaction to one employee, but frighten another.

Armstrong and Stephens go on to identify the benefits of a total reward approach:

- The variation of the different components of reward will result in a longer-lasting impact on the motivation and commitment of employees.
- The employment relationship is enhanced by the balance of transactional and relational rewards.
- The total reward approach allows greater flexibility to meet the individual needs of employees.
- The relational rewards have a direct positive impact on the psychological contract which can make the organisation an 'employer of choice'.

This approach could serve to address the overall weakness of trying to use financial reward as a motivator. As we have already identified, not all employees are motivated by money and hence the direct link between motivation and pay has to be questioned. However, if the reward package has a more holistic approach it is much more likely that there will be some element of it that is motivating to an individual, and hence there is much more opportunity to motivate through effective use of the reward package.

KEY POINTS FROM THIS CHAPTER

- Reward is related to the value placed on an individual by the organisation.
- Reward has three objectives: to recruit and retain employees, to motivate employees and to encourage commitment to required behaviours and rules.
- Although motivation can be affected by reward there is no direct link between reward and motivation.
- A perceived unfairness with reward can have a negative impact on the psychological contract.
- Contingency-based pay is basing an element of the reward on specific factors identified by the organisation.
- Team-based pay encourages teamwork, rather than individual achievements.
- It can be difficult for employees to see how they contribute towards organisation-wide reward schemes.
- The Equal Pay Act 1970 was introduced to eliminate differences in pay between men and women.

- There is still an average pay difference of 18 per cent between men and women.
- Total reward covers both transactional and relational rewards, and takes a holistic approach to reward

1. At a meeting of departmental managers the general view is aired that employees are demotivated. A suggestion is made that a review of the reward package is carried out to address this issue. However, the suggestion is opposed because other managers believe that the issue is not related in any way to reward. Use motivation theory to suggest why both groups of managers could be correct.
2. Explain the relevance of reward to the employment relationship.
3. To what extent do you think that the concept of total reward addresses the difficulties produced by a purely financial approach to reward? Are there any weaknesses of the concept that you can identify?

(Suggestions of answers to the examples can be accessed by tutors at www.cipd.co.uk/tss).

Townsleys is a retail organisation specialising in men's fashions. It has a head office in Cardiff, with a network of 34 branches, primarily in Wales and the south-west. It is a well-established organisation with around 750 employees.

As is typical of the retail sector, there is a significant level of competition. Over recent years Townsleys has remained profitable, but this has proved to be more and more difficult as time has passed. The competition is growing as designer goods become more affordable, and there have also been a number of ladies fashion outlets that have started to include men's fashions amongst their products as they diversify in response to competition.

The senior management at Townsleys firmly believe that the success or failure of a branch depends on the motivation of the management. Hence, it has long been the practice to pay the store managers in accordance with the profitability of the store. The current pay structure is as follows:

- base pay paid on a scale according to the size (in square metres) of the store
- bonus paid according to the sales and profits each month
- additional bonus paid according to the promotion of specific ranges, altered on a monthly basis.

At a recent management conference the store managers complained about the way that their bonuses are calculated. Put simply they do not think that the bonus structure is fair. They do not have any local advertising or promotion budget – all of that is controlled by head office. Hence, they think that they have very little influence over the level of sales in their individual stores. Also, they are given very little discretion over pricing, and hence they cannot make any adjustments to help boost sales.

You are the HR manager and your observation is that the current pay structure is actually demotivating the store managers, rather than motivating them. You do think, therefore, that there needs to be some action taken to change the current reward structure.

You have considered a range of options, primarily looking at contingency-based pay. You could opt for an approach that is based on:

- *Competence*: paying the store managers for the competencies that they have developed in their roles.
- *Skill*: paying the store managers for the skills that they demonstrate in their roles.
- *Contribution*: paying the store managers for a mix of their skills and their competencies.
- *Performance*: although this could be seen to be very similar to the current approach it is still attractive. However, in setting up such a pay system you would want to be paying the store managers for things that they can really influence.

Before deciding how you want to proceed you have drawn up some basic requirements of the new pay system.

- It must motivate the store managers to increase their sales, and their profits.
- It must be attractive when recruiting new store managers.
- It must be manageable.
- It must be a system that the store managers trust. You do not want to introduce a system that introduces suspicion into the way that pay is being calculated.

Questions

1 Evaluate the four approaches to reward that have been identified by the HR manager, considering the advantages and disadvantages of each.
2 Match the four approaches to the basic requirements that have been identified.
3 On the basis of the evaluations that you have carried out in answering the first two questions, recommend a way forward for the store managers' pay, justifying your recommendations.

Discipline and Dismissals

CHAPTER 11

The objectives of this chapter are to:

- explore why discipline is required in the workplace
- consider why people break the rules
- outline the procedure for fairly handling discipline
- explore the law relating to dismissals
- explore the law relating to redundancies.

In this final section of the book we are moving to look at the law that underpins the employment relationship. Although the following chapters explain the relevant legislation, our interest is also in considering the impact that the law has on the employment relationship.

We start, in this chapter, by looking at the issue of discipline and dismissals. In Chapter 12 we move on to look at the law that relates to trade union activities. In Chapter 13 we look at how the law gives employees individual protection, and consider how this level of protection has grown rapidly in recent years.

We need to look at the issue of discipline alongside that of reward, which was discussed in Chapter 10. Discipline is largely used to punish and regulate unwanted behaviour. However, behaviour can also be regulated through the use of reward – an approach that many would argue is much more positive, and often more appropriate.

THE USE OF DISCIPLINE

According to the CIPD survey *Managing conflict at work* (2004), organisations experienced an average of 30 formal disciplinary cases (including formal warnings through to dismissal) and nine grievance cases each year. The average number of cases within sectors varied considerably, as shown in Table 11.1. It is interesting to consider why there is this difference between sectors. The survey does not give any answer to this question, and hence no definitive answer can be given.

The organisations surveyed reported that a significant number of days per year are spent managing disciplinary and grievance cases. They account for this through adding together 4.6 days of management time, 5.6 days of HR staff time and 1.8 days of in-house lawyers' time.

ACTIVITIES

Find out how many disciplinary warnings have been issued in the organisation where you work, or in an organisation with which you are familiar. If possible, find out the reasons that the warnings have been given. Ask the person responsible for HR whether these are typical figures. Does the head of HR think that using the disciplinary procedure has been effective in reducing the unwanted behaviours?

This survey would suggest that discipline is a relatively common issue faced by organisations. Why is discipline and punishment necessary in organisations?

If we go back to the behaviourist psychologists that we quoted briefly in Chapter 10 we can see that punishment can be used to shape behaviour. Skinner (1938), working with pigeons, found that following a response with an aversive stimulus could be effective in eliminating the behaviour. So, applying this to human behaviour, he found that giving some form of punishment following an unwanted response would help to eliminate that behaviour.

However, Skinner also found that the results of the punishment were relatively short-lived, and hence punishment only has a temporary effect on deterring unwanted behaviour rather than eliminating it totally. He also found that punishment has a more permanent effect if the desirable behaviours are rewarded at the same time as punishing the undesirable behaviours. In a work setting, for example, this would suggest that punishing an employee who regularly turns up late for work will be more effective if that employee is also rewarded when s/he turns up for work on time.

Collins (1995) suggests a number of reasons that punishment often fails to achieve the goals required. These include:

- *It hurts.* In the work situation the hurt is not physical pain (like it could be when smacking a child as a punishment), rather it is likely to be the emotional/mental pain felt as a result of the humiliation of being disciplined.
- *Those who are punished often drop out of the situation.* In a work situation this could mean that the employee decides to resign. However, it could also mean that the employee withdraws from group activities and works alone, which could be to detriment of successful working relationships.
- *Punishment can create anger and hostility.* If this is not addressed the working relationships can become very damaged over time.

Table 11.1 Average number of disciplinary and grievance cases by sector

	All respondents	Manufacturing and production	Voluntary, community, not for profit	Private sector	Public sector
Disciplinary cases	30	22	6	51	13
Grievance cases	9	4	3	15	7

This survey is based on 1,190 organisations. 288 were in the manufacturing and production sector, 473 in the private sector, 355 in the public sector and 88 in the voluntary, community and not-for-profit sector.

- *Punishment brings with it the reward of getting attention*. If an employee views punishment in this way it will not be successful.

Regardless of the difficulties associated with punishment it is used, along with rewards, to regulate behaviour within organisations (Salamon 2000).

Using discipline in the organisation is a process of both control and of power. Weber (1978) defined power as the ability to get others to do what you want them to do, even if this is against their will. Alternatively, it is to get them to do something they otherwise would not do. In earlier chapters we have also seen the six bases of power as defined by French and Raven (1959). These two theorists would suggest that power could be used by management to force employees to work in a particular way. If they do not, management also has the power to punish (coercive power), and if they do as required, management has the power to reinforce those responses (reward power).

Wilson (2004) suggests that disciplinary procedures used by management are the micro-techniques of power within the organisation. This suggests that management has an overall power because it is in control – and disciplinary procedures are the processes used at the most basic level in order to exercise this power. The purpose of the disciplinary procedure, she goes on to suggest, is to use managerial power to ensure that all employees conform to the rules of the organisation.

Salamon (2000) suggests that the rules that employees are required to comply with can be divided into three categories:

- general society rules relating to personal behaviour (such things as fighting, swearing, stealing etc)
- rules from external legislation (health, safety and hygiene, discrimination)
- managerially determined general work control rules (timekeeping and work performance).

These rules are used to identify the norms of behaviour in an organisation. Norms of behaviour are specific to individual organisations. For example, different organisations have different tolerances of general society rules. This can result in behaviour that is generally seen as acceptable in an organisation being seen as unacceptable by others. When there is a difference of understanding of the norms, it is not always clear to all employees that rules have been broken.

ORGANISATION
EXAMPLE

Moonsar v Fiveways Express Transport Ltd (2004)

Moonsar (a female) complained that, on three occasions, men with whom she worked in the same office had downloaded pornography onto their computers. The pornography had not been shown to her, but she was aware of what was happening and subsequently argued that it led to an intimidating atmosphere and offended her dignity.

In this case we can see how there is a difference in the interpretation of what is an acceptable norm of behaviour. Moonsar's view was that looking at pornography in this setting was unacceptable behaviour. However, the male employees involved did not take the same view.

Interestingly, the case went to an employment appeals tribunal, which found that downloading and displaying pornographic images where a woman could see them amounted to less favourable treatment for the purposes of sex discrimination legislation. The tribunal commented that such behaviour, carried out by male workers in the presence of a female worker, whether or not actually directed towards her, was an obvious affront to her dignity and would constituted a detriment. The behaviour therefore amounted to direct sex discrimination.

Within an organisation the employee can break the rules in two different ways. First, the employee can understand the rule and accept that the rule is legitimate but still go ahead and break the rule. In this situation the employee is less likely to question the right of management to exercise the disciplinary procedure. For example, there is a requirement for all employees to be at work in a retail outlet at 9 am, because that is when the doors open to customers. An employee is persistently late in turning up for work. The employee understands the rule, and accepts that it is a legitimate rule. However, for some reason the employee keeps breaking that rule, accepts that it has been broken it and that sanction must follow.

Alternatively, there is the employee who understands the rule but does not accept that it is legitimate. In this situation the employee will consider it unreasonable for the disciplinary procedure to be used. In our example, another employee is persistently late for work, but does not accept that it is right that all employees should be at the workplace by 9 am. This is because there are very rarely any customers there at this time, and also because the management often require employees to stay late, for which they are not paid overtime. The employee considers that he/she is working his full amount of contractual hours (through staying late) and hence the 9 am rule is unfair. He/she challenges any disciplinary action that is taken.

Apart from seeing a rule as unfair there are other reasons that employees might break the rules:

- According to control theory (Hirschi 1969), social ties influence the tendency to break the rules. Hence, if the employee has a strong commitment to the organisation s/he is less likely to break the rules.
- Differential association theory (Sutherland *et al* 1992) suggests that different groups have different standards for behaviour. The employee, therefore, chooses which group to associate with, and adopts their standards. Within the workplace this might mean that the employee adopts the standards of a group who generally flout the rules within the organisation.

Jones v Tower Boot Company (1997)

Jones was a 16-year-old of mixed race origin. From the start of his employment at Tower Boot he was subjected to abuse from two colleagues. They burned him with a hot screwdriver, threw metal bolts at his head and subjected him to a series of verbal abuse. He resigned and successfully claimed racial discrimination.

The employer claimed that it did not know what the employees were doing to Jones, and that it did not support such racist activities. Although the employees might have known what

> the standards for behaviour were within the organisation, they adopted the standards of behaviour of another group, and in doing so broke the organisation's rules.

Although there might be the perception by an employee that exercising the disciplinary process is unfair, the perception of other employees also needs to be considered. Most people accept that those who deviate from the required behavioural standards should experience some sort of unpleasant consequence.

It is also important that there is consistency in response from the management. Indeed, employment tribunals will take into consideration how previous situations have been dealt with when considering whether an employer has acted fairly in dismissing an employee.

THE PROCEDURE FOR HANDLING DISCIPLINARY ISSUES

The Employment Act 2002 introduced the requirement for all organisations to follow a Statutory Dismissal and Disciplinary Procedure. The requirement to follow the procedure became part of UK law from 1 October 2004. If the procedure is not followed the dismissal will be deemed to be automatically unfair.

The standard procedure has three steps:

1. The employer must set down in writing the issue that it wants to address through the disciplinary procedure. This written statement must be sent to the employee, making it clear what the basis of the complaint is.
2. The employer must invite the employee to a meeting to be held at a reasonable time and place in order to discuss the issue. The employee must take all reasonable steps to attend. After the meeting the employer must inform the employee about the decision it has made, and offer the employee the right to appeal against that decision.
3. If the employee wants to take up the option of appealing s/he must inform the employer. The employer must then arrange a further meeting for the employee to attend at which the appeal will be heard. Wherever possible this meeting must be held by a more senior manager than the one who held the meeting at step 2. At the end of the meeting the final decision must be communicated to the employee.

The standard procedure must be followed in all situations where there is a possibility that dismissal could be the end result. This includes, therefore, situations of redundancy and of the non-renewal of a fixed-term contract.

The law does allow for a modified procedure to be used when it is not possible or appropriate to use the three-step procedure. This will usually be in cases of gross misconduct (although in most cases of gross misconduct the standard procedure could be used). The modified procedure has two steps:

1. The employer must set down in writing the nature of the alleged misconduct that has led to the decision to dismiss. The employer must explain the evidence that has resulted in this decision. The written document must be sent to the employee. The employee must be informed of the right to appeal against the decision.
2. If the employee wishes to appeal s/he must inform the employer. The employer must then

invite the employee to a meeting at which the appeal will be heard, and the final decision must then be communicated to the employee.

It should be noted that the modified procedure is unlikely to be applicable in many situations. There is not yet sufficient case law on the issue to give clear guidelines. However, it will probably only be applicable in cases such as when an employee has been found guilty of a criminal offence that has an impact on his/her employment.

Not only is there legal doubt over how extensively the modified procedure can be used, there should also be doubt from the perspective of maintaining good employment relationships. Dismissing an employee is a serious step, and not allowing the employee an opportunity to give his/her side of the story prior to dismissal does not promote good employment relations.

Sections 10–15 of the Employment Relations Act 1999 gave workers the right to be accompanied by a fellow worker or trade union representative to any disciplinary or grievance hearing that falls within the following definitions:

- the giving of a formal warning to a worker by the employer
- the taking of some other action to a worker in relation to a disciplinary matter
- the confirmation of a warning or other action that has been taken.

If the hearing is informal there is no statutory right to be accompanied. It must also be emphasised that the right is to be accompanied by a fellow worker or a trade union representative – not a solicitor, member of the family or any other person who does not fall within the given definition.

The emphasis so far has been on the dismissal process. This process can only be the start of the disciplinary process if the alleged incident is classified as gross misconduct (see later in the chapter) and could potentially result in summary dismissal (dismissal without notice). However, most disciplinary issues are not this serious and hence are dealt with through a series of disciplinary warnings.

The law does not specify how many warnings should be given by an employer prior to dismissal, but employment tribunals will look to see whether the employer has followed a process similar to that laid down in the *ACAS code of practice on disciplinary and grievance procedures in employment 2003*. A code of practice is not categorised as legislation, but deviation from it has to be for an acceptable reason. The *ACAS code of practice* advises that a disciplinary procedure should be constructed in the following way:

- an oral warning
- a written warning
- a final written warning
- dismissal.

Each warning has a 'life', which is the period during which the disciplinary sanction remains on record. If during that period the same breach of discipline is repeated, the employer can move up to the next level of sanction. If a further breach of discipline happens after the 'life' has ended, the employer has to return to the start of the disciplinary procedure. The recommended 'life' for a written warning is six months, and the recommended 'life' for a final written warning is 12 months.

In understanding this process of discipline it is important to remember the purpose of the disciplinary procedure. Although the ultimate sanction is dismissal, the employer should see it as a means of improving behaviour, rather than a step-by-step approach to dismissal.

The disciplinary procedure, therefore, is a mix of sanction and a corrective approach. To achieve this it is important that the employee understands not only what is wrong (which has led to the dismissal) but also what the required standards are. Many organisations set specific targets that are then reviewed within the 'life' period of the warning. By linking the targets to the period of the warnings clear focus is given on the need to make improvements. This links back to our earlier comments about the need for employees to understand the acceptable norms of behaviour in their organisation.

FAIR REASONS FOR DISMISSAL

If disciplinary action results in dismissal, the legal question that becomes relevant is whether the dismissal is fair or unfair. If an employee believes that the dismissal is unfair, there is the potential to take a claim to an employment tribunal. To do this, the employee must have at least one year's continuous employment with the organisation.

Section 98 of the Employment Rights Act 1996 lists five potentially fair reasons for dismissal. They are shown in Figure 11.1.

Capability or qualifications

The Employment Rights Act 1996 defines capability as 'skill, aptitude, health or any other physical or mental quality'. Qualifications are defined as 'any degree, diploma or other academic, technical or professional qualification relevant to the position which the employee holds.'

The employer should, at the recruitment stage and in the subsequent period of induction, make sure that the employee understands the requirements of the job. The employer should determine any training needs that exist and act upon them. The employer should also make clear to the employee the likely penalty of failing to meet the required standards. If the employee does not

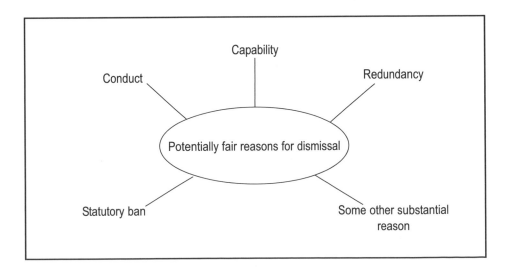

Figure 11.1 Five potentially fair reasons for dismissal

meet the required standards of performance the employer would be expected to try to assist that employee through further training and education before taking disciplinary action.

As we have already noted, punishment alone does not necessarily have a lasting impact on behaviour. Hence, many organisations are taking a more holistic approach to discipline and viewing it as part of the general performance management process.

Armstrong and Baron (1998) define performance management as:

> A strategic and integrated approach to increasing the effectiveness of organisations by improving the performance of the people who work in them and by developing the capabilities of teams and individual contributors.

Performance management has, at its centre, the appraisal process. Targets are set for all employees and the performance against these targets is regularly assessed.

The process of appraisal focuses on improvement and development. If an employee has not achieved a target the focus is on how the employee can be helped to improve in the future, rather than on what sanctions can be imposed. This suggests that the first approach in addressing an issue relating to capability should be through looking at approaches to improvement and development, rather than discipline.

If the capability issue relates to ill health the employer must consider the nature of the illness, the actual and potential length of the absence and the employer's situation (eg the size of the business and the impact that the absence is having on the organisation).

In addition, the employer must consider whether the ill health amounts to a disability under the definition given by the Disability Discrimination Act 1995. (A disabled person is defined as having a 'physical or mental impairment that has a substantial and long-term adverse effect on a person's ability to carry out normal day-to-day activities'.) If the employee is disabled, the employer has to make reasonable adjustments to meet the needs of the employee, and not rush to use the disciplinary procedure.

Even if the employee does not meet the definition of disabled there is still a need to act reasonably, as illustrated by the following case.

Rolls-Royce Ltd v *Walpole (1980)*

Despite having a good attendance record for his first four years of his employment, during the next three years prior to his dismissal Walpole's attendance record averaged 50 per cent. There was no pattern to the attendance. Rolls-Royce followed its procedures in making Walpole aware of its concerns, and could not foresee any reason that the situation would improve. The company dismissed Walpole. He made a claim of unfair dismissal, which was supported by the employment tribunal. The Employment Appeals Tribunal (EAT) overruled the employment tribunal's decision, stating that it was perverse. Dismissal was a reasonable response to an attendance record as poor as that of Walpole.

ORGANISATION EXAMPLE

It is important that the employer's response is reasonable in the particular circumstances of each situation. Although an absence record may be poor, the employer must consider the reasons for this in deciding how to react.

Kerr v Atkinson Vehicles (Scotland) Ltd (1973)

Kerr was severely disabled. He was moved from a role where his absence was interfering with his work, to another role in the organisation. Although his work was satisfactory he was dismissed because of his absences. Kerr successfully claimed unfair dismissal because his employer should have anticipated the absence pattern, and taken steps to accommodate it.

In the same way, the employer must act reasonably in addressing capability issues that relate to performance in the job. The following case illustrates the need to ensure that adequate training and supervision is provided.

Mansfield Hosiery Mills Ltd v Bromley (1977)

Bromley responded successfully to an advertisement for a boiler service fitter. Although the advertisement stated that training would be given, he received none. He performed well and was promoted to maintenance supervisor. In this role a number of issues occurred and he was eventually dismissed. The employment tribunal found that he had been given inadequate supervision, insufficient direction and encouragement, and hence the dismissal was unfair. The EAT supported this finding.

If the employer has taken action to try to help the employee improve the standard of performance, but capability remains an issue, the dismissal can potentially be fair.

Gozdzik & Scopigno v Chlidema Carpet Co Ltd (1979)

The two employees were employed as winders. Because of the effects of the recession the employer introduced a new bonus system aimed at improving the productivity of the winders. The two employees did not meet the new standards and were given further training by the employer. They still did not meet the new standards and they were dismissed. Their claim for unfair dismissal failed because the employer had acted reasonably in providing them with additional training before taking the decision to dismiss.

How much is the responsibility for capability held by the employer, and how much by the employee? If the employer has recruited or promoted someone who is not able to do the job, what action should the employer reasonably be expected to take? What approaches can the employer take to determine the reason for the lack of capability, and how much effort do you think the employer should reasonably be expected to take to determine this?

Conduct

Conduct is typically divided into two categories:

- *Gross misconduct, which can result in summary dismissal (dismissal without notice).* Examples of gross misconduct include theft, assault, vandalism and falsification of records.
- *Misconduct, which comprises less serious offences which are usually dealt with through disciplinary warnings.* If the behaviour does not cease, there is the possibility that the employee will be dismissed. Examples of this include bad language, poor time-keeping and improper wearing of uniform.

A dismissal for misconduct is potentially fair, but the employer must show that he/she has acted reasonably in reaching the decision to dismiss. The role of the employment tribunal is not to determine whether the employee committed the act of misconduct, but whether the employer investigated the situation thoroughly, had a reasonable belief that the employee committed the act, then took a reasonable course of action. This is referred to as acting within the 'range of reasonable responses'.

This test of reasonableness is illustrated in the following cases. An important case is *British Home Stores* v *Burchell (1978)*. This case demonstrates the need for the employer to have a reasonable belief in the guilt of the employee.

British Home Stores v *Burchell (1978)*

Burchell was dismissed because of irregularities in staff purchases. Evidence was obtained from dockets relating to purchases of Burchell and other staff, and a statement from another employee. Burchell took a claim of unfair dismissal to the employment tribunal, which supported her claim, stating that BHS had not clearly established Burchell's guilt. The EAT overturned this decision, stating that the employment tribunal had tried to apply tests more fitting to a criminal investigation. This strict standard of proof was not required. What was required was that the employer had a reasonable belief based on a reasonable investigation. The EAT identified three key elements to this process:

- The fact underlying the belief must be established.
- The belief must be held on reasonable grounds, after an appropriate investigation.
- The investigation must be reasonable, in the circumstances.

It is important to note that the level of investigation and belief required in order to proceed with a dismissal is not the same level as that required in a criminal prosecution.

The reasonableness of a dismissal can also relate to the previous disciplinary record of an employee.

Bartholomew v *Post Office Telecommunications (1981)*

In this case an employee was dismissed for making a 20-minute private overseas telephone call. The employers investigated, and Bartholomew could give no explanation for the call. As Bartholomew had already been given a number of warnings for misconduct, the decision was taken to dismiss him. Both the employment tribunal and the EAT supported the decision to dismiss, in the light of Bartholomew's employment history. However, making the decision to dismiss an employee who had made such a telephone call, and had no record of any past disciplinary issues would probably be seen as unreasonable.

Harris & another v *Courage (Eastern) Ltd (1982)*

If an employee is charged with a criminal offence it can be reasonable to proceed with a dismissal, even if that employee will not co-operate with any dismissal hearings. This is demonstrated in this case. The tests established by *BHS v Burchell* are relevant here.

Courage believed that Harris and another had stolen some beer, and the police charged them both. Courage also started disciplinary proceedings. On legal advice the two employees did not attend the disciplinary hearings, and were not prepared to co-operate with any investigation by Courage. Courage carried out an investigation to the best of its ability, including the taking of witness statements. On the basis of the evidence it had gained it dismissed the two employees. The claim for unfair dismissal was rejected because Courage had carried out a reasonable investigation, and had a reasonable belief that the employees had stolen the beer. It was found that there was no requirement to wait until after a criminal trial. (In the actual criminal trial the employees were acquitted.)

There are many cases of unfair dismissal that are regularly reported in the personnel press. Read some recent cases and apply the 'Burchell test' to them. Try to develop an understanding of what the employment tribunal sees as a 'reasonable response' from an employer.

The issue of acting reasonably is central to the relationship between the employer and the employee when addressing alleged actions of misconduct. Do you think that there is a sufficiently clear definition of reasonableness to give guidelines to both the employer and the employee? Do you think there is a fair balance in the way that the test of reasonableness is applied?

Redundancy

We explore this issue in more detail later in the chapter (see page 264–272).

Statutory ban

This is when it is unlawful to continue working because of a legal restriction or duty. An example of this is an employee who has the job of a driver within an organisation but then loses his/her driving licence because of motoring offences. Clearly, the individual cannot continue to work in the role of driver while the ban is in place.

Again, the concept of reasonableness is central to the reaction of the employer. The employer should consider the length of time that the restriction is likely to be in place. If, to continue the use of our example, the driver has lost his licence for three months it might be possible to find alternative duties during this period. If, however, the driver lost his or her licence for five years, there would be the need to completely redeploy him or her, which might be more difficult.

ORGANISATION EXAMPLE

This issue is illustrated in the case of *Roberts* v *Toyota (GB) Ltd (1981)*. Roberts was an area sales manager, and there was an implied term in his contract that he would have a driving licence. He was convicted of driving whilst over the legal alcohol limit, and lost his licence for 12 months. He offered to purchase a company car and provide a driver to drive him during this 12-month period, but the employer went ahead and dismissed him, viewing the option of using a driver as impractical. His claim of unfair dismissal was rejected, because there was clear evidence that the requirement to have a driving licence was an implied term of his contract of employment.

The need to act reasonably in reaching the decision to dismiss was demonstrated in *Sutcliffe and Eaton Ltd* v *Pinney (1977)*. Pinney was a hearing aid dispenser, and it was a requirement of the profession that he passed a series of examinations within a five-year period. He repeatedly failed the examinations, although he did pass the oral examination just before the five years expired. The employer dismissed him because they believed that he would never pass the examinations, and continuing to employ him would breach the professional requirements. The day after his dismissal he applied for an extension to the examination period, and was informed nearly three months later that an extension had been granted. He claimed unfair dismissal and this claim was supported by the employment tribunal.

The employer, in this situation, had acted too quickly. If Pinney had not been granted the extension we can presume that there would have been a fair dismissal. However, in not seeking an extension and waiting to hear the response to the request the employer had acted unreasonably.

Again, we see the importance of the employer acting reasonably. Although this is an important test in law, it must also be noted that it is an important element of how the employment relationship is being managed. If the employer is acting unreasonably it suggests that the employer is breaching the psychological contract in some way, which will then go on to have a negative impact on the employment relationship.

Some other substantial reason

This category allows the employment tribunal to consider any dismissal that does not fall under one of the other four headings, and to consider the reason and its fairness. Examples under this heading are discussed below.

Pressure from an external source to dismiss

In *Scott Packing and Warehousing Co Ltd* v *Paterson (1978)* the US Naval Authorities refused to have Paterson working on their contract due to alleged incidents of misconduct. This was a major part of Scott Packing's business. The employment tribunal found that Paterson had been unfairly dismissed because the employer had not investigated the issue of misconduct and established a reasonable belief in Paterson's guilt. However, the EAT overturned this decision, stating that the issue here was not one of conduct, but of 'some other substantial reason'. In this case the employer had not acted unreasonably because he had acted in accordance with the wishes of his major customer.

Although customers might refuse to have an employee working with them, the requirement on the employer to act reasonably remains. The above case was referred back to the employment tribunal for it to consider whether there was other work to which Paterson could have been moved. Even if there is pressure from a customer to remove an employee, the employer cannot dismiss without exploring all the options for continued employment.

Reorganisation of the business

If an employer needs to reorganise a business and can show that it is essential to make alterations to an employee's working pattern, there is a potentially fair reason. Again, the employer must show that all the options have been considered and that the conclusion that dismissal is the solution has been reached after reasonable consideration. This occurred in the following case.

Davey v *Daybern Co Ltd (1982)*

Davey worked in a sweet kiosk. Business was poor, and it was decided to reorganise the working hours in order to cut wage costs. The reorganisation meant that Davey would be required to work two evenings, which she was unable to do because of family commitments. A temporary arrangement was put in place, but eventually Davey was dismissed. Her claim of unfair dismissal was unsuccessful because the employment tribunal found that the employer had acted fairly. It was able to demonstrate the commercial needs for the reorganisation, and hence the reason for the dismissal was reasonable under the heading of 'some other substantial reason'.

Mistaken belief

If an employer has a genuine belief that the reason for dismissing an employee is fair, the dismissal could come under the heading of 'some other substantial reason' even if it is later shown that the belief was actually mistaken. This categorisation refers back to the need for an employer to carry out a reasonable investigation, which leads to a reasonable belief.

This is demonstrated in *Bouchaala* v *Trust House Forte Hotels Ltd (1980)*. Bouchaala was a Tunisian student who was given limited leave to enter and remain in the UK. Trust House Forte employed him as a trainee manager, but was then informed by the Department of Employment that he did not qualify for a work permit and continuing to employ him would be illegal. He was dismissed. The Department of Employment then informed the employer that Bouchaala had been given indefinite leave to remain in the UK and hence a work permit was not required. Bouchaala made a claim of unfair dismissal. This claim was not supported because the employer had a genuine belief that there was a substantial reason for the dismissal of Bouchaala. Although that belief was later shown to be mistaken the dismissal, at the time, was still fair.

CONSTRUCTIVE DISMISSAL

In the last section we looked at the five potentially fair reasons for dismissal, and all of these relate to actions that the employer can take to either terminate the contract of the employee, or start the process of termination. However, there are also situations where the employer does not actually dismiss the employee, but the actions of the employer are such that they breach the contract of employment, and that breach goes to the very root of the contract. In this case the employee can terminate the contract of employment and claim constructive dismissal.

In order to show that there has been a constructive dismissal the employee must demonstrate that:

- there was a fundamental breach of the contract on the part of the employer
- the breach of the contract caused the employee to resign
- there was no significant delay in resigning.

A way that the contract can be breached is if the mutual trust and confidence between the employer and the employee is irretrievably damaged:

Isle of Wight Tourist Board v Coombes (1976)

Mrs Coombes was the personal secretary to the director of the board. One day they had an argument and, in the presence of another employee, the director stated that Mrs Coombes 'is an intolerable bitch on a Monday morning'. Mrs Coombes resigned and claimed constructive dismissal. She was successful in her claim, because it was judged that the words of the director had shattered any trust and confidence in the relationship.

It can be difficult to determine whether the behaviour of the employer has actually breached the employment contract. It is not important to consider what the employer intended to do. The employment tribunal will focus on the actual behaviour of the employer, and whether an employee cannot reasonably have been expected to tolerate such behaviour.

The important factor in determining whether constructive dismissal has taken place is whether the actions (or inaction) of the employer have amounted to a breach of the contract. The specific part of the contract that has been breached must be identified, and it must then be possible to show that the breach is fundamental.

Another way to look at this is to consider, again, the psychological contract. If the employer has seriously breached the expectations of the contract it is possible that there is a situation of constructive dismissal. Clearly, however, the breach must go to the very root of the contract – as explained in the definition of constructive dismissal at the start of this section.

AUTOMATICALLY UNFAIR REASONS FOR DISMISSAL

There are situations in which a dismissal is automatically unfair. This means that the one-year qualifying period required to bring a claim of unfair dismissal is not required. This includes situations where the reason for a dismissal relates to:

- the employee's membership (or non-membership) of a trade union
- the employee's pregnancy or any maternity-related issue
- a transfer of employment (see Chapter 12 for further explanation)
- the refusal of a retail employee to work on a Sunday
- a conviction that is, according to law, deemed to be 'spent' (see Chapter 13)
- activities carried out in the role of health and safety representative
- asserting a statutory right
- making a protected disclosure under the Public Disclosure Act (see Chapter 12)
- asserting the right to be paid in accordance with the National Minimum Wage Act 1998
- disclosing fraud or corruption.

WRONGFUL DISMISSAL

Wrongful dismissal occurs when the employer terminates the contract of employment, and in doing so breaches the contract of employment. The breach of contract can be:

- giving no notice of termination, or insufficient notice (presuming that a summary dismissal was not justified)
- where the dismissal is in breach of a contractual disciplinary procedure
- where the dismissal is in breach of a contractual redundancy procedure
- the termination of a fixed-term contract before the date it is due to expire.

If the employee is claiming that a wrongful dismissal has taken place, he/she must be able to show that the employer has terminated the contract of employment, and that such termination has been a breach of the contract. To defend the action of termination the employer must demonstrate that the employee had conducted him/herself in such a way as to show no intention to be bound by the contract of employment.

If an employee successfully shows that wrongful dismissal has taken place, he/she is entitled to compensation for the breach of the contract. This will usually be equal to the loss of salary between the date of the termination and the date of the hearing when wrongful dismissal is determined.

Alternatively, the employee can ask for an injunction against the dismissal being carried out, or a declaration by the court that the dismissal is invalid. In most cases the remedy given is damages.

Although injunctions are not common, the granting of one was allowed in the case of *Irani* v *Southampton and SW Hampshire Health Authority (1984)*. In this case Irani was a part-time ophthalmologist working in a clinic for the health authority. Irreconcilable differences developed between Irani and the consultant in charge of the clinic. The health authority decided that the only solution was for one of the employees to leave the clinic. As Irani was the more junior employee, and worked part time, he was dismissed. The health authority did not determine that there was any particular fault with Irani.

Irani successfully obtained an injunction against the dismissal because the correct procedures had not been followed. The injunction meant that the dismissal was suspended until the issues had been correctly considered. Irani did not work during this period.

REDUNDANCY

Although redundancy is in the list of the five potentially fair reasons for dismissal, it has been decided to look at it separately because it is different from the other reasons in one fundamental way. The decision to make an employee redundant is related to the performance of the organisation, and not any attribute related to the individual.

Redundancy is an unpleasant situation for both the employer and the employee, and the important task for the employer is to try to manage it so that the employment relationship is not damaged by the process. One way of doing this is to follow carefully the quite detailed legislation, which is primarily focused on ensuring that redundancies are handled fairly. Even an employee selected for redundancy can feel that s/he has been treated fairly if the situation is handled well.

The focus of the redundancy situation on the organisation can be seen by looking at the legal definition of redundancy that can be found in Section 139(1) of the Employment Rights Act 1996. According to this definition employees are regarded as redundant if their dismissals are attributed, primarily or partially, to:

The fact that the employer has ceased, or intends to cease, to carry on the business for the purposes for which the employee was employed

This is illustrated in the case of *Hindle* v *Percival Boats (1969)*. Hindle was employed as a boat builder. Percival Boats moved from its traditional methods of making boats from wood, to making them from fibreglass. Hindle was unable to adapt to the new methods of working, and was made redundant on the grounds that the employer had ceased to carry on the business for which Percival had been employed.

However, it was ruled that Hindle was not in fact redundant. He was employed to make boats, and Percival Boats were continuing as boat builders. Hence, there was no redundancy.

If Hindle was unable to make boats out of fibreglass and could not be lawfully made redundant, what action could Percival Boats take? Would a dismissal on the grounds of capability be potentially fair?

The fact that the employer has ceased, or intends to cease, to carry on that business in the place where the employees were employed

If an employee has a clause in his or her contract of employment requiring him or her to be 'mobile', it is possible that a redundancy will not occur if the location where the employee works is closed, but other locations remain open. The mobility clause may allow the employer to move the employee to a different location. The employer would need to show that such a request was reasonable.

This is demonstrated in *Bass Leisure Ltd* v *Thomas (1994)*. Thomas worked at Bass Leisure's Coventry depot that closed. She was asked to move to another depot that was 20 miles away, and refused because of family commitments. There was a mobility clause in her contract, which the employer relied on in requesting her to make the move. After a trial period she left employment and claimed a redundancy payment. The EAT ruled that she should be paid a redundancy payment because, given her family commitments, travelling 20 miles was an unreasonable request.

The fact that the requirement of that business for employees to carry out work of a particular kind, or for employees to carry out work of a particular kind in the place where they were employed, has ceased or diminished or is expected to cease or diminish

In the case of *Safeway Stores plc* v *Burrell (1997)*, the EAT gave a clear approach to follow in determining whether there has been a reduction in the need for employees. In this case Burrell was employed as a petrol station manager. Following a reorganisation the role of manager disappeared and was replaced with the role of filling station controller, at a lower salary and with less status. Burrell decided that he did not want this role and he was dismissed with a redundancy payment. He claimed the dismissal was unfair, because there was no diminution in the duties that he had been carrying out. Someone else was carrying them out. The employment tribunal supported his claim.

In considering the appeal made by Safeway against the decision, the EAT laid out the following approach to determining whether someone has been dismissed for redundancy:

1. Has the employee been dismissed?
2. Had the requirements of the employer's business ceased or diminished, or were they expected to do so?
3. If so, was the dismissal the whole or primary result of the cessation or diminution?

In applying this test the EAT found that the dismissal of Burrell was due to redundancy and was fair. His duties as a manager had diminished, because not all the duties would be carried out by someone of lower status, hence applying this test there is a redundancy situation.

According to the *Labour force survey 2004,* redundancy rates in 2004 were running at 5.5 per 1,000 employees. In the previous 10 years the peak had been at 8.7 per 1,000 employees in the period from November 1998 to January 1999. Redundancy rates are higher for men than for women, and have been for the whole ten-year period. In September 2004 men had a redundancy rate of 6.4 per 1,000 employees compared with a rate of 4.5 per 1,000 employees for women.

The manufacturing industry consistently has the highest rate of redundancies, with 31.9 redundancies per 1,000 employees. (At the time of writing there are no figures available taking in the spring of 2005, when the figures are likely to have increased significantly because of the collapse of the MG Rover Group.) Rates for the banking, finance and insurance sector have increased steadily since 1995 to 18.4 per 1,000 employees, which is a similar level to the distribution, hotels and restaurant sector.

The survey also found that those in the 25–49 year age group were less likely to be made redundant than older and younger employees.

ACTIVITIES

Although mass redundancies have not been seen in the UK since the recession of the late 1980s/early 1990s, the announcement of redundancies is still a regular occurrence. Over a four-week period keep a record of all the redundancies you can find announced in the national and local press. You might be surprised at how many you become aware of.

Selection

Although an employer might have a situation that classifies as a redundancy under the definition we have just considered, it is still possible for the dismissal to be unfair if the selection of the redundant employee(s) is unfair.

It is important to emphasise that it is the job that is made redundant. Therefore, if there is more than one person carrying out similar jobs and only some of those jobs are to disappear, there must be a fair way of determining who is to be selected for redundancy.

The first step is to determine the selection 'pool'. These are the employees that all carry out a similar job, and hence are all potentially at risk from the redundancy. In some cases this is quite straightforward. For example, presume that a company operating a call centre needs, for economic reasons, to make 10 call centre operators redundant. The call centre has 50 call centre operators who all do broadly similar work. The call centre has no other operations. In this case the selection of 10 redundant employees must be made from the 50 call centre operators.

However, consider the example of another call centre that handles three separate contracts. One is for a car breakdown company, one is for a home shopping company and one is for a tourism information company. The home shopping company's business has reduced and hence there is a need to make five employees redundant. Should the selection be made from only those call centre operators working on the home shopping company account? Would your decision change if you were told that the employees working on each contract move around when necessary to cover absence?

The general rule gleaned from case law is that the employer should err on the side of including employees in a pool. This is illustrated in *Bristow and Roberts* v *Pinewood Studios Ltd (1982)*.

ORGANISATION EXAMPLE

Bristow and Roberts were two of 14 drivers employed by Pinewood. The drivers were employed in four different sections of the business. Bristow and Roberts were employed in the commercial section, along with two other drivers. Pinewood announced the need to make two drivers redundant, and following consultation with the trade union it was agreed that the selection would be made solely from the commercial section. As a result Bristow and Roberts were selected for redundancy. The EAT ruled that the redundancy had been an unfair dismissal, because no good reason had been given for the restriction of the selection pool.

Once the correct selection pool has been determined, the method of selection must then be agreed. The process of selection must be fair and must be as objective as possible. In the past the most common method of selection has been LIFO (last in, first out). This is totally objective, because the employees with the shortest period of service are those selected for redundancy. However, many employers have moved away from this approach to selection, because of the impact it can have on the balance of the skills mix in the organisation.

This is particularly true if an organisation has been working hard over recent years to improve the standards of the recruitment and selection procedures. If the result of the redundancy is to terminate the contracts of all the employees who have been recruited because of their levels of skills and qualifications, all the effort that has been put into the recruitment and selection has been wasted.

The approach of LIFO was challenged in the case of *Blatchfords Solicitors* v *Berger and others (2001)*.

Blatchfords announced that it was going to close two of its three offices. The cashier at one of the offices that was to close was put in a selection pool for redundancy with two other cashiers working in the other offices. The selection of the cashier to be made redundant was made solely on the length of service.

The employment tribunal found that the employer was unable to give any reason for LIFO being the only criterion that was considered in the selection process, and the selection pool was also unexplained. The tribunal's view was that no reasonable employer would use LIFO as the sole reason for selection. The EAT rejected that opinion because the tribunal was imposing its own view of the best selection criteria to be used, and it was a perverse finding that LIFO could never be a reasonable criteria.

However, in looking more widely than at length of a service as a selection tool, the employer must choose appropriate criteria. Guidelines for this were laid down in *Williams* v *Compair Maxam (1982)*.

In this case employees were selected for redundancy by three departmental managers listing those they felt should be retained for the best long-term viability of their departments and the company. The employer justified this approach because the reasons for the redundancy were that the business was struggling, and long-term viability was a real issue.

However, the EAT found that the selection criteria were completely subjective. There had been no attempt to agree objective criteria with the trade union representatives, and hence the selection was unfair. In making the ruling on this case a number of points were made that should be followed to ensure a fair redundancy:

- As much warning as possible should be given of any impending redundancies.
- Consultation must take place over the selection criteria, with a view to agreeing those criteria.
- The criteria chosen must be able to be checked objectively (eg against attendance records or records of performance).
- The criteria must be applied fairly in carrying out the selection.
- If possible, alternative employment must be offered in preference to making an employee redundant.

Any selection that is carried out must be completed by assessors who know all the employees in the selection pool, and are able to assess each of the criteria correctly.

In devising selection criteria it is important to note that no criteria must be directly or indirectly discriminatory. For example, deciding to terminate all the part-time employees before considering the full-time employees is likely to be indirect sex discrimination because significantly more women than men work part time. Also, choosing criteria that relate to physical attributes (eg strength) are likely to be indirect sex discrimination because the average man is biologically stronger than the average woman.

It is also important for long-term employment relationships that the employees understand the process of selection and see that it is fair. If there is the perception that the criteria are fair, and that they are fairly applied, then the damage caused to the employment relationship by the process can be minimised.

Consultation

If no consultation takes place prior to employees being made redundant, the redundancy will usually be unfair. If the employer can show that any consultation would have been a futile exercise, it could be found that consultation was not necessary. However, this is an unusual finding.

The length of time that must be spent in consultation is laid down in the Trade Union and Labour Relations (Consolidation) Act 1992 (TULRCA):

- If the proposed redundancies involve more than 100 employees, the consultation must take place over at least 90 days.
- If the proposed redundancies involve more than 20, but less than 100 employees, the consultation must take place over at least 30 days.

If less than 20 employees are to be made redundant the redundancy is not covered by the above legislation relating to collective redundancies. However, case law has demonstrated a clear requirement on the employer to consult with the individual who is potentially affected by the proposed redundancy. This consultation must take place over a 'reasonable' period of time.

It should be noted that any employer intending to make more than 20 employees redundant at one establishment is required to inform the Secretary of State for Trade and Industry in writing at the time that the intention is announced, using form HR1.

Some key requirements of the consultation period were laid down in the Court of Sessions ruling in *King and others* v *Eaton Ltd (1995)*. Eaton Ltd announced a redundancy, and consultation took place with the trade union representatives. During this consultation period the issues relating to selection were not addressed. The employment tribunal found that the redundancies were unfair because there had been insufficient consultation. The EAT disagreed with this view, but it was supported by the Court of Sessions. In making the decision it laid down the following guidelines:

- The consultation must take place when the proposals are still at a formative stage (ie, starting the consultation when all decisions have already been made does not lead to a meaningful consultation).
- The employer must give adequate information and give adequate time for a response to be given.
- The employer must give 'conscientious consideration' to the points made during the consultation process.

Section 188(4) of TULRCA 1992 also determines that certain information must be given in writing by the employer at the start of the consultation:

- the reason for the proposed redundancies

- the number and description (ie the types of jobs involved) of the employees it proposes to make redundant
- the total number of employees at the establishment who are to be affected
- the proposed method of selection
- the procedure to be followed in dealing with the redundancies
- the method of calculating the redundancy payment, if it differs from the statutory payment.

A meaningful period of consultation cannot start until the employees (or employee representatives) have been supplied with all the required information regarding the redundancy.

ORGANISATION EXAMPLE

In *Green and Son (Castings) Ltd and others* v *ASTMS and AUEW (1983)* a redundancy was announced, but details of the proposed selection methods were only given to the trade unions eight days before the dismissals took effect. In this case it was ruled that there was insufficient time for meaningful consultation to take place regarding the selection criteria.

If the employer fails to consult, the dismissal will not be automatically unfair, although that is a possible conclusion. However, a protective award will be made when the appropriate length of consultation has not been observed. The protective award is the wages that the employee would have earned during either the 30 or 90-day consultation period, if that period of consultation had taken place.

At the end of the consultation period with the trade unions or employee representatives, the employer then has to formally go through the process of making the individual employees redundant. To do this the employer must follow the three-step statutory disciplinary procedure that was explained earlier in this chapter. This allows the employee an opportunity to argue against the redundancy, and to suggest alternatives to being made redundant.

Redundancy compensation

An employee is entitled to a statutory redundancy payment if s/he has been employed for more than two continuous years at the time of the dismissal, and if s/he is aged over 18 years. If the employee is aged over 65 years no redundancy payment will be made (although this will be changed when age discrimination legislation is introduced in October 2006).

The statutory redundancy payment is calculated in the same way as the basic award. This is calculated by determining the employee's period of continuous service with the employer (up to a maximum of 20 years). The calculations are as follows:

- 1.5 weeks' pay for each year when the employee was between the ages of 41 and 64 years
- 1 week's pay for each year when the employee was between the ages of 22 and 40 years
- 0.5 weeks' pay for each year of employment between the ages of 18 and 21 years.

A week's pay is subject to the statutory maximum, which is currently (July 2005) £280. This figure is reviewed by the government in February each year.

(Note that clearly the calculation of the basic award is based on age. This is potentially a breach of age discrimination legislation, and hence the formula for calculating the basic award is very likely to change before October 2006, but no details are currently available.)

In addition to the statutory redundancy payments outlined above, some organisations have an additional company redundancy scheme that gives enhanced payments to employees.

If an employee is offered suitable alternative employment and refuses this unjustifiably, that employee loses his/her entitlement to a redundancy payment.

Suitable alternative employment

Section 141 of the Employment Rights Act 1996 provides that if the employer makes an offer to renew the contract of employment, or to re-engage the redundant employee under a new contract which is to take place when the old contract expires, or within four weeks of the contract expiring, then *if* the capacity and place of employment, and the other terms and conditions of employment do not differ from the previous contract *or* the terms and conditions of the proposed contract differ, but the proposal constitutes an offer of suitable employment, *and* in either case the employee unreasonably refuses that offer, *then* the employee will not be entitled to a redundancy payment.

The employer has the burden of showing that the offer of employment was a suitable alternative, and that the refusal of it was unreasonable. In assessing these points consideration needs to be given to the extent that any terms and conditions might vary, and the impact that this might have upon the individual employees concerned.

ORGANISATION
EXAMPLE

Little v *Beare and Son Ltd (1980)*

Little was employed at Rathbone Place, when, following a redundancy situation, his job was moved to Barnet (an additional 30 miles). Beare and Son bought him a van to assist in the travelling. There was then a further move to Hemel Hempstead, which involved an additional 70 miles of travel, the cost of which his employers agreed to pay. He refused the second move, but the employment tribunal found he had refused a suitable offer of alternative employment.

It should be noted that, in considering such issues, consideration would normally be given to the mode of transport available to the employee and any impact that the extra travelling time might have.

If the employee accepts an offer of alternative employment he is entitled to a statutory minimum trial period of four weeks. If, during that period, the employee finds the job to be unsuitable he can resign and claim a redundancy payment.

Survivor syndrome

As we have seen, from an exploration of the legislation, the process of making employees redundant is reasonably lengthy (especially if large numbers are involved) and involves a detailed period of consultation. Hence, all the employees in the organisation experience a period of several weeks when they are nervous about their job security.

Presuming that the purpose of the redundancy has not been to terminate all jobs (ie to close down the site or the organisation) the employer needs to think about how to maintain healthy employment relationships with the employees who remain. In trying to preserve healthy relationships the employer needs to think both about how the redundant employees are being treated, and how the remaining employees are treated.

The reactions of the employees who remain will partly be influenced by whether they perceive that the redundancies were necessary. If they perceive that they were required, and that they were handled fairly, their perception about the employer will be more positive. If they also perceive that the employees have been treated well (eg been paid fairly and have been given assistance in finding alternative employment), then the perception of the employer will also be more positive.

Despite this, a number of commentators have still reported that the remaining employees are likely to suffer from a number of emotions such as guilt (at not being chosen for redundancy when others have), disenchantment, pessimism and stress. This is known as 'survivors' syndrome'. As well as the emotional impact there can also be frustration if employees that remain are asked to take on extra work (especially if it is work that was previously done by redundant colleagues) or if there is poor communication from the employer about the future of the organisation.

It is important that organisations not only communicate clearly with employees, but also check that employees are hearing the messages correctly. Blakstad and Cooper (1995) found that three sets of stimuli can interfere with communication, and one of these is internal stress. Hence, a message might not be heard clearly and correctly by employees who are suffering from stress

Within the communication it is important that employees who remain are clear about why the redundancies were necessary, whether there is the likelihood of any further redundancies, and what the strategic plan for the future of the organisation is.

ACTIVITIES

Talk to a number of people that have experienced a redundancy situation in their organisation. Ask them about the emotions that they experienced, and ask them to try to link these to the way that the redundancy process was handled by the organisation. Ask them, if they have 'survived' a redundancy, whether there were any long-term effects on the employment relationship.

KEY POINTS FROM THIS CHAPTER

- According to CIPD research, organisations experience an average of 30 formal disciplinary cases each year.
- The effects of punishment are relatively short-lived.
- Discipline is a process of both power and control.
- Employees break rules for a variety of reasons.
- When disciplining an employee the statutory disciplinary and dismissals procedure must be followed.
- Employees have a right to be accompanied by a colleague or a trade union representative in a formal disciplinary hearing.
- If the offence is not serious enough to warrant summary dismissal a series of warnings must be given to the employee.

- There are five potentially fair reasons for dismissal: capability, conduct, redundancy, legal restriction and some other substantial reason.
- Constructive dismissal is where the employer breaches the contract and the employee resigns as a result of this conduct.
- Wrongful dismissal is when the employer terminates the contract of employment, and in doing so breaches that contract.
- If an employer is proposing to make more than 20 employees redundant the employer must follow clear guidelines on the length of the consultation period.
- The consultation period must be meaningful, and employees must be supplied with certain minimum information in writing.
- Statutory redundancy payments are calculated in accordance with the basic award.
- An employee who refuses an offer of suitable alternative employment forgoes the right to a redundancy payment.
- Those in the organisation who are not selected for redundancy might suffer from 'survivor syndrome'.

EXAMPLES TO WORK THROUGH

1. Mary is an employee who is often late for work. After monitoring her punctuality for a month it was decided to give her a verbal warning. For about three weeks her timekeeping improved, but then she started being late again. It was decided to give her a formal written warning, and again her timekeeping improved for a while, and then started to deteriorate. The employer does not want to dismiss Mary because she is a good worker, but it seems that a final written warning is the next inevitable step. Why might the improvements keep deteriorating and what else could the employer consider doing?

2. The organisation where you are the HR manager has been performing badly for six months, and it has been decided that there are no alternatives but to make 50 employees redundant. Work out a communication plan that meets the needs of both the employees who will be made redundant, and those who will survive.

3. You work for one of the organisations that has been selected as being in the top 10 of the *Sunday Times* survey of 100 best companies to work for. Your managing director states that there is no need to have a disciplinary procedure in such an organisation. Do you disagree or agree? Justify your answer.

(Suggestions of answers to the examples can be accessed by tutors at www.cipd.co.uk/tss).

CASE STUDY

You are the general manager of a leisure centre. Each Friday, for several months, you have been concerned that the takings in the till at the end of the day do not match with the amount that should be there according to the till record.

The till is used for a variety of transactions. These include customers paying for sessions when they arrive, the sales of snacks and beverages, and the sale of leisure products such as goggles, swimming costumes and towels. All the staff in the leisure centre have access to the till, because they could all be involved in selling a product to a customer.

You have started to keep a record of which staff are present when the takings appear to be incorrect. From this basic investigation you have worked out that only Fred and Julie have been at work every time there has been a discrepancy. You took the decision, therefore, to suspend both Fred and Julie pending a potential dismissal. During this period of suspension it was your intention to talk to the other employees and see if they were aware of any improper transactions taking place, and hopefully to work out which of Fred and Julie was the culprit.

However, things have not worked out as you planned. When you called Fred in to suspend him he became very angry. He insisted that he had not done anything wrong, and accused you of manipulating the investigation to implicate him. Several months ago your girlfriend left you, and then started a relationship with him, and he believes that this is your way of getting back at him. He has made a complaint to the area manager and has refused to accept his suspension.

When you called Julie in she became very emotional. She said that you had obviously decided she was guilty and she was resigning with immediate effect. She then walked out and went home. An hour after she had left the leisure centre, she phoned you and said she had 'taken advice' and was going to 'take a claim of constructive dismissal'. She has also complained to the area manager.

You are very upset at the outcome, because you were convinced that you were doing everything in accordance with the law, and in accordance with good HR procedure. Clearly, however, things have gone very wrong. Your area manager has asked to see you tomorrow morning and has asked you to be prepared to answer three questions:

a) Explain the procedure you took in suspending Fred. Highlight anything you did wrong, and also explain how the procedure you followed matched with the relevant legislation.
b) Explain the procedure you took in suspending Julie. Explain, with reasons, whether you think her claim for constructive dismissal will be successful.
c) Tell her what you plan to do now to resolve the situation.

The Law Relating to Employee Relations

CHAPTER 12

The objectives of this chapter are to:

- explain the process of trade union recognition
- examine the legislation surrounding the bargaining process
- outline the legislation that governs industrial action
- explain the difference between lawful and unlawful industrial action
- examine the prevalence of industrial action
- consider the protection given by law to a trade union member
- examine the role of the trade union member in health and safety and learning issues.

This chapter is a further look at the law that affects employment in the UK. In this chapter we concentrate on the law that governs employee relations, and primarily that which relates to trade union activities. As we have already noted in this book, trade union membership has declined in the UK, but trade unions are still an important part of many workplaces, and hence it is important that we understand how they are allowed to operate. In Chapter 13 we move away from this view of collective legislation, and concentrate on the growing area of individual protection.

TRADE UNION RECOGNITION

In Chapter 6 we started by defining a trade union. In this chapter we shall start by considering how a trade union becomes recognised in the workplace.

It is important to understand the process of recognition. An individual employee can join any trade union, presuming that any required levels of eligibility are met (for example, one must be a member of the teaching profession to join the National Union of Teachers). However, if the trade union that the employee joins is not formally recognised in the workplace, the employee cannot invite that trade union to negotiate on workplace issues. The issue of recognition, therefore, is of prime importance for those who want trade union activity in their workplace.

Recognition is a formal agreement between the management and the employees that the trade union represents, either all of the employees in the workplace or a specific group of employees in that workplace. It is an agreement that all, or specific issues, are to be determined through the process of collective bargaining. As Torrington and Hall (1998) state, it is agreement to a system of rules and processes to which both management and the employees will operate. It is, therefore, a crucial first step in the formalisation of the trade union's role in a workplace.

Prior to the 1970s trade union recognition was an informal process that was largely achieved through employees putting pressure on management. It was often the result of a significant number of employees joining a trade union, and then demonstrating a combined desire for recognition in the workplace. Indeed, this pressure could include industrial action in a bid to try to force management to agree to recognition.

In 1971 the Industrial Relations Act and in 1975 the Employment Protection Act, introduced a statutory process that trade unions could use to try to persuade management to agree to trade union recognition. According to Salamon (2000), during the period 1976–79 Acas handled 2,066 recognition cases under its voluntary conciliation process and 1,168 claims under the statutory procedure. As a result of these claims 1,524 recognition agreements were entered into, covering 130,000 employees.

However, the statutory procedure did not succeed in addressing the employer who was determined not to allow recognition. This is evidenced in the following case, which became somewhat infamous as an example of the flaws of the procedure:

ORGANISATION EXAMPLE

The Grunwick dispute (1977)

Grunwick was a photo processing plant in London that employed predominantly east African and south Asian females. It was known as having some of the worst employment conditions in the industry, with racial harassment and bullying being commonplace. It also had one of the lowest rates of pay in the industry.

When one worker, a Mrs Desai, refused to work overtime (which was typically unannounced, but was compulsory), she and her son (who also worked at Grunwick) resigned. She then formed a picket outside the factory demanding trade union recognition for the employees. She asked other workers to sign a petition requesting the recognition, and eventually more and more employees joined the picket lines. There resulted a strike that lasted for around two years, and during that time ongoing discussions took place about trade union recognition. The management refused recognition, however, and dismissed a number of employees who took part in the industrial action. It refused to co-operate with any conciliation process or statutory process conducted by Acas. In the end, the industrial action crumbled and the goal of trade union recognition was not achieved.

The Grunwick dispute illustrated the fact that, although a statutory process was in place, and a majority of employees requested trade union recognition, management was still able to resist the request.

As we have already noted, when the Conservative Party came into government in 1979 one of its major tasks was to change the balance of power in the employment relationship, seeking at least an equilibrium, but definitely a reduction in the power of the employees. It is therefore of little surprise that the Conservatives repealed the statutory procedure for union recognition in 1980, rather than seeking a way of strengthening the existing process.

There remained no formal means of gaining trade union recognition until the Employment Relations Act 1999, and trade union recognition became part of the Trade Union and Labour Relations (Consolidation) Act 1992. This procedure has four alternative routes:

1. Voluntary, when the agreement is made voluntarily between the employer and the trade union.

2. Semi-voluntary, when the trade union makes a formal approach to the employer in writing, which the employer then agrees to.
3. Automatic recognition.
4. Recognition by ballot.

The last two routes can be a result of the statutory recognition procedure. This applies only when the employer has at least 21 employees (although the employees potentially represented by the trade union can be of a smaller number). For the statutory recognition procedure to be invoked the trade union making the request must have a certificate of independence.

The statutory recognition process is as follows:

- The trade union seeking recognition makes a written request to the employer for recognition. This must identify the trade union and the bargaining unit.
- The bargaining unit is the group of workers that the trade union is seeking to represent. This might be all employees, or it could be a specific group.
- If the employer and the trade union cannot agree on the definition of the bargaining group the Central Arbitration Committee (CAC) will decide. The CAC can only become involved in the discussions if there are at least 10 per cent of trade union members in the proposed unit and the majority of workers in the unit are likely to favour recognition.

The CAC is an independent body that has statutory powers, the main one being the adjudication on decisions relating to recognition or derecognition of trade unions. Although the body is independent, the committee members are appointed by the Department for Trade and Industry following discussions with Acas (see Chapter 3).

Go to www.cac.gov.uk and become more familiar with the work and the constitution of the Central Arbitration Committee.

ACTIVITIES

The Employment Relations Act 2004 added instruction about the process that must be followed if the two parties have failed to agree on an appropriate bargaining unit. The CAC must first consider the bargaining unit that has been proposed by the trade union. If it does not consider that this is an appropriate unit, it must make an alternative proposal. In doing this the CAC will consider the need for the unit to work within current management and bargaining arrangements. It will also try to avoid small fragmented units in an organisation.

Once the bargaining unit has been decided the next question is whether the trade union should be recognised as representing the workers. If the CAC is satisfied that at least 50 per cent of the workers in the unit are union members, the CAC will issue a declaration that the trade union is recognised for the purpose of collective bargaining. This is the route of automatic recognition.

However, the CAC can decide to proceed with the route of a ballot if one of three qualifying conditions is fulfilled. These are:

- The CAC determines that a ballot is the best way of proceeding for the purpose of good employee relations.
- A significant number of the members of the trade union in the bargaining unit tell the CAC that they do not want the trade union to carry out collective bargaining on their behalf.
- The CAC has evidence that leads to doubts that a significant number of trade union members do want the union to represent them.

In addition, if less than 50 per cent of the workers are union members, a ballot of the workers in the bargaining unit will be held.

If the CAC decides to proceed with a ballot it will appoint an independent person to carry this out. The ballot must take place within 20 working days of the appointment unless there are good reasons for an extension to that period of time. If a majority of those who vote support recognition, and at least 40 per cent of the workers in the bargaining unit support recognition, the CAC will issue a declaration that the union is recognised.

The Employment Relations Act 2004 introduced legislation to address the possibility of intimidation, by the employer or the trade union, during the ballot process. The legislation requires both the employer and the trade union to take no actions that might unduly influence the employees who are taking part in the ballot. Such actions are classified as 'unfair practices', and include such things as undue coercion, offering any form of inducement to vote in a particular way, the threat of disciplinary action and the threat of dismissal. It should be noted that this also applies to any action taken by either party to try to force an employee to reveal how s/he intends to vote.

Once the declaration of recognition has been given, the two parties have 30 days to agree a process for conducting collective bargaining. They can agree an extension to this period of time if required. If the two parties are unable to reach an agreement the CAC may be asked to assist. The CAC has 20 days in which to help the parties reach agreement, although this period of time may be extended by agreement. If the parties are unable to reach agreement the CAC will specify the method of collective bargaining that is to be used.

Once an agreement is reached it is a legally enforceable contract.

If there are significant changes to the original bargaining unit, either party may apply to the CAC asking for a decision on the appropriate bargaining unit. If the CAC accepts that the bargaining unit has changed, it can issue a declaration ending the current bargaining arrangements or making a declaration on a more appropriate bargaining unit.

Although there is now a formal process for trade union recognition, it is interesting to consider the potential impact this might have on employee relations. Gall (2005) states that initially the processes were controversial. Employers saw the procedures as legal interference in their ability to run their organisation in the way they saw best, and trade unions were critical of the restrictive nature of the provisions. Gall goes on to report that the CAC initially predicted it would be dealing with around 150 applications each year. However, during the first five years in which the legislation was in place it received about half that number of applications. CAC activity to 11 May 2005 was reported by Gall as shown in Table 12.1.

Gall suggests that the reason for this lower level of applications is partly the complex nature of the process. As there is a three-year ban on reapplying for recognition should the initial application fail, there has been some reluctance to follow a formal procedure. He also suggests that some

Table 12.1 CAC activity to 11 May 2005

First stage	
Applications made to the CAC:	482
Applications withdrawn before adjudication	117
(15 per cent were later resubmitted)	
Applications accepted (including resubmissions)	279
Applications rejected	68
Final outcomes	
Voluntary agreements solicited using CAC application	86
Automatic recognitions	57
Recognitions won by ballot	71
Ballots lost by union	42

trade unions doubt that they can achieve genuine collective bargaining from truly reluctant employers, and hence there is little point in gaining formal recognition.

However, it would be wrong to presume that the lower number of applications to the CAC means that fewer recognition agreements have been reached. During the period June 2000 to December 2004, 1,730 new deals were signed, covering just over 788,500 employees. Only 206 of these had resulted from statutory applications (covering 36,500 employees). In interpreting these figures it must not be presumed that this is indicative of increased overall trade union presence in workplaces. As well as new recognition agreements there have also been closures of unionised workplaces, and overall no significant gains have been achieved.

In considering the overall impact of the new agreements on employee relations Gall suggests that there are three categories of experience:

- mutual gains
- business as usual
- conflict continued.

Mutual gains

In this category are the employers and trade unions that feel the introduction of formal recognition has been of benefit to both parties. Although this might seem to be very indicative of a partnership agreement forming, less than 20 per cent of new agreements have actually been reported as being partnership agreements.

However, there are a number of organisations that have reported fruitful results of the recognition, with outward signs including new reward systems being negotiated or other terms and conditions being formally agreed.

Honda UK, based in Swindon, signed a recognition deal in 2003. Two years after the deal was signed a new overtime agreement was reached. The Amicus trade union representative reported that this was first time that a policy within Honda UK had been changed through the negotiation process. The management and trade unions at Honda UK are increasingly working towards a partnership-style agreement.

Business as usual

In this category it is reported that the recognition agreement has brought little difference to employee relations. Gall suggests that this could be because the trade union representation is too weak, or too poorly trained, to have any impact. Alternatively it could be because the management have not taken part in any genuine dialogue, basically rendering the recognition agreement useless.

It is possible that the trade union recognition has brought no noticeable impact because employee relations were already well conducted within the organisation and there was no need for change. Although this is definitely a possible explanation it seems reasonably unlikely, because if this were the case one has to ask why the trade union would trigger formal recognition requests (and why sufficient employees would support the request).

In his article, Gall suggests that one organisation that has not made genuine attempts at working within the recognition agreement with the GMB is Richmond Mirrors. Although the CAC ruled in favour of recognition, the organisation was actually undergoing a reorganisation at the time and was placed into administration. It was subsequently bought by the current owners, along with another organisation. Richmond Mirrors then applied to the CAC for derecognition as the original bargaining unit had ceased to exist, and it was successful in the application.

Conflict continued

Gall reports that, in about 8 per cent of new agreements, old conflicts do continue. This could be the result of unresolved differences which simply continue to exist within a new framework. Alternatively, it could be the result of raised expectations as a result of the recognition agreement. Employees, employers and trade union representatives might all enter the agreement with some uncertainty over the impact on their relationships, and hence the uncertainty could have an ongoing negative impact on the relationship whilst the new processes become part of the way of working.

Although it might not always be simple to identify the impact on employee relations, it is very unlikely that the introduction of a new process of conducting the relationship will have no impact. This impact could have a significant effect on the psychological contract, especially where the introduction of the recognition agreement gives the employees raised expectations regarding the employer.

As well as a process for recognition, there is a formal process for derecognition. An application for derecognition of the trade union can only be made after a minimum of three years after the declaration of recognition. The application can only be made if:

- the size of the workforce is now less than 21
- there is no longer majority support for the collective bargaining arrangements
- the original declaration was made on the basis of 50 per cent union membership and the rate of membership has now fallen below this level.

ACTIVITIES

Find out whether the organisation you work in, or an organisation with which you are familiar, has a formal recognition agreement with a trade union. If it has, find out how long it has been in existence and what prompted it. If it has not, find out why not and whether there has ever been a request for recognition.

Talk to at least one manager about this, and try to understand how the recognition or lack of recognition affects the way that employee relations is managed within the organisation.

LEGISLATION ON THE PROCESS OF COLLECTIVE BARGAINING

Disclosure of information

As we have seen in the last section, a recognised trade union negotiates with the employer on issues covered by collective bargaining. Examples of such issues are terms and conditions of employment, disciplinary matters and grievances. However, although a formal mechanism for collective bargaining can be agreed, the employees could be seen to be at a disadvantage, as it is likely that the employer will always have the majority of information pertaining to any work-related issue. As Moore (1980) states, the very fact that disclosure is an issue suggests that there is in existence an inequality in access to information.

If we go back to Gall's three categories of experience post-recognition, this would suggest that there are employers who will willingly disclose information (mutual gains), those who disclose information in the same way as previously (business as usual) and those who do not willingly make disclosures (conflict continued). Although this analysis might be somewhat inaccurate, it does highlight that different employers will take different attitudes to disclosure.

As we saw in Chapter 6, 'openness and transparency' is one of the six fundamental principles of partnership as defined by the TUC. We also saw in Chapter 6 how the Information and Consultation of Employees Regulations 2004 impact on the rights of employees to receive information about the organisation for the purposes of consultation. However, within the Trade Union Labour Relations (Consolidation) Act (TULRCA) 1992 there is also specific legislation relating to information that the employer is required to disclose in order for the collective bargaining process to proceed effectively. Information should be disclosed which:

- Is information without which the union would be impeded to a material degree in carrying out collective bargaining with the employer
- is information which it would be good industrial relations practice to disclose.

Clearly there could be a range of interpretations of these two definitions. The code of practice produced by Acas (*Disclosure of information to trade unions for collective bargaining purposes*) gives useful additional guidance. Some important guidelines to consider are:

- Any information that is requested must be relevant to the issue being addressed through the collective bargaining.
- The information must be of importance to the negotiations.
- The level at which the negotiations are taking place must be considered.
- The relevance of the type and size of the organisation must be taken into account.

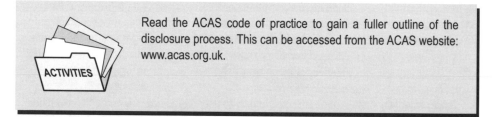

ACTIVITIES

Read the ACAS code of practice to gain a fuller outline of the disclosure process. This can be accessed from the ACAS website: www.acas.org.uk.

The need for the requested information to relate to the matters being discussed in collective bargaining is illustrated in the case of *R* v *Central Arbitration Committee ex parte BTP Tioxide Ltd (1981)*.

ORGANISATION EXAMPLE

In this case BTP Tioxide entered into a limited bargaining agreement with ASTMS. ASTMS subsequently asked the employer to disclose information regarding a job evaluation process which was not part of the area covered by the bargaining agreement. BTP Tioxide refused to disclose the information, and ASTMS took a complaint to the CAC. The CAC ordered BTP Tioxide to disclose the information, and it appealed to the High Court. The appeal was upheld. The High Court stated that the CAC had been misdirected because the information did not relate to the representational function of the trade union.

There are certain classifications of information that the employer is not required to disclose. These include:

- information that might affect national security
- information that can only be disclosed by contravening other legislation (for example, the Data Protection Act 1998)
- information that has been given to the employer in confidence
- information relating specifically to an individual unless he/she gives consent
- information that could significantly damage the employer's undertaking
- information obtained by the employer for the purpose of defending or bringing legal proceedings.

Any information that is disclosed by the employer can only be used for the purposes of collective bargaining.

If the trade union considers that the employer is failing to comply with the requirement to disclose information it can make a complaint to the CAC.

The difficulty with the fair operation of this legislation is that the employee does not always know what s/he does not know. This means that the employee will not always make the request for information simply because there is no realisation that it exists. Alternatively, the employee might request information and be supplied with it, but will have no way of knowing whether all the relevant information has been given. An employer who has no intention of meeting the requirements for disclosure of information, therefore, could get round the legislation by complying at only a very minimal level.

Although it is not legislation relating to the collective bargaining process, it is important to consider the impact of relatively recent legislation requiring public sector organisations to be more transparent. On 1 January 2005 the Freedom of Information Act 2000 (FOIA) came into force. This Act gives a legal right for any person to ask an organisation within the public sector for access to information that it holds. The aim of the FOIA is to promote a culture of openness and accountability among public sector organisations and to improve the understanding of how public sector organisations operate. If employees involved in the process of collective bargaining in the public sector wanted additional information, they could use this legislation alongside their rights under TULRCA 1992.

PROTECTION FOR THE TRADE UNION MEMBER

As we saw when we considered the issue of trade union recognition, there are employers who resist trade union involvement in their organisations. It is also true that there are employers who will want to dissuade individuals from becoming trade union members, or from becoming trade union representatives. The law therefore protects individuals who are trade union members from any detriment that might result from their membership.

The first level of protection comes at the stage of recruitment. TULRCA 1992 makes it unlawful to refuse employment to people because:

- they are or are not members of a trade union
- they refuse to accept a requirement that they become a member or cease to be a member, or a requirement that they suffer deductions if they fail to join

(Lewis and Sargeant 2004).

Hence, an employer cannot try to select employees who it is perceived will not join a trade union, maybe with a view to reducing the numbers of trade union members and therefore making it impossible for a recognition request to be pursued. Neither can an employer try to promote membership of a particular trade union, or indeed membership of any trade union.

Moving on to existing employees, it is also unlawful for the employer to subject employees to any detriment in relation to their trade union activities. Detriment includes:

- preventing or deterring employees from joining an independent trade union, or penalising them for doing so
- preventing or deterring them from taking part in any activities of an independent trade union, or penalising them for doing so
- compelling them to join a trade union
- forcing them to make one or more payments because they refuse to join or to leave a trade union.

TULRCA 1992 goes on to address the issue of dismissal for trade union activities. A dismissal will be automatically unfair (ie the qualifying period of one year's continuous service will not be required) if the principal reason for the dismissal was:

- the employee proposed to become a member of an independent trade union
- the employee took, or proposed to take, part in the activities of an independent trade union at an appropriate time
- the employee refused to become, or proposed to refuse to become, a member of a trade union (Lewis and Sargeant 2004).

The summary of these provisions is that employees have the freedom to make their own decision over trade union membership, and cannot be penalised for this. Along with recognition legislation this takes away any control that the employer has over the nature of collective representation within the workplace.

Trade union representatives have additional protection. Employers must allow official representatives of independent trade unions that they recognise a reasonable amount of paid time off during working hours. The allowed time should be for the purpose of:

1. Carrying out duties relating to negotiations with the employer.
2. Carrying out duties connected with their role (specifically listed in section 178(2) of TULRCA 1992) and duties that the employer has agreed they may carry out. The most likely examples are representing their members at disciplinary and grievance hearings.
3. Receiving information from the employer.
4. Undergoing training relevant to their trade union duties, which is approved by their trade union or the TUC (Trade Union Congress).

The trade union representative is not required to have a minimum length of service before these entitlements apply.

ACTIVITIES

If possible talk to a trade union representative and gain an understanding of the amount of time that s/he takes off from normal work duties to carry out trade union duties. Do you think that this amount of time is reasonable? If you cannot find a trade union representative phone a local branch of a trade union and ask it if it can give you an idea of the typical amount of time spent on trade union activities by one of its local representatives.

INDUSTRIAL ACTION

As we have already noted in Chapter 2, the Winter of Discontent (1978/79) was the prelude to the Conservative Party coming into government. One of the tasks that this government undertook immediately was trying to rebalance the power between employers and employees in the employment relationship. As we have already noted, legislation was passed making it unlawful to take industrial action without going through a ballot process.

In this section we examine the legislation surrounding industrial action, and try to understand how this legislation has affected the balance of power in the employment relationship. An important starting point, however, is to understand the prevalence of industrial action in the UK. The data in Table 12.2 is taken from information supplied by the Office of National Statistics:

Although the numbers do not show clear trends, it is certainly true that, prior to TULRCA being introduced in 1992, the number of working days lost and the number of stoppages in progress was generally much greater than after the introduction of the legislation. TULRCA contained the provisions introduced by the Conservative government requiring a ballot to take place before strike action commenced (as we shall see later in this chapter).

Although the working days lost and the stoppages in progress have fallen as the years have passed, it would be very wrong to conclude that industrial action is a thing of the past. For the last full year reported (2004) there were 493 stoppages, which is far from insignificant.

 Over a four-week period keep a record of all the industrial action you can find reported in the news. Look at newspapers (local and national), and also access the BBC news website (www.bbc.co.uk /news) which is a very useful source of information. You will probably be surprised at how many instances you record.

A fundamental part of the law relating to employment relations is that there is a right to organise strikes and other industrial action. However, whenever workers strike or take some other form of industrial

Table 12.2 The prevalence of industrial action within the UK

	Working days lost (1000s)	Stoppages in progress	Workers involved (1000s)
2005*	68	81	48
2004	906	493	409
2003	408	185	198
2002	1323	224	1022
2001	526	259	221
2000	499	270	371
1995	192	315	222
1990**	1903	822	382
1985	6400	1173	
1980	11964	839	
1975	6012	3082	
1970	10979	4832	

*   This covers only the first seven months of 2005.

**   Data regarding the numbers of workers involved is only available for 1990 onwards

action they are acting in breach of their contract of employment. Therefore, when a trade union calls for organised industrial action it is inducing its members to take action in breach of their contracts.

Under common law it is unlawful to induce people to act in breach of a contract, and therefore trade union officials would face legal action each time they called for strike action. To overcome this there are special immunities granted in relation to the calling of industrial action. The immunity from legal action only applies to actions that are in preparation for, or involved in the activities of, a trade dispute.

The immunities relate to:

- inducing a breach of contract
- intimidation
- conspiracy
- interference with a business by unlawful means
- inducing a breach of a statutory duty.

A trade union's immunity from any legal action will only apply to actions that are in contemplation or furtherance of a trade dispute. This immunity is known as the 'golden formula'. To understand the immunity in more detail we shall look at the first three of those listed above as they are most commonly encountered.

Inducing a breach of contract

Direct inducement is when pressure is put on a person to break a contract. A tort (wrong) is committed if the person putting the pressure on knows that the result of the pressure will be a breach of the contract. Indirect inducement is where pressure is put on a person to do an unlawful act to another body, which then results in that other body breaching a contract.

TULRCA gives immunity from any legal action in relation to the tort of inducing a breach of contract, presuming that the inducement relates to the contemplation or furtherance of a trade dispute.

Timeplan Education Group Ltd v *National Union of Teachers (1997)*

ORGANISATION EXAMPLE

In this case Timeplan (a recruitment agency for teachers) had agreed to place a series of advertisements in a magazine run by a teachers' union in New Zealand (NZEI). However, the NUT was in dispute with Timeplan at this time, regarding the terms and conditions of the teachers that it supplied. As the NZEI was a sister organisation of the NUT the NUT contacted it to inform it of the ongoing dispute with Timeplan and to request that the advertisements cease. After some correspondence NZEI agreed to withdraw the advertisements. Timeplan then took action against the NUT claiming that it had unlawfully interfered with the contract between Timeplan and NZEI.

The Court of Appeal held that the NUT had not been aware of any contract that existed between NZEI and Timeplan and hence could not be found guilty of persuading, procuring or inducing the NZEI to breach a contract. Therefore the NUT had not committed the tort of inducement to breach a contract.

Intimidation

This tort is committed when a person is threatened. For example, Fred is convicted of stealing the funds of the local football club. He is also an employee at Bloggs Ltd. A number of the employees at Bloggs Ltd are also members of the football club. They are no longer prepared to work with Fred and their trade union representative tells the management of Bloggs Ltd that the employees will take industrial action unless Fred is dismissed. If such a threat is made in contemplation or furtherance of a trade dispute TULRCA gives immunity from any legal action.

Conspiracy

This occurs when two or more people combine to damage the employer by unlawful means with intent to damage the employer (for example, gathering together to take industrial action to protect jobs. Any industrial action is likely to damage the employer). Alternatively it can occur when two or more people combine together to harm the employer by using unlawful means.

TULRCA gives immunity if the action is taken in contemplation or furtherance of a trade dispute, unless the act would be subject to legal action if it had been carried out by one person (that is, it is effectively criminal action).

It is important to note that this statutory immunity is forfeited if the action that is being taken is unlawful. Prior to the introduction of legislation by the Conservative government of 1979–97 to rebalance the power in the employment relationship, almost all forms of industrial action were covered by these statutory immunities. Today, statutory immunity only applies if the industrial action:

- Is about employment related matters, and is between the employers and their own employees. (As we shall see later, taking 'sympathy action' – known as secondary action – is not lawful, and hence is not subject to statutory immunity.)
- Is the result of a ballot conducted in the way laid out in law (see later in this section). Hence, simply walking out on the job is not subject to statutory immunity.
- Does not involve unlawful picketing (see later).
- Is not action that has been carried out to support an employee who was dismissed while taking unofficial industrial action.

Lawful industrial action

As has already been noted, TULRCA 1992 initially explained the process that must take place for any industrial action to be lawful. Further alterations to this have been made by the Employment Relations Acts of 1999 and 2004. The current process is as mapped out below:

At least seven days before any ballot is held the trade unions must inform the employers (in writing) of all employees involved in the ballot. They must tell the employers that a ballot is to be held, when the ballot will take place, and give the employer information that the trade union holds which will help the employer to make plans and bring information to the attention of those employees who are to be balloted.

This requirement does not mean that the trade union must supply the names of all those who are to be involved in the ballot, but the numbers, categories of employees and workplaces are to be disclosed. The trade union must give the total number of employees in each category and in each workplace. The trade union must take all reasonable steps to ensure the accuracy of the information.

If the trade union intends to organise industrial action at more than one place of work it must carry out separate ballots at each of those places of work. An independent scrutiniser must be appointed to oversee the ballot process, and the counting of the votes.

All those who are entitled to vote must be given a reasonable opportunity to vote. This includes giving the opportunity for a postal vote when this is appropriate. The voting paper must clearly state the name of the independent scrutiniser, the address to which the ballot paper is to be returned (presuming there is the option of a postal vote) and the date by which it must be returned, be marked with a number which is one of a series of consecutive numbering, must allow the voter to clearly indicate a 'yes' or 'no' response to the willingness to participate in strike action, and identify the person authorised to call industrial action. The voting paper must also contain a clear statement as follows:

> If you take part in a strike or other industrial action you may be in breach of your contract of employment. However, if you are dismissed for taking part in a strike or other industrial action which is called officially and is otherwise lawful, the dismissal will be unfair if it takes place fewer than eight weeks after you started taking part in the action, and depending on the circumstances may be unfair if it takes place later.

The voting must be secret and the ballot papers must be fairly and accurately counted. As soon as reasonably possible the trade union must inform all those concerned of the result of the ballot. If the result is in favour of industrial action the trade union must give the employer seven days' notice of the industrial action. Any industrial action must commence within an agreed period. This is usually four weeks, but could be longer if agreed between the employer and the trade union. If the industrial action does not commence within the agreed period a new ballot must take place.

The notice to take industrial action must give the employer sufficient information to make plans and to bring information to the attention of those who are likely to be involved in the action. The trade union must explain whether the industrial action is intended to be continuous or on specific days or at specific times (and explain what days and times those are to be). If the action is to be continuous the date it will start must be given.

If this procedure is not followed in any significant way the ballot can be declared void.

The somewhat lengthy procedure for ensuring lawful industrial action, introduced by TULRCA 1992, was criticised for weakening the employee's strength in an industrial dispute. Some believe that, by the time the balloting process is completed, some of the initial 'passion' has gone out of the situation and employees are less likely to vote in favour of industrial action. Others would argue that this is the very point of the legislation – making sure that any action taken has been thought about, rather than being an emotional reaction to a set of circumstances.

It is also true that the lengthy process allows the employer to make some plans to cope with the stoppage. The process of planning from the employer's side, and giving advance notice of action from the trade union's side, is illustrated well in the following example.

ORGANISATION EXAMPLE

In January 2005 there was a dispute between Glasgow Underground Workers (represented by the Transport and General Workers Union, TGWU) and Strathclyde Passenger Transport (SPT). The dispute was over pay. Following a lengthy period of negotiations no agreement was reached and the TGWU balloted its members for strike action. There was a majority vote for industrial action, and the TGWU informed SPT that its members would take industrial action each Monday over a four-week period. From this we can see how the process was working – a ballot was held and then the employer was informed of the type of proposed action (strike) and the dates of the action (Mondays). In addition, the TGWU informed the SPT that there would be an immediate overtime ban.

This advance warning meant that the SPT was able to make plans for some provision for customers. It laid on some free replacement bus services to help passengers who would have been travelling on the underground on those days. Although the industrial action did go ahead the SPT was able to put in place some plans because it knew the detail of who would not be at work, and were able to understand the impact that this would have on its operations.

The other purpose of the lengthy ballot process is to allow additional time to resolve the dispute. This desire to see disputes resolved mirrors the introduction of the Statutory Disciplinary Procedures that we examined in the Chapter 11, and the Statutory Grievance Procedures that we examined in Chapter 9. All these procedures give more time and more opportunity for disputes to be resolved without escalating to any form of further action.

Unlawful industrial action

Unlawful action is action that takes place without a ballot, or following a ballot that is void because it did not follow the procedure in some way. Unlawful action is also referred to as 'wild cat' strikes.

ORGANISATION
EXAMPLE

The Royal Mail has suffered a number of occasions of unlawful industrial action over recent years. A specific example took place in April 2004 when workers walked out over allegations of bullying and harassment of some of their colleagues. The problems occurred in Oxfordshire, initially at one sorting office, and spread as employees at other sorting offices in the area joined the unofficial action in support of their members.

In this situation the employer, here the Royal Mail, has no time to make any contingency plans to keep the post moving.

If unlawful industrial action is taken the employer can apply for an injunction to stop any further action being taken. Given the immediacy of the situation (ie the desire to stop unlawful action that is already occurring) it is usual for an employer to start by trying to obtain an interim injunction. This gives an order for the unlawful action to cease until a particular date. It is hoped that, by the given date, the matter will have been considered at a full hearing and either the application will have been refused or a permanent injunction will have been granted.

In deciding whether to grant an interim injunction the courts will consider first whether there is a serious issue to address. The courts will then need to consider the balance of convenience – in other words is the granting of an interim injunction in the interests of both parties (and is there any relevant public interest?)? The court also needs to consider the likelihood of the trade union being able to give a defence under the immunities that we examined earlier in this chapter.

If it can be shown that a person has suffered loss as a result of unlawful industrial action he or she can bring an action for damages. Claims are usually brought against trade unions, although they can be brought against individual participants.

The level of damages that can be awarded by the court is subject to limits imposed by TULRCA. The limits vary according to the size of the union:

- £10,000 – if the union has less than 5000 members
- £50,000 – for 5,000 to 25,000 members
- £125,000 – for 25,000 to 100,000 members
- £250,000 – for 100,000+ members.

Secondary action

Secondary action (also known as 'sympathy action') is when employees take action regarding a matter that is not an issue with their own employer. An example of this occurred in August 2005.

Gate Gourmet, based at Heathrow Airport, supplies airline meals to British Airways. As a result of financial difficulties it announced a restructuring that would include redundancies. In addition, it proposed to recruit temporary seasonal staff as it had done each year previously. As a result of this a significant number of employees (reports vary from 300 to 667) took unlawful industrial action. Gate Gourmet dismissed all staff who took unofficial action.

Many of the British Airways employees based at Heathrow knew workers from Gate Gourmet. Indeed, some of the workers were former British Airways employees because the airline company used to supply its own meals. Enraged at what they saw as the unfair treatment of the dismissed Gate Gourmet employees, a number of British Airways employees (baggage handlers, ground staff and loaders) took secondary action, and walked out. This was secondary action because the dispute was between Gate Gourmet and its employees, and was nothing to do with British Airways and its employees.

The British Airways staff who took secondary action belonged to the same trade union (TGWU) as the Gate Gourmet employees. The secondary action lasted for around two days, grounding hundreds of British Airways flights during the peak holiday season.

Although the British Airways staff did eventually return to work, the dispute with the Gate Gourmet employees is currently unresolved (September 2005). Indeed, it has been a key subject at the start of the recent TUC conference, with a number of key trade union representatives calling for the government to repeal legislation making secondary action unlawful. This request has been clearly refused by the government.

Picketing

TULRCA 1992 allows for a person who is contemplating or acting to further a trade dispute to attend at or near his/her place of work or (if he/she is a trade union official) at or near the place of work of a member of the trade union he/she is representing for the purpose of peacefully communicating information or peacefully persuading a person to abstain from working.

Picketing, therefore, is not unlawful in itself although there are situations in which actions taken in relation to picketing may be deemed to be unlawful. For example, it is unlikely that mass picketing will be considered lawful, because it is unlikely to be picketing for the purposes of 'peaceful persuasion'.

ORGANISATION EXAMPLE

Maybe the most violent picket line scenes in recent memory occurred during the miners' strike of 1984. A specific case that went to the courts was *Thomas v National Union of Miners (South Wales) (1985)*. When a number of miners started to return to work, although the dispute continued, large groups of pickets assembled at the entrances to the mines. Although there were only six official pickets groups, 60–70 miners would gather shouting abuse at those who crossed the picket lines. It was found that this was no longer 'peaceful persuasion' and was also restricting the miners from using the highway to get to work. An injunction was placed on the NUM restricting it to the placing of just six pickets at the mine gates.

There are other civil and criminal offences that could potentially be committed in the process of picketing:

Civil

- Inducing a breach of contract. This could occur if a driver from another organisation is persuaded not to cross a picket line. In this situation the driver is being induced to breach his/her contract of employment.
- Trespass to the highway. This could occur if the regular passage along the highway is disrupted.
- Private nuisance. This could be interference with a person's use of nearby land or premises. It could also be action that makes it unpleasant for a person to access premises, such as using foul language or beating on cars as they drive through.

Criminal

- obstruction of the highway
- causing a breach of the peace
- obstruction of a police officer in the execution of their duty
- riot, affray, violent disorder
- public nuisance
- criminal damage to property
- harassment.

The law does not specify a limit on the number of pickets that may be in one place. However, the Department of Employment code of practice on picketing suggests that in general the number of pickets should not exceed six at any entrance/exit to the premises, and often a smaller number will be appropriate. The police have the discretion to take any necessary measures to ensure that picketing is peaceful and orderly, and this can involve restricting the number of pickets at any one place.

Dismissal of employees involved in industrial action

When the Employment Relations Act 1999 was introduced, it made it unlawful to dismiss those involved in strike action for the first eight weeks of any strike. After the government had reviewed the Act it stated that there were no major changes planned. However, the trade unions continued to press for a number of changes, including an increase to this eight-week period. According to the *IDS brief 766* (2004), they were concerned that employees could become involved in long-running industrial action, only to find that they were dismissed at the end of it. However, the government refuted this, stating that most industrial action was short in length, and hence this problem would rarely arise. However, just before the Employment Relations Act 2004 received Royal Assent a last-minute amendment was tabled by the House of Lords, which resulted in the eight-week period being extended to 12 weeks.

The Employment Relations Act 2004 also excludes any period of lockout from the period of protection. 'Lock-out' occurs when the place of employment is closed, the employer suspends all work, or an employer refuses to continue to employ employees because of a dispute, which is done with a view to compelling those persons to accept the terms and conditions that are the subject of the dispute. Hence, it is a period that is imposed by the employer and is different in nature to an employee taking industrial action.

It should also be noted that, if an employer unreasonably refuses to take up conciliation or mediation services, the period of protection against dismissal can be extended. This section of the Employment Relations Act 2004 has been inserted to try to encourage employers to resolve disputes.

After the 12-week period the dismissal of employees involved in industrial action is fair if the CAC judges that all reasonable action has been taken by the employer to end the strike. However, if an employer dismisses all employees involved in industrial action and then re-engages a selection of those employees within a three-month period the dismissal of those who are not re-engaged is likely to be unfair.

OTHER TRADE UNION DUTIES

It would be wrong to presume that the trade union representative is only involved with conflict, including representation in the disciplinary process and in the industrial action process. The law also gives the trade union representative rights to be involved in specific areas of representation:

Health and safety

The Health and Safety at Work Act 1974 provides for the appointment by recognised trade unions of safety representatives. The safety representatives must be employees, and may be elected or appointed. The employer has a duty to consult with these representatives about all measures to ensure the health and safety of employees at work.

The main duties of the safety representatives are to investigate potential hazards and dangerous occurrences, investigate complaints by their colleagues about health and safety-related issues, make general representations regarding health and safety to their employer, carry out inspections and to attend safety committees.

Trade union safety representatives are allowed paid time off to carry out their duties during normal working hours. Safety representatives are also allowed paid time off for relevant training.

If at least two trade union safety representatives submit a written request, employers must establish a safety committee. This must be formed after consulting with those who made the request, and any other representatives of recognised trade unions, and within three months of the request being made. The function of the committee is to review measures being taken to ensure the health and safety at work of employees.

Although there is the potential for conflict with regard to the handling of health and safety issues, the nature of this role is different in that it is focusing on promoting good practice rather than dealing with conflict. However, according to WERS (1998) fewer than 40 per cent of workplaces had health and safety committees, and only one-third of these committees had a representative appointed by a trade union. Direct consultation with health and safety representatives took place in less than 30 per cent of workplaces.

Learning representative

The Employment Act 2002 introduced the role of 'trade union learning representative'. A learning representative can be appointed by a trade union in an organisation where it has a recognition agreement. Learning representatives have a number of formal duties, for which they are allowed paid time off. These are:

- analysing learning and training needs
- providing information and advice about learning or training matters
- arranging learning or training
- promoting the value of learning
- consulting the employer about such activities
- undergoing training for their union learning representative role.

Learning representatives are generally trained on a course run by the TUC, or on a course run by their own trade union. Some learning representatives will have prior experience in teaching or training, although that is not a prior requirement.

According to the CIPD (2004), the thought behind the development of the role of union learning representatives is to provide support and encouragement to their colleagues in seeking and receiving training opportunities. They are of particular value where the employer provides few training opportunities, or where the employee is not sure how to explain his/her training need, or where the employee works in an area that is not covered by traditional learning opportunities.

As well as providing advice and encouragement to their members a key purpose of the role is to help change attitudes towards learning. This fits well with the current Labour government's desire to see lifelong learning on the agenda. In the Government green paper *The learning age: a renaissance for a new Britain* (February 1998), the proposals for lifelong learning were a central theme. The government is committed to seeking ways for employees to develop new skills and to update old skills. The introduction of learning representatives in the workplace is one means of encouraging employees to see the importance of ongoing learning.

This is important because the UK is increasingly composed of knowledge-based industries, rather than the more traditional industries based on manual labour. If the employees in UK organisations do not have leading-edge knowledge, the organisations will become uncompetitive and ultimately the UK economy will suffer.

This theme of lifelong learning, therefore, is also reflected in the partnership agreements that have developed between some trade unions and management. If you refer back to Chapter 6 and the section on partnership you will see how learning is a fundamental basis to the success of many of the partnership criteria.

It is also a fundamental part of the ongoing psychological contract between the employee and the employer. As we have already noted, the employee expects development and increased employability from the employer in return for loyalty and hard work. This is a change from the job security that the employee might have expected 20–30 years ago. A fundamental part of development and employability is continued learning.

ACTIVITIES

The role of learning representative is still a growing area within the UK. Talk to the person responsible for learning and development within the organisation where you work, or an organisation with which you are familiar. Ask that person if he or she sees a role for a learning representative (if the organisation is non-unionised consider the role being taken by a non-union representative) in the workplace.

In this chapter we have looked at a wide range of trade union responsibilities and relevant legislation. It is important to recognise that the role of the trade union is not just about industrial action, although the law is probably most detailed in this area. There is also a role for the trade union in taking positive action in promoting such things as learning in the workplace.

KEY POINTS FROM THIS CHAPTER

- Trade union recognition is a formal recognition of bargaining rights between management and employees.
- There are four routes to trade union recognition: voluntary, semi-voluntary, automatic recognition and recognition by ballot.
- A bargaining unit is the group of employees to be covered by a recognition agreement.
- The Central Arbitration Committee is an independent body that has statutory powers to mediate in disputes relating to trade union recognition and related matters.
- The Employment Relations Act 2002 made it unlawful to intimidate any employees involved in the balloting process of trade union recognition.
- Derecognition cannot be applied for within three years of recognition being gained.
- After recognition has been agreed organisations seem to fall into one of three categories: mutual gains, business as usual and conflict continued.
- The employer is legally required to disclose information to employees to assist in the bargaining process.
- An employee has protection against detriment or dismissal in relation to trade union activities (or lack of trade union activities).
- A trade union representative is allowed time off to carry out his/her duties.
- The 'golden formula' gives the trade union statutory immunity from legal action when lawfully taking or contemplating industrial action.

- Lawful industrial action follows a clearly defined balloting process.
- Unlawful industrial action is action without a ballot or following a void ballot.
- Secondary action is action in response to a dispute between another employer and employees.
- Picketing must be for the purpose of peaceful persuasion.
- Employees cannot be dismissed for the first 12 weeks of any lawful industrial action.
- A trade union can appoint a health and safety representative in the workplace
- The role of a trade union learning representative is to encourage and support employees in seeking additional learning and successfully taking part in that learning.

1. The employees in your organisation have made a request for trade union recognition. Your managing director wants to reach an agreement that meets her requirements as well as the requirements of the employees. How will you advise her to proceed, giving good employee relations practice and also the requirements of the law?

2. You are the HR manager and a line manager has complained to you that one of his employees, who is a recognised trade union representative, is recruiting new members in work time. When asked to stop, the trade union representative has informed the line manager that it is one of his trade union duties and he is allowed paid time off for such duties. What do you advise?

3. After a ballot for industrial action the trade union informed you that it was taking strike action every Friday for the next six weeks. A number of employees, who are trade union members, have been to see you and told you they are unhappy about this situation because they thought they had only voted for an overtime ban. How could this situation have been avoided, and what would you advise the employees?

(Suggestions of answers to the examples can be accessed by tutors at www.cipd.co.uk/tss)

Speedy Delivery is a courier company specialising in the delivery of parcels anywhere within the UK in 24 hours. It has a network of offices throughout the UK, and employs about 1,500 people. The biggest group of employees are the van drivers and the parcel handlers at the six depots situated in main cities throughout the UK.

For many years now Speedy Delivery has been plagued with employee relations problems. It is heavily unionised, with 87 per cent of all employees belonging to the recognised trade union. The trade union has a rather traditional view of working practices, and is very reluctant to agree to any changes proposed by the management.

The main confrontation between management and the trade unions has been over the handling of the unpredictability of the work. Although Speedy Delivery does have a number of regular contracts with organisations, about 45 per cent of the work is attributed to customers simply phoning up and asking for a parcel to be transferred from A to B. This work is unpredictable, not only in volume but also in where in the country it will be required.

The current practice is that van drivers are entitled to a 'stand by' payment. They are on the rota to work a certain number of core hours, then they have additional stand by hours when they are not required to be present for work unless specifically requested. However, during the stand-by hours they must be easily contactable and they must be able to drive (for example, they must not consume any alcohol for five hours before or during the stand-by period).

The management is finding that this process is very uneconomical, because drivers are only required to work for about 35 per cent of the time that they are on stand by. They have proposed, therefore, to stop the stand-by hours process and to replace it by the use of freelance drivers. The proposal is that they will build up a register of drivers they can contact at short notice, all of whom would be trained to work according to Speedy Delivery standards. Existing drivers could add their names to this register, and would be called if they had not already worked their full quota of hours for that day.

The trade unions have refused these proposals outright, saying that it is taking work away from their members. They called a mass meeting of all the van drivers and called for a show of hands in favour of industrial action. They have reported back saying that they have a majority in favour of taking immediate strike action and that this will start in two hours' time if the proposals are not withdrawn.

Speedy Delivery cannot afford to have industrial action because it seriously fears it will lose valuable customer contracts. However, it is tired of the trade unions refusing every proposal that involves change. At the same time, it knows it must improve the employee relations within the organisation or this type of confrontation will happen again and again.

Questions

a) Given that Speedy Delivery cannot afford to have immediate industrial action, what should it do? What are the implications for the future if it does this?

b) Given that Speedy Delivery wants to stop the trade unions refusing every proposal it puts forward, in the longer term what should it do? What are the implications for the future if it does this?

c) Given the conflict between taking action for the short term and action for the long term, what is the best course of action for Speedy Delivery?

Individual Legal Protection

The objectives of this chapter are to:

- explain how individual legal protection has grown in recent decades within the UK
- consider whether individuality is promoted by current legislation
- outline how legislation can be used to address a concern within society
- examine how legislation can promote ways of behaviour for both the individual and management
- consider how legislation can help determine a way of working
- examine how individual legislation can underpin partnership agreements.

In a number of instances in this book we have suggested that one of the reasons for the decline in the trade union movement is the growth of protection that the law offers to the individual. The purpose of this chapter is to take an overview of the growth in this area of legislation, and to consider how it has affected employment relations within the UK.

It must be emphasised that this chapter is very much an overview of the law. Employment law is a fast-growing area, and a complex one, and it is not possible to cover it all in one chapter. Nor is the intention to do this: our examination is very much from the standpoint of the impact on employment relations.

THE GROWTH OF INDIVIDUAL LEGAL PROTECTION

At the start of the 1970s there was very little legal protection for employees. Much of what we take for granted within employment today was not part of the employment relationship. For example, at this time it was still possible for employers to dismiss employees without the employee having any recourse. If we consider, therefore, the balance of power in the employment relationship at this time it was something like that shown in Figure 13.1.

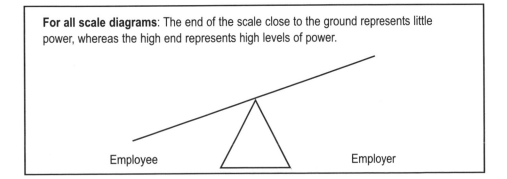

For all scale diagrams: The end of the scale close to the ground represents little power, whereas the high end represents high levels of power.

Employee   Employer

Figure 13.1 The balance of power in the employment relationship

During the 1970s a number of key pieces of legislation were passed. These included legislation relating to unfair dismissal (1971), the Equal Pay Act 1970, the Health and Safety at Work Act 1974, the Sex Discrimination Act 1975 and the Race Relations Act 1976. By the end of this decade an employee had considerably more protection. However, the employment relations scene had not become less confrontational. The Winter of Discontent took place in 1978/79, one of the bitterest examples of breakdown in the employment relationship. Although the issues within the Winter of Discontent were not related to the areas listed above (it was primarily a confrontation over levels of pay), it would be wrong to conclude that the introduction of the wide-ranging legislation had resolved all issues in the employment relationship.

At the end of this decade the Conservative Party came into government, and as we have already seen, it took action because it saw an imbalance in power in the employment relationship. However, this was not an imbalance in individual protection, rather it was seen to be an imbalance in the power of employees as a group. Hence, when we return to our scales we see two things happening, as in Figures 13.2 and 13.3.

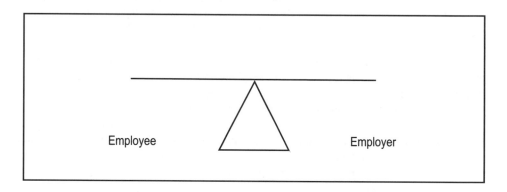

Figure 13.2 Balance of power on an individual basis

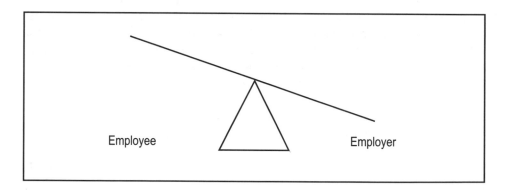

Figure 13.3 Balance of power on a collective basis

It is difficult to suggest exactly how these lines should fall, because the assessment is somewhat subjective. However, I would suggest that the range of legislation introduced in the 1970s had brought considerably more protection for the employee.

The action of the Conservative government through the 1980s, and into the early 1990s was to address the collective imbalance. It did this through the legislation that we examined in Chapter 12. On an individual basis there was very little new legislation introduced during this time. To understand this lack of new individual legislation we have to consider a number of key points:

- As we saw in Chapters 2 and 3, the Conservative government of 1979–97 refused to sign the Social Chapter. This meant that a number of changes that would have been introduced had this been signed were not addressed.
- There was a big emphasis on bringing control back to the trade union/employer relationship, and this might have well have detracted from thinking about any reforms needed at an individual level.
- The miners' strike of 1984 fell during this period and was symptomatic of a huge power struggle between the Conservative government and the trade unions. It might be that the Conservative government would not have seen this to be an appropriate time to give additional legal protection to employees.
- The 1980s were a period of great growth, with many people experiencing more wealth than ever before. Although this was followed by a sharp recession in the late 1980s/early 1990s, during most of this decade many groups of employees were generally quite happy with their situation, and there was relatively little pressure for change.

The mid-1990s was a time in which the individual and collective relationships between the employee and the employer were seen to be balanced. However, this was the start of a period where a considerable amount of legislation giving individual protection was introduced. According to Hopkins and Warren (1993), the European Community had a goal to harmonise and increase health and safety standards throughout the community. As we shall see later in this chapter, this resulted in a range of health and safety legislation being introduced in the UK in 1992.

In 1995 there was the first alteration to discrimination legislation for 19 years, with the introduction of the Disability Discrimination Act 1995. In 1996 the Employment Rights Act was introduced, which among other things revised legislation relating to unfair dismissal.

Towards the end of the 1990s we start to see the impact of the Labour Party taking government (in 1997) and signing the Social Chapter. The National Minimum Wage Act 1998 is an excellent example of the impact of this. We also see, at this time, more legislation coming from Europe. One of the best examples of this is the Working Time Regulations 1998, which gave considerable new protection to employees, as we shall see later in this chapter.

By the end of the 1990s employees had considerably more protection than just 10 years earlier. At this time there started to be some concern from employers that the balance of power had moved in favour of the employee. It was noted that employees' rights had increased dramatically in a relatively short period of time (Painter *et al* 1998). Again, the drawing of the scales reflecting the period is somewhat subjective, but there was definitely concern from employers that the situation was as in Figure 13.4 (overleaf).

As we enter the twenty-first century employment legislation has grown yet further, and at great speed. As a result of European directives, discrimination legislation has been increased to cover sexual orientation, religion/belief and (from October 2006) age. As we referred to in Chapter 5, the Flexible Working Regulations were added in 2002. The Employment Act 2002 introduced statutory procedures relating to discipline and grievance, which gave a more formalised route for employers

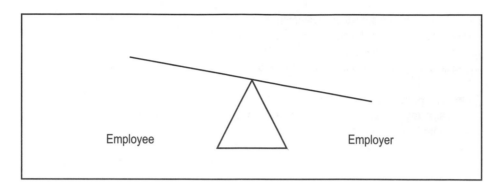

Figure 13.4 The scales redrawn to reflect the 1990s

to use in the workplace (see Chapter 11). Legislation was added giving more protection to part-time workers (2000) and fixed-term contract workers (2002).

Farnham (2005) states that the increase in employment law has put extra pressures on management. They need to be aware of their obligations, and also have to ensure that subordinate employees do not breach the legislation. This frustration that some employers feel was summed up in a statement given by Sir Digby Jones, the chief executive of the CBI (13 September 2005). Speaking in advance of the annual TUC Conference, Jones stated that meeting the demands of the trade unions (which included a doubling of statutory redundancy pay, increased rights for part-time workers as well as extending the scope of collective bargaining) would totally undermine the development of the UK as a competitive economy. He stated that employers have had to absorb a series of new employment rights in a positive and constructive manner, but the growth of organisations will be hampered if the trade unions' demands were met.

However, a survey by CIPD and Lovells (2005) presents a more positive attitude to the recent changes in employment law. In this survey less than one-sixth of the employers surveyed saw employment law as getting in the way, or detracting from business. The majority saw employment law as making a positive contribution to employee relations, and increasing the employees' sense of trust in their employer. However, the survey does state that it is difficult to make general statements about the impact of employment law.

More than 50 per cent of employers welcomed the changes to discrimination legislation and family-friendly legislation. However, far fewer employers felt as positive about legislation relating to statutory trade union recognition, freedom of information, statutory dispute resolution or informing and consulting with employees.

The majority of employers saw the introduction of the right to request flexible working (see page 112 for more explanation of this) as a driver of good employment practice. Only 15 per cent saw this as resulting in unnecessary red tape. Most found it relatively straightforward to comply with the legislation in this area. However, only 22 per cent of employers reported that the Working Time Regulations (see page 313) had had a positive impact on their organisation, with most reporting that the impact was negligible or negative. It is difficult, therefore, to know how to draw the final set of scales in this section. It is very likely that some employers would draw scales that look like Figure 13.5. However, it might be optimistic to presume that employee representatives would draw them as in Figure 13.6.

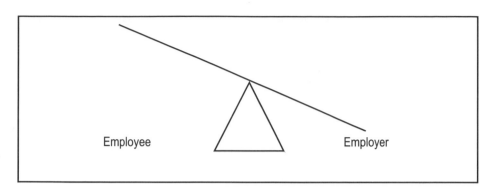

Figure 13.5 The scales redrawn according to some employers

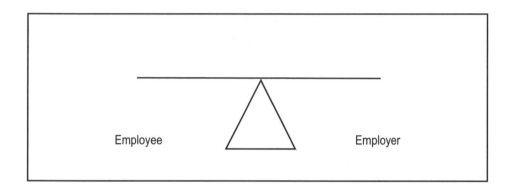

Figure 13.6 The scales redrawn by employee representatives on an optimistic presumption

ACTIVITIES

Talk to a number of different employers and employees and ask them for their impression of the balance of power in the employment relationship. If possible, ask them to draw the relationship scales from their point of view. Do you see a lot of variation in your findings?

USING LEGISLATION TO PROMOTE INDIVIDUALITY

Most of the protection that is given in the employment relationship is to employees. It is important, therefore, that we understand who is, and who is not, an employee. There are two alternatives for those who work in an organisation. They can be hired to work under a contract of service (an employee) or under a contract for services (an independent contractor).

Section 230 (1) of the Employment Rights Act (1996) defines an employee as 'an individual who has entered into or works under a contract of employment'. Section 230 (3) of the same Act states that a worker is 'an individual who either works under a contract of employment or works under any other contract where that individual agrees to personally perform work or services for another party'. Although these definitions are of some use they do not tell us exactly who should be given a contract of employment. This is primarily because situations of employment are very varied and there can be no one clear rule.

To overcome this lack of clarity the courts have, over time, developed a series of tests that can be applied to determine who is an employee. The examination of these tests is outside the scope of a textbook on employee relations, but it is important to be aware that there are structured approaches in existence to address this issue.

For employees, a key document is the employment contract. Farnham (2005) refers to a contract as an exchange of promises. Indeed, the contract of employment is an exchange of promises explaining what the employer agrees to do, and what the employee agrees to do in return.

The concept of a contract of employment has been part of employment legislation since 1963. However the detail of what would must be specified in the contract was not set out until the Employment Rights Act 1996. The contract is fundamental to the employment relationship, and is increasingly symptomatic of the individualism of this relationship. Whereas groups of employees would once have had identical contracts, increasingly employees are negotiating the terms of their contracts on an individual basis.

The contract of employment describes the basis of the employment relationship. It can be in writing, or it can be agreed orally. It is of great importance in the event of any dispute, because the contract of employment explains the way in which the employer and employee have agreed to work together.

The terms of the contract of employment can be classified as express terms and implied terms. Express terms are terms that have been discussed and agreed between the employer and employee. They might not be in writing. It must be emphasised that express terms cannot diminish statutory rights given by law. For example, if an employer writes a rate of pay into a contract of employment that is less than the national minimum wage (NMW) it does not mean that the NMW does not apply. Implied terms are those that have not been specifically agreed between the employer and employee but are derived from the following sources:

- collective agreements
- statute (the law)
- custom
- the courts
- work rules.

Written statement of initial employment particulars

As already noted, the Employment Rights Act 1996 set out what items must be specified in the contract of employment. The employer is required to issue all employees with a written statement of initial employment particulars not later than two months after the beginning of employment. The statement must include:

- The names of the employer and the employee.
- The date when employment began.
- The date when continuous service with the employer began (ie taking into account any previous service with the employer prior to this appointment).
- The job title, or a brief description of the job duties.

- The rate of remuneration, the way in which it is to be calculated (eg the terms of a bonus scheme) and the periods at which the employee will be paid. This includes all financial benefits as well as basic pay.
- Terms and conditions relating to hours of work (eg this should include basic hours; shift patterns and rules regarding overtime).
- Terms and conditions relating to holiday pay (eg, this must specify the numbers of days holiday to which the employee is entitled each year, and the period in which this is to be taken).
- The place of work, or the employer's address if the employee will be moving between a number of places of work.
- Terms and conditions relating to payments given if incapacitated due to sickness or injury.
- Details of pension schemes.
- The length of notice the employee is required to give, and the employer is entitled to receive to terminate the contract of employment.
- Where the employment is not intended to be permanent, the period for which it is expected to continue must be stated, or if it is a fixed-term contract, the date it is to end.
- Any collective agreements that will directly affect the employee including, where the employer is not a party, the persons by whom they were made.
- If the employee is required to work outside the UK for more than one month, the period of work outside the UK must be specified; the currency of the remuneration must be specified and any additional remuneration or benefits applicable to the work must be detailed. In addition, any terms and conditions relating to the employee's return to the UK must be detailed.
- Details of disciplinary rules that apply to the employee.
- Details of grievance procedures, and the name of the person the employee should apply to if he or she is dissatisfied with any disciplinary decision, or to air a grievance.

Despite this lengthy list of contents the statement is not the contract of employment, it is simply a statement of the main terms and conditions of employment. Indeed, it should be noted that the law does not actually require employees to sign the statement, or to give any indication that they have received the statement. The statement is the employer's version of the terms and conditions, and is not an indication of any agreement being reached between the employer and the employee. If the employee accepts the terms and conditions, and works in accordance with them, it could be argued that the employer's version has contractual effect because of the lack of any challenge. In practice, a court will usually accept that the statement is strong evidence of the terms agreed by the employer and employee. However, as the statement is not a contract either party can challenge the accuracy of the statement.

When an employee seeks employment from an employer it is usually the employer who determines the terms and conditions of employment. Apart from senior employees who typically negotiate the terms of their employment in some detail, employees are usually offered a job on the basis of 'These are the terms, if you don't like them don't take the job.' Given that situation it is not surprising that the initial statement is seen as the employer's interpretation of the terms and conditions of employment.

However, as the statement can be issued any time during the first two months of employment it is quite possible that the employee has started employment when the statement is received and has possibly left other employment to take the job. 'Don't take the job' might not be a fair solution if the statement is not as the employee expected. It could be argued, therefore, that although the contract of employment does represent the individual relationship between the employer and the employee, there is not equal power in the development of this contract.

ACTIVITIES

How much flexibility did you have in determining the last employment contract that you were given? Do you feel that this contract was really an indication of your individual relationship with the employer, or was it simply the general terms offered to all employees? What would you have liked to change, if anything?

USING LEGISLATION TO ADDRESS EXTERNAL FACTORS IN THE EMPLOYMENT RELATIONSHIP

In Chapter 2 we looked at a variety of external factors that can impact on the employment relationship. Within the heading of social factors we looked at the impact of family issues. The government has specific concerns over issues relating to families and work. As we saw in Chapter 5, this is partly related to the issues surrounding work–life balance. The political issues are complex, but there is no doubt that action has been taken to make it easier for parents to work.

The Maternity and Parental Leave Regulations 1999 led the way in addressing this issue by introducing a minimum framework of rights for parents. The legislation allowed employees with at least one year's continuous service, who have the responsibility for a child, to take up to 13 weeks' unpaid leave for the purpose of caring for the child (this is increased to 18 weeks if the child is entitled to a disability living allowance). This right applies during the child's first five years of life (18 years for a disabled child). The leave must be taken in blocks of at least one week, but must not be more than four weeks in any one year. Although this legislation led the way in addressing an important social factor relating to employment, it did not have a big impact. This is possibly because the leave is unpaid, and hence is not a particularly attractive option to the employee.

The Employment Act 2002 added a range of additional provisions:

- *Increased statutory maternity protection* The legislation extended the full period of absence to 52 weeks for women with the eligible length of service (26 continuous weeks by the beginning of the 14th week before the week when the baby is expected to be born).
- *Adoption leave* The legislation introduced leave that is identical to maternity leave for all those who adopt a child.
- *Paternity leave* For the first time the statutory right to take paternity leave was introduced. The leave is for a maximum of two weeks, paid at the lower rate of statutory maternity pay (currently £106 per week).

However, the most dramatic change was the introduction of the Flexible Working Regulations 2002. This gives an employee the statutory right to request flexible working. It does not give a right to be granted flexible working hours.

It is also important to note that the rights are only available to those who have a child aged less than 6 years, or a disabled child aged less than 18 years. This aspect of the regulations has given employers some concern. Is it fair to expect those with no children, or older children, to work 'non-flexible' hours, while colleagues with younger children are treated differently? In looking at the detail of the legislation we shall attempt to address this concern.

To qualify for the right to make a request for flexible working, the employee must have had at least 26 weeks' continuous service on the date of making the request, must be the mother, father, adopter, guardian or foster parent of the child or be married to the child's mother, father, adopter, guardian or foster parent, and must expect to have responsibility for the child's upbringing. In considering these qualification criteria it is important to note that:

- The legislation is not restricted to women.
- The request does not have to be made at the end of maternity leave; it can be made any time that the child is aged less than 6 years (18 for a disabled child).
- The purpose of the request must be to care for the child. It cannot just be because the parent would like to work different hours for his or her own benefit.

In requesting flexible working employees can request changes to:

- the hours they work
- the times they work
- the place they are required to work.

An employee must write to his/her employer requesting a change to flexible working. Once the employer has received the request it must arrange a meeting with the employee within 28 days to discuss the request. The employee has the right to be accompanied to this meeting by a fellow worker or a trade union representative. Within 14 days of the meeting the employer must give a written response to the request.

If the request is granted the changes that have been agreed must be specified in writing, and a date for the start of the changes must be confirmed. This will be a change of contract and will be considered a permanent change. In other words, the employee has no right to expect a change back to the current terms and conditions of employment at some future date. Therefore, it should also be noted that the new working patterns will continue after the child reaches his/her sixth birthday.

The legislation sets out a number of grounds on which the employer can turn down the request. They are:

- burden of additional costs
- detrimental effect on the ability to meet customer demand
- inability to reorganise work among existing staff
- inability to recruit additional staff
- detrimental impact on quality
- detrimental impact on performance
- insufficiency of work during the periods the employee proposes to work
- planned structural changes
- any other ground the secretary of state may specify by regulations.

If the employee's request is refused he/she may appeal against the decision. If the employee's request is still turned down he can refer the issue to an employment tribunal. The employment tribunal has a limited role to play. It cannot challenge the validity of the employer's decision, and it cannot make its own judgement on whether the request should have been granted. Its role is simply to consider whether the employer has given the request serious consideration, whether the reason for refusal was one permitted by the legislation, whether the facts used to assess the request were correct and whether the employer has acted in accordance with the statutory procedure.

The introduction of this legislation gives rise to a number of concerns for employers. These concerns relate to the impact on the relationship between the employer and the employee *and* on the relationship between employee and employee. The major concerns are:

- *Setting precedents* An employer might receive a request from an employee for flexible working, and decide to grant the request. If another employee in the same department then makes the same request, can the employer refuse that employee? Each request is handled separately, so it might be possible to refuse a further request because, for example, the employer was able to reorganise work among existing staff when only one employee was working different hours, but cannot achieve this when two employees are working in this way.
- *Interpretation of the business grounds* How much inconvenience is the employer expected to accept? It might be possible, for example, to still meet customer demands, although the flexible working of a member of staff makes this more difficult. To what extent must the employer accept a certain level of difficulty before it becomes classed as a 'detrimental effect'?
- *Expectations of employees* It is true that the legislation was heralded in the popular press as the opportunity for all parents of young children to work the hours they requested. Although the legislation does not state that, there is definitely an increased expectation of some level of flexibility. How does the employer address this and maintain good employee relations?
- *The impact on non-eligible employees* If those who are entitled to request flexibility are seen to get the more popular hours or times of work, other employees could become very dissatisfied and demotivated. However, a negative impact on other employees is not one of the grounds on which an application for flexibility can be refused. The reaction of the TUC to this problem is to call for all employees to be allowed to seek flexibility, for whatever reason. However, the employer could find it very difficult to manage such a scenario.

Many employers have addressed these types of issues by formulating a clear policy on dealing with employee requests. Obviously the policies must incorporate the statutory procedure, but writing a company policy gives time for employer and employees to consider the issues before any conflict occurs.

Concern has been expressed about the strength of the legislation. At the CIPD's annual employment law conference (2003) there was debate over the likelihood of the legislation being flouted. The concern is that employers only have to give a 'business reason' for refusing the request, and that employment tribunals cannot investigate those reasons, they can only instruct firms to 'go back and think again'. It was confirmed by the head of the DTI's Employment Relations Directorate that the government was committed to reviewing the new rights in April 2005, and would consider bringing in some test of objective justification, or possibly a right to flexible working, if there was widespread evidence that the rules were being ignored.

Daniels and Macdonald (2005) report that, according to a major piece of research by the CIPD and Lovells (2003), in the first six months from the date of the regulations coming into force over a quarter of organisations saw an increase in the number of requests for flexible working. Sixty-two per cent of employers have agreed to these requests, either fully or in a modified form of what was originally requested. Seventy-two per cent of employers stated that they were prepared to consider requests from all employees, even if they were not legally entitled to make such a request.

Of those that made the request for flexible working, 44 per cent were clerical workers, 21 per cent were managers, 20 per cent were technical staff and 27 per cent were classed as professionals. The most commonly requested form of flexibility is part-time work and coming in late or leaving early. As we saw in Chapter 5, additional research from the CIPD has found that 47 per cent of employers are concerned that staff without children resent the flexibility that colleagues with children are allowed. In addition, the secretary of state for trade and industry has hinted that the government might consider extending the rights to flexible working to employees who care for elderly or disabled relatives, although no firm proposals have made.

The TUC leader, Brendan Barber, has been quoted as saying that flexible working is one of the most important pieces of legislation introduced by the Labour government. However, a CBI/Pertemps survey (September 2005) found that organisations were reporting that they were spending too long on processing claims for flexible working, which was distracting them from managing the business. Overall, 26 per cent of the 420 organisations surveyed reported a negative impact on the organisation from 'family-friendly legislation' (up from 11 per cent in the previous year).

While it is clear that the government has made a significant impact on the social factor of 'the family' through the use of legislation, it is not fully clear how successful this has been. It is certainly true that a number of employees have benefited from it, but it has to be questioned whether the issue has been partly resolved through the legislation, or whether the legislation has simply created other problems – namely, tensions in the relationships between employer and employee or between employee and employee.

ACTIVITIES

What do you think? How much do you think that the employment relationship has been helped by family-friendly legislation, and how much do you think it has been damaged? If you were a government adviser, what would your advice be for any future changes?

USING LEGISLATION TO DETERMINE ACCEPTABLE BEHAVIOUR IN THE EMPLOYMENT RELATIONSHIP

Individual employment legislation does bring certain rights to the employee, such as rights under the Working Time Regulations 1998 (see page 313). In addition, some aspects of individual legislation determine behaviours that are and are not acceptable in the employment relationship.

One area of legislation that does this is discrimination. As we have already noted, three pieces of legislation date back to the 1970s (the Equal Pay Act 1970, Sex Discrimination Act 1975 and Race Relations Act 1976). Since the 1970s the legislation has extended to include disability, gender reassignment, part-time workers, fixed-term employees, sexual orientation and religion/belief. From October 2006 age will be added to this list.

In Chapter 5 we looked at some of the negative impacts on the employment relationship that can occur through the development of prejudice and discrimination. It is important to realise that such behaviour can happen in the relationship between employer and employee, and in the relationships between employees. However, it is also important to note (particularly for the employer) that the employer is responsible for the actions of employees in the course of employment. This is known as 'vicarious liability'. An example is found in the following case.

Jones v *Tower Boot Company Ltd (1997)*

Jones was a 16-year-old man of mixed-race origin. When he started work at Tower Boot Company he was subjected to a campaign of verbal and physical assaults from two colleagues. This included him being burnt by a screwdriver and having metal bolts thrown at his head. After one month he resigned and brought a claim of race discrimination. Tower Boot Company argued that the colleagues had been acting outside of their work duties, and hence the employer was not liable for the discrimination. However, the Court of Appeal ruled that the employer was vicariously liable for the discriminatory acts as they had happened in the course of employment.

It is also important to note that, if the employer is aware that discriminatory acts are taking place, it is expected to stop those acts. If the employer does not take any action to stop any discriminatory acts and is aware that they are happening, the employer will become directly liable for the discrimination, rather than vicariously liable.

Discrimination legislation covers behaviour that is both direct and indirect. Direct discrimination is where an individual is treated less favourably than another on one of the grounds listed above. The treatment must be less favourable; being different is not sufficient to classify as discrimination. The law allows for direct discrimination to be found where the comparator is hypothetical, as well as where there is an actual person who can be identified as being treated more favourably.

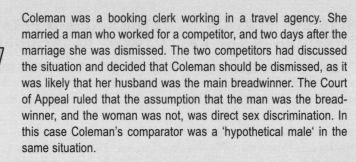

Coleman v *Skyrail Oceanic Ltd (1981)*

Coleman was a booking clerk working in a travel agency. She married a man who worked for a competitor, and two days after the marriage she was dismissed. The two competitors had discussed the situation and decided that Coleman should be dismissed, as it was likely that her husband was the main breadwinner. The Court of Appeal ruled that the assumption that the man was the breadwinner, and the woman was not, was direct sex discrimination. In this case Coleman's comparator was a 'hypothetical male' in the same situation.

Indirect discrimination is where an employer applies to both sexes, both races (etc) a criterion that adversely affects a considerably larger proportion of one sex, race or other group than another, it is to the detriment of the person that s/he cannot comply, and it cannot be justified, irrespective of sex, race or other discriminatory factor. This definition might seem rather complicated, but it is well illustrated in the following example:

R v Secretary of State ex parte Equal Opportunities Commission (1995)

At the time of this case full-time employees had to have served for at least two consecutive years to gain statutory rights (eg for claiming unfair dismissal) whereas part-time employees had to serve for at least five consecutive years. The Equal Opportunities Commission challenged the government over this because a significantly larger proportion of women than men work part-time, and hence this qualifying period was claimed to be indirectly discriminatory. The claim was upheld and the qualifying periods were changed to be identical (and are now one year for both full and part-time employees).

Here we see that there is a criterion (length of continuous service) that affects a larger proportion of one gender than another (affects more women), it is to detriment of the women that they cannot comply (they take longer to gain statutory rights), and it cannot be justified on the grounds of gender.

Although the presence of legislation does not mean that discrimination does not happen, it has brought increased awareness of what is and is not acceptable behaviour in the employment relationship. Here we see, therefore, legislation being used to promote acceptable behaviour, both among employees, and between the employer and the employee. However, legislation will not change attitudes. As we saw in Chapter 5, attitudes can develop through prejudice, and can be very difficult to change.

Has discrimination legislation made any difference? Access one of the websites of the three main bodies addressing discrimination issues:

www.eoc.org.uk Equal Opportunities Commission
www.cre.gov.uk Commission for Racial Equality
www.drc-gb.org Disability Rights Commission

Gain an understanding of the main issues that you identify within the workplace. Do you think that further legislation would address these issues, or is a change of attitude required that legislation cannot bring about?

USING LEGISLATION TO PROMOTE WAYS OF WORKING

According to Bratton and Gold (2003), approximately 1,000 employees were killed at work during the 1960s. Every year of that decade around 500,000 employees suffered injuries of varying degrees of severity, and 23 million working days were lost each year as a result of industrial injury or disease.

The Health and Safety Executive reported that in 2004/05 there were 220 fatal injuries at work. In 2003/04 159,809 employees were injured at work, and it is estimated that 2.2 million employees were absent from work as a result of illness they believed was caused or made worse by work. In total, in 2003/04 39 million working days were lost, 9 million because of work related injuries and 30 million because of work-related ill health.

In 1972 Lord Robens was commissioned by the government to review the provisions for health and safety in the workplace. The Health and Safety at Work Act 1974 (HASAWA) encompasses most of the recommendations that were made as a result of his report. A key conclusion of the Robens Report was that the creation of improved health and safety required the shared responsibility of employer and employee.

The joint responsibility is shown within the HASAWA through the duties that are specified for both the employer and the employee. The duties of the employer are to provide:

- safe and adequate plant and equipment
- safe premises and/or place of work
- competent and safe fellow employees
- a safe system of work.

The duties of employees are to:

- take reasonable care for the health and safety of themselves and others who may be adversely affected by their acts or omissions at work
- co-operate with their employer as necessary to enable health and safety requirements to be met.

However, the impacts of good standards within health and safety go beyond compliance with the law. Beer *et al* (1984) suggest that going beyond compliance with the law has a strong positive effect on the psychological contract. This is due to a strengthening of employee commitment, motivation and loyalty. Bratton and Gold (2003) suggest that union–management relations are improved when employers satisfy the health and safety needs of their employees.

Given the value to the employment relationship of having a positive approach to health and safety, it is possibly surprising that concerns about health and safety are one of the growing areas of conflict within the employment relationship. This is specifically with relationship to work-related stress. According to the Health and Safety Executive, work-related stress, depression or anxiety is the leading cause of working days lost through work-related injury or ill health, with an estimated 12.5 million days a year lost in 2003/4. Each reported case of stress leads to an average of 28.5 days lost.

There is no legislation specifically addressing the issue of workplace stress. Rather, it is covered by the general duties of care that the employer has under the HASAWA (as outlined earlier). Hence, specific guidance on the responsibilities for stress within the workplace has been built up through a series of case law. One of the first, and often quoted, cases relating to stress is explained below.

ORGANISATION
EXAMPLE

Walker v *Northumberland County Council (1994)*

Walker was a social worker. There was a heavy workload in the area in which he worked, largely because of the increased reporting of child abuse cases. On a number of occasions Walker discussed the workload with his employer, expressing his concern at the pressure he was under. No solution was found. In November 1986 Walker suffered a nervous breakdown, and he was absent as a result of this breakdown until March 1987. During his period of absence he discussed the workload with his employers again, and certain support mechanisms (including the temporary assignment of extra staff to help with the work) were agreed. When Walker returned to work most of this support mechanism did not appear, and any that did was withdrawn within a month. Walker suffered a second breakdown, and in February 1988 was dismissed on the grounds of permanent ill health.

He claimed that the employers had been negligent in not providing him with a safe system of work. The High Court ruled that the employer was not liable for Walker's first breakdown because it was not reasonably foreseeable that this would occur. However, it was liable for the second breakdown because he had already suffered the first breakdown, and the agreed support mechanisms had been withdrawn. An out-of-court settlement of £175,000 was eventually agreed.

The fact that the damages were awarded for the second breakdown only is very significant. For an employer to be liable for damages resulting from the stress of an employee, the illness resulting from the stress must have been reasonably foreseeable. This point was emphasised further in a judgement given by the Court of Appeal when considering appeals on four cases that were grouped together.

ORGANISATION EXAMPLE

Sutherland v Hatton and three other cases (2002)

In this appeal damages had been awarded in four unrelated cases, and in each one the employer was appealing against the decision.

Hatton had been awarded £90,766. She was a teacher who had suffered stress and depression and had eventually retired early on the grounds of ill health. Her workload had not been exceptionally heavy, and she had not told the school she was struggling. The history of events included her being attacked in the street in January 1994, and suffering the anxiety of her son being hospitalised in April 1994 for a considerable period. Neither of these events related to her work. In August 1994 she first saw a stress counsellor, but did not tell the school. In October 1995 she went absent because of sickness, and never returned to work. She eventually took ill health early retirement in August 1996. The appeal of the employer succeeded, and the award of damages was withdrawn. There could be no liability because the illness relating to stress was not foreseeable, because the school had not been made aware that she was struggling.

Barber was also a teacher. He worked at a difficult school, but did not have a particularly heavy workload in comparison to other teachers. He became depressed in August 1995, and did not tell his employers at that time. In October 1995 he talked to the deputy head teacher and told him he was struggling, and the deputy head helped Barber to prioritise and delegate some work. He continued to experience symptoms of stress but did not tell anyone (not even his doctor) until his collapse in November 1996. In March 1997 he took early retirement on the grounds of ill health. He took a claim for damages relating to stress-induced injury and was awarded £101,042. The employers won the appeal. Barber had not told anyone he was suffering medical symptoms as a result of stress, and hence the employer could not foresee the problem and could not be liable.

Jones worked as an administration assistant. Hers was a unique job in the organisation, which involved working very long hours. The employer commented that it was a gamble to expect one person to do the job, which was really two or three people's work. She complained of the workload and was offered extra help, but it never materialised. She then wrote a five-page document explaining the problems in detail and invoked the formal grievance procedure. She was threatened with the loss of her job if she continued to complain. In January 1995 she became ill with anxiety and depression and never returned to work. Towards the end of 1996 the centre where she worked closed and as a result she was made redundant. She was awarded £157,541 on her claim for damages relating to stress-induced illness on the grounds of the employer's negligence.

The employers lost this appeal. The outcome was clearly foreseeable: Jones had complained in detail about the problems, and the employer had accepted that the workload was too great.

Bishop was a factory worker. His organisation was bought by another and there was a reorganisation. He had to move to a new job, and found it hard to adjust. He complained and asked for his old job back, but it no longer existed. The pressures in the new job were not seen to be excessive, but Bishop could not cope with the changes. He saw his GP with symptoms of depression, but did not tell his employer. His employer knew he was unhappy, but was not aware of any medical impact this was having on him. In February 1997 he had a breakdown and attempted suicide. In 1998 his employment was terminated. He brought a claim for damages relating to a stress-induced illness, and was awarded £7,000 plus loss of earnings.

The employer won the appeal. At no time had the employer been made aware that the difficulties at work were having any impact on Bishop's health, and hence the outcome was not foreseeable.

These rulings are important because they result in some clear guidelines for dealing with claims of negligence relating to stress. The key points to note are:

- The ordinary principles of employer's liability apply to any psychiatric injury, in the same way as they apply to any physical injury.
- An essential question is whether the harm was reasonably foreseeable. In particular, was an injury to health attributable to stress at work (as opposed to stress from personal difficulties)?
- Forseeability has to depend on what the employer knows (or ought to know – the employer cannot decide to ignore obvious signs, and then claim ignorance). If the employer is not aware of any problems he/she is entitled to assume that there are none.

In considering whether an event was reasonably foreseeable, consideration must be given to the type of work being carried out, and the demands placed on an employee in comparison to other employees in similar work.

Although these cases help us to understand how the courts will deal with claims of stress, an equally important issue is to understand stress in the workplace and try to minimise it. If an employee perceives that s/he is being put under excessive stress by the employer, the balance of the psychological contract will be negatively affected, which could lead to the perceived stress being exacerbated.

Another area of increased legislation which actually relates to health and safety is the Working Time Regulations 1998. The Regulations do not apply to mobile workers in the transport sector (they are covered by legislation specific to their individual industries), jobs in domestic service, managing executives, family workers and workers officiating at religious services in churches and religious communities. The restriction on the length of the working week is being phased in for junior doctors.

The purpose of the Regulations is to make the working environment safer (employees who are tired have more accidents) and also to stop unscrupulous employers requesting unacceptable hours of work. The Regulations cover a range of aspects of working time.

Annual leave

Workers are entitled to four weeks' paid leave, which includes public and any other state holidays. The entitlement is only to that holiday entitlement which has been accrued, one-twelfth of the four weeks being accrued each month. Workers are entitled to be paid a sum equivalent to a week's pay for each week of leave. This will be the basic week's pay; non-contractual overtime (overtime which is not guaranteed) is not included in calculating the amount.

Maximum working week

The number of hours worked, including overtime, must not exceed an average of 48 hours per week over a 17-week reference period. Therefore, it is not correct to state that a worker cannot work more than 48 hours in any week. A worker can, as long as less than 48 hours are worked another week, to give an average of no more than 48 over the 17-week period.

A worker can opt out of this requirement. Any agreement to opt out must be in writing, and either relate to a specific period of time or apply indefinitely. Within the agreement there must be the right for the worker to give seven days' notice (or a greater period of notice, agreed between the two parties – but this must not be more than three months) to terminate the agreement. The employer is also required to keep up-to-date records of all the workers who have signed such an agreement.

The opt-out was negotiated by the UK government with the European Community when the Regulations were first introduced. In 2005, the European Community reviewed the provisions relating to the opt-out and suggested a variety of potential changes, from removing it altogether to limiting it to a one-year period. The UK government and employer groups are arguing hard against the opt-out being removed, claiming that it will severely damage the competitiveness of the UK economy, and the freedom of employers to manage their businesses. However, employee representatives argue that working longer than 48 hours per week damages employee health, and negatively affects the work–life balance. At the time of writing no conclusion to this discussion had been reached.

Night work

The protection given to night workers is as follows:

- If the work involves any special hazards or physical or mental strain, the night worker must not work for more than eight hours in any 24-hour period.
- An entitlement to a free health assessment before starting night work, and at regular intervals thereafter.
- An entitlement to adequate rest periods if the nature of the work is likely to cause health problems.

If the health assessment shows problems that might be connected with night work, the employer should make every attempt to move the worker to work that is not night work.

In the regulations 'night work' is defined as a period that is not less than seven hours in length and includes the normal hours of 12 midnight to 5 am. A 'night worker' is a worker who normally works at least three hours of working time during this period of 'night work'. Therefore, an employee who normally works a shift from 6 pm to 2 am is not a 'night worker' because only two hours fall in the period defined as 'night work'. However, an employee who works from 10 pm to 6 am is a 'night worker' because five hours fall in the period defined as 'night work'.

It is not necessary for the worker to work these night hours each week. It is required that the hours are a regular feature of the pattern of work.

Rest breaks

All adult workers are entitled to at least 11 consecutive hours rest in every 24-hour period. Young workers (those aged under 18) are entitled to a consecutive rest period of not less than 12 hours in every 24-hour period.

A worker is entitled to at least 24 hours uninterrupted rest in every seven-day period. The weekly rest period can be averaged over a period of 14 days (eg 12 hours in one seven-day period and 36 hours in the following seven-day period). If a worker's daily work lasts for more than six hours, the worker is entitled to a rest period. The length of time allowed for the break can be agreed in a collective agreement, but it must be at least 20 minutes, and the worker must be entitled to spend that period of time away from the workstation. Young workers are entitled to a break of at least 30 minutes if their working time is more than four and a half hours.

In looking at the Working Time Regulations we see a further example of how legislation can be used to regulate an aspect of the employment relationship.

USING LEGISLATION TO UNDERPIN THE MOVE TO PARTNERSHIP DEALS

In Chapter 6 we looked at the new approach to relationships between the trade union and the employee, partnership deals. In this we looked at the six principles, identified by the TUC in 1999, which underpinned a genuine workplace partnership between unions and management. They are:

- a commitment to the success of the organisation
- a focus on the quality of working life
- a recognition and respect of the legitimate roles of the employer and the trade union

- a commitment to employment security
- openness and transparency
- adding value to all concerned.

It is interesting to see how a variety of the legislation supports these principles. For example:

- The 'family friendly' legislation, and particularly the Flexible Working Regulations 2002 support the focus on the quality of working life.
- The Employment Rights Act 1996 supports the rights of employees not to be unfairly dismissed, therefore adding some support to the commitment to employment security.
- The Information and Consultation of Employees Regulations 2004 support openness and transparency in the employment relationship.

It could be argued, therefore, that the growth in individual legal protection supports increased individualism, but also gives some of the foundations on which collectivism is based.

- Legislation giving protection to the individual employee developed in the 1970s, and then started to grow again significantly during the mid-1990s.
- The contract of employment contains the terms and conditions that spell out the individual relationship between the employer and the employee.
- By introducing a range of family-friendly legislation the government has attempted to address one of the external factors impacting on the employment relationship ('social').
- The wide range of discrimination legislation helps to determine the required behaviour of both the employer and the employee within the workplace.
- Health and safety legislation promotes acceptable ways of working.
- The Working Time Regulations 1998 are an example of legislation being used to regulate the employment relationship.
- A range of legislation underpins the principles of partnership agreements.

1. If you were in government today, which area of the employment relationship would you want to address most urgently through increased legislation? Explain the reasons for your choice.
2. If employees have deeply ingrained prejudicial attitudes, do you think discrimination legislation can have any impact? Justify your answer.
3. Given the amount of working days lost as a result of stress-related illness each year, this is clearly an area of concern within the workplace. What ways would you recommend to tackle the problem?

(Suggestions of answers to the examples can be accessed by tutors at www.cipd.co.uk/tss)

Social workers in one of the London boroughs are known to have to work long hours in difficult circumstances. One of the teams specialises in cases of child abuse, and many of the situations that the social workers have to face are emotionally upsetting and draining.

In the social work team dealing with child abuse there are 15 social workers. Each one has his or her own case load of children for whom he or she is responsible. The workers do discuss cases at a weekly case conference, but much of the work is carried out alone because of staff shortages.

Last week all the social workers attended the annual conference run by all the social work departments operating within the London borough. One of the sessions was run by a leading consultant in the area of stress management. She explained the symptoms of stress, and the purpose of her session was to advise social workers who were experiencing stress of ways that they could manage the stress more effectively.

At this week's case conference the subject of stress has been raised. All the 15 social workers within the team have reported to the manager leading the case conference that they are experiencing symptoms of stress. Each of them blames the high case load and the nature of the work. As a group they have asked the manager to reduce the stress that the work is causing them.

The manager has explained that she can do nothing. She cannot reduce the number of cases because the number of referrals is something out of her control. Nor can she reduce the number of cases given to each social worker. She knows that the department needs more social workers, but despite regular advertising she has been unable to attract any new recruits. She says there is nothing she can do. However, she did ask the social workers to think of anything that might help resolve the problem, and to put the ideas to her.

After the conference a number of the social workers discussed the matter further and decided they were far from satisfied with the response. They did not think it was satisfactory to simply say that no solution could be found.

Questions

1. Is the manager's response satisfactory? Answer this with reference to relevant legislation.
2. What else could/should the social workers do to make their dissatisfaction clear?
3. If, in the future, one of the social workers was absent with an illness related to stress, what possible action might the manager be able to take?

Bibliography

BOOKS AND ARTICLES

ADAMS, J. (1965) Injustice in social exchange. In: L. Berkowitz (ed). *Advances in experimental psychology*. New York: Academic Press.

Advisory Conciliation and Arbitration Service (Acas). (2003) *ACAS code of practice on disciplinary and grievance procedures in employment*. London: Acas.

Acas. (2003) *Code of practice: disclosure of information to trade unions for collective bargaining purposes*. London: The Stationery Office.

Acas. (2004a) *Acas annual report 2003/04*. London: Acas.

Acas. (2004b) *Acas code of practice on disciplinary and grievance procedures*. London: Acas.

ARMSTRONG, M. (2002) *Employee reward*. 3rd ed. London: CIPD.

ARMSTRONG, M. and BARON, A. (1998) *Performance management: the new realities*. London: CIPD.

ARMSTRONG, M. and STEPHENS, T. (2005) *A handbook of employee reward management and practice*. London: Kogan Page.

ASCH, S.E. (1955) Opinions and social pressure. *Scientific American*. No. 193. 31–35.

ATKINSON, J. (1984) Manpower strategies for flexible organisations, *People Management*. August. 28–31.

BARON, R.A. and GREENBERG, J. (1990) *Behaviour in organisations*. 3rd ed. London: Allyn and Bacon.

BASS, B.M. (1985) *Leadership and performance: beyond expectations*. New York: Free Press.

BEER, M., SPECTOR, B., LAWRENCE, P.R., QUIN MILLS, D. and WALTON, R. E. (1984) *Managing human assets*. New York: Free Press.

BELBIN, M.R. (1981) *Management teams: why they succeed or fail*. London: Heinemann.

BELBIN, M.R. (1996) *Team roles at work*. London: Butterworth-Heinemann.

BLAKSTAD, M. and COOPER, A. (1995) *The communicating organisation*. London: CIPD.

BLAIR, A. (1998) *The third way: new politics for the new century*. London: Fabian Society.

BLYTON, P. and TURNBULL, P. (2004) *The dynamics of employee relations* 3rd ed. Basingstoke: Palgrave Macmillan.

BOLKESTEIN, F. (2000) *The future of the social market economy.* Speech by Commissioner Frits Bolkestein, Brussels, 5 December.

BOOTH, A. (1989) What do unions do now? Discussion paper. *Economics.* No. 8903, Brunel University.

BOYATZIS, R.E. (1982) *The competent manager.* London: John Wiley.

BRATTON, J. and GOLD, J. (2003) *Human resource management: theory and practice.* 3rd ed. Basingstoke: Palgrave.

BRAVERMAN, H. (1974) *Labour and monopoly capital: the degradation of work in the twentieth century.* New York: Monthly Review Press.

BRIDGFORD, J. and STIRLING, J. (1994) *Employee relations in Europe.* Oxford: Blackwell.

BRITISH COMPUTER SOCIETY. (2003) *Information overload: organisation and personal strategies.* London: BCS and Henley Management College.

BRODBECK, F. *et al.* (2000) Cultural variation of leadership prototypes across 22 European countries. *Journal of Occupational and Organisational Psychology.* No. 73. 1–29.

BULLOCK COMMITTEE (1977) *Review of the committee of inquiry on industrial democracy.* London: HMSO.

BURCHILL, F. (1997) *Labour Relations.* 2nd ed. Basingstoke: Macmillan.

BURNS, J.M. (1978) *Leadership.* New York: Academic Press and Harper & Row.

CANNELL, M. (2004) *Trade unions: a short history.* Factsheet. London: CIPD.

Central Arbitration Committee (CAC). (2004) *CAC annual report 2003/04.* London: CAC.

CERTIFICATION OFFICER. (2003/04) *Report 2003/04.* London: Certification Office. Online version available at: www.certoffice.org [accessed 13 January 2006].

CHAMBERLAIN, N. and KUHN, J. (1965) *Collective bargaining.* New York: McGraw-Hill.

Chartered Institute for Personnel and Development (CIPD). (2001) *Employee well-being and psychological contract survey.* London: CIPD.

CIPD. (2003) *Corporate social responsibility and HR's role.* London: CIPD.

CIPD. (2004a) *Flexible working and paternity leave, survey report.* London: CIPD.

CIPD. (2004b) *Managing conflict at work.* London: CIPD.

CIPD. (2004c) *Trade union learning representatives, joint research between the CIPD, TUC and LSC*. London: CIPD.

CIPD. (2004d) *Work–life balance*. Factsheet. London: CIPD. Online version available at: www.cipd.co.uk [accessed 13 January 2006].

CIPD. (2005a) *Recruitment, retention and turnover*. London: CIPD.

CIPD. (2005b) *Reward management*. London: CIPD.

CIPD. (2005c) *Quarterly trends and indicators, winter 2004*. CIPD survey. London: CIPD.

CIPD. (2005d) *Flexible working: impact and implementation, an employer survey*. CIPD survey. London: CIPD.

CIPD. (2005e) *European Works Councils*. Factsheet. London: CIPD.

CIPD/Department of Trade and Industry (DTI). (2004) *High performance work practices: linking strategy and skills to performance outcomes*. London: CIPD.

CIPD/LOVELLS. (2003) *A parent's right to ask: a review of flexible working arrangements*. London: CIPD and Lovells.

CIPD/ LOVELLS. (2005) *Employment and the law: burden or benefit?* Report. London: CIPD and Lovells.

CLUTTERBUCK, D. (2003) *Managing work–life balance: a guide for HR in achieving organisational and individual change*. London: CIPD.

COLLINS, C. (1995) Spanking is becoming the new don't. *New York Times*. C8. 1995.

CONFEDERATION OF BRITISH INDUSTRY (CBI)/PERTEMPS. (2005) *Employment trends survey*. London: CBI.

CRESSEY, P. (1998) European works councils in practice. *Human Resource Management*. Vol. 8, No. 1. 67–79.

CULLY, M., WOODLAND, S., O'REILLY, A. and DIX, G. (1998) *Workplace employee relations survey*. London: Routledge.

CULLY, M., WOODLAND, S., O'REILLY, A. and DIX, G. (1999) *Britain at work as depicted by the 1998 workplace employee relations survey*. London: Routledge.

DAFT, R.L. (1998) *Organisation theory and design*. 6th ed. Cincinnati, Oh.: South-Western College Publishing.

DANIELS, K. (2004) *Employment law for HR and business students*. London: CIPD.

DANIELS, K. and MACDONALD, L. (2005) *Equality, discrimination and diversity: a student text*. London: CIPD.

DAVIES, J. (1998) Labour disputes in 1997. *Labour Market Trends.* June.

DEPARTMENT OF EMPLOYMENT. *Department of Employment code of practice on picketing.* (available at www.dti.gov.uk)

DTI. (2002) *High performance workplaces.* London: DTI.

DTI. (2004a) *Work–life balance and flexible working: the business case.* London: DTI. Online version available at: www.dti.gov.uk [accessed 13 January 2006].

DTI. (2004b) *Flexible working.* London: DTI. Online version available at: www.dti.gov.uk [accessed 13 January 2006].

DONOVAN, P. (2005) Mayor announces London living wage. *People Management.* 21 April.

DONOVAN, T.N. (1968) *Royal commission on trade unions and employers' associations* (Cmnd. 3623). London: HMSO.

DUNCAN, R. (1979) What is the right organisation structure? decision tree analysis provides the answer. *Organisational Dynamics.* Winter. No. 429.

EAGLY, A.H. and CHAIKEN, S. (1993) *The psychology of attitudes.* Fort Worth, Tx.: Harcourt Brace Jovanovich.

EDWARDS, P. (1995) Strikes and industrial conflict. In: P. Edwards (ed). *Industrial relations: theory and practice in Britain.* Oxford: Blackwell.

ELLIOTT, R.F. (1981) Some further observations on the importance of national wage agreements. *British Journal of Industrial Relations.* Vol 19.

ENGINEERING EMPLOYERS' FEDERATION (EEF). (2001) *Catching up with Uncle Sam.* London: EEF. Online version available at: www.eef.org.uk [accessed 13 January 2006].

EUROPEAN COMMISSION. (2001) *Promoting a European framework for corporate social responsibility. Commission Research Paper No.3.* London, HMSO.

EYSENCK, H.J. and WILSON, G. (1975) *Know your own personality.* London: Maurice Temple Smith.

FARNHAM, D. (2000) *Employee relations in context.* 2nd ed. London: CIPD.

FARNHAM, D. (2005) *Managing in a strategic business context.* London: CIPD.

FATCHETT, D. (1989) Workplace bargaining in hospitals and schools: threat or opportunity for the unions? *Industrial Relations Journal.* Vol. 20, No. 4.

FLANDERS, A. (1968) Collective bargaining: a theoretical analysis. *British Journal of Industrial Relations.* Vol. 6, No. 1.

FORD, H. (1923) *My life and work.* London: Heinemann.

FOX, A. (1966) *Industrial sociology and industrial relations*. Royal Commission Research Paper No.3, London: HMSO.

FRENCH, J. and RAVEN, B. (1958) The bases of social power. In: D Cartwright (ed). *Studies in social power*. Ann Arbor, Michigan: Institute for Social Research.

GALL, G. (2005) Happy anniversary. *People Management*. 2 June.

GEARY, J.F. (1994) Task participation: employees' participation enabled or constrained? In: K. Sisson (ed). *Personnel management: a comprehensive guide to theory and practice in Britain*. 2nd ed. Oxford: Blackwell.

GENNARD, J. and JUDGE, G. (2005) *Employee relations*. 4th ed. London: CIPD.

GOLDTHORPE, J.H., LOCKWOOD, D., BECHHOFER, F. and PLATT, J. (1969) *The affluent worker in the class struggle*. Cambridge, UK: Cambridge University Press.

GOLEMAN, D. (1996) *Emotional intelligence: why it can matter more than IQ*. London: Bloomsbury.

GOODMAN, J. (1984) *Employment relations in industrial society*. Oxford: Philip Allan.

GREAT BRITAIN DEPARTMENT FOR EDUCATION AND EMPLOYMENT (1998) *The learning age: a renaissance for a new Britain*. HMSO.

GREENHALGH, L. (1986) Managing conflict. *Sloan Management Review*. No. 27, Summer.

GRIFFITHS, G. (2005) Driving force. *People Management*. 7 April.

GUEST, D.E. and CONWAY, N. (2004) *Employee well-being and the psychological contract*. London: CIPD.

GUEST, D.E., CONWAY, N., BRINER, R. and DICKMAN, M. (1996) *The state of the psychological contract in employment*. London: CIPD.

GUPTA, N. and SHAW, J.D. (1998) Financial incentives are effective! *Compensation and Benefits Review*. March/April 26. 28–32.

HALL, K. (2005) Global division. *People Management*. 24 March. 44–45.

HALSEY, A.H. (1995) *Change in British society from 1900 to the present day*. Oxford: Oxford University Press.

HANEY, C., BANKS, W.C. and ZIMBARDO, P.G. (1973) A study of prisoners and guards in a simulated prison. *Naval Research Review*. No. 30. 4–17.

HARRIGAN, K.R. (1987) Managing joint ventures, part 1. *Management Review*. February. 24–41.

HEERY, E., SIMMS, M., DELRIDGE, R., SALMON, J. and SIMPSON, D. (2000) Union organising in Britain: a survey of policy and practice. *International Journal of Human Resource Management*. Vol. 11, No. 5.

HELLRIEGEL, D. and SLOCUM, J.W. (1978) *Management: contingency approaches*. Reading, Mass.: Addison-Wesley.

HERIOT, P. (1995) The management of careers. In: S. Tyson (ed) *Strategic prospects for HRM*. London: Institute of Personnel and Development (IPD).

HERZBERG, F., MAUSNER, B. and SNYDERMAN, B. (1957) *The Motivation to Work*. New York: John Wiley.

HILTROP, J. (1995) The changing psychological contract: the human resources challenge. *European Management Journal*. Vol. 33, No. 3. 286–294.

HIRSCHI, T. (1969) *Causes of delinquency*. Berkeley: University of California Press.

HOLLINSHEAD, G. and LEAT, M. (1995) *Human resource management: an international and comparative perspective*. London: Pitman.

HOLLINSHEAD, G., NICHOLLS, P. and TAILBY, S. (2003) *Employee relations*. 2nd ed. London: FT/Prentice Hall.

HOPKINS, M. and WARREN, M. (1993) *Health and safety: are you at risk?* Bicester: CCH Editions.

HUCZYNSKI, A. and BUCHANAN, D. (1991) *Organizational behaviour*. 2nd ed. Hemel Hempstead: Prentice Hall.

HUTCHINSON, S. and PURCELL, J. (2003) *Bringing policies to life: the vital role of line managers in people management*. London: CIPD.

HYMAN, J. and MASON, B. (1995) *Managing employee involvement and participation*. London: Sage.

HYMAN, R. (1994) Changing trade union identities and strategies. In: R. Hyman and A. Ferner (eds). *New frontiers in European industrial relations*. Oxford: Blackwell.

INCOME DATA SERVICES (IDS). (2004) *IDS Brief 766*. October. London: IDS.

INDUSTRIAL RELATIONS SERVICES (IRS). (2002) Don't nurse a grievance: resolving disputes at work. *Employment Trends*. No. 759, September.

IRS. (2004) UK working hours changing. *IRS Employment Review*. 11 August.

INVOLVEMENT AND PARTICIPATION ASSOCIATION (1989). *Industrial Participation*. Autumn. London: Involvement and Participation Association.

JANIS, I.L. (1982) *Victims of group think: a psychological study of foreign policy decisions and fiascos*. 2nd ed. Boston, Mass.: Houghton Mifflin.

JEHN, K.A. 1995. A multimethod examination of the benefits and detriments of intragroup conflict. *Administrative Science Quarterly*. No. 40. 256–282.

JONES, D. (2005) *Unions' employment law demands would be disastrous for UK economy*. 13 September. London: CBI. Online version available at: www.cbi.org.uk [accessed 13 January 2006].

KELLY, J. (1998) *Rethinking industrial relations: mobilization, collectivism and long waves*. London: Routledge.

KODZ , J., HARPER, H. and DENCH, S. (2002) *Work–life balance: beyond the rhetoric*. IES Report No. 384. Brighton: Institute for Employment Studies.

KOHN, A (1998) Challenging behaviourist dogma: myths about money and motivation. *Compensation and Benefits Review*. March/April, 27. 33–377.

LABOUR FORCE SURVEY (2004). Office for National Statistics.

LATHAM, G. and LOCKE, E.A. (1979) Goal setting: a motivational technique that works. *Organisational Dynamics*. Autumn. 68–80.

LAWLER, E.E. (1990) *Strategic pay*. San Francisco: Jossey-Bass.

LEARY-JOYCE, J. (2004) *Becoming an employer of choice*. London: CIPD.

LEWIN, K. (1951) *Field theory in social science*. New York: Harper and Row.

LEWIN, K. and WHITE, R.K. (1939) Patterns of aggressive behaviour in experimentally created 'social climates'. *Journal of Social Psychology*. No. 10. 271–299.

LEWIS, D. and SARGEANT, M. (2004) *Essentials of employment law*. 8th ed. London: CIPD.

LEWIS, P., THORNHILL, A. and SAUNDERS, M. (2003), *Employee relations: understanding the employment relationship*. London: FT Prentice Hall.

LIKERT, R. (1961) *New patterns of management*. New York: McGraw-Hill.

LIPPITT, R. and WHITE, R. (1959) An experimental study of leadership and group life. In: E. Maccoby, T.M. Newcomb and E.L. Hartley (eds). *Readings in social psychology*. 3rd ed. London: Methuen.

LOHR, J.M. and STAATS, A. (1973) Attitude conditioning in Sino-Tibetan languages. *Journal of Personality and Social Psychology*. No. 26. 196–200.

LORSCH, J.W. (1970) Introduction to the structural design of organisations. In: G.W. Dalton, P. R. Lawrence, and J.W. Lorsch, JW (eds). *Organisational structure and design*. Homewood, Ill.: Irwin and Dorsey.

MACHIN, S. (2003) Trade Union decline, new workplaces and new workers. In: H. Gospel and S.

Wood (eds). *Representing workers: trade union representation and membership in Britain*. London: Routledge

MACHIN, S. and BALNDEN, J. (2003) *Cross-generational correlations of union status for young people*. London: Centre for Economic Performance Discussion Paper, No. 553, London School of Economics.

MACPHERSON, S. (1999) *The Stephen Lawrence inquiry*. London: HMSO.

MANT, A (1996) *The psychological contract*. Unpublished address to the IPD National Conference.

MANUS, T.M. and GRAHAM, M.D. (2002) *Creating a total rewards strategy: a toolkit for designing business-based plans*. New York: American Management Association.

MARCHINGTON, M. (2001) Employee involvement at work. In: J. Storey (ed). *Human resource management: a critical text*. 2nd ed. London: Thomson Learning.

MARCHINGTON, M., GOODMAN, J., WILKINSON, A. and ACKERS, P. (1992) *New developments in relations practice*. London: Kogan Page.

MARSDEN, D. and RICHARDSON, R. (1994) Performing for pay? the effects of 'merit pay' in a public service. *British Journal of Industrial Relations*. June. 243–261.

MASLOW, A. (1954) *Motivation and personality.* New York: Harper and Row.

McLELLAN, D. (1999) *Capital: an abridged edition*. Oxford: Oxford University Press.

McLOUGHLIN, I.P. and GOURLAY, S.N. (1994) *Enterprise without unions: industrial relations in the small firm*. Buckingham: Open University Press.

METCALF, D. (2005) Highway to hell? *People Management*. 15 September.

MICHENER, H.A., DELAMATER, J.D. and MYERS, D.J. (2004) *Social psychology*. Belmont CA: Wadsworth/Thomson.

MILGRAM, S. (1963) Behavioural study of obedience. *Journal of Abnormal and Social Psychology*. No. 67. 371–378.

MOORE, R. (1980) Information to unions: use or abuse? *People Management*. Vol. 34, May.

NAYLOR, J. (2004) *Management*. 2nd ed. Essex: Pearson Education.

OFFICE OF NATIONAL STATISTICS (ONS). (2002) *Labour Force Survey 2002*. London: TSO

ORGANISATION FOR ECONOMIC CO-OPERATION AND DEVELOPMENT (OECD). (1976). *Annual report 1976*. Paris: OECD.

PAINTER, C., PUTTICK, K. and HOLMES, A. (1998) *Employment rights*. London: Pluto.

PALMER, G. (1983) *British industrial relations*. London: Unwin Hyman.

PAVLOV, I. (1927) *Conditioned reflexes*. London: Oxford University Press.

People Management. (2005) Aslef members form breakaway drivers union. 27 January.

PERLMUTTER, H.V. (1999) On deep dialog. *Knowledge@Warton Newsletter*

PFEFFER, J. (1998) Six dangerous myths about pay. *Harvard Business Review*. May–June.

PHILPOTT, J. (2005a) Where's the party? *People Management,* 21 April. 36–39.

PHILPOTT, J. (2005b) Work audit. In: *Impact 11*. London: CIPD.

PLATT, L. (1997) Employee work–life balance: the competitive advantage. In: F. Hesselbein, M. Goldsmith and R. Beckhard, *The Drucker foundation: the organisation of the future*. San Francisco: Jossey-Bass.

POLZER, J.T., MILTON, L.P. and SWANN, W.B. Jr. (2002). Capitalizing on diversity: interpersonal congruence in small work groups. *Administrative Science Quarterly*. No. 43. 296–324.

PORTER, M.E. (1990) *Competitive strategy: techniques for analysing industries and competitors*. New York: Free Press.

PRICE, A. (2004) *Human resource management in a business context*. 2nd ed. London: Thomson Learning.

PUBLIC ACCOUNTS CTTEE (PAC). (2003). *Public Administration Committee report on targets in the public sector*. London: TSO.

PURCELL, J. and SISSON, K. (1983) Strategies and practice in the management of industrial relations. In: G. Bain (ed). *Industrial relations, theory and practice in Britain*. Oxford: Blackwell.

RAMSAY, H. (1997) Fool's gold? European works councils and workplace democracy. *Industrial Relations Journal*. Vol. 28, No. 4. 315–316.

RICHARD, O.C. and SHELOR, R.M. (2002). Linking top management team age heterogeneity to firm performance: juxtaposing to mid-range theories. *International Journal of Human Resource Management*. No.13. 958–974.

RICHTER, A., VAN DICK, R. and WEST, M. (2004) *The relationship between group and organisational identification and effective intergroup relations*. Academy of Management best conference paper 2004. In press.

RIKETTA, M. and VAN DICK, R. (2005) Foci of attachment in organisations: a meta-analytic comparison of the strength and correlates of workgroup versus organisational identification and commitment. *Journal of Vocational Behaviour*, Vol. 67. 490–510

ROETHLISBERGER, F.J. and DICKSON, W.J. (1939) *Management and the worker*. Cambridge, Mass.: Harvard University Press.

ROWTHORN, B. (1986) The passivity of the state. In: D. Coates and J. Hillard (eds). *The economic decline of modern Britain: the debate between left and right.* Brighton: Wheatsheaf.

ROYAL COLLEGE OF NURSING (RCN). (2005) *UK nursing labour market commentary 2004/05.* Report at the RCN conference, April.

SALAMON, M. (2000) *Industrial relations.* 4th ed. Harlow: Financial Times/ Prentice Hall.

SCHEIN, E. (1988) *Organisation psychology.* 3rd ed. Englewood Cliffs, NJ: Prentice Hall.

SCHUSTER, J.R. and ZINGHEIM, P.K. (1992) *The new pay.* New York: Lexington.

SCHWAB, R.C., UNGSON, G.R. and BROWN, W.B. (1985) Redefining the boundary-spanning environment relationship. *Journal of Management.* No.11. 75–86.

SCULLY, J.A. (1994) Top management team demography and process: the role of social integration and communication. *Administrative Science Quarterly.* No. 39. 412–438.

SHAW, M.E. (1978) Communication networks fourteen years later. In: L. Berkowitz (ed). *Group processes.* New York: Academic Press. 351–361.

SHERIF, M. (1956) Experiments in group conflict, *Scientific American.* No. 195. 54–58.

SINCLAIR, J. (1999) Trade unions. In: G. Hollinshead, P. Nicholls and S. Tailby (eds). *Employee relations.* London: FT/Pitman.

SKINNER, B. (1938) *The behaviour of organisms: an experimental analysis.* New York: Appleton.

SMITH, K.G., SMITH, K.A., OLIAN, J.D., SIMS, H.P., O'BANNON, D.P. and SPINDLER, G.S. (1994) Psychological contracts in the workplace: a lawyer's view. *Human Resource Management.* Vol. 33, No. 3. 325–333.

SPINDLER, G.S. (1994) Psychological Contracts in the workplace: a lawyer's view, *Human Resource Management*, Vol. 33, No. 3. 325–33

SPRIGG, C.A., SMITH, P.R. and JACKSON, P.R. (2003) *Psychosocial risk factors in call centres: an evaluation of work design and well being.* London: Health and Safety Executive.

STANDING COMMISSION ON PAY COMPARABILITY. (1981) *Final report.* London: HMSO.

STERN, C.W. and STALK, G. (1998) *Perspectives on strategy from the Boston consulting group.* New York and Canada: John Wiley.

STOGDILL, R.M. (1948) Personal factors associated with leadership: a survey of the literature. *Journal of Psychology.* No. 25. 35–71.

SUNDAY TIMES. (2003) *100 best companies to work for 2003.* 2 March.

SUNDAY TIMES. (2005) *100 best companies to work for 2005.* 6 March.

SUTHERLAND, E., CRESSEY, D. and LUCKENBILL, D. (1992) *Principles of criminology*. 11th ed. Dix Hills, NY: General Hall.

TAJFEL, H. (1970) Experiments in intergroup discrimination. *Scientific American*. No. 223. 96–102.

TAYLOR, F.W. (1911) *Principles of scientific management*. New York: Norton.

THOMPSON, J.D. (1967) *Organisations in action*. New York: McGraw-Hill.

THOMPSON, M. (1992) Pay and performance: the employee experience. *IMS Report No 218*. Brighton: Institute of Manpower Studies

TORRINGTON, D. (1972) *Face to face*. London: Gower

TORRINGTON, D. and HALL, L. (2002) *Human resource management*. 5th ed. London: Prentice Hall.

TORRINGTON, D. and HALL, L. (1998) *Human resource management*. 4th ed. London: Prentice Hall.

TOWNLEY, B. (1994a) *Reframing human resource management*. London: Sage.

TOWNLEY, B. (1994b) Communicating with employees. In: K. Sisson (ed). *Personnel management: A comprehensive guide to theory and practice in Britain*. 2nd ed. Oxford: Blackwell.

TSUI, A.S., EGAN, T.D. and O'REILLY, C.A. (1992) Being different: relational demography and organizational attachment. *Administrative Science Quarterly*. No. 37. 549–579.

TUCKMAN, B. and JENSEN, N. (1977) Stages of small group development revisited. *Group and Organisational Studies*. Vol 2. 419–427.

UNITED NATIONS (UN). (1997) *Trade and development report: globalisation, distribution and growth*. London: UN.

VAN DICK, R. (2004) My job is my castle: identification in organisational contexts. In: C.L. Cooper and I.T. Robertson (eds). *International review of industrial and organisational psychology*. New York: John Wiley.

VAN DICK, R. *et al*. (2004) Role of perceived importance in intergroup contact. *Journal of Personality and Social Psychology*. Vol. 87, No 2. 211–227.

VROOM, V. (1964) *Work and motivation*. New York: John Wiley.

WALL, T.D. and LISCHERON, J.A. (1977) *Worker participation*. London: McGraw-Hill.

WALTON, M. (1992) *The Deming management method*. London: Mercury Business Books.

WATSON, W.E., KUMAR, K. and MICHAELSEN, L.K. (1993) Cultural diversity's impact on interaction processes and performance: comparing homogeneous and diverse task groups. *Academy of Management Journal*. No. 36. 590–602.

WEBB, S. and WEBB, B. (1902) *Industrial democracy*. London: Longmans Green.

WEBBER, S.S. and DONAHUE, L.M. (2001) Impact of highly and less job-related diversity on work group cohesion and performance: a meta-analysis. *Journal of Management*. No. 27. 141–162.

WEBER, M. (1978) *Economy and society: an outline of interpretive sociology*, ed. G. Roth and C. Wittich. Berkeley, Calif.: University of California Press.

WEST, M.A. (2002). Sparkling fountains and stagnant ponds: creativity and innovation implementation in work groups. *Applied Psychology*. No. 51. 355–386.

WHEATLEY, M. (2003) When change is out of our control. In: M. Effron, R. Gandossy and M. Goldsmith (eds). *Human resources for the 21st century*. London: John Wiley.

WHITEHEAD, M. (1999) Rover's return. *People Management*. 16 September.

WILDER, D.A. (1990) Some determinants of the persuasive power of in-groups and out-groups. *Journal of Personality and Social Psychology*. No. 59. 1202–1213.

WILLIAMS, K.Y. and O'REILLY, C.A. (1998). Demography and diversity in organizations: a review of 40 years of research. In: B. Staw and L. Cummings (eds). *Research in organizational behavior* (Vol. 20, 77–140). Greenwich, Conn.: JAI Press.

WILSON, F.M. (2004) *Organisational behaviour at work: a critical Introduction*. 2nd ed. Oxford: Oxford University Press.

WOODRUFFE, C. (1991) Competent by any other name. *Personnel Management*. September, 30–33.

YOUNSON, F. (2002) Power struggles. *People Management*. 12 September.

YUKL, G. (2001) *Leadership in organisations*. 5th ed. London: Prentice Hall.

LEGISLATION

Disability Discrimination Act 1995

Employment Act 2002

Employment Equality (Religion and Belief) Regulations 2003

Employment Equality (Sexual Orientation) Regulations 2003

Employment Protection Act 1975

Employment Relations Act 1999

Employment Relations Act 2004

Employment Rights Act 1996

Employment Rights (Dispute Resolution) Act 1998

Equal Pay Act 1970

Flexible Working (Eligibility, Complaints and Remedies) Regulations 2001

Flexible Working (Procedural Requirements) Regulations 2002

Freedom of Information Act 2000

Health and Safety at Work Act 1974

Health and Safety (Display Screen Equipment) Regulations 1992

Industrial Relations Act 1971

Industrial Training Act 1964

Information and Consultation of Employees Regulations 2004

Information and Consultation Regulations 2004

Management of Health and Safety at Work Regulations 1998

Manual Handling Operations Regulations 1998

Maternity and Parental Leave Regulations 1999

National Minimum Wage Act 1998

Part-time Workers (Prevention of Less Favourable Treatment) Regulations 2000

Personal Protective Equipment at Work Regulations 1998

Provision and Use of Work Equipment Regulations 1998

Race Relations Act 1976

Sex Discrimination Act 1975

Sex Discrimination (Gender Reassignment) Regulations 1999

Trade Union and Labour Relations (Consolidation) Act 1992

Working Time Regulations 1998

Workplace (Health, Safety and Welfare) Regulations 1992

CASES

Arw Transformers Ltd v *Cupples (1977)* IRLR 228

Bartholomew v *Post Office Telecommunications (1981)* EAT 53/81

Bass Leisure Ltd v *Thomas (1994)* IRLR 104

Blatchfords Solicitors v *Berger and others (2001)* EAT 25.4.01.

Blue Circle Staff Association v *Certification Officer (1977)* ICR 224

Bouchaala v *Trust House Forte Hotels Ltd (1980)* ICR 721

Bracebridge Engineering Ltd v *Darby (1989)* IRLR 3

Bristow and Roberts v *Pinewood Studios Ltd (1982)* EAT 600/81-601/81

British Airways v *Starmer*, EAT 21.7.05 (0306/05)

British Home Stores v *Burchell (1978)* IRLR 379.

Campbell v *Union Carbide (2002)* EAT 034/01

Capper Pass v *Lawton (1977)* ICR 83

Coleman v *Skyrail Oceanic Ltd (1981)* IRLR 398

Davey v *Daybern Co Ltd (1982)* EAT 710/81

Driskel v *Peninsula Business Services Ltd & ors [2000]* IRLR 151

Enderby v *Frenchay Health Authority (1993)* IRLR 591

Gozdzik & Scopigno v *Chlidema Carpet Co Ltd (1979)* EAT 598/78

Green and Son (Castings) Ltd and others v *ASTMS and AUEW (1983)* IRLR 135

Harris & another v *Courage (Eastern) Ltd (1982)* IRLR 509.

Hayward v *Cammell Laird (1984)* IRLR 463

Hindle v *Percival Boats (1969)* WLR 174

Irani v *Southampton and SW Hampshire Health Authority (1984)* IRLR 203

Isle of Wight Tourist Board v *Coombes (1976)* IRLR 413

Jones v *Tower Boot Co Ltd (1997)* IRLR 168

Kerr v *Atkinson Vehicles (Scotland) Ltd (1973)* IRLR 36

King and others v *Eaton Ltd (1995)* IRLR 199

Little v *Beare and Son Ltd (1980)* EAT 130/1980

Mansfield Hosiery Mills Ltd v *Bromley (1977)* IRLR 301

Midland Cold Storage v *Turner (1972)* ICR 230

Moonsar v *Fiveways Express Transport Ltd (2004)* EAT 0476/04

NCB v *Galley (1958)* 1 WLR 16

Navy, Army and Air Force Institutes v *Varley (1976)* IRLR 408

Outlook Supplies v *Parry (1978)* IRLR 12

R v *Secretary of State ex parte Equal Opportunities Commission (1995)* 1 AC 1

R v *Central Arbitration Committee ex parte BTP Tioxide Ltd (1981)* IRLR 60

Roberts v *Toyota (GB) Ltd (1981)* EAT 614/80.

Rolls-Royce Ltd v *Walpole (1980)* IRLR 343

Safeway Stores plc v *Burrell (1997)* IRLR 200

Scott Packing and Warehousing Co Ltd v *Paterson (1978)* IRLR 166

Springboard Sunderland Trust v *Robson (1992)* IRLR 261

Stanley Cole (Wainfleet) Ltd v *Sheridan (2003)* IRLR 52

Sutcliffe and Eaton Ltd v *Pinney (1977)* IRLR 349

Sutherland (Chairman of the Governors of St Thomas Becket RC High School) v *Hatton and three other cases (2002)* IRLR 263

Thomas v *National Union of Miners (South Wales) (1985)* IRLR 136

Timeplan Education Group Ltd v *National Union of Teachers (1997)* IRLR 457

Walker v *Northumberland County Council (1994)* IRLR 35

Williams v *Compair Maxam (1982)* IRLR 83.

WEBSITES

www.acas.org.uk

www.amicustheunion.org

www.bbc.co.uk/news

www.cac.gov.uk

www.ceep.org

www.coe.int.

www.cre.gov.uk

www.curia.eu.int

www.dti.gov.uk

www.drc-gb.org

www.echr.coe.int

www.eoc.org.uk

www.employersforworklifebalance.org.uk

www.etuc.org

www.europa.eu.int

www.europarl.org.uk

www.hse.gov.uk

www.kingsmillreview.gov.uk

www.nhsemployers.org

www.partnership-institute.org.uk

www.statistics.gov.uk

www.tuc.org.uk

www.unice.org

www.womenandequalityunit.gov.uk

Index

Also from CIPD Publishing . . .

Personal
Effectiveness

Diana Winstanley

Written by a leading author in this field, this new text on Personal Effectiveness is designed to give students a basic understanding of study skills and management skills, and to give context to other studies.

Suitable for use on a range of undergraduate and postgraduate modules, including those relating to self development, personal skills, learning and development, management skills, study skills and coaching modules, and as part of general business or HR degrees, this text seeks to be both comprehensive and accessible through the use of learning aids.

Each chapter includes:
- learning objectives and a synopsis of content;
- vignette examples to illustrate key points;
- exercises with feedback;
- a self-check exercise and synopsis at the end of the chapter; and
- references and further sources of information.

Order your copy now online at www.cipd.co.uk/bookstore or call us on 0870 800 3366

Diana Winstanley has over 15 years experience of training staff, students and managers in personal effectiveness, as well as in human resource management, and is already a well respected author of a number of books and articles. She has also led, designed and supported a number of PhD and postgraduate programmes in transferable skills and personal effectiveness, and is currently Professor of Management and Director of Postgraduate Programmes at Kingston Business School. Previously she has been Senior Lecturer in Management and Personal Development, Deputy Director of the full-time MBA programme and Senior Tutor at Tanaka Business School, Imperial College London. She also has professional qualifications as a humanistic counsellor.

| Published 2005 | 1 84398 002 9 | Paperback | 256 pages |

The Chartered Institute of Personnel and Development is the leading publisher of books and reports for personnel and training professionals, students and all those concerned with the effective management and development of people at work.

Also from CIPD Publishing . . .

Personnel Practice

4th edition

Malcolm Martin and Tricia Jackson

Personnel Practice is widely acclaimed as the definitive introduction to human resource management. It is designed specifically to cater for the CIPD Certificate in Personnel Practice and is invaluable for all students taking the Certificate as well as anyone seeking an overview of the subject area.

This new edition offers an updated look at the subject area, with coverage of up-to-date legislation and information management. Each chapter has a clear overview and concise summary, providing ideal points for revision and reference. The text also contains detailed sources of further information, alongside activities and case studies to test knowledge and link knowledge to practice.

'Personnel Practice should be the standard reference text for all line managers, HR practitioners and undergraduate HR and personnel students developing an interest in and/or responsibility for HR issues who need an understanding of maximising people performance in today's competitive environment.' Alan Lund MCIPD, Programme Manager, East Lancashire Business School

Order your copy now online at www.cipd.co.uk/bookstore or call us on 0870 800 3366

Malcolm Martin BSc, MCMI, FCIPD has been involved in the design and delivery of the Certificate in Personnel Practice programmes for many years, primarily at the training provider, MOL. He has worked for British Steel, Dunlop, Guthrie and the BBA Group, where he held managerial positions in industrial relations, project management and personnel. Since then he has directed numerous CPP courses for corporate clients and for public programmes.

Tricia Jackson BA, MSc (Personnel Management), MInstAM, Chartered FCIPD is a freelance training and personnel consultant, specialising in employment law. Tricia has many years' experience as a generalist practitioner in both the public and private sectors. She is currently involved in tutoring on open-learning and college-based CIPD programmes, competence assessment, identifying and providing training solutions, personnel consultancy and representing clients at employment tribunals.

| Published 2004 | 1 84398 102 5 | Paperback | 240 pages |

The Chartered Institute of Personnel and Development is the leading publisher of books and reports for personnel and training professionals, students and all those concerned with the effective management and development of people at work.

05401631